The Price of Love

The selected works of Colin Murray Parkes

Colin Murray Parkes

Routledge
Taylor & Francis Group

LONDON AND NEW YORK

First published 2015
by Routledge
27 Church Road, Hove, East Sussex BN3 2FA, UK

and by Routledge
711 Third Avenue, New York, NY 10017

Routledge is an imprint of the Taylor and Francis Group, an informa business

First issued in paperback 2015

British Library Cataloguing in Publication Data
A catalogue record for this book is available from the British Library

Library of Congress Cataloging-in-Publication Data
Parkes, Colin Murray.
  [Works. Selections]
  The price of love : the selected works of Colin Murray Parkes / Colin
Murray Parkes.
     pages cm
  1. Bereavement. 2. Grief therapy. 3. Loss (Psychology) I. Title.
  BF575.G7P3772 2014
  155.9'37—dc23
  2014005056

ISBN 978-0-415-66271-0 (hbk)
ISBN 978-1-138-02610-0 (pbk)
ISBN 978-1-315-76146-6 (ebk)

Typeset in Sabon
by ApexCovantage, LLC

CONTENTS

Foreword   *ix*
Acknowledgements   *x*
Introduction   *xii*

PART 1
Love and grief   **1**

1   **All in the end is harvest**   3

From Introduction. In Agnes Whitaker (ed.) *All in the end is harvest: an anthology for those who grieve* (pp. ix–xii). London: Dartman, Longdon & Todd in association with Cruse Bereavement Care, 1984.

2   **'Seeking' and 'finding' a lost object: evidence from recent studies of the reaction to bereavement**   7

Extracted from 'Seeking' and 'finding' a lost object: evidence from recent studies of the reaction to bereavement. *Social Science & Medicine* 4: 187–201, 1970.

3   **Is grief a universal phenomenon?**   20

Extracted from Comments on Dennis Klass's article 'Developing a cross-cultural model of grief'. *Omega* 39(3): 153–178, 1999.

4   **Evaluation of a bereavement service**   23

From *Journal of Preventive Psychiatry* 1(2): 179–188, 1981.

5   **Broken heart: a statistical study of increased mortality among widowers**   31

Reprinted from *British Medical Journal* 1: 740–743, 1969.

6 Guidelines for conducting ethical bereavement research   38

   From *Death Studies* 19: 171–181, 1995.

7 Helping bereaved people from other cultures   45

   From Bereavement: understanding grief across cultures
   Psychiatry in Practice 17(4): 5–8, 1998.

8 Love and loss   51

   Extracts from Parkes, C.M. *Love and loss: the roots of grief and
   its complications.* London and New York: Routledge. Portuguese
   edition *Amor e Perda* Trans. Maria Helena Pereira Franco.
   SP Brasil: Summus Editorial, 2006.

9 Complicated grief: the debate over a new DSM-5 diagnostic category   63

   From Kenneth J. Doka (ed.) *Living with grief before and after
   the death* (pp. 139–152). Washington, DC: Hospice
   Foundation of America, 2007.

10 Dangerous words   73

   From *Bereavement Care* 26(2): 23–25, 2000.

PART 2
Crisis, trauma and transition   79

11 Psychiatric problems following bereavement by murder
    or manslaughter   81

    From *British Journal of Psychiatry* 162: 49–54, 1993.

12 Psychosocial transitions: a field for study   90

    From *Social Science and Medicine*, 5: 101–115, 1971.

13 What becomes of redundant world models? A contribution
    to the study of adaptation to change   106

    From *British Journal of Medical Psychology* 48(2): 131–137, 1975.

14 Bereavement dissected – a re-examination of the basic components
    influencing the reaction to loss   115

    From *Israeli Journal of Psychiatry* 38(3–4): 151–156, 2001.

15 Assumptions about loss and principles of care   123

    From Parkes, C.M. and Markus, A. (eds.) *Coping with loss:
    helping patients and their families* (pp. 131–138). London:
    BMJ Books, 1998.

16 An experiment that failed: perceptions of a family-oriented
     crisis service by referrers and clients   129

     From Perceptions of a crisis service by referrers and clients.
     Psychiatric Bulletin 16(12): 748–750, 1992.

PART 3
Death and dying   137

17 Attachment and autonomy at the end of life   139

     From R. Gosling (ed.) *Support, innovation and autonomy*
     (pp. 151–166). London: Tavistock, 1973.

18 Terminal care: evaluation of in-patient service at St Christopher's
     Hospice. Part I. Views of surviving spouse on effects of
     service on the patient   148

     From *Postgraduate Medical Journal* 55: 517–522, 1979.

PART 4
Disasters   157

19 Bereavement following disasters   159

     From M. S. Stroebe, R. O. Hansson, H. Schut and W. Stroebe (eds.)
     *Handbook of bereavement research and practice: advances in theory
     and intervention* (pp. 463–484). Washington DC: American
     Psychological Association, 2008.

20 Psychosocial effects of disaster: birth rate in Aberfan   176

     Reprinted from *British Medical Journal* 2: 303–304, 1975.

21 Help the Hospices Tsunami Project: consultant's report and
     recommendations   180

     Parkes, C. M. and Dent, A. Help the Hospices Tsunami Project:
     consultant's report and recommendations. Prepared for Help the
     Hospices, 2004.

PART 5
War and terrorism: breaking the cycle of violence   195

22 Grief and reconciliation: extracts from an address to celebrate the
     tenth anniversary of the foundation of Cruse Bereavement
     Care in Northern Ireland   197

23 Genocide in Rwanda   199

From *Bereavement Care* 14(3): 34, 1995.

24 Reflections on Cruse's response to 9/11: extracts from the
diary of Colin Murray Parkes   203

From *South West Herts Bereavement Network Newsletter*, 2002.

25 Making and breaking cycles of violence (abridged)   209

From R. G. Stevenson and G. Cox (eds.) *Perspectives on
violence and violent death* (pp. 223–238). Amityville, NY:
Baywood Publishing, 2007.

26 Can the cycle of terrorism be broken?   222

From Synthesis and conclusions. In C. M. Parkes (ed.)
*Response to terrorism: can psychosocial approaches break the
cycle of violence?* (pp. 230–235). London and New York:
Routledge, 2014.

Final conclusions – love is the key   229
Index   233

FOREWORD

This is a fascinating selection of Colin Murray Parkes's favourite and most influential articles and chapters. Each paper is prefaced by a thought-provoking introduction on both its origins and its place in the current context. These reflections reveal the humanity, modesty, generosity and wisdom of a man whose lifelong endeavour has been to further our understanding of bereavement and to provide effective support to those who struggle with it. This book uncovers his developing interests as both a researcher and a practitioner, moving from the significance of attachment to the establishment of volunteer-based community bereavement services, and from disasters to armed conflict. This volume provides unique historical insights into the evolution of what was in the seventies a newly emerging field of study and clinical engagement and underlines Colin Murray Parkes's pre-eminent role within it.

Professor Dame Barbara Monroe
Chief Executive, St Christopher's Hospice,
United Kingdom

ACKNOWLEDGEMENTS

In the course of my life's journey I have had the good fortune to work alongside remarkable people who have guided, provoked and encouraged me to struggle on and sometimes to blaze a trail. They include my paternal grandfather, James Parkes, who opened my eyes to the intellectual beauty of the natural world and enabled me to see mankind as only one among a panoply of evolving species; my lawyer father, Eric Parkes, who taught me the value of logical thinking in the face of received opinions; John Bowlby, whose high intelligence and ability to draw together evidence from many different disciplines and areas of research made him the father of Attachment Theory (the theory of love) and, for many years, my mentor; Gerald Caplan, the pioneer of Crisis Theory and Community Mental Health, on whose team I worked at Harvard's Laboratory of Community Psychiatry; and Robert Lifton, the Harvard psycho-historian, whose studies of responses to historical events and circumstances of our time include the Hiroshima bomb, concentration camp doctors, torture, thought reform ('brain washing'), terrorist attacks and much else. He taught me that psychiatric theories have real contributions to make outside the field of mental illness. Then there was Cicely Saunders, the single-minded mother of palliative care ('hospice'), with whom I shared our anger at the scandalous ways our fellow doctors were treating patients faced with death and their families, and who enabled me to play a part in the planning and development of St Christopher's Hospice from its inception; and Margaret Torrie, the founder of Cruse Clubs for Widows, who was similarly stubborn in her determination to empower widows at a time when women had little to look forward to when their husbands died; she trusted me, and others, to turn this organisation into Cruse Bereavement Care for all bereaved people.

Thanks to them I have had the opportunity to carry out research, to develop new ways of thinking about the problems associated with love and grief and to assist in the development of services for people faced with bereavement, death, disasters and wars.

I am also grateful to the publishers of the following papers for permission to include them in this volume:

To Taylor & Francis/Routledge for Introduction (pp. 1–6) and Conclusions (pp. 272–278) from *Love and Loss: The Roots of Grief and its Complications*, Routledge, London and New York, 2006; Dangerous words *Bereavement Care* 26(2), 23–25, 2000; Genocide in Rwanda: personal reflections *Mortality* 1(1), 95–110, 1998; Attachment and autonomy at the end of life (pp. 151–166) from *Support, innovation and autonomy* Robert Gosling (ed.) London: Tavistock, 1973; and Synthesis and conclusions (Chapter 16) from *Response to terrorism: can psychosocial approaches break the cycle of violence?* C. M. Parkes (ed.) Routledge, 2014.

To Elsevier for 'Seeking' and 'Finding' a Lost Object: Evidence from recent studies of the reaction to bereavement *Social Science and Medicine* 4, 187–201, 1970 and Psychosocial transitions: a field for study *Social Science and Medicine* 5, 101–115, 1971.

To Baywood for Comments on Dennis Klass's article 'Developing a Cross-Cultural Model of Grief' *Omega* (39)3: 153–178, 1999 and Making and breaking cycles of violence (abridged) (pp. 223–238) from *Perspectives on violence and violent death* R. G. Stevenson and G. Cox (eds.) Amityville, NY: Baywood Publishing, 2007.

To the Royal College of Psychiatrists for Psychiatric problems following bereavement by murder or manslaughter *British Journal of Psychiatry* 162, 49–54, 1993 and Services for families in crisis in Tower Hamlets: perception of a crisis service by referrers and users. *Psychiatric Bulletin* 16(12), 748–753, 1992.

To Wiley/Blackwell for What becomes of redundant world models? A contribution to the study of adaptation to change *British Journal of Medical Psychology* 48(2), 131–137, 1975.

To the British Medical Association for Broken Heart: A statistical study of increased mortality among widowers *British Medical Journal* 1, 740–743, 1969 and for Terminal care: evaluation of in-patient service at St Christopher's Hospice. Part I. Views of surviving spouse on effects of service on the patient *Postgraduate Medical Journal* 55, 517–522, 1979.

To the American Psychological Association for Bereavement following disasters (Chapter 22, pp. 463–484) from *Handbook of Bereavement Research and Practice: Advances in Theory and Intervention* Margaret Stroebe, Robert Hansson, Henk Schut and Wolfgang Stroebe (eds.) American Psychological Association, 2008.

Every effort has been made to trace copyright holders and original publishers of the papers included in this book.

INTRODUCTION

In the course of a long working life as a psychiatrist I have found myself faced with many problems that did not, at first sight, seem to have much relevance to my main topic of study, bereavement. As time has passed, however, I have discovered that losses and threats of loss underlie many of the problems that bring people into psychiatric care and even play a part in cycles of distress and violence at family, group and global levels. This has steered my researches into new directions. Indeed I have found myself entering several parallel areas of discourse in which my ideas have relevance and which also feed back into the field of bereavement.

Rather than sticking to a strict time sequence and including papers in the order in which they were written – which would have meant dodging back and forth between the worlds of bereavement, traumatic stress, palliative care, disaster care and the study of war and terrorism – I have devoted a different part of this book to each of these fields. And within each field I have chosen papers that will, I hope, show how ideas have developed, how they can contribute to the prevention and solving of psychological problems and why they have implications for the future.

In selecting papers and extracts for this book I have not included much of the statistical, quantitative data that support my conclusions; this can easily be accessed today by computer searches. Instead, I have tried to balance the historical significance of my ideas against their current readability and relevance. For instance I have not included many of my earlier papers whose conclusions have been built upon and superseded by subsequent research. These early papers may have acted as a starting point for others but have little remaining interest today. This said, while trawling through these early papers, I have come across some whose ideas and conclusions remain relevant today and have included some later papers that review the earlier work and put it in a current perspective.

It is rather like solving an exceedingly large jigsaw puzzle. Little by little another piece is added and the picture becomes clearer. Sometimes we get stuck and have to move to another part of the board, which then fills in a gap and enables us to move on. And sometimes we find that a piece has been put into the wrong place and must be taken out and placed elsewhere. You, my reader, are engaged in the solution of the same puzzle, which will never be finished, but it is my hope that you will find in this selection some ideas and assumptions that make sense of your own corner of the puzzles of life and death.

PART 1

LOVE AND GRIEF

In many respects, then, grief can be regarded as an illness. But it can also bring strength. Just as broken bones can end up stronger than unbroken ones, so the experience of grieving can strengthen and bring maturity to those who have previously been protected from misfortune. The pain of grief is just as much a part of life as the joy of love; it is, perhaps, the price we pay for love, the cost of commitment. To ignore this fact, or to pretend that it is not so, is to put on emotional blinkers which leave us unprepared for the losses that will inevitably occur in our lives and unprepared to help others with the losses in theirs.

This extract from the first edition of *Bereavement: Studies of Grief in Adult Life* (1972) sums up the main findings of my early researches into the psychology of bereavement. These ideas have justified and motivated much of what has followed in a career that has led into some dark places and challenging situations.

In searching for the roots of grief I started by comparing the griefs of small children with the griefs of other species. With John Bowlby and others I helped to develop the new field of Attachment Theory and to show how love and loss are intertwined to the point where problems in attachments to parents were shown to explain some of the problems in grieving that had emerged from empirical research. Out of these studies it became possible to identify people at the time of bereavement who were at greater risk of a range of problems and to develop cost-effective services aimed at reducing the risk and solving some of those problems.

New thinking often gives rise to new language but then becomes incomprehensible to those who do not speak it. I have always preferred to make use of existing words, whenever possible, but this requires clarity and consistency. Part 1 ends with a warning about the ambiguities and misperceptions that have arisen in our discourse about love and loss, most of which can be avoided by the careful and consistent use of words. Poetic language has its own precision and the right words in the right order can both inform and inspire.

CHAPTER 1

ALL IN THE END IS HARVEST

From Introduction. In Agnes Whitaker (ed.) *All in the end is harvest: an anthology for those who grieve* (pp. ix–xii). London: Dartman, Longdon & Todd in association with Cruse Bereavement Care, 1984.

Although written as my introduction to Agnes Whitaker's anthology of poems and quotations about bereavement, the following can also be read as an additional introduction to this book of selections from my own prose.

To a lover of books, libraries are a fearsome blessing – we approach them with awe, conscious of the treasures they contain, but half paralysed by the necessity of choice. In the same way, to a lover of poetry, anthologies are awesome.

We may be tempted to simplify the need for choice by reading them cover to cover, or we may prefer to open the book at random and read on. In either case, we are likely soon to find ourselves suffering from a condition which psychologists have termed 'reactive inhibition', but which is more usually referred to as 'too much of a good thing'.

This anthology is more awesome than most because it treats of a species of poetry and prose which most of us find hard to take. Much of the greatest writing is about death and grief, but to concentrate it together under one cover is to expect a lot of the reader – particularly if that reader has been bereaved or come close to death.

Yet these are the very readers who are most likely to seek out a book of this kind. Grief fills the mind and, for a while, it may be difficult to think of anything else. Since grief cannot be avoided, we might as well accept it and find some way to think about it and to make sense of it. But as every relationship is different, so every grief is different, and we should not expect to find much uniformity in the response to loss or in the solutions which people find to the problems of loss. Words which give comfort to one person may seem like sentimental pap to another. Symbols which to one person are charged with meaning evoke no response in another. Advice which has proved helpful to one person may even harm another.

And yet there is a common chord beneath all this diversity. There are things which most bereaved people have in common, and there are meanings which emerge again and again in the writings of those who find themselves impelled to write about grief.

One function of poetry is to express emotion, fear, despair, anger, bewilderment, rage – all reflect some aspect of the impact of bereavement. We share the poet's grief and in doing so we make our own grief easier to accept, more real, more earthy, more controlled. A sorrow shared may not reduce that sorrow, but it does remind us we are not alone. Grief is the price we pay for love and we must all be prepared to pay it.

Why should this happen to me, and me, and me? Why not? God never promised you a rose garden. Why should you be exempted from the laws of chance or mischance? Life was never fair.

This book reflects bewilderment and outrage, naked fear and flat despair. It echoes the heartache of disappointed hopes, the agonies of regret and the ugly images which haunt the memory when death comes violently in the night. It is not a comfortable book.

But it also contains positive emotion. Some deaths can be a triumph and some people in the face of loss feel joy and pure delight burst unexpectedly upon their minds. Laughter explodes at the most awkward moments and modern man's capacity for pricking the bubbles of pomp and seeking out hypocrisy shows most keenly in the face of solemn condolence.

Some find the 'peace that passes all understanding' in the successful completion of a life well lived together. Some celebrate the passage of the one they hold most dear from this 'vale of tears' into a better place and time. Some simply feel relief that suffering is done. It is an arguable question whether these different reactions result from various philosophies of life or whether philosophy itself reflects emotion. Some hold that faith arises from divine enlightenment ('enthusiasm' – to be possessed of gods), others that logical conviction (by the use of scientific method) is the only road; others cynically deride man's objectivity and point out that those beliefs to which we hold most strongly are the ones about which we have least evidence.

The poet struggles with ideas in ways which give offence to logic. Yet there is a truth in poetry and myth that can transcend dry reason. Just as a dream, being the creation of a person's sleeping mind, plays out the meaning of unconscious mental traffic, so the poet plays with symbols in a game whose truth arises from the feelings it contains. How we interpret dream and poem depends on our ability to learn the rules of the game and the meanings of the symbols, And, since poets, like dreamers, are inclined to change the rules and to play upon the ambiguities of symbols, the meanings which we glean will be elusive. Yet there are common themes, ideas of potent imagery and meaning, which emerge again and again throughout this book. One is the theme of hope, hope that, however bad grief may be, it has a meaning; hope that all the good that can come out of love is not lost; hope that the meaning of life extends beyond life.

Another theme is the idea that, however dimly we comprehend it, everything relates to everything else; all is not chaos. Light and shade, pain and pleasure, love and loss are elements of a pattern whose details we perceive, even though we can never hope to perceive the whole. Each one of us is a part, and only a part, of something bigger and more important than ourselves, and that something is ordered by a natural order which is so all-pervading that we find it difficult to name, though some call it 'God'.

And there is another theme which cuts across and includes the others, the theme of transcendence. This is, perhaps, the hardest to contain with words; it struggles and bolts to leap free. It develops out of despair into resignation, from resignation to surrender, from surrender to renunciation, from renunciation to acceptance and from acceptance to transcendence. In this process fear is transmuted into anger and anger into peace.

Death may happen in a moment but grief takes time; and that time is both an ordeal and a blessing. An ordeal in the sense that grief is often one of the most severe mental pains that we must suffer, and a blessing in the sense that we don't have to do it all at once. We can, to a degree, ration out our grief in bearable dosage; according to our circumstances we may choose to give full vent to grief, and like the Maoris, cry and shout and chant three days and nights on end; or we may stultify our grief, avoiding public show, and leak it, drip by drip, in secret, over many months. But sooner or later, in time, our grief will out, like truth, a harsh reminder of our own mortality.

There are many turning points in the progression of our grief, occasions when events bring home its impact: anniversaries, meetings, recapitulations. At first we think these only serve to aggravate our pain, break down our brittle structures of escape. But, with experience, we learn to treasure them for what they are, reminders of the good things that make up our lives, evidence that 'he (or she) lives on in my memory'. At last it becomes possible to look back with pleasure and look onward now with hope.

This book is a tribute to the work of Cruse Bereavement Care. Cruse is an unlikely body, a group of people with no other aim than to ameliorate the griefs of others. From small beginnings it has grown to offer counsel and support to widows, widowers and their families all over Britain. Those who know Cruse know grief, but they also know compassion and a kind of love – the love which each of us can offer to each other at times of loss. Cruse is an instrument and a symbol of change. We look back at its history with pride, but also with sadness. Many of the people who gave life to Cruse have died; helpers are now bereaved; age and sickness take their toll. But despite these losses, and because of them, the life of Cruse continues. Those who have taken passage through the storms of grief and reached calm waters may return as pilots, and although a major loss is not the only way to know the needs of the bereaved, it adds conviction to the words, 'I understand'. So the bereaved who come for help may stay as helpers, and the cycle is renewed . . .

[Agnes included in her anthology quotations from two Annual Reports of Cruse that would otherwise have been forgotten.]

All is not lost

There is no magical anaesthetic for the pain of grief . . . We cannot give to the bereaved the one thing they most want; we cannot call back Lazarus or Bert or Harry from the dead. The bereaved know that. They know that 'There is nothing you can say.' And they have seen others turn away, embarrassed by their uselessness. But anyone who turns towards the widow and the widower, and gives confidence that they do have something to offer at moments of utter despair, helps to reassure them that all is not lost. Goodness is not gone from the world because one good person has died. Meaning has not gone from life because one who meant so much is no longer present. The loss of one trusted person need not undermine trust in all of those who remain.

The old pattern and the new

We are one people, one community and the death of one is the concern of all. In the face of death man can achieve grandeur, but if he turns his back on death he remains a child, clinging to a land of make-believe. For death is not the ending of the pattern of life's unwinding, but a necessary interruption. Through the painful work of grieving we rediscover the past and weave it afresh into a new reality.

Our aim cannot be to cancel out the past, to try to forget, but to ensure that the strength and meaning which gave beauty to the old pattern is remembered and reinterpreted in the pattern now emerging. Every man must die but the world is permanently changed by each man's existence. At the point of death we meet the forces of social evolution. We may back away in fear, refuse the chance to change, drown our pain in drugs or alcohol or meaningless activity, or we may accept the pains of grief and begin the long struggle to rediscover meaning in a life whose meaning can no longer be taken for granted. There is no easy way through the long valley but we have faith in the ability of each one to find his own way, given time and the encouragement of the rest of us.

CHAPTER 2

'SEEKING' AND 'FINDING' A LOST OBJECT: EVIDENCE FROM RECENT STUDIES OF THE REACTION TO BEREAVEMENT

Extracted from 'Seeking' and 'finding' a lost object: evidence from recent studies of the reaction to bereavement. *Social Science & Medicine* 4: 187–201, 1970.

Written while I was working with John Bowlby at the Tavistock Institute of Human Relations, this paper provides evidence for a theory that lies at the root of much of my thinking about grief. It recognises the importance of the emotion of 'pining' or 'yearning' that distinguishes grief from other emotional states, and provides an explanation for this emotion and for the behaviour that accompanies it. This was one of several issues on which Bowlby and I found ourselves at odds with Freud's theories. Re-reading it today I am uncomfortable with the use of the term 'object' for all of the objects of love. It does, however, serve to remind us that it is not only human beings to whom we become attached.

Grief is the reaction to the loss of an object of love. It is a complex process which, as Bowlby (1961) pointed out, passes through a succession of phases before it is resolved. This article is concerned with one aspect, the most obvious and, to many, the pathognomonic feature of grief, restless pining for the lost object. It is our contention that this represents a frustrated search common to all social animals who maintain attachments to other objects in the life space.

'The urge to recover the lost object' has been described by Bowlby as a principal component of the reaction to loss. The evidence which he cites is largely derived from studies of animals and young children, and although much of it is anecdotal in form, its consistency and clarity carry weight. The behaviour patterns which Bowlby finds in accounts of the separation behaviour of several different species and from which he deduces a common urge to recover a lost object are crying, searching and angry protesting, all of which are directed towards the object. These behaviour patterns have evolved and have obvious value in ensuring the survival of the individual and/or the love object. Thus crying and searching help the separated parties to find each other, and protesting, according to Bowlby, punishes all concerned with the loss and makes it less likely that it will occur again.

It is not intended to repeat here the evidence upon which Bowlby bases his theory nor to cite evidence for the occurrence of this behaviour in children and animals. There is a need for systematic studies in this area and current work such as that of Hinde (1959) on the behaviour of infant rhesus monkeys separated from their mothers can be expected to throw further light on the situation.

In this paper evidence will be drawn from a series of studies of bereaved human adults which have been carried out by the writer in recent years. These studies show that when an adult human being learns of the death of a person to whom he is attached he tends to call and search for that person; at the same time his awareness that such a search is useless, reinforced by lifelong restrictions on the expression of 'irrational' behaviour and the knowledge that fruitless searching is painful, causes him to avoid, deny and, in many ways, restrict the expression of the search. The result is a compromise, a partial expression of the search which varies in degree from person to person and even, within a single person, over time.

Focussing on searching, rather than on crying and protesting as Bowlby does, is not intended to belittle the importance of these other features. But both crying and protesting are relatively nonspecific phenomena. A bereaved person has many reasons for tears and many causes for anger. It is only when the anger and tears are clearly related to the lost person that they can be regarded as a specific part of grief. Searching, by its very nature, implies the loss or absence of an object; it is thought to be an essential component of grief and important to an understanding of the process.

The data drawn upon comes from three sources:

1   Unselected widows

Twenty-two unselected widows under the age of sixty-five who were interviewed systematically at intervals during their first year of bereavement. They were identified by their general practitioners and whilst there were a few who declined to volunteer for the project those who did agree to be seen seemed to constitute a representative sample of London widows. Case examples from this series are prefixed by the letter U.

Most of the information on which the conclusions of this paper are based comes from this study which was concerned with the typical grief of typical London widows. But there is much to be learned about the normal from studying the abnormal and it has been found helpful to include two further studies in which information was obtained from psychiatrically disturbed bereaved patients. To avoid confusion with data obtained from the unselected widows case, examples taken from the two psychiatric studies will be prefixed by the initials I and C and enclosed in brackets. All numerical data and statistics refer to the sample of unselected widows.

2   Psychiatric interviews

Twenty-one psychiatric patients whose illness had come on within six months of the death of a spouse, parent, child or sibling. These were interviewed at the Bethlem Royal and Maudsley Hospitals. Additional information was abstracted from their case notes. Other details of this and the series which follows are described elsewhere (Parkes 1965). Case examples are prefixed by the letter I.

3   Psychiatric case notes

Other examples are taken from the case notes of ninety-five psychiatric patients who had suffered a bereavement during the six months preceding their illness. Members of this group were not accessible for interview. Case examples from this series are prefixed by the letter C.

The components of searching

Although we tend to think of searching in terms of the motor act of restless movements towards possible locations of the lost object, it also has perceptual and ideational components. Thus in the normal course of events the motor activity of searching is likely to bring the lost object within the perceptual field. The perceptual apparatus must be prepared to recognize and pay attention to any sign of the object. Signs of the object can only be identified by reference to memories of the object as it was. Searching the external world for signs of the object therefore includes the establishment of an internal perceptual 'set' derived from previous experience of the object.

A woman is searching for her missing son. She moves restlessly about the likely parts of the house scanning with her eyes and thinking of the boy; she hears a creak and immediately associates it with the sound of her son's footfall on the stair; she calls out, 'John, is that you?' The components of this behaviour sequence are:

1   *Motor hyperactivity* – Restless movement about and scanning of the environment;
2   *Preoccupation with thoughts of the lost person;*
3   Developing a *perceptual 'set' for the person,* namely a disposition to perceive and to pay attention to stimuli which suggest the presence of the person and to ignore those that are not relevant to this aim;
4   *Directing attention towards those parts of the environment in which the person is likely to be found;*
5   *Calling for the lost person.*

Each of these components is to be found in bereaved men and women. In addition some grievers were:

6   *Consciously aware of the urge to search for the lost person.*

Evidence for each component as it appeared in the three studies under discussion will be presented:

1   *Motor hyperactivity*

All save two of the unselected widows studied said they felt restless and fidgety during the first month of bereavement and none of them felt retarded or anergic. The interviewer's observations confirmed this report and assessments of restlessness at interview averaged over the whole year were found to correlate highly with estimates of general muscle tension ($r = 0.83$, $p < 0.001$). These findings confirm Cobb and Lindemann's quantitative study of bereaved subjects using the Interaction Chronograph technique (1943). Lindemann's account of this feature cannot be bettered:

> The activity throughout the day of the severely bereaved person shows remarkable changes. There is no retardation of action and speech; quite to the contrary, there is a rush of speech, especially when talking about the deceased. There is restlessness, inability to sit still, moving about in aimless fashion, *continually searching* for something to do. There is, however, at the same time, a painful lack of capacity to initiate and maintain normal patterns of activity. (my italics)

(Lindeman 1944: 156)

Table 2.1 Correlation coefficients of average scores in the first year of bereavement of variables described in text

	Preoccupation with thoughts of deceased	Clear visual memory of deceased	Sense of presence of deceased	Tearfulness	Irritability or anger
Restlessness	0.18	0.04	0.08	0.32	0.65[†]
Preoccupation with thoughts of deceased		0.73[†]	0.58[†]	0.54[†]	−0.05
Clear visual memory of deceased			0.56[†]	0.38	−0.18
Sense of presence of the deceased				0.42[*]	0.02
Tearfulness					0.41

* p. less than 0.05
† p. less than 0.01

It is contended that in fact the searching behaviour of the bereaved person is not 'aimless' at all. It has the specific aim of finding the one who is gone. The bereaved person, however, seldom admits to having so irrational an aim and his behaviour is therefore regarded by others and perhaps even by himself as 'aimless'. His search for 'something to do' is bound to fail because the things which he can do are not, in fact, what he wants at all. What he wants is to find the lost person.

Taken alone restlessness cannot be regarded as convincing evidence of search. There are other factors such as anger which are also likely to give rise to restlessness.

Table 2.1 shows cross-correlations of six components described in this paper. Quantitative assessments were made at each of five interviews during the course of the first year of bereavement and the mean figures *['variables']* obtained in each case were cross-correlated. Further details of the component features are given below.

[For readers unfamiliar with statistics it is worth noting that all correlations are scored between 0 and 1.0. A correlation coefficient (r) of 1.0 indicates complete agreement between two variables (e.g. all toffs wear toppers), while 0 correlation means there is no relationship between them (e.g. toffs are no more likely to wear toppers than other people) and −1.0 indicates a complete negative association (no toffs wear toppers). Intermediate scores give an idea of the extent to which the variables are associated. The significance of these associations (p.) is affected by the number of people studied. p. = 0.05 indicates that the association could have occurred by chance alone in 5 per cent of cases, and is referred to as 'moderate significance', while 0.01 indicates that only 1 per cent could have occurred by chance and is 'highly significant'.]

It will be seen that whilst 'preoccupation with thoughts of the deceased', 'clear visual memory', 'sense of presence' and 'tearfulness' correlate significantly together, 'restlessness' and 'anger' correlate mainly with each other.

Despite this there was one widow whose motor activity *[restlessness]* did seem clearly related to the urge to look for her husband; she (Case U 1) showed a tendency to keep glancing over her right shoulder. She did this, she said, 'Because he was always on my right'.

2   *Preoccupation with thoughts of the lost person*

While we have no sure means of knowing the thought content of young children and animals during the period of searching, it seems reasonable to suppose that their thoughts are focussed on the lost object and maybe on the events and places associated with the loss. This is certainly the case with adult humans for whom preoccupation with thoughts of the lost person and *[thoughts of]* the events leading up to the loss is the rule.

During the first month of bereavement nineteen of the twenty-two unselected widows interviewed were preoccupied with thoughts of their dead husbands ('I never stop missing him,' Case U 4); twelve of them still spent much of their time thinking of their husbands a year later. Throughout the year a clear visual picture of the dead persons remained in the minds of most of the widows and they reported no blurring as preoccupation grew less. This visual image was sometimes so clear that it was spoken of as if it were a perception. U 22 said, 'I can picture him in any given circumstances . . . I can almost feel his skin and touch his hands,' U 1, 'I keep seeing his very fair hair and the colour of his eyes,' U 5, 'I can always see him,' U 11, 'I can see him whenever I want to,' U 16, 'I still see him, quite vividly, coming in the door,' U 24, 'I can see him sitting in the chair'. The amount of preoccupation with thoughts of the dead persons assessed at interview and the widows' reports of a clear visual picture of their husbands were highly correlated (r = 0·73, p < 0·001). Although there were a few times when widows complained that they were unable to recall the appearance of their spouses, such episodes were transient blocks in recall rather than lasting states of mind.

It is postulated that maintaining a clear visual memory of the lost person facilitates the search by making it more likely that the missing person will be located if, in fact, (s)he is to be found somewhere within the field of search.

3   *Perceptual 'set' for the lost person*

Clear visual memories are associated with a change in the perceptual 'set' such that incoming sensory data is scanned for evidence of the lost object. From time to time ambiguous sensory data will fit the image of the lost object. When this occurs attention is focussed on the data and further evidence sought to confirm the initial impression. Occasionally, an ambiguous sensation is misidentified as deriving from the lost person. Nine of twenty-two widows described actual illusions of the lost person at some time during the first month of bereavement. These usually involved the misidentification of existing environmental stimuli. Case U 3 thought she heard her husband at the door; U 4 repeatedly heard him cough at night; U 7 heard him moving about the house; U 10 said, 'I think I catch sight of him in his van, but it is the van from down the road'. U 11 woke to hear her husband calling her in the night; U 14 repeatedly misidentified men in the street who seemed to resemble her husband; a Nigerian girl, U 15, said 'Everywhere I looked I saw his picture. Ordinary things would have his face.' U 20 thought she heard the door opening and her husband coming in.

4   *Focussing of attention on those parts of the environment which are associated with the person*

Half the widows said that they felt drawn towards places or objects which they associated with their dead husbands. For example, Case U I kept visiting old haunts and planned to go to spiritualist meetings in the hope of making contact with her husband. (Spiritualist meetings were also attended by six psychiatric cases: C 34, C 39, C 46, C 95, I 99 and I 111.) U 3, U 4 and I 119 were unable to leave home without experiencing a strong impulse to return there. U 11 and U 21 felt drawn towards the hospital where their husbands had died and the latter actually walked into the hospital before realizing that such behaviour was pointless. U 3, U 21, U 24, C 7 and I 97 felt drawn to the cemetery and six of the unselected widows returned compulsively to places which they had visited with their husbands. As U 18 said, 'I walk around all where we used to go'. Nineteen widows treasured possessions which they associated with their husbands and four returned repeatedly to these, for instance, U 2 kept searching and gazing at her husband's clothes.

Even when conscious efforts were made to avoid painful reminders of the dead person there was a sense of conflict as if the bereaved person was pulled two ways. U 14 for instance tried sleeping in the back bedroom to get away from her memories but found she missed her husband so much that she had to go back to the front bedroom to be near him.

Several turned over in their minds the idea of killing themselves in order to join the dead person in an afterlife. One girl, aged twelve (Case I 101), was admitted to hospital because of serious weight loss after the death of her mother. She had refused to eat and her father said, 'You'll become like mother,' whereupon she replied, 'That's just what I want to do, I want to die and be with Mummy'. Suicidal ideas were also expressed by I 106 who had seen the face of her husband after death: 'He looked so happy in death,' she said, 'it made me think he was with her (his first wife).'

5   Calling for the lost person

'Dwight, where are you? I need you so much,' wrote Frances Beck in her *The Diary of a Widow* (1965). Crying is, of course, a frequent feature of grief and one which occurred in sixteen out of twenty-two widows when discussing their husbands a month after bereavement. The fact that they cried does not, of course, mean that they were necessarily crying for their husbands. Had they been asked it is doubtful if many would have acknowledged that a cry needs to have an object at all. On occasion, however, the object towards whom the cry was directed was quite clearly the husband. For instance, faced with the fact that she would never have her husband back again, one widow (U 4) shouted out, 'Oh Fred, I do need you,' and then burst into tears. (Case C 94 cried out for her dead baby during the night. Similarly Case I 111 called to her dead sister at night; she went to several spiritualist meetings and dreamed repeatedly that she was searching for her sister but couldn't find her.)

Tearfulness correlated significantly with preoccupation with the memory of the dead person ($r = 0 \times 54$, $p < 0.001$), sense of the presence of the dead person ($r = 0 \times 42$, $p < 0.05$), overall negative affect ($r = 0.73$, $p < 0.001$) and tension ($r = 0 \times 43$, $p < 0.05$). All of these features are associated with severe grief and with the focussing of ideation and perception. The association seems to suggest that, whatever other factors contributed to causing these widows to cry, an important one was the memory of their lost husbands.

6   Consciously aware of the urge to search for the lost person

The adult human being is well aware of the fact that searching for a dead person is irrational and will therefore resist the suggestion that this is what he wants to do following a bereavement. Exceptions occur among those who recognize the irrational components of their own behaviour, in psychotic patients and in children who are less bound by reality than adults.

The following statements were made by four of the twenty-two unselected widows interviewed: Case U l. 'I walk around searching for him.' 'I felt that if I could have come somewhere I could have found him.' She was tempted to go to a spiritualist séance but decided against it.

Case U 3. 'I go to the grave . . . but he's not there.' Case U 9. 'I'm just searching for nothing.' Case U 21. 'It's as if I was drawn towards him.'

Searching for the lost person was also apparent in several bereaved psychiatric patients: Case C 78. An Australian woman lost her adoptive son and her true son in the war. Their deaths were announced within a few weeks of each other. When told of her son's death she refused to believe him dead and eventually persuaded her husband to bring her from Australia to England in search of him. On arrival in Britain she thought she saw her son coming towards her on the stair; she became very depressed and cried for the first time since her bereavement. Case C 79. Received a report that her son had been killed in action in Belgium. She reacted severely and four years later, when the war was over, persuaded her husband to take her to visit her son's grave to make sure that he was dead. Returning home, she said, 'I knew I was leaving him behind forever.' Case I 116. After the death of her baby this patient kept going to the bedroom in search of her dead baby. Case I 117 admitted that she went to the street door to look for her husband. She found this kind of behaviour so painful that she consciously resisted it: 'I think, there's no good going into the kitchen, he'll never come back.'

Children who persisted in a search for lost parents into adult life have been described by Stengel (1939, 1941 and 1943) who believes that some wandering fugues can be accounted for in this way. A young man seen at a case conference in Professor Romano's department in Rochester had been an adoptive child and had spent large sums of money in hiring private investigators to locate his true mother. A singular change occurred when he succeeded in finding his mother. She came to stay with the patient and he was disappointed that she did not live up to his idealized picture of her. Their relationship, however, did become quite good and the patient's restless anxiety diminished considerably.

To sum up, each of the components which go to make up searching behaviour has been shown to play a part in the reaction to bereavement. Motor restlessness, preoccupation with a clear visual memory of the lost person, development of a perceptual 'set' for the lost person, direction of attention towards those parts of the environment in which the person is most likely to be found, and calling to him or her have been found in some or all of the bereaved people studied. In addition, despite the irrationality of such behaviour a number of bereaved persons were consciously aware of the impulse to search.

The studies from which this evidence is derived were not designed to test the 'search' hypothesis. If they had been there are a number of other questions which could have been asked and which might have thrown further light on the problem. For instance in none of these studies were the respondents asked whether they were aware of the need to search. There is a danger, however, that if such an intention had been in the mind of the investigator he could have phrased his questions in such a way that he would have exerted undue influence on the respondent to give replies which would confirm his expectations.

Additional evidence could be cited from dreams and from interpretation of behaviour which seems to represent displaced searching, but the chain of inference in such cases grows long and it has been thought preferable to confine attention to the evidence presented. Searching is only one aspect of the reaction to bereavement. Other components such as anger, guilt, identification phenomena and loss of appetite for food and other forms of gratification are not relevant to this paper. Neither is it intended to describe in detail the forms of secondary elaboration which modify the components of the search. It is, however, necessary to describe another major aspect of bereavement which is, at first sight, the antithesis of searching, disregard of the fact of loss.

Disregard of the fact of loss

When searching the bereaved person feels and acts as if the lost person were recoverable although he knows intellectually that this is not so. Similarly, bereaved people may feel and act as if the dead person were still present even though they know that this is not so. Here we have used the terms 'disregard' and 'disbelief' in preference to the more traditional term 'denial' to avoid ambiguity. Loss is seldom explicitly denied.

Commonly disregarding and searching alternate with periods of each occurring many times in the course of a day. Disregard of the fact of loss, however, is most prominent in the earliest stage of bereavement whereas searching does not reach its peak until a week or so later. Disregard of the fact of loss is seen most clearly during the final illness and immediately after the loss. This involves disbelief in the fact that the loss has or is about to occur, but this is seldom complete; for instance, one bereaved patient (Case I 99) said, 'I just didn't want them to talk about it because the more they talked the more they'd make me believe he was dead.'

Of twenty-two widows nineteen had been warned of the seriousness of their husbands' illnesses before their demise. They were later asked how they had reacted to this information. Twelve said that they did not believe what they were told; either they disbelieved the correctness of the diagnosis or they accepted the diagnosis but questioned the correctness of the prognosis. Seven said that they believed what they were told but at least three of them described how they had subsequently distorted the information or 'pushed it to the back of their minds'.

The significance of death itself is also likely to be disregarded. Half (eleven out of twenty-two) of the widows described feelings of 'numbness' or 'blunting' during the first few days following bereavement. The feeling was variable in its intensity and was well described by one widow (Case U 3) whose husband died during an attack of asthma. She had found the body hanging over the banisters and her first thought was to get her children out of the house. As the door closed behind them she recalls that she heard herself wailing: 'I suddenly burst. I was aware of a horrible wailing and knew it was me. I was saying I loved him and all that. I knew he'd gone but I kept on talking to him'. Shortly afterwards she began to feel 'numbed solid' – 'It's a blessing . . . everything goes hard inside you – like a heavy weight'. It enabled her to carry on without crying.

Even after the numbness had passed most widows still had difficulty in accepting the reality of what had happened and realizing its implications. In twelve cases this was still present from time to time a year later, although in only one case was it a pronounced feature. Four widows said they felt they were waiting for their dead husbands to come back and most of them consciously attempted to avoid situations and thoughts which would remind them of their loss and bring about painful pangs of longing.

Fifteen of the twenty-two widows experienced a comforting sense of the presence of their lost husbands. This was often associated with a temporary reduction in restlessness and pining which seems to indicate that this phenomenon is accompanied by mitigation of searching. Case U 4 said, 'I still have the feeling he's near and there's something I ought to be doing for him or telling him . . . He's with me all the time. I hear him and see him although I know it's only imagination.' U 12 said, 'I still feel that he's around'. U 14, 'Spiritually he's near'. U 21, 'When I'm washing my hair it's the feeling he's there to protect me in case someone comes in through the door.' The sense of his presence was particularly strong in the cemetery – 'It's terrible if it's raining. It's as if I want to pick him up and bring him home.' Later the feeling became more general: 'He's not anywhere in particular, just around the place. It's a good feeling.'

Whilst these examples are probably illusions, hypnagogic hallucinations occurred in other cases. These were clearly unrelated to pre-existing sensory stimuli. Thus U 13 saw her husband coming through the garden gate, C 39 saw her dead father standing by her bed at night and C 62 saw her dead husband gardening with only his trousers on whilst she was relaxing in a chair on a Sunday afternoon. Some bereaved subjects actually spoke to or did things for the absent person whilst others were aware of resisting the impulse. 'If I didn't take a strong hold on myself I'd get talking to him,' said U 14. U 4 often became tearful in bed at night: 'I talk to him and I quite expect him to answer me.' It almost seems that for these people the search has been successful.

That 'seeking' and 'finding' occur close together is hardly surprising. Measures of 'sense of presence' correlated with 'clear visual memories of the deceased' ($r = 0 \times 56$, $p < 0.01$) and 'preoccupation with thoughts of the deceased' ($r = 0.58$, $p < 0.01$). It will readily be recognized that these phenomena, which have already been referred to as components of searching, can equally well be components of finding. In fact, it seems that whilst searching and finding cannot, logically, occur simultaneously, they may be so closely juxtaposed as to be inseparable. Thus a widow may be preoccupied with a clear visual memory of her husband. At one moment she is anxiously pining for him, and a moment later she experiences a comforting sense of his presence near her. As time passes and the intensity of the affects diminish pain and pleasure are experienced as the 'bitter-sweet' mixture of emotions which characterize nostalgia. 'Memorials' are built to 'keep alive' the memory of a dead person. To many of the bereaved they seem to bring the same sense of comfort of having 'found' the lost one as that which is obtained from the sense of presence.

Perhaps the most striking illustration of the way the search for a lost person can be associated with a sense of the presence of that person was found in Case I 99. This was a woman of thirty who had been very attached to her dominating mother. When her mother died her search was consciously directed towards making contact with the departed spirit. At her sister's home she improvised a planchette and 'received' messages which she believed came from her mother. At the same time she noticed a Toby jug which resembled her mother. She became convinced that her mother's spirit had entered into this jug and persuaded her sister to give it to her. During the next few weeks she kept the jug in a prominent position at home but became increasingly frightened by it. Against her will her husband eventually smashed the jug and she noticed that even the pieces 'felt hot', presumably a sign of life. Not long afterwards she was offered a little dog. Her mother had said that if she returned it would be in the form of a dog. When interviewed by the writer three years after her bereavement she said of the dog, 'She's not like any other animal, she does anything. She'll only go for walks with me and my husband. She seems to eat all the things that mother used to eat. She doesn't like men.'

Another type of ideation which seems to imply a partial disregard for the fact of loss is the repeated reviewing of memories of events leading up to the death. More than half of the widows studied reported unhappy reminiscences of such events – 'I go through that last week in the hospital again and again . . . It seems photographed on my mind' (Case U 14). 'I think if only I'd woken up early, perhaps I could have saved him,' (Case U 3). This is associated with a great deal of anxiety and cannot be regarded as a comforting defence.

Such reminiscences obtrude upon the mind much as anticipatory worrying preoccupies people who fear a possible misfortune. This anticipation has been called 'worry work' (Janis 1958) and when it occurs before a misfortune it has the effect of focussing attention on possible dangers and providing an opportunity for appropriate planning. Once the misfortune has occurred, however, this is no longer possible and the most that can be hoped for is that the affected person will learn something from the 'post mortem' which might prevent a similar occurrence in the future. In practice, the painful reminiscences which follow bereavement are particularly fruitless. Not only is there nothing which can now be done to bring back the dead person but there is rarely anything which can be learned from such reminiscence which will prevent future disasters. Anxious reminiscence thus resembles the searching behaviour of bereaved people in being a behavioural sequence which, in the normal course of events, is a valuable activity but which, in the special case of permanent loss, has little positive value.

Ego defence and the 'grief work'

Disregard of either the fact of loss or its permanence has, in the past, been regarded as a consequence of ego defence and the principal mechanism postulated has been denial. More recently, Maslow and Mittelmann (1941) have preferred the term 'coping mechanisms' when speaking of crisis reactions in order to stress the positive value of such processes in helping the individual to cope with an otherwise intolerable situation.

But there are difficulties arising from such terms which limit their usefulness in the special case of grief. In the first place ego defence mechanisms are usually presumed to reduce anxiety. Disregard of the fact of loss certainly does this but searching and the type of reminiscing described earlier in this paper can hardly be said to reduce anxiety. Furthermore bereaved persons often go to great lengths to avoid such painful thoughts; in terms of ego defence they are defending themselves against a defence or using one coping mechanism to cope with another.

Similar difficulties arise when we try to understand the 'function' of grief. Freud asserts that the function of 'mourning' is 'to detach the survivor's memories and hopes from the dead' (1913), yet in 'searching' behaviour we have an important component of mourning which seems to have the opposite function, the restoration of the object. We know, however, that even in animals unrewarded searching does not persist forever. With repeated failure to achieve reunion the intensity and duration of searching diminish, habituation takes place, the 'grief work' is done. It seems that the human adult must also go through the painful business of pining and searching if he is to 'unlearn' his attachment to a lost person . . .

'Searching' and 'finding' in contemporary psychology and ethology

It is necessary to relate the search for a lost object to a more general conceptual framework. Traditional theories of psychology have paid little attention to this category of behaviour and only recently has the significance of searching been recognized.

In analysing animal behaviour ethologists have assumed most behaviour to be 'chain-organized'. That is to say it is made up of behaviour sequences which commonly lead to a biologically useful end result. The appetitive and consummatory (terminating) activities which make up these sequences do not presuppose awareness of the end result in the animal itself.

Miller, Gallanter and Pribram (1960) point out that most human behaviour (and some animal behaviour also) is not 'chain-organized' but is planned so as to achieve a preset goal: successive behaviours are repeatedly modified as their consequences relative to the overall goal become apparent, and cease only when the goal is reached. Thus the organization of the behaviours resembles that of a homing missile. To distinguish behaviour organized on these lines Bowlby (1969) has proposed the term 'goal-corrected'.

It is clear that searching behaviour is normally 'goal-corrected' and is consequently likely to be more adaptable and versatile than it would be if it were 'chain-organized'. But what happens if none of the usual paths look like leading to the goal? At this point the behaviour can be said to be 'frustrated'. The term 'frustration' can be used to indicate both the situation of a person or animal whose goal-corrected behaviour is baulked and the subjective discomfort to which this characteristically gives rise.

C.S. Lewis (1961) has described the sense of frustration of the mourner:

> I think I am beginning to understand why grief feels like suspense. It comes from the frustration of so many impulses that had become habitual. Thought after thought, feeling after feeling, action after action had H. (his wife) for their object. Now their target is gone. I keep on through habit fitting an arrow to the string; then I remember and I have to lay the bow down. So many roads lead through to H. I set out on one of them. But now there's an impassable frontier-post across it. So many roads once; now so many *culs de sac*.

In all goal-corrected behaviour there is an element of searching, of finding the right 'fit' between action and perception. In the behaviour which mediates attachment to a human being the search element is more explicit. We speak of love as a 'tie'. The strength of a tie is its resistance to severance. The behaviour patterns mediating attachment are patterns of interaction; clinging, smiling, following, searching, calling and so on. Some of them, such as smiling and clinging, require the presence of the object for their evocation. Others, such as calling and searching, occur only in the absence of the object.

The situation to which these behaviour patterns normally lead is an optimal proximity to the loved person, and when this is achieved the behaviour ceases. When the loved person is lost, however, the behaviour persists and with it the subjective discomfort which accompanies unterminated striving. This is experienced as 'frustration'.

However, the behaviour patterns mediating attachment are not the only behaviour patterns to be evoked following bereavement. There are many activities which require or have benefited from the collaboration of the lost person but which are not themselves examples of attachment behaviour. Some of these are habits established over the years, in which both parties shared; getting the children off to school on time, planning leisure activities, washing up. When circumstances cause these patterns to be initiated the sense of frustration and restlessness occurs but alternative means of doing without the lost person are likely to be readily available and the bereaved person soon learns to cope.

When, however, attachment behaviour is evoked (e.g. a woman reaches for her husband in bed or interprets a noise as the gate slamming at a time when he is due home from work) no substitute is acceptable. It is this that accounts for the persistence of the impulse to search for the lost person long after habits such as laying the table for two have been unlearned. C.S. Lewis was right in regarding the persistence of habit as a cause of frustration but it is not the only cause. The suspense which he describes would seem to indicate the expectation that something important is about to happen. To the griever the happening which seems most important is the finding of the one who is lost. And in social animals from their earliest years the behaviour pattern which is evoked by loss is searching.

Less clear is the occurrence of consummatory behaviour following the frustration of searching. There are many examples of this phenomenon in the form of the 'vacuum activities' described in the ethological literature. For instance, the behaviour of the male stickleback, deprived of a mate, carrying out its 'courtship dance' in an empty tank (Tyhurst 1951) is reminiscent of the widow (U 4) who regularly talked to her husband in bed at night and the mother (C 94) who got up at night to rock the cradle of her dead baby. It seems reasonable to postulate that in such cases there is a sensorimotor 'set' which predisposes the individual to seek for and to find something, however tenuous, towards which consummatory behaviour can be directed . . .

The paper ends, somewhat abruptly. It will be clear to the reader that, at this time, I was grappling with the recognition that the psychoanalytic explanation for grief was inadequate. Since that time the discovery of fMRI scanning has enabled researchers to study what is happening in the brain while people are grieving. When a woman with a persistent complex bereavement disorder (see Chapter 9) is shown a picture of her dead husband, electrical changes take place in her 'nucleus accumbens' (the so-called reward centre of the brain). But her subjective experience is a pang of grief (O'Connor et al. 2008). It seems that, for a moment, her search for her husband has been rewarded, but a moment later she is forced to recognise that a picture is not enough.

What is emerging is a recognition of the conflict in the mind of every bereaved person between a deep-seated and frustrating urge to seek for someone who is lost and a conscious recognition that searching is fruitless. Or is it? Among the various 'solutions' the bereaved people found, some were more lasting and comforting than others. In years to come much attention has been given to the 'continuing bond' to the people now lost to whom we remain attached and to the idea that while it may be necessary for the bereaved to let go of dead people outside themselves there is a very real sense in which they do 'live on' in our memory. All is not lost.

References

Beck, F. *The Diary of a Widow*. Beacon Press, Boston, 1965.

Bowlby, J. Processes of mourning. *International Journal of Psychoanalysis*, 62, 317, 1961.

Bowlby, J. *Attachment and Loss*. Vol. 1. Attachment. Hogarth, London, 1969.

Cobb, S. and Lindemann, E. Neuro-psychiatric observations of the Coconut Grove Fire. *Annals of Surgery,* 117, 814, 1943.

Freud, S. Totem and taboo. *Complete Psychological Works.* Vol. 13. Hogarth, London, 1913.

Hinde, R. A. Some recent trends in ethology. In S. Koch (ed.) *Psychology: A Study of a Science.* Study 1, Vol. 2, 561–610, McGraw-Hill, New York, 1959.

Janis, I. *Psychological Stress.* John Wiley, New York, 1958.

Lewis, C. S. *A Grief Observed.* Faber & Faber, London, 1961.

Lindemann, E. The symptomatology and management of acute grief. *American Journal of Psychiatry,* 101, 141, 1944.

Maslow, A. H. and Mittelmann, B. *Principles of Abnormal Psychology: The Dynamics of Psychic Illness.* Harper, London, 1941.

Miller, G. A., Gallanter, E. and Pribram, K. H. *Plans and the Structure of Behaviour.* Henry Holt, New York, 1960.

O'Connor, M. F., Wellisch, D. K., Stanton, A. L., Eisenberger, N. I., Irwin, M. R. and Leiberman, M. D. Craving love: enduring grief activates brain's reward center. *Neuroimag,* 42, 969–972, 2008.

Parkes, C. M. Bereavement and mental illness. Part I. A clinical study of the grief of bereaved psychiatric patients. Part II. A classification of bereavement reactions. *British Journal of Medical Psychology,* 38, 1–26, 1965.

Stengel, E. Studies on the psychopathology of compulsive wandering. *British Journal of Medical Psychology,* 18, 250, 1939.

Stengel, E. On the aetiology of the fugue states. *Journal of Mental Science,* 87, 572, 1941.

Stengel, E. Further studies on pathological wandering. *Journal of Mental Science,* 89, 224, 1943.

Tyhurst, S. S. Individual reactions to community disaster. The natural history of psychiatric phenomena. *American Journal of Psychiatry,* 107, 764, 1951.

CHAPTER 3

IS GRIEF A UNIVERSAL PHENOMENON?

Extracted from Comments on Dennis Klass's article 'Developing a cross-cultural model of grief'. *Omega* 39(3): 153–178, 1999.

In considering the wide variation in responses to bereavement, both among and within cultures, Klass wrote:

> *There may be no 'grief' only griefs. Like religion, grief may not be a separate entity, but something that touches many aspects of our inner and our social life. . . . So, the search for the universal must proceed carefully and not create a concept that we reify in a way that blocks, rather than carries forward, our understanding of human experience.*
>
> *(Klass 1999)*

Given that bereavement, the loss of a loved person, is an event that can have many psychological consequences, which include grief, Klass's challenge set me thinking about the basic elements that underlie the responses that follow. Among these it is its resistance to severance that is closest to what most people mean by 'grief'. 'Social animals' include most mammals, many birds, a few reptiles and even some insects. 'Attachment behaviours' include patterns of behaviour that maintain attachments (e.g. clinging and following) and those that facilitate reunion when separated (e.g. crying and searching).

In my view grief is not itself a unitary and universal phenomenon but is derived from the interaction of several components which are themselves universals. These are easiest to comprehend if we accept the wide differences that exist among individuals, cultures and species and seek for the similarities, the things that they have in common. When we do this we find that the following do seem to justify inclusion as universals, at least among social animals:

1 All social animals, by definition, tend to make and maintain attachments to each other. In the environment of evolution such attachments were, and to a large extent still are, necessary to our survival.
2 It is in the nature of attachments that they resist severance. When an animal perceives a threat to an attachment, as when separations occur, neuro-physiological arousal takes place and behavioural tendencies are initiated with the set goal of achieving reunion with the object of the attachment. In many, but not all, species these include crying (or calling) and searching. While we have no means of knowing if the distressing emotion which accompanies this situation in human beings is shared by other species it is not unreasonable to guess that it is.

3   Because attachments have high survival value, attachment behaviours take priority over many other tendencies of lesser importance. But there are other priorities which can and often do take priority over attachment behaviours. These include the perception of other direct and indirect threats to the survival of the individual.
4   If the set goal of a behaviour pattern is not attained the behaviour will gradually diminish and the individual becomes open to other external and internal stimuli (psychologists term this extinction by non-reinforcement). As well as attending to other situational needs the individual may also become open to the exploration of alternative means of reaching the set goal.

Although I take responsibility for the formulation adopted here the ideas are not new. They derive from the work of Bowlby (1969, 1973 and 1980) and others who share my view that the phenomena of grief are best understood from an evolutionary perspective.

I would suggest that the acceptance of these basic mechanisms is compatible with the wide range of reactions to bereavement that is found in human beings. Thus the inhibition of crying and searching may sometimes result from perceived threats to survival as during times of war or other emergency. Bereavements are often times of insecurity (danger) and it is not surprising to find that fears for one's personal survival sometimes take priority over grieving. In addition, the intelligent human being knows that it is illogical and antisocial to cry aloud and to search for a dead person and this may provide us with powerful reasons for inhibiting our natural reactions. In cultures such as the Rwandese, Apache and Navajo, which prohibit grieving, this is seen as a warrior virtue favouring the chances of survival in a hostile environment.

Freud's concept of grief work (1917) reflects his observation that avoidance of grief is sometimes associated with delayed reactions, an observation that is still occasionally confirmed in clinical practice. This could be explained by the fact that attachment behaviour cannot be extinguished if it is not expressed. People who avoid grieving by giving attention to other priorities may find that their grief emerges, unbidden, at a later date.

Opponents of the grief work hypothesis point out that people who grieve intensely from the outset often continue to do so but this too can be explained if we recognise that there are good reasons why some attachment patterns are difficult to extinguish. Thus the work of Ainsworth and others on secure and insecure attachments explains why insecure attachments give rise to lasting problems when interrupted by death (see p. 57). The concept of grief work only ceases to be useful if it is seen as the *only* explanation for pathological grief.

Klass claims that pathological grief is a peculiarly Euro-American concept, yet elsewhere in the same paper he states that in Egypt, emotions are to be expressed, for mental health is damaged if they are held in (Klass 1999: 168). Other cultures such as the Tahitian interpret many responses to bereavement as evidence of illness or fatigue (Levy 1984), and others, including the Ifaluk of the Pacific islands, define continued grieving as pathological (Lutz 1985).

Continuous grief is not of course to be confused with the continuing bonds which Klass, Silverman and Nickman (1996) described in many bereaved people and which are seldom pathological. They often seem to be acceptable alternative means of achieving the set goal of reunion with the lost person. Belief in a spirit world may also reflect this although this opens the door to the dangers of hostile spirits or ghosts.

. . . Deaths and other major events producing change in our lives cause us to move from one subculture to another; a married woman becomes a widow, a child becomes an orphan . . . As Klass, quoting Blauner, says, death disrupts the social structure and it is this disruption that necessitates transition to a new identity. It also implies that those of us who attempt to study and assist bereaved people should do our best to understand the cultures and subcultures from which and to which they move.

I agree with Klass that the systematic exploration of the causes and consequences of cultural differences in reactions to death and bereavement is an important task which will add much to our understanding. It is inevitable that, at the outset, each of us will perceive such differences through our own cultural blinkers, for we have no other way of seeing them. But this does not mean that we cannot learn to see through the eyes of others and to do this without necessarily discarding those of our existing ideas which continue to prove useful and valid. . . . I am, perhaps, more confident than *[Klass]* that much of the hard-won psychology that we have found relevant and clinically useful to our own culture can also prove relevant and of value to others.

References

Ainsworth, M.D.S. Attachments and other affectional bonds across the life cycle. In C. M. Parkes, J. Stevenson-Hinde and P. Marris (eds.) *Attachment across the Life Cycle*. Routledge, London and New York, chapter 3, 1991.

Blauner, R. Death and social structure. *Psychiatry* 29, 378–394, 1966.

Bowlby, J. *Attachment and Loss. Vol. I, Attachment*. Hogarth, London, 1969.

Bowlby, J. *Attachment and Loss. Vol. II, Separation: Anxiety and Anger*. Hogarth, London, 1973.

Bowlby, J. *Attachment and Loss. Vol. III, Loss: Sadness and Depression*. Hogarth, London, 1980.

Freud, S. Mourning and Melancholia, *The Standard Edition of the Complete Psychological Works of Sigmund Freud*, under the general editorship of James Strachey, in collaboration with Anna Freud, assisted by Alix Strachey and Alan Tyson. Hogarth, London, 1953–. Vol. 14, 1917.

Klass, D. Developing a cross-cultural model of grief. *Omega* 39(3), 153–178, 1999.

Klass, D., Silverman, P. R. and Nickman, S. (eds.) *Continuing Bonds: New Understandings of Grief*. Taylor & Francis, Washington, DC and London, 1996.

Levy, R. I. The emotions in comparative perspective. In K. R. Scherer and P. Ekman (eds.) *Approaches to Emotion*. Erlbaum, Hillsdale, NJ, 397–412, 1984.

Lutz, C. Depression and the translation of emotional worlds. In A. Kleinman and B. J. Good (eds.) *Culture and Depression*. University of California, Berkeley, 63–100, 1985.

CHAPTER 4

EVALUATION OF A BEREAVEMENT SERVICE

From *Journal of Preventive Psychiatry* 1(2): 179–188, 1981.

This paper provided a model for low-cost support to bereaved people at risk of psychiatric problems. In later years it was rightly criticised for the small size of the sample of bereaved people studied and for the failure of subsequent studies to replicate my findings. Raphael's study, which is discussed here, used a very similar methodology and came up with even better results, but is it possible for practitioners to evaluate their own work impartially? (See Chapter 6, p. 40.)

Most random-assignment studies have shown little evidence that most bereaved people benefit from counselling, but most grief is transient and only a minority need help from outside their own families. Current research shows that, within that minority, no single intervention will help everyone. We are now, twenty-five years later, much better able to identify the particular problems for which help is needed and likely to be effective thanks largely to the methods developed in this study.

Ours was the first service to offer counselling to the minority most at risk. My finding that men benefitted more than women from a method of intervention which, at the time, encouraged people to express emotion explains why subsequent research showed that women, who are less inhibited than men, may need help of a different kind. Schut and his colleagues (1997) have found that, although men who seek help benefit from the kind of intervention we espoused, among women seeking help after bereavement, cognitive, problem-solving approaches were more effective than emotional expression.[1]

This said, we should not assume, from statistical studies of this kind, that all men require emotive therapy and all women cognitive. Most members of both sexes will cope perfectly well without specialist help and among those who do not there are many exceptions to the rule that women weep and men bottle their feelings.

The main statistical test used in this study is the Chi-squared test which is used to determine the extent to which differences could have been obtained by chance alone. The important statistic is the value of p. If $p = 0.10$ there is a one in ten chance of error, $p\ 0.05$ indicates a one in twenty chance of error and is referred to as 'statistically significant' and $p\ 0.01$ indicates a one in a hundred chance of error and is 'highly significant'.

Abstract

A service for selected bereaved families of patients dying in St Christopher's Hospice, Sydenham, is described. Surviving spouses of 181 patients who died during 1970–1974 were followed up around twenty months after bereavement. A predictive questionnaire was used to assess the risk of poor outcome after bereavement. Respondents predicted to have poor outcome were assigned at random to two groups, one of which was given the support of the Bereavement Service.

A significant association was found between 'high risk' and 'poor outcome' in the control (unsupported) group. Comparison of supported and unsupported groups indicated that bereavement support reduced the risk in the 'high-risk' group to about that of the 'low-risk' group. In particular it reduced the consumption of drugs, alcohol and tobacco by the bereaved and reduced the number of symptoms attributable to anxiety and tension from which they suffered. The service is shown to be effective, humane and economical.

Despite the awe which each of us must feel in the face of death, clinical observation forces one to conclude that it is easier to die than to survive. If conditions of care are good, the distress of the dying is rarely as severe as the grief of those who love him, nor does it last so long. The patient's troubles will soon be over; those of his nearest and dearest may just be beginning.

As members of the 'caring' professions we appropriately consider what actions we can take to reduce this suffering and to prevent some of the psychological and psychosomatic problems which so often follow bereavement.

In theory the risk of bereavement might be reduced by actions taken before and/ or after bereavement, before bereavement death education programs have been introduced, but I am not aware of any substantial evidence for their effectiveness. There is evidence that special services for the families of terminally ill patients, such as those provided by the hospices, reduce stress on the families before bereavement but not strong evidence to indicate that they influence adjustment after bereavement, except in those hospices which also provide post-bereavement support (v.i.). *[My account of six other studies that have all been superseded has been deleted here.]*

Raphael's 1977 study differs from the others in that she selected a group of bereaved people who were already thought to be at special risk. Recognizing that in any group of bereaved people most will come through the stress of bereavement without serious damage to health, she used a method for screening bereaved people which had been developed by Maddison and Viola (1968). Among a total of 194 widows she selected sixty-four high-risk widows, thirty-one of whom were counselled by Raphael herself and thirty-three of whom remained unsupported. Thirteen months after bereavement both groups were assessed using Maddison's 'health questionnaire'. This provides a health outcome measure derived from a checklist of fifty-seven symptoms which commonly take people to a doctor. Extra weight was given to symptoms which had led to medical consultation and hospital admission. At follow up 22 percent of the index group and 59 percent of the controls reported a 'bad outcome' (p < .02).

To sum up the findings of these studies, it seems that there is good evidence that bereavement counselling can be effective, but that the most impressive results have been obtained from a service – Raphael's – which, because it used a psychiatrist as a bereavement counsellor, would probably be too expensive to widely introduce.

The Family Service at St Christopher's Hospice in London has been in existence since 1970. It resembles Raphael's service in selecting bereaved family members for support, but most of this is given by carefully chosen volunteer counsellors, and the psychiatrist and social workers only take over if the volunteers run into difficulties. The Family Service also has some of the advantages of the P.C.U. Service at Montreal because it is part of the total program of care for the family with a dying member which St Christopher's Hospice provides.

The selection of bereaved people for follow-up is made by the nurses who have cared for the patient before death. At St Christopher's Hospice this usually means that they get to know the family well, and this has enabled them to complete an assessment form with respect to the key person most affected by the patient's death in 94 percent of the cases. This form is then handed to the social worker in charge of the Service who uses it to decide who should be followed up, to select a suitable person to provide support and to decide how soon the first visit should be made. In those cases where the family has been looked after by the Hospice's Home Care Service before the patient's death, bereavement support is usually given by the Home Care nurses, but in most other cases one of a group of six to eight voluntary counsellors is asked to make a visit.

A form which these visitors complete after the first visit gives information about this visit. In reporting this data, however, I must admit that I have not found it easy to persuade volunteers to fill in forms. The following findings come from 123 first visits from a total of 249 during the period of study. I have no reason to believe that they are unrepresentative.

The Key Person (or K.P.) was most often a widow (65%) or widower (22%), but support was also offered to six people (5%) who had lost a son or daughter, seven (6%) who had lost other relatives and three (3%) who had lost a friend.

In most instances the visitor agreed that help had been needed, but in a quarter of cases (29) the bereaved family seemed to be coping quite well with their bereavement and were well able to support each other. Two-thirds of the K.P.s (84) needed to talk about their bereavement and over a half (65) were thought to have benefited from expression of feelings about this. In 11 percent, the assessment of suicide risk was thought to have been important. A quarter (30) needed to talk about interpersonal problems, 19 percent about housing, 18 percent about financial problems and 13 percent about problems relating to wills and the disposal of possessions. In most of these cases the visitor had felt that it was sufficient to listen patiently without offering advice, but in 10 percent advice was offered or information given.

Nineteen percent of bereaved respondents were thought to be in need of friendship, and this was something which was easily offered by the visitor; but there were several cases in which help was needed from other sources. Thus 7 percent were referred to their G.P., 7 percent to a social worker, 6 percent to a clergyman, 2 percent to the social security office and 1 percent (one person) to a psychiatrist (myself). Ten percent were recommended to join the Hospice's social club, which meets monthly and provides patients, family members and staff with a chance to meet.

In an extended version of the assessment form, which was completed by visitors after fifty first visits during 1974–1975, it was observed that 84 percent cried at some time during the interview, 44 percent seemed severely anxious or agitated, 26 percent appeared angry or bitter and 24 percent talked more than a little about the loss. In twelve cases (24%) there was thought to be some suicide risk, but in nine of these the risk was remote and none did attempt suicide. Problems reported included insomnia (18%), actual physical illness (14%), keeping existing home (12%), excessive crying (10%), inability to cry (8%), eating too little (8%), haunting memories (8%) and difficulty in maintaining relationships (8%).

Our method of selecting bereaved people for support derives from the Harvard Bereavement Study. This was a longitudinal study of widows and widowers, which was carried out in Caplan's Laboratory of Community Psychiatry in Boston. It provides us with a list of eight predictive factors which can be assessed at the time of bereavement and which correlated with poor outcome a year later (Parkes 1975). With only slight modification, it was possible to use these same assessments to create a short questionnaire (Table 4.1) which could be completed by nurses at the time of a patient's death. The final question was intended to allow nurses to

Table 4.1 Questionnaire

RING ONE ITEM IN EACH SECTION.
LEAVE BLANK IF NOT KNOWN.

Tick here if Key Person (K.P.) not well enough known to enable these questions to be answered.

A. *Age of K.P.* (only applies if K.P. is spouse)	B. *Occupation of principal wage earner of K.P.'s family.*	C. *Length of K.P.'s preparation for patient's death.*
1. 75+	1. Professional and executive	1. Fully prepared for long period.
2. 66–75	2. Semi-professional	2. Fully prepared for > 2 weeks.
3. 56–65	3. Office and clerk	3. Partially prepared.
4. 46–55	4. Skilled manual	4. Totally unprepared.
5. 15–45	5. Semi-skilled manual	
	6. Unskilled manual	

D. *Clinging or Pining*	E. *Anger*	F. *Self-Reproach*
1. Never	1. None (or normal)	1. None
2. Seldom	2. Mild irritation	2. Mild – vague, general
3. Moderate	3. Moderate – occasional outbursts	3. Moderate – some clear self-reproach
4. Frequent	4. Severe – spoiling relationships	4. Severe – preoccupied with self-blame
5. Constant	5. Extreme – always bitter	5. Extreme – major problem
6. Constant and Intense		

G. *Family*	H. *How will K.P. cope?**
1. Warm, will give full support	1. *Well,* normal grief and recovery without special help
2. Doubtful	2. *Fair,* probably get by without special help
3. Family supportive but live at distance	3. *Doubtful,* may need special help
4. Family not supportive	4. *Badly,* requires special help
5. No family	5. *Very badly,* requires urgent help

---

*All scoring four and five on H will be followed up.

use their own intuitive judgement regardless of the preceding parts of the form. Any person scoring four or five on this last question was assigned to Group A, the Imperative Need Group (and excluded from the study). They were followed up, whatever they might have scored on the rest of the questionnaire.

The questionnaire was scored by adding the scores for each question; eighteen was taken as our cut-off point and anyone with eighteen or more was assigned to the 'high-risk' group (Group B). Persons with scores of under eighteen (Group C) were not refused help if they asked for it, but no initiative was taken by us in offering it and in fact few received any.

Over the four-year period of study Group B, the 'high-risk' group, was randomly assigned, by tossing a coin, to an Experiment Group (BH) and a Control Group (BT). The Experimental Group was offered the services of a bereavement counsellor, the Control Group was not.

Members of all four groups were followed up at about twenty months after bereavement by an interviewer from the Tavistock Institute of Human Relations

(Mrs Cynthia Coleman). She administered a shortened version of the Health Questionnaire which had been developed in the Harvard Bereavement Study to assess psychosocial adjustment a year after bereavement (Parkes and Brown 1972). This had enabled the identification of four measures which differentiated one-year bereaved from non-bereaved persons at statistically significant levels. Thus there was an 'Autonomic Symptom' list comprising thirteen symptoms, which are commonly reported as accompaniments of anxiety and tension. A 'Depression' score was obtained by adding together replies to twenty-four questions concerning feelings of sadness and discontent. A 'Habit Change' score was derived from assessment of any increases in the consumption of tranquillizers, sedatives, alcohol and tobacco; and three questions were asked concerning the utilization by the respondent of health care systems during the course of the preceding year. In addition, a 'Worry' score was also obtained by including a list of ten external sources of anxiety, and a 'Physical Symptom' score was derived from ten questions about general health. Neither of these scores had distinguished bereaved from non-bereaved groups in the Harvard study.

Finally an 'Overall Outcome' score was obtained by assigning more or less equal weight to each of these outcome measures and adding them together. Three hundred and two respondents were approached for follow-up, of whom sixty-one (20%) could not be traced, nineteen (6%) were dead or too ill to be interviewed and forty-one (13%) declined an interview. This rate of refusal is to be expected in any study of bereaved people and we did not think it ethical to press them if they preferred not to participate.

The 181 who were followed up were distributed as shown in Table 4.2.

We did not attempt to follow up all Group C cases (who are, of course, a proportionately larger group than the others), but the ninety-three whom we did contact were chosen at random and can be regarded as representative of the total group.

Although the sexes were analysed separately, there were few major differences between them – and ninety-two widowers and eighty-nine widows have been lumped together in the main analysis. The mean age of the group was sixty-six (± 11 years).

The first question we wanted to answer concerned the ability of our predictive questionnaire to correctly identify a 'high-risk' group. We had no means of knowing whether the questions which had correctly predicted outcome in a younger group of widows and widowers in Boston, Massachusetts, would do so in London.

Table 4.3 shows how the unsupported control group (BT), which had a predictive score of more than eighteen and was therefore regarded as at 'high risk' compared with the 'low-risk' group (C) who were also unsupported on our overall outcome, measures twenty months after bereavement. Fifty-seven percent of the 'high-risk' group had outcome scores in excess of three compared with 32 percent

Table 4.2 Group categories and numbers

		n.
Group A	Imperative Need	21
Group B	Predicted 'High-Risk' Group	32
	BH 'Supported' Group	35
	BT Control Group	
Group C	Predicted 'Low-Risk' Group	93
	TOTAL	181

28   *Love and grief*

Table 4.3 Overall outcome and predictive groups

	High-Risk Group (BT) Predictive score 18+ n. 38	Low-Risk Group (C) Predictive score < 18 n. 93
Poor Outcome (Overall Outcome score 3.0+)	22 (57%)	30 (32%)
Good Outcome (Overall Outcome score < 3.0)	16 (42%)	63 (68%)

Yates' χ^2 = 6.37, 2 d.f., p < .02

of the 'low-risk' group. This difference is significant at the 2 percent level widows (Chi squared 5.37, 1 d.f., p < .02). Widows and widowers in the 'high-risk' group were twice as likely to have four or more autonomic symptoms than the 'low-risk' group, and almost twice as likely to have increased their consumption of drugs, alcohol or tobacco (both of these findings are significant, p. < .01).

Even so these results are far from ideal, and a stepwise regression was carried out in order to discover which questions constituted the best predictors of overall outcome. It was clear that the best question is D, 'Clinging', and that the sex of the K.P. is important, women having poorer outcome than men.

Older age is also an indicator as is Question H – the nurses' own prediction of outcome. All of these correlated significantly with outcome as did Question F, 'Self-reproach'.

As a result of these findings we have modified the questionnaire, omitting Question G and substituting a question which allows us to give extra weight to women with young children at home. This has been done because Brown has found, in an adjacent part of South London, a high incidence of depression among women who suffer losses while they have children at home (Brown, Bhrolchain and Harris 1975). Also, of course, this may place the children themselves at risk.

The main purpose of our study was to discover if our intervention had affected the health outcome twenty months after bereavement and, if so, in what ways. This we could do by comparing our various outcome measures in Groups BH and BT, the 'high-risk' experiment and control groups.

The Bereavement Service was initiated in October 1970, and it was hardly surprising that our results with the first five individuals whom we visited were not good. The visitors lacked experience, and it would have been unfair to judge the success of their efforts on the basis of the first few months. It was decided, therefore, to discard these cases and the seven controls from the same period and to base our evaluation on the twenty-eight in the experiment group and the twenty-nine in the control group who entered the project during 1971–1973. Because many scores were not normally distributed, it was decided to use non-parametric methods of analysis. The Mann-Whitney U test (two tailed) was the test of significance employed.

Table 4.4 shows that the experiment group differed from the control group at significant or borderline levels on each of the four measures which had been found to distinguish one-year bereaved respondents from non-bereaved controls in the Harvard study and on the overall outcome measure.

Table 4.4 Mean outcome scores around twenty months after bereavement (1971–1973)

n.	Experimental Group BH 28	Control Group BT 29	p
Autonomic Symptom score	2.2	3.5	0.05
Depression score	5.5	7.9	0.14
Worry (external anxiety) score*	1.25	1.83	0.46
Physical Symptom score*	2.2	2.5	0.44
Habit Change (Drugs, Alcohol and Tobacco) score	0.36	0.85	0.02
Health Care score	1.3	1.59	0.17
OVERALL OUTCOME	2.78	3.93	0.03

*These measures did not distinguish one-year bereaved from non-bereaved respondents in the Harvard Bereavement Study (Parkes and Weiss 1983)

When the sexes were analysed separately, the sample size (15 men and 13 women in group BH, and 19 men and 10 women in group BT) reduced the likelihood that statistically significant differences would be obtained. In fact male experimentals did differ from male controls on depression (p = .06), habit change (p = .02) and overall outcome (p = .10). Female experimentals and controls did differ in the expected direction, but the differences were less striking than those of the male respondents, and none approached statistical significance.

The inclusion of figures for the first months of the project reduces the significance of the overall outcome measure to p = .12, but autonomic symptom scores (p = .05) and habit change scores (p = .04) remain significantly lower in experiment than control groups. To complete the picture let us look at the overall outcome scores in the other two groups (Figure 4.1). Group A, the Imperative Need Group, is rightly regarded as being in special need of help. Since they were excluded from the process of randomization, we have no means of knowing whether their overall outcome scores were influenced by the help which they received from the service.

Group C, the 'low-risk' group, had lower scores than the 'high-risk' controls (Group BT), but were not appreciably different in outcome from the 'high-risk' experiment group. It seems, therefore, that the effect of the service has been to reduce the health risk of the 'high-risk' group to about the same level as the 'low-risk' group.

It seems reasonable to conclude that the introduction of the service for bereaved people at St Christopher's Hospice has produced a real improvement in health outcome which remains nearly two years later. In particular the service reduces the need for drugs, alcohol and tobacco among the bereaved and reduces the number of symptoms attributable to anxiety and tension from which they suffer. It may also reduce the use which they make of doctors and improve their overall level of contentment (particularly if they are men).

In economic terms it seems likely (but not conclusive) that the introduction of the service has reduced the cost of physical health care to the bereaved relatives of patients who have died in the Hospice. These savings have to be set against the

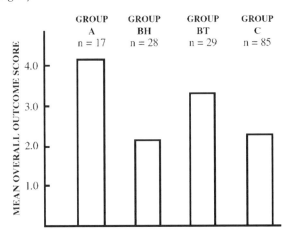

Figure 4.1 Overall outcome × group

costs of the service itself. But, since most of the visiting is conducted by volunteers, the costs to the health service are little more than the time of the social worker and psychiatrist who provide support. On present showing this amounts to about three days of the time of a social worker and three to four hours per month of the time of a consultant psychiatrist. This allows us to screen 400–500 families a year and to follow up about 100 bereaved individuals.

The only possible conclusion which can be reached on grounds of humanity as well as economics is that bereavement services of this type should be more widely introduced.

Note

1   Schut, H.A.W., Stroebe, M., van den Bout, J. and de Keijser, J. Intervention for the bereaved: gender differences in the efficacy of two counselling programs. *British Journal of Clinical Psychology* 36, 63–72, 1997.

References

Brown, G.W., Bhrolchain, M.N. and Harris, T. Social class and psychiatric disturbance among women in an urban population. *Sociology* 9, 225–254, 1975.

Maddison, D. and Viola, A. The health of widows in the year following bereavement. *Journal of Psychosomatic Research* 12, 297–306, 1968.

Parkes, C.M. Determinants of outcome following bereavement. *Omega* 6, 303–323, 1975.

Parkes, C.M. and Brown, R.J. Health after bereavement. A controlled study of young Boston widows and widowers. *Psychosomatic Medicine* 34, 449–461, 1972.

Parkes, C.M. and Weiss, R.S. *Recovery from Bereavement*. Basic Books, New York, 1983.

Raphael, B. Preventive intervention with the recently bereaved. *Archives of General Psychiatry* 34, 1450, 1977.

CHAPTER 5

BROKEN HEART

A statistical study of increased mortality among widowers

Colin Murray Parkes, Bernard Benjamin and Roy G. Fitzgerald

Reprinted from *British Medical Journal* 1: 740–743, 1969.

In 1963 a paper was published by Young, Benjamin and Wallis reporting a significant increase in the death rate in widowers during the first six months after the deaths of their wives. Subsequently I wrote to Bernard Benjamin, the director of studies at the Research and Intelligence Unit at the Greater London Council, to ask if the data from death certificates that had been used in that study included information on the causes of death. He confirmed that they did and agreed to collaborate with me and with Roy Fitzgerald, who was on attachment from the National Institutes of Mental Health in the United States, to analyze those data.

This was to be the first study to show that there was substance to the old belief that people can die of a 'broken heart'. It gave rise to much interest in the press and stimulated many further studies which confirmed the finding and extended it to include widows and parents losing children. In the following extract analysis of the influence of social class and of concordance of causes of death in both the widower and the deceased partner has been deleted as other and larger studies have superseded our findings.

Summary

A total of 4,486 widowers of fifty-five years of age and older have been followed up for nine years since the deaths of their wives in 1957. Of these 213 died during the first six months of bereavement, 40% above the expected rate for married men of the same age. Thereafter the mortality rate fell gradually to that of married men and remained at about the same level.

The greatest increase in mortality during the first six months was found in the widowers dying from coronary thrombosis and other arteriosclerotic and degenerative heart disease. There was also evidence of a true increase in mortality from other diseases, though the numbers in individual categories were too small for statistical analysis. During the first six months 22.5% of the deaths were from the same diagnostic group as the wife's death. Some evidence suggests that this may be a larger proportion than would be expected by chance association, but there is no evidence suggesting that the proportion is any different among widows and widowers who have been bereaved for more than six months.

Introduction

To most of us death from a 'broken heart' is a figure of speech, yet the term reflects a bygone belief that grief could kill, and kill through the heart.

In 1963 a report was published of a follow-up of a cohort of all men of fifty-five years and older who were widowed in England and Wales during January and July 1957 (Young, Benjamin and Wallis, 1963). This showed that during the first six months of bereavement the mortality rate was 40% greater than the mortality rate for married men of the same age, and that this increase gradually fell thereafter to the level of the rate for married men.

More recently Rees and Lutkins (1967) reported the results of a survey of the death rate among 903 relatives of patients dying in a semi-rural area of Wales. They found that 4.8% of bereaved close relatives died within a year of bereavement compared with 0.68% of a non-bereaved control group. The greatest increase was found among widows and widowers, their mortality rate being ten times greater than that of the matched controls. After the first year of bereavement mortality rates fell off sharply and were not significantly higher than in the control group.

The study by Cox and Ford (1964) of mortality rates among widows shows a rise during the second month but not during the first six months of bereavement. This study relies on the widow having applied for a contributory pension, but, as the authors pointed out, many widows who become ill and die during the first six months after the death of their husbands may never have applied for a pension.

None of these studies has attempted to determine the particular diagnoses which contribute to the increased post-bereavement mortality rate, and none has followed up a cohort of bereaved persons for more than six years.

This paper reports a nine-year follow-up of the widowers studied by Young and colleagues (1963), with additional information, which was not previously reported, concerning certified causes of death and social class.

Method

A total of 4,486 widowers of fifty-five years of age and older were identified from the death certificates of their wives. The punch cards of the N.H.S. Central Register were then tagged so that the death of any of these men would automatically be reported. Information concerning age, occupation and the certified cause of death was obtained from the death certificates of the widowers.

Results

Figures showing the overall mortality rate as a proportion of the mortality rate for married men of the same age during the first four years of bereavement have been published (Young *et al.* 1963). At that time the possibility of a further subsequent rise was discussed.

Figure 5.1 shows the findings extended to include the first nine years of bereavement. It can be seen that the increment in mortality rate of 40% which occurred during the first six months of bereavement is subsequently followed by a gradual return to around the level for married men of the same age and that there is no subsequent rise in mortality.

The number of deaths during the first six months is now found to be 213 as compared with 214 in the original paper, a false posting to the N.H.S. Central Register having been discovered.

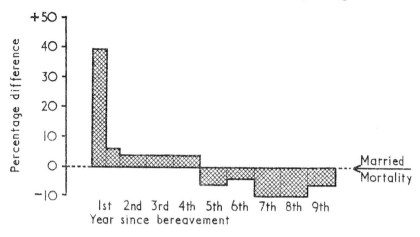

Figure 5.1 Percentage difference between mortality rate of widowers over fifty-four and that of married men of the same age, by years since bereavement. N = 4,486.

Cause of death of widowers

Table 5.1 shows the causes of death among the 213 widowers who died within six months of their wives. These are compared with the number which would have been expected had these widowers had the same mortality rate as married men of the same age in England and Wales during 1957.

Figure 5.2 shows the mortality rate among these widowers as a proportion of the expected rate. The greatest increase was in the group diagnosed as 'coronary thrombosis and other arteriosclerotic and degenerative heart diseases'. Seventy-seven deaths were attributed to this cause, an increase of 67% above the expected number. The 99% confidence interval for the expected deaths from coronary thrombosis and other arteriosclerotic heart disease (together) is 25–67. The actual number of deaths is seventy-seven, so that the excess is significant at the 1% level.

The second greatest increase was found in the group diagnosed 'other heart and circulatory disease'. Twenty-four deaths occurred in this group, an increase of 60% over the expected number. Taken together diseases of the heart and circulatory systems accounted for two-thirds of the increase in mortality during the first six months of bereavement.

No disease group other than 'coronary thrombosis and other arteriosclerotic and degenerative heart diseases' showed a statistically significant increase, but when all other causes of death were combined the 99% confidence interval for expected deaths is 77–137 and the actual deaths number 136. The excess is therefore only just short of significance at the 1% level . . .

Discussion

In the original paper by Young and colleagues (1963) the mortality was traced up to the end of the fifth year after bereavement and it was noted that the mortality of widowers in the general population is in the region of one to four times that of married men of the same age. But it was shown that the increased mortality in this sample of 4,486 widowers is almost confined to the first six months of

Table 5.1 Cause of death among the 213 widowers who died within six months of their wives compared with the number expected from the mortality rate of married men of the same age in England and Wales during 1957.

Cause of Death	Number of Deaths	
	Actual	Expected
Coronary thrombosis and other arteriosclerotic and degenerative heart disease	77	46
Influenza, pneumonia and bronchitis	29	20
Other heart and circulatory diseases	24	15
Cancer of other sites	22	19
Cancer of lung and bronchus	8	7
Infectious diseases	4	1
Other causes	27	23
Total	213	153

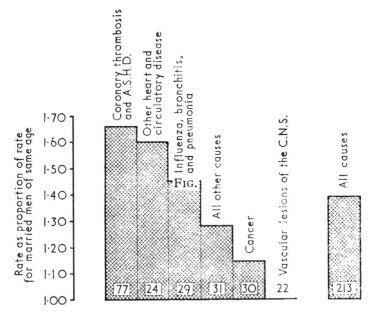

Figure 5.2 Mortality rate of widowers during first six months of bereavement as a proportion of rate for married men of the same age, by cause of death. Figures = number of deaths among 4,486 widowers.

bereavement, after which it falls to that of married men of the same age. The possibility was mooted that a subsequent rise in mortality would take place which would bring the mortality rate of the sample into line with that of the general population of widowers.

Now that the sample has been followed up to the end of the ninth year it seems clear that no such rise is likely to take place; in fact from the fifth year of bereavement the mortality rate is slightly below that of married men of the same age.

Various possible explanations for this were discussed in the previous article, and we have no means of deciding between them. For the sake of completeness we list them here:

1   The average age of widowers in any age group is about one year older than the average age of married men within the same age group. This might explain up to a quarter of the excess overall mortality among widowers.
2   Widowers may be under-enumerated in the census.
3   Widowers may be over-enumerated in the deaths.
4   It *is* possible that only the healthier widowers remarry. Because widowers who remarry are not removed from our cohort we may be studying a population who are fitter than the general population of widowers.
5   Some tagged cases may have been 'lost' – that is to say, some of the widowers whose N.H.S. Central Register cards were tagged may not have been reported to the Registrar General's Office on their demise. This would result in a spuriously lower mortality rate in all years following bereavement.

Another matter which requires explanation is the difference between the 25% increase in mortality found in our study during the whole of the first year of bereavement and the tenfold increase (nineteen deaths in the bereaved group with only two deaths in the control group) in the study of widows and widowers in Llandidloes by Rees and Lutkins (1967). In fact the mortality rate among the widowers studied by us, 8.5%, is not much different from the mortality rate of 12.2% Rees and Lutkins found among their widows and widowers. What is different is the low figure of 1.2% which they give as the mortality rate of their control group of married persons. This is probably lower than the mean rate for married persons of the same age in England and Wales (4.9% in our study), and it seems must reflect some local peculiarity in the population studied. Despite these differences it seems fair to conclude that there is a true increase in mortality among widowers during the first six months after bereavement. We must now consider the possible causes of this.

The findings reported make it clear that the increased mortality is not explained by an increase in deaths from accident or infectious disease which might have been shared with the wife. In fact the greatest increase is found in the group diagnosed 'coronary thrombosis and other arteriosclerotic and degenerative heart disease', which accounts for 53% of the increased mortality. In addition, there is some evidence of a true increase in mortality from other diseases, though the number in individual disease categories is too small for statistical analysis.

Death certificates are not necessarily a reliable source of information concerning cause of death. In a survey carried out by the General Register Office (1966) of 995 cases of death attributed by clinicians to coronary and arteriosclerotic heart disease there were 278 cases (28%) in which the diagnosis was changed after post-mortem examination. A similar number of cases were changed from other diagnoses to coronary and arteriosclerotic heart disease by the pathologist, and misdiagnoses were attributed to many different diseases. While these observations throw some doubt on the reliability of our findings there is no reason to believe that the heart disease group is any more heavily weighted with incorrect diagnoses than other diagnostic groups.

If we accept that the increased mortality is largely attributable to coronary and arteriosclerotic heart disease we still have to explain this increase. Young and colleagues (1963) listed 'homogamy' (the tendency of unfit to marry unfit) and 'joint unfavourable environment' (the fact that husband and wife share a pathogenic environment) as possible explanations of the increased six-month mortality. Either of these were factors one would expect husband and wife to die from the same or similar diseases. This study has shown that there is a tendency for this to occur. But if this were the main cause of the increased mortality following bereavement one would expect to find the greatest concordance in diagnosis in those diagnostic groups that account for the increased mortality rate. This is not the case, and in fact the number of husbands and wives who died from arteriosclerotic and other degenerative heart diseases was only three greater than expectation. Furthermore, the overall concordance rate in this study, which was 24% above chance expectation, is not much different from Ciocco's (1940) figures for married couples whose respective deaths were not limited to the first six months of bereavement. He found the concordance rate 18% above expectation. These findings do not disprove the possible contribution which homogamy and joint unfavourable environment make to the increased mortality following bereavement, but they do make it less likely that these factors explain more than a part of the increased six-month mortality.

The finding that bereavement is associated with an increased mortality from coronary thrombosis does not necessarily mean that it is associated with an increase in the incidence of the disease. It may be that it simply increases the proportion of patients who died after having a coronary thrombosis. Even if the thrombosis itself does not occur until after bereavement it will presumably occur only if the coronary arteries are already diseased. In other words, bereavement may act as an aggravating or a precipitating factor in coronary thrombosis, but in either case it is unlikely to be the sole cause of death.

Psychological stress has long been thought to be a factor in this disease. For example, Weiss, Dlin, Rollin, Fischer and Bepler (1957) found evidence of emotional stress in 86% of forty-three coronary thrombosis cases compared with 9% of matched controls. But how such stresses influence the formation or course of the thrombosis remains a matter for conjecture. It is possible that emotional stress acts by altering the consumption of fats, sugar, coffee or tobacco,[1] all of which have been shown to be statistically related to the mortality from coronary artery disease (Hammond and Horn 1958; Paul *et al.* 1963; Yudkin 1967). On the other hand, emotional stress alone has been shown to affect pulse rate, stroke volume, cardiac output, peripheral resistance, arterial blood pressure, exercise tolerance and clotting time, and to produce arrhythmias and electrocardiographic changes (Schneider and Zangari 1951; Stevenson and Duncan 1950). In patients with known hypertension, angina pectoris or other structural heart disease such changes have been shown to have pathological effects (Hickham, Cargill and Golden 1948). All of which leads one to suspect that it may well be the emotional effects of bereavement, with the concomitant changes in psycho-endocrine functions, which are responsible for the increased mortality rate . . .

If the findings of this study are typical we must conclude that nearly 5% of widowers over the age of fifty-five die within six months of the deaths of their wives, and that nearly a half of these deaths are from heart disease. Research is needed to discover whether widowers under fifty-five and widows are similarly at risk and to determine what intervention is possible to minimize this risk. Already much is known about the psychological and social consequences of bereavement, and if, as seems most likely, the baneful effects of bereavement on physical health are a response to psychological stress then anything which mitigates that stress can be expected to reduce the risk of its physical effects.

Programmes for the primary prevention of physical and mental illness by public and professional education and the provision of services to help people at times of crisis are in a stage of development (see, for instance, the outline of a primary prevention programme by Caplan 1964), and it is an area which practicing clinicians can ill afford to ignore.

Thanks are due to the staff of the Registrar General's Office for their assistance in the execution of the survey; to Dr Michael Young and Dr Christopher Wallis for permission to carry out this study of the cohort of widowers originally described by them; and to Dr C. J. Gavey and Dr John Bowlby for their helpful criticism of the draft.

The work was supported by research grants from the Mental Health Research Fund, the Ministry of Health and the National Institute of Mental Health, Washington, DC.

Note

1   Doll and Hill (1956) showed that the association between smoking and mortality from coronary heart disease is almost confined to patients under the age of fifty-five who would not, of course, have been included in this study.

References

Caplan, G. *Principles of Preventive Psychiatry*. Basic Books, New York, 1964.
Ciocco, A. *Human Biology* 12, 508, 1940.
Cox, P. R. and Ford, J. R. *Lancet* 1, 163, 1964.
Doll, R. and Hill, A. B. *British Medical Journal* 2, 1071, 1956.
General Register Office. *Studies on Medical and Population Subjects*, No. 20. H.M.S.O., London, 1966.
Hammond, E. C. and Horn, D. *Journal of the American Medical Association* 166, 1159, 1958.
Hickham, J. B., Cargill, W. H. and Golden, A. *Journal of Clinical Investigation* 27, 290, 1948.
Paul, O., et al. *Circulation* 28, 20, 1963.
Rees, W. D. and Lutkins, S. G. *British Medical Journal* 4, 13, 1967.
Schneider, R. A. and Zangari, V. M. *Psychosomatic Medicine* 13, 289, 1951.
Stevenson, I. and Duncan, C. H. *Research Publication of the Association of Nervous and Mental Diseases* 29, 799, 1950.
Weiss, E., Dlin, B., Rollin, H. R., Fischer, H. K. and Bepler, C. R. *Archives of Internal Medicine* 99, 628, 1957.
Young, M., Benjamin, B. and Wallis, C. *Lancet* 2, 454, 1963.
Yudkin, J. *New Scientist* 33, 542, 1967.

CHAPTER 6

GUIDELINES FOR CONDUCTING ETHICAL BEREAVEMENT RESEARCH

From *Death Studies* 19: 171–181, 1995.

I recall the anxiety with which I approached my first interviews with bereaved people. Was I intruding on private grief? What should I do if they became upset? The ethical committees who had to approve the research were equally uncertain. Would they receive angry letters of complaint? Was this researcher a suitable person to approach people at this most vulnerable time in their lives?

In the end it was the bereaved subjects who reassured me. True, many were already upset and they cried as they shared their stories, but far from blaming me, most of them were grateful for the opportunity to talk and share feelings about issues that preoccupied their minds and they were glad to bring something good out of the bad thing that had happened. 'I think it's wonderful what you are doing!' said one of my first interviewees.

This has been one of my most popular papers and has been republished in the Indian Journal of Palliative Care and elsewhere. Several researchers have enclosed copies of this article with their applications for approval by ethical committees along with reassurance that their proposed research meets my list of criteria.

Abstract

It is unethical to introduce services for the bereaved that are not well founded and evaluated; yet there are special difficulties in conducting research with bereaved people. This situation has deterred some from carrying out research in this field and has caused others to place obstacles in the way of would-be researchers. The ethical difficulties of bereavement research are described, and guidelines are provided that should enable investigators to carry out research without harming those who offer their help and without violating the scientific value of the research.

It is only by conducting systematic research that it has been possible to establish an ethical basis for bereavement care. One could go so far as to say that it is unethical to introduce any kind of service without carrying out research to find out whether it does good or harm. Even so, this is a sensitive area in which there is a real danger that researchers will cause distress for bereaved persons and may even harm them.

All plans for research should be scrutinized by an ethical committee. Problems are likely to arise for several reasons, and ways to resolve these problems are described in the following sections.

Gaining access to bereaved people

Access to bereaved people can be obtained in a variety of ways, including public records of death registrations, hospital records, obituary/notices, referrals from funeral directors and referrals from general practitioners. Guardians of these sources are right to be cautious in checking the credentials of the researcher and the ethical validity of the research but they often err on the side of being overzealous, depriving bereaved people of the opportunity to help with well-founded research and forcing researchers to make use of non-random methods of sampling.

It is impossible to say how many researchers have been put off by obstacles of this kind, but the number of well-conducted projects in this field remains small. Special difficulties exist in obtaining access to bereaved children. Parents are understandably protective, and it is necessary for researchers to spend time with them before parents are likely to trust them to talk to their children.

Obtaining informed consent

The families of people who are dying or have recently died are often emotionally upset; they find it difficult to take in explanations and may be easily persuaded to agree to procedures or interviews that they will subsequently regret. Alternatively, they may refuse to help with a project that, were they in a calmer frame of mind, would present no problems to them. These problems are less likely to arise if respondents are sent a clearly written explanation of the project that they can study at their leisure and discuss with their families. In this written explanation, researchers should establish their credentials by citing their qualifications for carrying out work of this kind and reassuring respondents that they are backed by a responsible and trustworthy institution to whom reference can be made if any doubt remains in respondents' minds. Ethics committees should always read and endorse these written explanations. Of course, because not every respondent will read or understand such a letter, it is essential that it be followed up by a telephone call or explanatory visit, at which time researchers can explain their credentials verbally and answer any questions.

Preventing possible harm to respondents

Bereaved people, particularly those who are newly bereaved, are vulnerable. Strong emotions can impair their judgement, their confidence, their ability to concentrate and their ability to appraise risks. Some are so desperate for help that they will accept any person who approaches them in a friendly way; others are deeply hurt and unduly suspicious. The credulous are vulnerable to exploitation and need to be protected from unscrupulous or potentially harmful intervention, be it by researchers or therapists; the suspicious may need the reassurance of an impartial and trusted person before they will agree to be interviewed.

A properly constituted ethics committee attached to a reputable organization can reduce these risks and is a source of reassurance to clients. How are the members of such committees to recognize potentially damaging research? In my view, the following criteria should be satisfied in all cases.

No personal gain to researcher

The researcher should obtain no personal gain from a particular research result. For example, researchers employed by a counselling organization to evaluate their counselling must have the right to make public the results of their evaluation regardless of the outcome of the research. Permission for publication should be written into any contract in advance of the research. Although it is not unreasonable for an employing body to have the right to see and to comment on research results before publication, it should not have the right to prevent publication if those results do not suit its commercial interests or prejudices.

Therapists and counsellors are often motivated to study the results of their own therapy; they are well able to collect data, and their special knowledge of the field may be considerable. They are, however, faced with serious ethical problems if the results of their research throw doubt on the value of their service and, for this reason alone, any project that sets out to test the value of a service should be carried out by a truly independent organization. Even then, it is important that all concerned recognize that any benefits to the researcher, whether financial or meritorious, derive from the quality of the research, rather than the results obtained.

No pressure on people to participate

The participants should not be subjected to any pressure, financial inducement or emotional blackmail to take part in the interview or to respond in a particular way, and they should be informed that they are free to withdraw from the research any time they wish. Financial payments should be limited to expenses incurred. It should be made clear to all participants that there are no correct answers to any of the questions. This can be difficult when the informant identifies the researcher with a particular viewpoint or service. Thus gratitude to a doctor or hospital can make it difficult for informants to criticize any aspect of the service provided, particularly if the research is being conducted by the doctor in question or by other representatives of the institution. Similarly, bereaved people who are under the care of a particular counsellor or therapist should not be asked by that person to evaluate the care they are receiving. These considerations add further weight to the necessity of any evaluation of services being carried out by individuals or organizations who are truly independent of the research and are seen by subjects to be independent of it.

Training of interviewers in the support of bereaved persons

Although researchers cannot be responsible for solving all the problems of the people who assist them with their research, they are responsible for any problems that arise as a result of the research itself. Interviewers should have received sufficient training in the support of bereaved people to ensure that they do no harm. If, in the course of an interview, the respondent becomes distressed, the needs of the respondent should take priority over the needs of the research. It is not always desirable to interrupt a research interview if the subject becomes distressed. Expressing grief can be a very therapeutic experience, and the interviewer need not attempt to block or inhibit such spontaneous expressions. Bereaved people expect the discussion of emotionally distressing events to be painful and may resent being told to calm down. The decision to interrupt or to discontinue the interview will depend on the response to the support given by the interviewer and the participant's wishes. This is no place for scientific detachment in the sense of the interviewer acting like a fly on the wall. If the respondent is in need of help, the interviewer should not hesitate to provide it. Interviewers should also be aware of other sources of help for bereaved people that are available in their area and should provide this information to any respondents who they think need it.

Supervision of interviewers

All interviewers should be closely and regularly supervised by someone with a sound knowledge of bereavement and counselling as well as a clear understanding of the purpose and method of the research and the ethical issues involved. Supervisors need to be particularly aware of the problems that can arise when an interviewer is either emotionally over involved (in which case, he or she may aggravate the subject's emotional response and bias the accuracy and the data) or too detached (in which case, the subject may feel unsupported and may conceal emotionally charged information). Given these safeguards, it is probable that the research will do good rather than harm to respondents.

Confidentiality

The confidentiality of the sources of all information obtained in the research should be protected in (a) all publications or other public communication arising from the research and (b) communications among supervisors and other colleagues about the research. Thus names, addresses and other information that could reveal the identity of a subject should be changed in ways that disguise the subject's identity without distorting the essential findings of the research. This can be difficult if, for instance, the details of a critical life event are widely known. For example, a psychologist who gave a lecture on the psychological aspects of murder was embarrassed when a newspaper reporter in the audience indicated that he had identified one of the cases under discussion. In such cases, it may be necessary to report results in general rather than specific terms.

If the researcher intends to exhibit videotaped interviews, confidentiality presents a particular problem. The usual method of ensuring confidentiality by concealing the face of the respondent may not be appropriate if the research is concerned with emotional expression. In such cases, potential subjects need to be fully aware of this implication. They should see any such material before it is released and give full consent to its release. Any limitation on audiences (e.g. that the tape should only be used for training doctors) should be strictly adhered to, but it is better not to make such restrictions in the first place, because it is very difficult to ensure that they will be met.

The information participants are given before their consent to the research is obtained should include a document stating that confidentiality will be respected.

Minimization of stress during the interview

The interview should be organized in such a way as to minimize the stress on the respondent and to maximize the accuracy of the information obtained. These two objectives seldom conflict because subjects are more likely to give accurate information if they are in a calm frame of mind than if they are upset or unsure of themselves. Thus questionnaires dealing with emotional issues and physical procedures such as taking blood samples, should, if possible, be left to the end of the interview. All interviews should give respondents time and opportunities to express their own needs as well as to meet the needs of the researcher. Verbatim comments often explain and enhance the value of the questionnaire findings, and researchers are wise to record both.

Tape recorders and video cameras are less often seen as intrusive today than they used to be, but interviewers should always inform subjects beforehand that they are willing to turn off these machines if they request it. There is no longer any need to take special lighting and camera teams into a person's home, but researchers should take care that equipment is working properly and that interviewers know how to use it. (There are few more annoying experiences to a researcher or subject than to find that a lengthy interview has been lost.)

Audio- or videotapes obtained for research purposes are the property of the researcher or his or her employing organization. Copies are sometimes given to research subjects as a reward for their help, but researchers should be aware that they will not thenceforth be able to control how that material is used. In one case, a bereaved patient who had been given a copy of a videotaped abreaction sold it to a television company!

Rigorous methodology

Although it is not the job of the ethics committee to teach science, it should protect the public from sloppy methodology. Research that can only confirm the prejudices of the researcher does more harm than good. Despite the technical difficulties in obtaining adequate samples and objective data, it is still important to be as rigorous as the circumstances permit and to include control groups whenever they are appropriate. In one study, for instance, Parkes and Weiss (1983) found that widows reported far more symptoms of bereavement than did widowers. We were tempted to conclude that women are more vulnerable to bereavement than men. However, a control group of married women, carefully matched with the widowed sample, also reported more symptoms than did the bereaved men. Two to four years after bereavement, the widows had no more symptoms than did the married women controls. In contrast, the widowers still had more symptoms than did a control group of married men.

Many of the instruments developed for use in psychiatric settings are inappropriate for use with community samples. Studies of the frequency of rarely occurring events (e.g. death rates) require large samples if findings are to reach statistical significance. Conversely, blockbuster studies (e.g. the American National Hospice Study), in which researchers attempt to gather data from huge samples, often lose the fine-tuning and sensitivity that are possible when small or moderate-sized samples are interviewed in depth. Small-sample methodology answers a different set of questions than does large-sample methodology. Examples of questions that can be answered only by means of large (1,000+) samples are:

Is bereavement a cause of death?
Can bereavement cause cancer, suicide, psychosis, duodenal ulcers, angina, ulcerative colitis, alopecia, etc.?

Examples of questions that can be answered only by detailed study of small (¯50) samples are:

How do men differ from women?
What are the common effects of bereavement on the immune response system?

Medium-sized samples (100–500) come into their own as soon as subdivision of samples is needed. That is, each time researchers divide their sample down the middle they need to double the sample size. For example, studying men separately from women and the suddenly bereaved separately from the gradually bereaved means that a minimum of eighty respondents is needed – twenty in each group. Because a researcher seldom finds equal numbers of men and women or sudden and gradual bereavements, his or her sample is more likely to end up as, say, 145, comprising 20 men and 30 women, 25 sudden bereavements and 70 gradual bereavements.

Such considerations should be borne in mind by investigators who are planning research, funding bodies and ethical committees, all of whom must satisfy themselves that the research will achieve its intended objectives.

A checklist of ethical criteria that bereavement research should meet[1]

Ethics committees and others concerned with research on bereaved subjects must satisfy themselves that the following ethical criteria are met:

I   All research proposals will be approved by a properly constituted ethics committee.
II All bereaved people who are invited to take part in research will receive a document that

   A   Explains the purpose and method of the research to them.
   B   Reassures them of the qualifications and good faith of the researcher.
   C   Informs them that the research has been approved by a particular ethics committee.
   D   Identifies the organisation under whose auspices the research is conducted.
   E   Introduces any person who will be contacting them to arrange an interview.
   F   Explains the precautions that will be taken to ensure their anonymity in any publication or report.
   G   Explains their right of access to any records made about them.
   H   Assures them of their right to withdraw from the research or to ask for recording equipment to be switched off at any time.
   I   Reassures them that they will not be penalized in any way should they choose to withdraw.
   J   Gives them the name, address and telephone number of the project officer and invites them to contact him or her if they have any questions, comments or criticisms.
   K   Invites them to sign one copy of the document (to ensure that the document has been read) and informs them they will receive a second copy of it.

III If children or mentally impaired persons are the subjects of the research, information similar to that detailed in II will be given to parents or guardians, who must give their consent. In most cases, a face-to-face interview with the parent or guardian should be carried out before any attempt is made to contact the child or mentally impaired person. The researcher will also explain the research to the subjects themselves in language appropriate to their age and state of mind and must take seriously their views regarding participation.

IV   No financial inducement or other pressure will be put on potential respondents.

V   The individual who is to interview bereaved people for the purposes of research has received sufficient training in counselling to ensure that he or she will do no harm. The interviewer will receive regular supervision of his or her work from someone with advanced-level training and experience in counselling the bereaved.

VI   When a respondent becomes distressed, the interviewer will be guided by the respondent and by his or her own understanding in deciding whether to interrupt the interview. If tape recorders or video cameras are used, the respondent will be reminded that they will be turned off on request.

VII   The researcher will obtain no financial gain from a particular research result and is independent of any commercial pressures. Evaluation of the quality or effectiveness of care will not be carried out by the people providing the care.

VIII   Apart from giving emotional support, the interviewer will confine himself or herself to the research and will not proselytize, advertise or advocate particular treatments. However, when help seems needed, the interviewer should be able to point the bereaved person to possible sources of impartial assessment and advice.

IX   If videotapes of respondents are to be exhibited, the researcher will take particular care to ensure that respondents are aware that confidentiality cannot be preserved and to satisfy himself or herself that consent to show the tape has been freely given.

X   The objectives of the research are worthwhile and likely to be met by the methods proposed.

XI   Out of courtesy, the project officer will write a letter of appreciation and thanks to all respondents.

Note

1   Drug trials require additional safeguards that are not covered in this section.

Reference

Parkes, C. M. and Weiss, R. S. *Recovery from Bereavement*. Basic Books, New York, 1983.

CHAPTER 7

HELPING BEREAVED PEOPLE FROM OTHER CULTURES

From Bereavement: understanding grief across cultures *Psychiatry in Practice* 17(4): 5–8, 1998.

Although my book Bereavement: Studies of Grief in Adult Life *(1972) obtained good reviews and has been translated into many languages, I was startled to receive a critical comment to the effect that I had treated the grief that follows conjugal bereavement in Britain and the United States as the 'norm' whereas people from other cultures grieve in very different ways. My critic was right. For each one of us our own culture is indeed our 'norm', for we have no other basis for comparison. Yet we have much to learn from other cultures.*

With this in mind I was delighted to be approached by a Hindu psychologist, Pittu Laungani, who suggested that we edit a book Death and Bereavement across Cultures *aimed at helping all who support bereaved people to understand and respond to the needs of bereaved immigrants. With the help of a child psychiatrist, Bill Young, we recruited a wide range of contributors, most of them from the cultures which they described. That exercise aroused my interest and the spread of hospice and bereavement services across the world enabled me to travel widely and to expand my life space. As a result I have graduated from the narrow-minded love of England and the Empire to a more global international and ecological love of all that wondrous system of being.*

This paper summarizes some of the more practical lessons that are explored in depth in the book, now in its second edition.

Summary

There are wide differences across and within cultures in the ways people mourn. There is psychiatric evidence that extreme repression of grief can be harmful. When this is the case people may benefit from opportunities and permission to grieve. Conversely those who become preoccupied and obsessed with grief may need opportunities and permission to put their grief aside and help to review and re-plan their lives.

The strength and quality of attachments influence the reaction when these attachments end. Societies with large, extended family networks and shared living conditions may grieve less and cope better with bereavement than those in which small families and low mortality rates make death particularly traumatic. Systems of belief and the rituals that accompany bereavement may be helpful or harmful.

The cultural divide

While people from other cultures will often turn to their own for help in bereavement they sometimes seek help from outsiders. Professionals and volunteer counsellors should not draw back from responding to such requests. The process of explaining one's own culture to another can itself be therapeutic. We need to be prepared to give the time that is necessary if communication across cultural divides is to succeed. The rewards are considerable for us as well as for the people who seek our help.

Two very different mistakes are commonly made by members of the caring professions when faced with bereaved people from cultures different from our own. On the one hand, we may assume that, because grief is a universal experience, we understand their feelings and that the theories and techniques of counselling with which we are familiar can be applied without modification to meet their needs. On the other hand, those who are aware of the large differences among cultures in attitudes, rituals and beliefs about death and mourning may go to the opposite extreme. They may assume that we have nothing to offer.

In this paper an alternative view will be presented. This constitutes a middle way which acknowledges the large differences among cultures while accepting that we have sufficient in common with others to make communication and real help possible. This common understanding cannot be taken for granted and much of this paper attempts to examine and explain the most frequent differences across cultures. With understanding comes respect and the possibility that both sides will benefit from the interchange.

When Pittu Laungani, Bill Young and this author started work on our book *Death and Bereavement across Cultures* (1996) we expected that we would publish a sort of cookery book to tell our readers everything they needed to know about the main cultures met with in the English-speaking world. If you had a Hindu patient, look up Hinduism in the index and you would be told what to expect and how to help a dying or bereaved Hindu. Similarly you could learn what to wear at a Jewish funeral or a Maori Tangi.

In the event, the great world religions all turned out to be much more complex and variable than I had expected. All of them include a variety of sects which tend to emphasise different ways of practising the faith. It was sometimes difficult to see what distinguished members of a faith; as one cynical Hindu said, the only things that Hindus have in common is their Indian nationality and their veneration for the cow. However, each culture does have a way of looking at death which is unique and it is fascinating to compare each culture with one's own.

Cultural differences in the expression of grief

One of the biggest differences is in the expression of grief which is regarded as normal within each society. In societies such as the Apache Indians and the Rwandans it is normal to show very little grief by Western standards. By contrast, in many parts of Africa and the Caribbean and in certain Arab sects bereavement gives rise to a great deal of overt crying and wailing. The situation is made more complicated by the fact that, even within societies, what is normal for one group of people may be abnormal for another. Thus, Rosenblatt, Walsh and Jackson (1976), in studying anthropologists' reports on fifty-eight different cultures, found that whereas women often show more grief than men there is not a single culture in which men show more grief than women.

Given that most of the evidence on cultural differences is anecdotal and unsystematic, what seems to distinguish the cultures whose mourning customs discourage the expression of grief from those that encourage it?

Emotional control and survival

One possible difference has to do with the need to control emotions in the face of threats to survival. Gorer (1965) has suggested that the major change which took place in Europe between 1900, when Victorian tradition dictated that mourning be deep and public, and 1920, when the stiff upper lip had become established, was attributable to the high death rate in the trenches during the First World War. Similarly, during the course of visiting Rwanda a year after the genocide, I attended the reburial of 10,000 bodies that had been dug up from mass graves. Although this was a public event attended by thousands of people I did not see a single Rwandan cry. The Rwandans to whom I spoke about this agreed that Rwandans do not show grief. Those who arc familiar with African traditions tell me that this is highly deviant for Africa as a whole.

Others who show little grief are tribes such as the Apache and the Navajo, who pride themselves on their courage as warriors. The identity of the warrior, like that of the policeman, the fireman and the surgeon, requires them to stay calm in the face of danger. This is a matter of pride and is classed as a masculine virtue. I know it is fashionable today to deride macho attitudes, but it may well be that, in the environment of evolution, human beings would not have survived if men, in particular, had not had the capacity to inhibit their grief when danger looms.

Is there a price to be paid?

Psychoanalysts, who see repression of emotions as the root cause of much mental illness, have suggested that the repression of grief may be psychologically harmful. Some confirmation for their claims comes from Norbert Mintz, who worked in a mental health clinic serving the Navajo Indians in the United States. He reports (personal communication) that Navajo regularly 'repress and suppress death and grief'. When three days have elapsed after a death the names of the dead are no longer mentioned and several elderly, traditional Navajos whom he interviewed denied recalling the names of their dead parents. He found that 'about one third of all patients attending the mental health clinic had a history of the death of a close person within the past year.' He claimed excellent results for psychotherapy aimed at helping these patients to grieve and said that the results of therapy 'matched or exceeded the improvement in health for all [other] patients'.

Further evidence comes from a still unpublished study of a very different society by Eyrena Burgoine. She asked widows in the Bahamas the same questions that I had used in studying widows in London. Little lasting depression was found in Caribbean widows, who adopt traditional mourning customs which encourage great overt expression of a variety of strong emotions. By contrast London widows and widows from the higher socio-economic status groups in the Bahamas, who have adopted more attenuated Western patterns of mourning, showed more lasting depression.

Pittu Laungani, who has written the chapter on Hinduism in *Death and Bereavement across Cultures* (Parkes, Laungani and Young 1996), brought home the extent to which people in the West have become distanced from death. In India death and the rituals that follow it are family events which take place in the home and in which everybody has a role to play. Children witness death from an early age but do not seem to suffer emotional trauma as a result.

Other factors influencing the grieving process

Having said this I do not want to give the impression that failure to express grief is the sole, or even the main, cause of problems in bereavement. Many other factors play a part (For a more detailed review see Parkes *et al.*, 1996). For example, in the West, intense distress, expressed before and in the immediate aftermath of a bereavement, may be a sign of insecurity or of a dependent attachment. In either case it is likely to predict intense and lasting grief and other difficulties in adjustment. People in this category may need a different type of help to establish their confidence in themselves and to help them to re-plan their lives and move forward, rather than the more traditional approach which encourages them to look backwards and express grief. Evidence for this view was reported in a paper by Schut and colleagues (1997) in which they showed, in a well-conducted random-allocation study, that Dutch women who had sought help after bereavement responded best to a therapy that helped them to review and re-plan their lives while bereaved men, who have more difficulty in expressing grief than women, did best with a therapy which helped them to express their grief and other emotions.

What these researches seem to indicate is that the response to loss of an attachment is often a reflection of the nature of the attachment. This too may be culturally determined. For instance, the reaction to the death of a child may reflect the family size and expectations of the particular country in which the death occurs.

I recently spent a week with a Dayak guide visiting various Dayak settlements in Borneo. Dayaks have large families because they expect most of their children to die. Many of them are riverine people who live in houses on stilts built out over the river. Some children drown in the river; others die by catching gastro-enteritis from the polluted water. Despite this the Dayaks to whom I spoke seemed to show very little grief. In fact they were much more preoccupied with marital problems and losses of relationship than with their bereavements. The explanation seems to lie in the size of their attachment networks and their living arrangements. Large numbers of people live together in large houses and share in the care of the children. If a child dies there are always others to take its place, and if a parent dies there are similarly others to continue the parenting. This seems to take the edge off their grief. There is safety in numbers. Something similar may account for the relative lack of grief reported in Samoans (Ablon 1973). By contrast the small nuclear families which are prevalent in the West may be particularly vulnerable to bereavement.

Beliefs and rituals

The systems of belief and the rituals that attend death vary enormously. Some seem to an outsider to be harmful and others helpful. Thus it is difficult to see any justification for the widespread belief that death is caused by witchcraft and the practice of suttee, flagellation and other forms of mutilation inflicted on bereaved people can hardly be justified simply because they are normal within particular societies. Other beliefs and rituals are more obviously likely to be helpful. It seems reasonable to conclude that it is unwise to idealise the cultures of other people just as it is unwise to denigrate them.

Buddhists have a particular interest in death stemming from the importance which they attach to the transience of all things. Many of them hold to the view that this world is an illusion and that we should prepare ourselves for the transition into the next life by detaching ourselves from everything in this world, including those we love. This must be a hard task for the dying and for their families, yet we are told that they often achieve a peaceful death. In our Western, acquisitive world attachments to people and things are constantly promoted and take up a large part of our mental investment. This makes it all the more difficult for us to let go when we are faced with our own death or the deaths of the people we love. In Japan, where religious tolerance is high, most people attempt to have the best of both worlds; they have a Shinto wedding and a Buddhist funeral.

Among cancer patients in the Patients' Group at St Christopher's Hospice it has been repeatedly brought home to me how much people who are dying fear that they will die alone, and often their fears are justified. That would never happen in a Moslem country where family and friends gather at the bedside of any seriously ill person to forgive them their sins and, in return, to be given forgiveness. In this way they clean the slate so that the bereaved are not tormented by self-reproaches. I can remember being called to a ward at the Royal London Hospital when a Moslem patient was dying. The ward nurse thought that there were too many people camping at the bedside and wanted me to tell them to go away. I suggested that she make room for them all and warn the other patients that they could be expected to make a great noise when the patient died. Not all Moslems are noisy grievers but some Arabs see it as a tribute to the dead to wail loudly.

It seems reasonable to draw the conclusion that, by comparison with most other cultures, Westerners live in a world in which religion and the fundamental ideas with which it deals – birth, death and the purposes of life – have become the province of midwives, doctors, funeral directors and other professionals and downgraded in personal significance. Doubts about the value of traditional religion stem from logical inconsistencies in beliefs that do not stand up to rational scrutiny and fundamentalists who take their dogmas very literally often seem ridiculous. However, few people have entirely abandoned the idea that there is something beyond themselves of which they are a part or that there is a meaning in life and death however dimly this may be glimpsed.

The role of the professional

As a professional psychiatrist with a special interest in bereavement I have often been asked to see immigrants or members of subcultures within the polyglot society of London, England. Their cultural backgrounds differ from mine; should I refuse to see them and refer them instead to a member of their own culture or do I have something to offer them? The answer to this question is not, of course, a simple one. Some people who seek my help have already left their culture of origin and are seeking something different. They exist in a kind of cultural limbo. Others know my culture so well that it does not prove difficult to bridge the gap and still others can explain themselves to me and in the process explain themselves to themselves in ways that prove very therapeutic. Bereavement is a time for taking stock and the very act of stepping aside from one's private and public world and explaining it to another person helps us to do just that.

To some extent we are all from different cultures. Your life space is different from mine. Many of the words you use have different meanings from the meanings I attach to them and many of the assumptions you make about the world are different from mine. That is why counselling and psychotherapy take time. We have to learn to communicate with each other. The greater the cultural gap the longer it takes to communicate effectively. If we recognise that fact and set aside the time that is necessary then communication will be rewarding and both sides will benefit.

I also believe that the satisfactions to be derived from communication increase with the size of the gaps that have been successfully crossed. Visits to foreign lands are fascinating, not because they are just like home, but because they are different. When we succeed in making contact with a fellow human being across the divide of culture both parties can expect to find their horizons expanding. This makes the work rewarding for the counsellor as well as the client. For someone who is seeking help because they are stuck in some kind of cultural rut the opportunity to step outside that rut can be very therapeutic.

Key points

- The strength and quality of attachments influence the reaction when they end – societies with large, extended family networks and shared living conditions may grieve less and cope better with bereavement.
- In societies such as the Apache and the Rwandans, it is normal to show very little grief, whereas in other parts of Africa and the Caribbean, bereavement gives rise to a great deal of overt crying and wailing.
- In the West, religion and its related ideas – birth, death and life – have become the province of doctors, midwives, funeral director and other professionals.
- Bereavement is a time for taking stock, and the very act of stepping aside from one's private and public world and explaining it to another person helps us.

References

Ablon, J. Reactions of Samoan burns patients and families to severe burns. *Social Science and Medicine* 7, 167–178, 1973.

Gorer, G. *Death, Grief and Mourning in Contemporary Britain*. Cresset, London, 1965.

Parkes, C.M. (1st edition, 1972, 3rd edition, with Holly Prigerson, 2006) *Bereavement: Studies of Grief in Adult Life*. Tavistock/Routledge, London; Pelican, Harmondsworth and International Universities Press, New York.

Parkes, C.M., Laungani, P. and Young W. (eds.) *Death and Bereavement across Cultures*. Routledge, London, 1996.

Rosenblatt, P.C., Walsh, R.P. and Jackson, D.A. *Grief and Mourning in Cross-Cultural Perspective*. HRAF Press, Washington, DC, 1976.

Schut, H.A.W., Stroebe, M., van den Bout, J. and de Keijser, J. Intervention for the bereaved: gender differences in the efficacy of two counseling programs. *British Journal of Clinical Psychology* 36, 63–72, 1997.

CHAPTER 8

LOVE AND LOSS

Extracts from Parkes, C.M. *Love and loss: the roots of grief and its complications*. London and New York: Routledge. Portuguese edition *Amor e Perda* Trans. Maria Helena Pereira Franco. SP Brasil: Summus Editorial, 2006.

In the course of reviewing a book, by another author, in The Times, *Bel Mooney criticised the author's neglect of the classical literature on bereavement. She went on: 'it is even more astonishing that he makes no reference to the work of Colin Murray Parkes, whose seminal* Love and Loss: The Roots of Grief and Its Complications *(2006) manages to be both academic and written in prose that dances with love around its subject' (Mooney* The Times *Saturday, 12 January 2008).*

This unsolicited testimonial pleased me greatly but raised important questions in my mind. Had I been right to make use of emotive words such as 'love' rather than the more neutral term 'attachment' in the course of an analysis of the roots of grief and its complications? Is my love of the 'dance' of psychology impairing the calm logic of the science? The reader will have to decide whether the following introduction and conclusions to my book, in which I have not hesitated to use emotive language, undermine the scientific analysis which is spelled out in the course of the chapters. Or was I right to put back the feelings in order to recognise that love, by its very nature, is not a cognitive phenomenon and any attempt to understand it must include feelings as well as logic, must reunite the dry-as-dust cognitive analysis with its emotive roots?

Bel Mooney's choice of words suggests that there is an interface between the art and the science of psychology that can be crossed without detriment to either.

Introduction (pp. 1–6)

For most people love is the most profound source of pleasure in our lives while the loss of those whom we love is the most profound source of pain. Hence, love and loss are two sides of the same coin. We cannot have one without risking the other. Knowing this, some people choose not to invest in love, the risk is too great; others deny the equation, they fool themselves into thinking that they, and the ones they love, are immortal and inseparable. They take love for granted and are outraged if it is threatened or lost.

It is the very transience of life that enhances love. The greater the risk, the stronger grows the attachment. For most of us, the fact that one day we shall lose the ones we love, and they us, draws us closer to them but remains a silent bell that wakes us in the night.

Our intelligence often enables us to predict when we and those we love will die, to some degree we can grieve for the loss before it happens and much has been written about the value of anticipatory grief as a preparation for the losses to come (see, for instance, Rando's 1986 review of this literature); yet there is an important difference between the grief that comes before and that which follows loss. Whereas the grief that follows loss eventually declines as we learn to live without the living presence of the one we love, the grief that precedes loss leads to an intensification of the attachment and a greater preoccupation with the other person; mothers will sacrifice themselves and neglect the needs of their healthy children in order to cherish one who is sick; family and friends of a person who is close to death often maintain their vigil long after the dying one has lost all awareness of their presence.

Observations of this kind, which stem from common experience as well as psychological research, suggest that a set of rules governs love and loss, some kind of dynamic force that can be assessed and, to a degree, measured. We hesitate to express these measurements in mathematical terms, partly because no simple equation can measure anything as complex as love, but also out of a sense of reverence for the very subject of our equation. It seems too calculating for the head to measure the heart. Yet we already make use of such calculations when, for instance, an unattached single person chooses whether or not to make a date with a much older person or when parents who have lost a baby decide whether or not to try for another.

Scientists, whose lack of such scruples allows them to dissect the 'sacred temple' of the human body, have, in recent years, begun to measure aspects of love and grief and to unravel some of their mysteries. Their first attempts can already be seen as simplistic yet they were a necessary step towards a science of human relationships.

The work considered here may be another step along the way and will, in its turn, be superseded by others. It is offered, not out of arrogance or *lese majestie*, but in the hope that an increase in our understanding of the building blocks which explain our joys and our sufferings will help us to enhance the former and minimize the latter.

What is this thing called love? Love has many aspects but an essential component without which it cannot be said to be present is commitment. Love is the psychological tie that binds one person to another over a lasting period of time. Once established it is not easily severed and some argue that it can never be entirely broken (Klass, Silverman and Nickman 1996: 14–23). Be that as it may, it is the nature of a tie that it resists severance. In physical terms love resembles an elastic band rather than any other type of tether, that is to say it grows stronger the further apart the lovers are located. By contrast, lovers who are never separated are inclined to take each other for granted. A consequence of this is that love is easier to measure when the parties are separated than it is when they are together.

Infants, separated from their mothers, behave in ways that teach us a great deal about their relationship with this particular mother and about the way they view the world and themselves within it. Likewise adults who lose a loved partner behave in ways that teach us, not only about their relationship with the partner, but about much else beside. Love may not make the world go round but it is an important source of security, self-esteem and trust. Without these essential supplies, we feel and are endangered.

In the environment in which mankind evolved these dangers were dangers to survival. A child who became separated from its parents would not live long and even adults were at risk if they got lost or separated from those who kept them safe in a dangerous world. Even today there is evidence that separations and losses of the people we love can have significant effects on our health and they even increase the risk of mortality. These harsh facts may account for the special intensity of the emotions evoked by love and loss, but most of the current dangers are more psychological than physical. These psychological dangers include frank mental illnesses as well as lesser psychological difficulties (Parkes 1996). It is the purpose of this book to unravel the causal sequences that explain these dangers and to suggest ways they can be reduced. Along the way we may gain new perspectives on the nature of love.

Another important component of love is its 'monotropy' (Bowlby 1958); love is a tie to one particular person only. There can be no substitute for the parent, child or loved partner who has been lost. True, some of the pain of grief may be mitigated by making a new attachment, a bereaved parent may have another child or a divorced person may marry again, but people are not interchangeable and each new relationship will be unique in its own right. For this reason alone, each person we love is priceless; we cannot count their value alongside other objects which are replaceable and utilitarian. We may criticise the people we love for not being useful or meeting a particular criterion of beauty, but the very things we criticise are part of the uniqueness of the individual and we love them 'warts and all'.

These qualities – vital importance, uniqueness and persistence – account for the very special quality of love relationships. Not without reason are they the stuff of prose and poetry, the major preoccupation of the media and the source of endless delights in song from grand opera to pop. Love disturbs the even tenor of our ways, complicates our plans and upsets political machines. It is worshipped and deplored, longed for and dreaded. We take great risks when we embark upon love relationships and greater risks if we abjure them. One way or another we need to find a way of living with love.

Because of the emotional connotations and ambiguities of the word 'love' scientists have preferred to use other words to study it and to separate out its various forms. There are few today who continue to use Freud's ambiguous term 'libido' and the more recent term 'object relations' seems too impersonal; people are not 'objects'. The most widely used term is 'attachment' which John Bowlby (1969) used to indicate the child's tie to its mother. Because he was observing the child's behaviour his preferred term was 'attachment behaviour'. By contrast the mother's behaviour towards her child he referred to as 'maternal caretaking behaviour'. Subsequent workers have preferred to use the term 'nurturance' for this type of mother love and the term 'romantic attachment' has been proposed for love between adult peers although this love, as we shall see, is often very unromantic.

Most researchers now use the term 'attachment' for all bonds of love and qualify this by adding parent-child or child-parent and so forth when a more specific connotation is needed. This certainly makes for scientific objectivity but the very neutrality of the term 'attachment' may mislead us into thinking of love as cognitive and instrumental when, in fact, it is experienced as a complex of feelings and emotions. In this book I shall attempt to move back and forth between the objective and the subjective view and will try to attain a balanced overall view.

A recurrent finding in the research into attachments, which will be described henceforth, is their lasting influence. Relationships formed in infancy colour all future relationships.

The work reported here set out to investigate a proposal that, at first sight, may seem unlikely. Are the problems which cause bereaved adults to seek help from a psychiatrist attributable, in some degree, to the particular kinds of attachment, the patterns of loving, which these bereaved people made to their parents in their childhood?

In attempting to answer this question and to understand the chain of causation, I have had to take into account a number of likely causes and to figure out how they influence each other. This study has taken up a large part of my working life as a psychiatrist with a special interest in bereavement. It is rather like trying to solve a very large jigsaw puzzle. I have moved slowly from speculation to clinical judgements and finally to a systematic attempt to test the fit between theory and data. Sometimes the pieces of the jigsaw have fallen neatly into place and at other times they have not and it has been necessary to take another look at the evidence and revise my theories. Little by little, what has emerged is very much more than a treatise on the psychiatric problems of the bereaved. The issues are important, not only to the minority of bereaved people who need psychiatric help but also, I suggest, to a much wider range of people in many life situations.

Steve Grand, in a recent article, writes:

> The fundamental problem is that science is dull. It really is tremendously dreary and boring most of the time . . . But so what? Science is just a methodology, not a body of knowledge. We don't describe the graphic arts as 'mixing paint'. What really matters – what is deeply and tremendously exciting – is the universe in which we live, and science is merely the means by which this is revealed to us. Unfortunately, the luminous beauty of one is tarnished by the dull sheen of the other . . . Scientific research has uncovered much of the elegance and rational splendour of the world around us, and this is what matters, not science itself.
>
> (Grand 2004: 7)

Boring old science has enabled us to probe the limits of space and the minutiae of the microscopic world but I would suggest that its greatest challenge is not the world about us but the world within. It is inner space that now requires our urgent attention and this is of sufficient moment to justify the hard slog that may be necessary to reach our goals. In this volume the reader will have to be prepared for a certain amount of tedious spelling out of methodology and critical review of the work of other researchers. Hopefully the light that this will shed on the 'luminous beauty' of love will justify the effort.

My interest in bereavement as a topic of psychological research stemmed from a realisation that losses of one sort or another are very common. Bereavement by death is only one of the host of major life change events which we all face from time to time. It is, perhaps, one of the most severe and potentially harmful of stresses and this makes it an appropriate topic for clinical research, but the problems which cause people to seek psychiatric help after a bereavement are not unique to bereavement and the lessons which we can learn from studying them penetrate, as we shall see, to the roots of human psychology.

This work has not been carried out in a vacuum. Much has been learned in the past fifty years about the psychology of the attachments that people make to each other and about the consequences that arise when these attachments are interrupted by death. It has been my privilege to know and to work with many of the pioneers in this field whose studies will be reviewed in Chapters 1 and 2 and reconsidered in other places in this volume.

This *corpus* forms the background to the major research project by which I have attempted to link together the field of Attachment and the separate, but related, fields of Loss and Trauma. The rationale for this research and the way the various interacting factors were measured and turned into 'variables' is described in Chapter 3. Because the issues are complex this chapter contains a great deal of information. Although I have tried to make the argument accessible, by avoiding jargon terms and confining much technical detail to appendices, readers may find it necessary to dodge back to this chapter later in the book in order to understand better the meaning and the limitations of the data.

This introduction and the first three chapters make up the first part of the book. The second part reports the main findings of the study and reveals the powerful influence which patterns of childhood attachment, as recalled in adult life, were found to have on the reaction to bereavements arising much later in life.

Part III looks at the other influences that contribute to the reaction to bereavement and attempts to disentangle the interaction between these various elements. We examine how each chapter of life is reflected in a new pattern of loving and how one pattern leads to another. Only when all are taken into consideration can we hope to obtain a balanced view of the part played by early attachments in the later lives, loves and losses that follow.

In the final part we examine the wider context of a study that has, up to now, focussed on bereavement. The pattern of attachments is found to have played a significant part in contributing to many of the other problems which people brought to this psychiatrist, even when no bereavement by death had taken place. Indeed some of the problems that followed bereavement have more to do with the wider context than they have with the bereavement. Bereavement remains important, however, in providing us with an opportunity to understand better the interweaving of love, loss and change. The wheel has come full circle and my original expectation, that the study of bereavement would throw light on the meaning and consequences of other stresses, has been confirmed.

The question arises whether some of the more extreme variants of the problematic attachment patterns should be regarded as psychiatric disorders in their own right. Can there be disorders of loving? The existence of attachment disorders in childhood has already been widely accepted and the data presented in Chapter 17 [of 'Love and Loss'] enables us to examine the evidence for the existence of attachment disorders in adult life. Whether or not this categorisation is accepted it seems that attachment issues contribute to a wide range of problems throughout life and Chapter 18 examines the implications of these for the care given by others be they medical professionals, volunteers, friends or relatives.

Finally we attempt to take a broader view of the world in which these problems have arisen and draw some conclusions about the priorities which cause many of us to place our commitments to the large social units to which we belong (particularly the occupational niches to which our education has led us), above our commitments to our children, families and homes. Our attachments, it seems, remain our most important source of security, serenity and support at times of trouble. We neglect them at our peril . . .

Final conclusions (pp. 272—278)

We of the twentieth century have witnessed some amazing advances in science and the creation, in cities and towns across the world, of environments that are largely man-made. As a result more people are alive today than ever before and, for many of them, the advances in medicine, public health, agriculture, transport, information systems and the large-scale organisation of society have brought about a world where we are healthier, safer and better nourished than ever before.

Unfortunately the psychological and social sciences have not kept up with the physical sciences. The large-scale systems of organisation, which, in the 'developed world', have taken over from the family as our principal source of security, rely on workers of both sexes who are separated from their children throughout the working day and whose extended family, the traditional surrogate parents, now often live too far away to be of use. While teachers and others may be quite adequate to meet the attachment needs of many children, often they are not, particularly because the increase in sexual abuse by such carers has led to prohibition of the most effective sources of reassurance for distressed children of all ages, touching and cuddling. Thus the very social changes that have increased our objective security have undermined those functions of the family which maintain subjective security, the experience of a secure base for the developing child.

We are only now beginning to discover the cost of this neglect and it is to be hoped that this volume will contribute to redress the balance.

Research into attachments has contributed to our understanding of child development and has become a field of study in its own right. At long last a scientific basis for studying the influence of the experiences of early childhood has been established and bids fair to bring about a rational basis for the prevention and treatment of the problems that arise from attachments.

Another consequence of the success of medical science has been the prolongation of life. While this is a worthy aim it has often been pursued without regard for the quality of the life that is thereby prolonged. Pneumonia, once called 'the old man's friend' for its capacity to bring merciful relief from the sufferings of the wide range of diseases and disabilities that afflict the elderly, is now routinely treated with antibiotics. Cancers, which remain the third commonest cause of death, are treated by poisons which half kill the patient in order to fully kill, or at least slow down, the tumour. Our fear of death is such that many patients collude with this and may even press their doctors to prolong their lives at all costs. Yet, despite all of the advances of modern science, 100 per cent of people still die.

In recent years a growing awareness of these issues has focussed attention on the dying and on the families who care for and survive them. Hospices have led the way; they combine the best of physical care with psychological, social and spiritual care for people who are dying. So successful has this been that they have spread, within a few years, across the globe. These successes reflect both awareness of the problems and faith in possible solutions. As a result an entire new field of Palliative Medicine has come into being with its own journals and scientific literature.

Interest in the related topic of bereavement has also burgeoned but has grown more slowly. Within Palliative Medicine lip service has been paid to the importance of the patient's family both as a source of support to the dying patient and in its own right. After all, the patient's problems will soon be over; those of the family may just be beginning. On the other hand the blinkered outlook of professionals has not helped the development of an agreed theoretical understanding of bereavement from the various disciplines with an interest in the field. As a result we have theories derived from psychoanalysis, cognitive psychology, sociology and traumatology competing for the high ground and denigrating their competitors.

In the current volume I have attempted to draw together evidence from all of these fields, as well as from my own research, to propose an integrated model that embraces studies of attachment and loss extending across the life cycle. Where conflicting views or discordant evidence have become apparent I have attempted to suggest explanations and, although I do not doubt that further modifications to the overall model will be needed, the existing pieces of the jigsaw puzzle do seem to fit.

It is this, more than anything else, which reassures us that the technical limitations of the study that were addressed in Chapters 3 and 4, the possible effects of retrospective distortion, the problems of missing information, the inadequacies of the measures of adult relationships and doubts about the reliability of the clinical assessments, do not seriously undermine the overall conclusions.

The focus on a group of people who came for help after bereavement has turned out to illuminate the whole structure and focus of our thinking about love and loss. Whatever genetic factors may have contributed to their problems these people are not freaks or curiosities. We find in them aspects of problems that we all face, for no family is perfect and no one immune to loss.

But our conclusions are not limited to loss by death and the data reported in Chapter 16 make it clear that attachment patterns, separations and the assumptive world to which they give rise influence how we cope with many of the losses of life and shed light on a wide range of psychiatric problems.

We started by examining the assessments our respondents made of their parents and of themselves as children. The replies to the questions about parenting correlated with the measures of childhood and confirmed expectations based on Ainsworth and Main's systematic studies. This justified us in using measures reflecting their classification of the patterns of attachment as our principal predictors of later development.

We saw how problematic attachments in childhood, and separation from parents, can undermine the developing child's views – of the world as a safe place, of their own ability to cope by independent action (or by rewarding or coercing others) and of the extent to which they can trust others to protect, support and encourage them. Out of this mixture of expectations and assumptions emerges a set of strategies and a view of the world and of oneself within it which colours all of our relationships and our approach to novel or challenging situations. The loss of a close relative or partner emerges as one of the most challenging and one which brings home, more clearly than other life situations, the fallibility of our basic assumptions.

Even so, Ward's comparison group made us aware of the resilience of human beings. As in other studies of the effects of 'stress' on mental health, we found that many people, who have been forced by circumstances to learn to cope with parenting that is less than ideal, develop strategies for survival that prepare them for disappointments and other stresses and that often stand them in good stead in later life.

We found, in the patterns of attachment derived from Ainsworth's Strange Situation, a set of basic assumptions about the world and its meanings that made sense of many of the strange situations that we meet throughout our childhood and later life. Assumptions about ourselves, about our families and about the world at large enable us to interpret the meaning of each situation and to develop strategies that, we hope, will enable us to survive. If we do survive this is assumed to confirm the validity of the strategies.

Some bereavements are more traumatic than others, but even the most traumatic can only be adequately understood if we pay attention to the basic assumptions that are being overturned by the trauma. And these basic assumptions arise from an experience of life that is very limited.

The basic assumption that arises from secure attachment is that I am protected, worthwhile and secure. Much of the time it stands me in good stead for it gives me the confidence and trust to face strange and novel situations without undue anxiety. But it may let me down when disaster strikes and I am suddenly unprotected, weak and deskilled.

The basic assumption arising from anxious ambivalent attachments is that I am a weak vessel in a turbulent environment in which my only hope of survival in strange situations is to stay close to a greater power. As long as I can find my greater power I am safe enough, although the uncertainty inherent in this situation means that I must be sure to stay close. Without the greater power I am lost.

The basic assumption arising out of avoidant attachments is that I will survive if I maintain an appearance of strength and do not get too close to others. Much of the time this assumption holds true and I may even get status and credit for my performance. But this assumption is confounded by anything that brings home my weakness, reduces my status (i.e. my power to control others) or leaves me 'without a leg to stand on'. When this happens I may attempt to regain control by threats or, as the data on disability suggest, by 'going sick'.

The basic assumption underlying disorganised attachments is that I am weak and others cannot be trusted to protect me. Consequently I must be constantly on the alert for danger while remaining inconspicuous, staying in places of relative safety and avoiding any situation that might undermine my security. If this fails I panic; I may take to the bottle or I may even take an overdose.

Although many of these basic assumptions arise in early childhood our data indicate that they are not immutable. Thus, in childhood, boys were no more likely than girls to make avoidant attachments but, with the arrival of adolescence, bodily and psychological changes lead to an increase in strength and aggressiveness with a corresponding change in basic assumptions about self and others which resemble those of the avoidant pattern. Thereafter, boys are much more likely than girls to respond to threat or loss by assertiveness, by inhibiting the expression of grief (and other feelings) and by refusing any help that might undermine their status. Although these strategies are sometimes successful, when they fail, they are reflected in the personality disorders to which the bereaved men in our study were prone. The smaller number of men than women who sought help after bereavement may say more about men's reluctance to admit their need for help than it does about their actual need.

Each type of relationship has its functions, strengths and weaknesses that are themselves influenced by prior attachments. The weaknesses are sometimes reflected in disorders of attachment and they sometimes become apparent when the relationship is challenged by bereavement. This study has enabled us to compare the loss of parents, children and spouses. It has also thrown light on social relationships, which turn out to play an important role at times of bereavement.

Relationships to parents may be vital to our survival during childhood, but with the advent of adolescence their importance normally diminishes, separation becomes possible and the nature of the bond gradually changes, often from attachment to nurturance. We saw how problematic reactions to the loss of a parent, more than other losses, commonly reflect the continuation into adult life of unusually close and clinging attachments to that parent in childhood.

The main function of nurturance is the survival of our genes through our children. This function is diminished once the children can survive without us; separation then becomes desirable and the nature of the parent's nurturant bond may gradually change to one of attachment. The loss of a child is always painful but our study suggests that it is most likely to lead to requests for psychiatric help if it revives a dangerous assumptive world over which the child had little or no control and from which they could not learn a satisfactory model of parenting. This was most obvious in the people who had experienced disorganised attachments. They reveal the extent to which the assumptions that arise from attachment relationships in childhood are reflected in the nurturant relationships of adults.

Relationships with partners fulfil sexual, nurturant and attachment functions including the provision of a secure base in which to raise children. Although we have found that insecure attachments in childhood are associated with insecure attachments to spouses, these are not a slavish copy of the attachments to parents. Insecurity upsets the balance between giving and taking, nurture and attachment, which ensures the success of pair-bonds between adults. In this study, problems following the loss of a partner often resulted from an exclusive, insecure and mutually interdependent relationship with the partner that gave rise to high levels of anxiety, grief and loneliness when the partner died.

In most societies the network of attachments to the extended family plays an important part in child rearing as well as providing physical and emotional support to the parents. In Western society social and professional networks have largely subsumed these functions. The research reported here shows that both social support and living with others can mitigate some of the intensity of grief and loneliness, and social support emerged as one of the most salient factors distinguishing the psychiatric patients from Ward's controls. Even people who had experienced insecure attachments reacted to bereavement without lasting distress if their support networks were still intact.

Problems associated with social isolation and lack of social support were most apparent in old age. Sadly, those who had experienced insecure attachments, who are the people most in need of this support, were also the ones least likely to get it. Their lack of trust in others meant that they remained isolated and unsupported.

One group whom one might have expected to be insecure were the immigrants. Their history of persecution, poverty and separations from parents was such that it came as a surprise to find that their ability to cope and their reaction to bereavement in later life was no worse than that of the non-immigrants. It seems that many of them had the benefit of surrogate parents and extended family networks whose support had helped to mitigate these difficulties. It may also be the case that their experience of stress in childhood prepared them for some of the stresses to come.

Another source of insecurity is life-threatening illness. When, in the current study, this occurred in early childhood it affected the parents' treatment of the child and was associated with overprotection and anxious/ambivalent attachments or distancing and avoidant attachments. In later childhood and adult life it seems that an increased prevalence of avoidant attachments increased the risk of illness and disability. Illness in childhood often caused separations from parents, which also undermined security.

Given the high prevalence of disabilities and the numerous bereavements and other losses that occur in the lives of older people it is remarkable how many of them are able to lead reasonably contented lives. Among those older folk who sought psychiatric help in the current study, however, it seems that it was the combined effect of insecure attachments, physical disabilities and social isolation (many lived alone) which made the added burden of bereavement intolerable.

It will be obvious by now that parental love is difficult to get right. None of us can prepare our children for every eventuality; all we can hope to be is 'good enough'. The most perfect parents may not succeed in preparing their children for an imperfect world. Well-meaning parents who overprotect or over-control their children, parents who are intolerant of closeness and grieving or traumatised parents (whose overwhelming needs for nurture make it hard for them, consistently, to nurture their own children), all of these problems in loving undermine the child's security and trust in itself and others. Few of these parents lack love for their child, it is the way they express or fail to express that love which causes problems.

Sometimes, as we have seen, the problems are so serious that they justify the diagnosis of an Attachment Disorder. We have seen how such disorders start in childhood and persist into adult life when they may increase the risk of complicated grief and a variety of other psychiatric problems that sometimes arise after bereavement.

But the influence of insecure attachments is not limited to bereavement and this study shows that they also play a part in psychiatric disorders arising in people who have not been bereaved. This important observation opens the door to a major advance in our understanding of mental illness and its causes.

Since these passages were written, the influential Diagnostic Statistical Manual Volume 5 *(of which more later) has included in its pages an adult version of Separation Anxiety Disorder of Childhood which I described in Chapter 17 of* Love and Loss. *The inclusion of this condition that, in both childhood and adult life, is correlated with anxious ambivalent attachments to parents in childhood reflects the growing acceptance in the DSM of insecure attachments as a potential cause of mental illness.*

The DSM-5 criteria for diagnosing Separation Anxiety Disorder are: 'A developmentally inappropriate and excessive fear or anxiety concerning separation from those to whom the individual is attached, as evidenced by at least three of the following:

1 *Recurrent and excessive distress when anticipating or experiencing separation from home or from major attachment figures.*
2 *Persistent and excessive worry about losing major attachment figures or about possible harm to them, such as illness, injury, disasters or death.*
3 *Persistent and excessive worry about experiencing an untoward event . . . that causes separation from an attachment figure (e.g. getting lost, being kidnapped . . .).*
4 *Persistent reluctance or refusal to go out, away from home, to school, to work or to elsewhere because of fear of separation.*
5 *Persistent and excessive fear or reluctance about being alone or without major attachment figures . . .*
6 *Persistent reluctance or refusal to sleep away from home or to go to sleep without attachment figures.*
7 *Repeated nightmares involving the theme of separation.*
8 *Repeated complaints of physical symptoms (e.g. headaches, stomach aches, nausea and vomiting) when separation from major attachment figures occurs or is anticipated.*

B *The fear, anxiety, or avoidance is persistent, lasting at least 4 weeks in children and typically 6 months in adults.*
C *The disturbance causes clinically significant distress or impairment in social, academic, occupational, or other important areas of functioning.*
D *. . . not better explained by another mental disorder . . .'*
(DSM-5 2013: 190–195).

We shall see, in the next chapter, that this condition sometimes precedes and may give rise to a persisting complicated type of grief.

Finally we come to the most important question of all, what can be done to put things right? This study was not set up to answer that question but the implications

are clear. They include recognition of the importance of parenting and the imple-
mentation of a range of measures to free up, educate and support parents or their
surrogates so that they can devote as much time and attention as is needed to provide each child with a reasonably secure base from which it can learn an appropriate degree of trust in itself and others. Early warning systems are needed to ensure
that children with attachment problems are recognised and that their parents
receive the help which they will need to put things right. This does not imply that
parents are to blame for their child's problems. As we have seen, their problems
are often rooted in their own upbringing and they need understanding and support
rather than condemnation.

In later childhood teachers and others have greater influence and must take
every opportunity to provide effective antidotes to problematic attachments.

For those whose attachment problems continue into adult life, bereavements
and other critical life events constitute both a risk and an opportunity. Professionals and others who are around at times of loss and change can recognise those at
special risk and act to reduce that risk. The loss of 'significant others' is both a
cause for grief and a challenge to our basic assumptions about the world. Counsellors and others can provide the 'secure enough base' from which our clients
can begin to explore what they have lost and what remains. Out of the wreckage
of habitual assumptions can come a new view of the world, which may be more
appropriate and realistic than the one that preceded it. Those whose assumptive
world was distorted by mistrust of self and/or others have the opportunity to discover their own strength and the strength and goodwill of others.

Our role, as carers, is akin to that of the good parent who provides protection
when it is needed but also recognises that most of the time it is not needed and helps
the child to believe the same. It then becomes safe for the child or client to think and
talk about things that are unsafe, to do the things that will establish their strength
and autonomy and to take the risk of trusting others and forming new relationships.

Perhaps one of the most important and cheering aspects of the study is the
recognition from both the control group and the follow-up study that even the
most insecurely attached are not doomed. People can learn to cope with distressing
circumstances and events, both those that result from insecure attachments and
bereavement. Some will never need psychiatric help or counselling, but for those
who do it is important that they receive help that recognises and facilitates the
painful process of change.

The carer must be prepared to share in this process. We will suffer along with
our clients and must hold fast to the faith that people have the capacity to pass
through grief and achieve a new maturity. With time and experience we shall discover that, like parenting, therapy is worth the effort. Therapists have developed
their own language for the attachments that our clients make to us and we to our
clients. Terms such as 'transference' and 'counter-transference', 'therapeutic alli-
ance' and 'therapeutic relationship' recognise that this relationship is not a romantic attachment or a nurturant attachment; yet, if we are honest, we must admit that
it contains elements of both these relationships; in the end, it is a species of love.

It seems that love and loss provide the point and counterpoint of a symphony
whose first movement sets the colour and feeling tone of all that is to come. Succeeding movements introduce new themes, which may challenge, replace or develop the
earlier themes but cannot wipe them out. Order alternates with chaos as the music
of life progresses and the whole moves towards some kind of resolution that, in
great music, is always unexpected, subtle and deeply moving. The greatest music,
like the greatest drama, is the saddest, and its greatness stems from the emergence

of meaning out of discord, loss and pain. The sublime in music, as in life, reflects the human search for meaning, the grasping at eternity, the transcendence of the littleness of I.

References

Bowlby, J. The nature of the child's tie to its mother. *International Journal of Psychoanalysis* 39, 350–373, 1958.

Bowlby, J. *Attachment*. Volume I of *Attachment and Loss*. Hogarth, London, 1969.

Diagnostic Statistical Manual of Mental Disorders (DSM-5). American Psychiatric Association, New York, 2013.

Grand, S. 'I'm sorry, has your brain broken?' *Guardian: Life* 7, 29 January 2004.

Klass, D., Silverman, P. R. and Nickman, S. (eds.) *Continuing Bonds: New Understandings of Grief*. Taylor & Francis, Washington, DC and London, 1996.

Parkes, C. M. *Bereavement: Studies of Grief in Adult Life*. hb. Routledge/Taylor & Francis, London and International Universities Press, NY, ppb Pelican, Harmondsworth & Taylor & Francis, New York, third edition, 1996.

Rando, T. A. *Loss and Anticipatory Grief*. Lexington Books, Lexington, MA and Toronto, 1986.

CHAPTER 9

COMPLICATED GRIEF
The debate over a new DSM-5 diagnostic category

From Kenneth J. Doka (ed.) *Living with grief before and after the death* (pp. 139–152). Washington, DC: Hospice Foundation of America, 2007.

Since its inception in 1844, the Diagnostic Statistical Manual of Mental Disorders (DSM) has become the diagnostic Bible of psychiatry. It exists to ensure that psychiatrists have a common language, that when psychiatrists make a diagnosis everyone will know what they mean. Its widespread use reflects the major role its progenitor, the American Psychiatric Association, played in promoting a particular view of psychiatry, a view that the World Health Organization (WHO) did not leave unchallenged in Chapter V 'Mental and Behavioural Disorders' of its huge International Classification of Disease (IDC). To make things even more complicated ideas about what constitutes a mental illness are changing and both systems of classification have changed. While the DSM has gone through five revisions the ICD is now in its tenth. The very existence of two changing diagnostic systems in the world has complicated the collection of reliable data about mental illness from country to country. It has also put the authors of both systems on their metal to carry out research in order to resolve differences between them. As a result the two systems have become increasingly similar, with only minor differences between them. On the whole the DSM tends to lead the way with the ICD lumbering behind if only because the authors of the ICD have to satisfy representatives of 200 countries.

Perhaps the greatest problem with these competing systems is their conservatism. Minor tweaks are made from one edition to the next but major overhauls are difficult when the aim is to produce uniformity. For instance an attempt to introduce a new set of overarching categories in DSM-IV[1] was dropped in DSM-5[2] because readers had ignored it. As a result:

> *the diagnosis of psychiatric disorders has relied mainly on accurate delineation of symptoms rather than on the identification of causes. It resembles the descriptive diagnoses of eighteenth century medicine rather than the cause-related categories of the twentieth century. The diagnosis of post-traumatic stress disorder broke the mould and it is hoped that the attempt to delineate categories of attachment disorder . . . will take the process a step further.*
>
> *(Parkes 2006b: 246–247)*

Perhaps because of this built-in conservatism, diagnostic categories for pathological responses to loss, which were proposed after World War II by Lindemann (1944) and supported by much subsequent research, have remained unrecognised. The article that follows was my contribution to the debate preceding the publication of DSM-5. That edition introduced the term Persistent Complex Bereavement Disorder *(PCBD) for the condition referred to elsewhere as* Complicated Grief *(CG). This was included in a special category of* Conditions for Further Study *but was not formally recognised with a coding category, probably because of controversy surrounding the diagnosis. It will be described in this chapter.*

The authors did, however, allow PCBD to be included in the much broader category of Adjustment Disorders *which could 'be diagnosed following the death of a loved one when the intensity, quality or persistence of grief reactions exceeds what might normally be expected when cultural, religious, or age-appropriate norms are taken into account'* (Parkes 2006b: 287).

Much research has shown that bereavement, the loss of a loved person, can cause lasting distress and problems in physical and mental health (see Jacobs 1993 for a review). It can also lead to improvements in maturity and psychological strength (Neimeyer 2001). Much is now known about the risk factors that decide what kind of outcome we can expect (Stroebe and Schut 2002). Those who care for families before and after bereavement are in a position to identify the risks and to steer people towards needed help. Well-conducted studies have shown that 'the more complicated the grief process appears to be or to become, the better the chances of interventions leading to positive results' (Schut, Stroebe, van den Bout and Ter-heggen 2001).

Anxiety states and clinical depression are the most frequent psychological problems to follow major bereavements (Jacobs 1993). These problems are frequent in psychiatric patients; their precursors, diagnosis and treatment are well known and do not differ from reactions to other types of stress. Less frequent is post-traumatic stress disorder (PTSD), which can occur when a person has 'experienced, witnessed, or been confronted with an event or events that involved actual or threatened death or serious injury, or a threat to the physical integrity of self or others' and the person's response involved 'intense fear, helplessness, or horror' (American Psychiatric Association 1994). Indeed, bereavement can act as a trigger for almost any mental disorder to which an individual is vulnerable.

These problems differ from . . . *[Persistent Complex Grief Disorder (PCBD)]* which, as we will see, is peculiar to bereavement, takes a unique course and responds to different treatments from those prescribed for other conditions.

This disorder was first described by Eric Lindemann in 1944, yet it has *[only now]* been included in the influential *Diagnostic Statistical Manual of Mental Disorders* (DSM) of the American Psychiatric Association, . . . *[and that in an experimental category with a provisional set of diagnostic criteria]*, and its status remains debatable. If Lindemann was right, this uncertain status has given rise to a great deal of unnecessary suffering.

In recent years, much research has been carried out in this field with the aim of establishing rigorous diagnostic criteria and improving the care of those who suffer from CG *[PCBD]*. Two main schools of thought have emerged, one from Mardi Horowitz and his colleagues at the Langley Porter Psychiatric Institute at the University of California, and another from Holly Prigerson and her colleagues at the Department of Epidemiology and Psychiatry of Yale University. Both have used sophisticated methods of data collection and analysis to derive their own diagnostic criteria, which differ more in detail than in substance. A recent edition of *Omega* enabled the leading contenders to engage in a 'symposium' to clarify the issues involved (Parkes 2006a). Their conclusions will be summarised here. The debate continues, and it now seems likely that agreement has been reached on most important matters (*v.s.*).

The contributors to the *Omega* edition were asked three questions:

- Is there a type of grief that can justifiably be regarded as a mental disorder?
- If so, how should the disorder be classified in relation to other disorders?
- What criteria for diagnosis are best supported by systematic research?

This article summarises the answers to these questions.

Is there a type of grief that can justifiably be regarded as a mental disorder?

Horowitz's research followed his own major contribution to the development of diagnostic criteria for PTSD, for which he had developed the Impact of Events Scale (Horowitz, Wilner and Alvarez 1979). Although a subscale of this instrument has been used as a measure of severe grief, Holly Prigerson and her colleagues (1995a) developed a more useful diagnostic instrument, the Index of Complicated Grief (ICG), aimed specifically at CG *[PCBD]*. Neither of these instruments is intended as a substitute for clinical judgment. Rather, they are standardised substitutes, approximations, that are suitable for research purposes but insufficiently precise for individual diagnosis.

Using the ICG, Prigerson's group has confirmed beyond reasonable doubt that for a minority of bereaved people, grief, instead of declining in intensity over time, remains chronic and severe, giving rise to protracted misery and inability to function effectively in the roles that make life worthwhile (Prigerson et al. 1995a, 1995b, 1996a). Indeed, bereaved people with persistent high scores on the ICG are at substantial risk for serious outcomes, ranging from hospital admissions and high blood pressure to suicide (Prigerson et al. 1997). These findings confirm and give powerful credence to much other work; however, some doubt the wisdom of designating CG *[PCBD]* as a mental disorder. The main objections are a reluctance to label grief as 'abnormal', the stigma attached to psychiatric diagnoses and the danger that family and friends will withdraw their support (Stroebe and Schut 2006).

Prigerson's group has responded to these objections. The group's research demonstrates that CG is distinct from 'normal' grief not only in terms of its persistence and severity but also because of the other symptoms and disabilities associated with it. The researchers do not doubt that stigmatisation can take place, even when no psychiatric diagnosis has been made. In fact, it is not uncommon for bereaved people to imagine that they are going mad. However, a formal psychiatric diagnosis of CG *[PCBD]*, far from confirming such fears, enables the psychiatrist to reassure people that they are not psychotic. In a study of 135 bereaved persons, 96% stated that if they were told they met the criteria for CG, 'they would be relieved to know that they were not going crazy, that they had a recognisable condition and that the diagnosis would help their family members to understand better what they were experiencing' (Prigerson and Maciejewski 2006: 16). Likewise, in a recent nationwide study of a Norwegian population of parents who had lost a child, 74% of whom met Prigerson's criteria for complicated grief, Dyregrov concluded, 'by claiming to protect the individual from being powerless and dependent on professionals, the demedicalisation strategy prevents people in psychosocial crisis *[from obtaining]* access to professional help' (Dyregrov 2005: 9).

Overall, there seems to be good reason to accept a psychiatric disorder of grieving but also to ensure that, as with all mental illness, diagnosis is reserved for those for whom the benefits outweigh any potential harm. Such people are entitled to the care, compassion and privileges accorded to the sick by society: sanction to withdraw from occupational and other demands they are unable to fulfil, the right to receive treatment and the right to be compensated for any secondary losses resulting from the illness. In addition, when the bereavement is someone's fault the bereaved have a right to legal compensation for suffering, loss of earnings and cost of treatment.

How should the disorder be classified in relation to other disorders?

While Prigerson's group has shown that CG *[PCBD]* is distinct from clinical depression, PTSD and normal grief (Prigerson et al. 1996a, 1996b), a dispute has arisen between her contention that it is a disorder of attachment and Horowitz's claim that it is a stress response syndrome. Horowitz (2006) finds several points of similarity between CG and PTSD, including preoccupation with intrusive memories and avoidance of painful reminders. Prigerson and Vanderwerker (2006) point out that, whereas the intrusive memories of PTSD are painful, those of CG are usually positive memories of a loved person. Furthermore, CG is frequently associated with a history of insecure attachments that may go back to childhood. That said, Prigerson and Vanderwerker continue to include 'symptoms of traumatization' among their criteria for diagnosis.

Since the main function of the attachments we make throughout life is to provide security and support in times of trouble, it is no surprise to find that those with insecure attachments are more vulnerable than others to traumas of all kinds, including bereavement (Parkes 2006b: 70). In that sense, both Prigerson and Horowitz are right. Like a pathological fracture of a bone, CG*[PCBD]* is both a disorder and a traumatic reaction. However, the essential element of CG is intense pining and yearning for a lost person, which seems to place it firmly in the category of attachment disorders. Another attachment disorder that has been included in the DSM is 'separation anxiety disorder' . . . *[severe fear and intolerance of separation from others to whom the sufferer is attached was formerly regarded as a childhood disorder but has now, in DSM-5, been recognised as liable to continue into adult life]*; this disorder is often reported in the history of people with CG (Vanderwerker, Jacobs, Parkes and Prigerson 2006).

What criteria for diagnosis are best supported by systematic research?

Thus far, we have been considering complicated grief as if it were one disorder, but several complications of grief have been described. *[In addition to PCBD]* these include . . . delayed or inhibited grief, and identification syndromes (in which the bereaved person develops hypochondriacal symptoms resembling the illness or injury suffered by the person now dead).

Inhibited grief remains contentious. It is difficult, if not impossible, to measure grief that is not expressed. Researchers such as Keltner and Bonanno (1997) have demonstrated that, overall, people who show positive rather than negative emotions after bereavement have less distress later than do overt grievers. Without controlling for the strength of the attachment, it is hard to know whether lack of grieving results from repression of grief or paucity of attachment. Currently, the onus is on the proponents of repression theory to show that the inhibition of grief is a cause of subsequent problems.

One possible outcome of inhibition of grief is delay in its onset. This delayed grief is allowed for in Prigerson's CG [PCBD], provided that the grief that then appears is severe and protracted and fulfils her other criteria.

Many criteria for diagnosing CG have been proposed at one time or another. Currently, the researchers who have contributed most to the refinement of these criteria agree on the following: (1) persistent pining for a lost person is an essential criterion; (2) a period of [twelve] months or more should have elapsed since the bereavement; and (3) the syndrome should seriously impair the sufferer's ability to function in occupational or domestic roles and responsibilities.

While the precise wording of the remaining criteria remains under discussion, symptoms of traumatisation are also required – thus, feelings of emotional numbness may persist along with inability to accept the reality of the loss and to move forward. People with CG find that their assumptive world – the world they have always taken for granted – has been shattered (Janoff-Bulman 1992); life seems to have lost its meaning and direction.

Taken together, these criteria provide us with a firm basis for diagnosing the principal form of complicated grief. The inclusion of the diagnosis in the DSM will stimulate future research, and other forms of CG may then be added.

[Six years later the DSM-5 proposed the following criteria for diagnosing PCBD: (pp. 789–792) for further study (my emphasis).

Proposed criteria for PCBD in adults

A   *The individual has experienced the <u>death</u> of someone [in] . . . a close relationship.*

B   *Since the death <u>at least one of the following</u> symptoms . . . for at least twelve months after the death:*

1   *Persistent yearning/longing for the deceased.*
2   *Intense sorrow and emotional pain in response to the death.*
3   *Preoccupation with the deceased.*
4   *Preoccupation with the circumstances of the death.*

C   *Since the death at least <u>six of the following</u> symptoms . . . . <u>on more days than not</u> and to a clinically significant degree, and persisting <u>for at least twelve months</u> after the death.*

Reactive distress to the death

1   *Marked <u>difficulty accepting the death</u>.*
2   *<u>Disbelief or emotional numbness</u> over the loss.*
3   *<u>Difficulty in positive reminiscing</u> over the deceased.*
4   *<u>Bitterness or anger</u> related to the loss.*
5   *Maladaptive appraisals about oneself . . . [re.] the deceased or the death (e.g. <u>shame</u>).*
6   *Excessive <u>avoidance of reminders</u> of the loss (. . . individuals, places or situations . . .)*

Social/identity disruption

 7 A *desire to die* in order to be with the deceased.
 8 *Difficulty trusting* individuals since the death.
 9 *Feeling alone or detached* from others . . .
10 Feeling *life is meaningless or empty* without the deceased, or . . . one cannot function . . .
11 Confusion over one's role in life, or a diminished sense of one's identity (e.g. feeling that part of oneself died with the deceased).
12 Difficulty or reluctance to pursue interests . . . or to plan for the future.

D   The disturbance causes *clinically significant distress or impairment in social, occupational or other important areas of functioning*.
E   The bereavement reaction is *out of proportion to . . . the cultural, religious or age-appropriate norms*.

Specify if **with traumatic bereavement** *due to homicide or suicide with persistent distressing preoccupations [re.] the traumatic nature of the death* . . .

Proposed criteria for PCBD in children *include all of the above except:*

B   requirement reduced to six months after the death.
C   requirement reduced to six months after the death.

 1   . . . difficulty accepting death . . . depending on the child's capacity to comprehend the meaning and permanence of death.
 6   . . . avoidance of reminders . . . may include avoidance of thoughts and feelings . . . [re.] the deceased.]

Can complicated grief be prevented?

While many systematic random-allocation studies have been carried out on the effectiveness of bereavement services in improving outcome after bereavement, few have focused on their influence on CG [*PCBD*]. Even so, lack of clear benefits from such services, when offered to unselected or self-selected samples of bereaved people, gives little cause for optimism.

In their review of these studies, Schut, Stroebe, van den Bout and Terheggen note, 'In several of these studies, participants were screened for risk level before being offered intervention. This coincides almost completely with whether or not positive results were found, suggesting that selecting participants raises the chances of intervention leading to positive results' (Schut, Stroebe, van den Bout and Terheggen 2001: 725). Many palliative care units now use some method of risk assessment to focus bereavement support where it is most needed and, at the same time, to identify problems that will need attention. These methods include assessment of the circumstances of the loss (e.g. the extent to which it was unexpected, untimely or otherwise traumatic); assessment of the vulnerability of the bereaved person (e.g. previous psychiatric history, suicidal threats, attachment problems, current distressing symptoms); and social circumstances (e.g. isolation, dysfunctional family or lack of future meaningful life). See Stroebe and Schut (2002) and Parkes (2006b) for further details.

Of particular relevance to the prevention of CG is Kissane and Bloch's family-focused grief therapy model (2002). This model is intended for use in palliative care units and aims to prevent problems before they arise by increasing cohesiveness, opening communication channels and enhancing problem solving in dysfunctional families, which are at special risk for CG. A recent random-allocation study indicates that the model reduces bereavement risk in families low on cohesiveness and expressiveness, but not if they are also highly conflicted or hostile.

Treatment of complicated grief

The most persuasive argument for including CG *[PCBD]* as a psychiatric disorder would be to demonstrate that it can be cured. While we have some way to go to achieve this aim, evidence exists of substantial benefits from treatment.

Therapies for CG reflect the theoretical assumptions of their proponents, and few have been subjected to adequate scientific evaluation. In the period after World War II, when Lindemann was carrying out his research, delayed and inhibited reactions may have been more common than they are today. He emphasised the danger of repressing grief and developed a method of treatment aimed at facilitating its expression. Random-allocation studies by Mawson, Marks, Ramm and Stern (1981) and by Sireling, Cohen and Marks (1988) gave limited support to the value of Ramsay's adaptation of this 'guided mourning' therapy (1979), but in most cases the results were disappointing.

More recently the recognition of the importance of coping strategies in bereavement has led to the development of cognitive therapies. Both cognitive (problem-focused) and Lindemann's affective (emotion-focused) therapies have shown benefits in random-allocation studies. One study indicated that women benefit most from cognitive and men from affective interventions (Schut, Stroebe, van den Bout and de Keijser 1997a). The combination of cognitive with affective therapy seems ideal; in one study, it was shown to produce more benefit than cognitive therapy alone (Schut, de Keijser, van den Bout and Stroebe, 1997b).

None of these studies focused exclusively on the problem of complicated grief, but a recent evaluation by Shear, Frank, Houck and Reynolds (2005) of a new method of CG *[PCBD]* treatment has done so. This method uses Stroebe and Schut's dual process model (1999), which suggests that for healthy grieving to take place, it is necessary to alternate between pining for the lost person (loss orientation) and putting one's grief aside and beginning the painful process of rethinking and revising one's view of the world and future plans (restoration orientation). Consequently, Shear and colleagues' therapy includes both affective and cognitive components.

They randomly assigned bereaved people with high scores on Prigerson's ICG to two groups. One group received sixteen sessions of interpersonal psychotherapy, the other received the same number of sessions of complicated grief treatment.

The therapy included an introductory phase during which the therapist provided information about normal and complicated grief and described the dual process model. In the middle phase, both orientations were examined and exercises were undertaken, including 'revisiting exercises' in which the patient told the story of the death of the lost person and related it to the level of distress. These exercises were tape recorded and played between sessions. The loss orientation was also addressed during these sessions, in the form of imaginary conversations with the dead person, the aim being to evoke positive emotions. The restoration orientation was addressed by encouraging the patient to set goals and identify ways of working towards them. In the final phase, progress was reviewed, achievements acknowledged and further targets agreed on.

By twenty-four weeks after the start of therapy, 60% of those receiving complicated grief therapy and 25% of those receiving interpersonal therapy showed a decrease in the ICG score of twenty points or more; similar, statistically significant differences were observed by independent assessors. While these results are very encouraging, it would be a mistake to assume that complicated grief therapy provides the answer to complicated grief: about a quarter of patients dropped out from both groups in the course of therapy and nearly half showed little or no improvement.

Another promising intervention that is under development is Wagner, Knaevelsrud and Maercker's Internet-based therapy for complicated grief (2005). This therapy is of particular interest for its low cost and potential value in developing countries. It includes guided writing of letters to the dead and to a mythical friend who has symptoms of CG similar to those of the patient. *[A random-allocation study showed greater improvements in the treated group by comparison with a waiting-list control group (Wagner, Knaevelsrud and Maercker 2006)].*

The breakdown of the pattern of life that results from CG presents both a challenge and an opportunity. Most therapists believe that, out of the ruins of the assumptive world, a new world can arise – not, as some think, by forgetting the dead, but by recovering the memories, meanings and messages that continue to enrich us (Klass, Silverman and Nickman 1996). Both cognitive and affective strategies have their place. Our future can only be built on the past.

Conclusions

The inclusion of complicated grief *[Persistent Complex Bereavement Disorder]* in the DSM will not be the end of the story. If PTSD is a precedent, CG's inclusion will stimulate research that will lead to further modifications and developments. One development may well be the recognition that CG is not confined to bereavement by death. Many other life events give rise to lasting grief and loss of the assumptive world (Kauffman 2002). Other complications of grief may also need to be included, either as separate categories or subcategories . . .

Psychiatry has lagged behind the rest of medicine in relying on diagnoses based on descriptive phenomenology rather than etiology. Now that PTSD and CG have broken the mould, we can expect further changes in nosology and, with them, more effective methods of prevention and treatment.

As resistance fades to diagnosing CG as pathology, we may become more understanding of those who suffer from it. Few people today would accept that doctors should withhold treatment because 'suffering is good for the soul'; indeed, those who work in palliative care and bereavement continue to discover more evidence of the extent to which the alleviation of physical and mental pain leaves people more secure and better able to face their own mortality and that of those they love. Therapy will never remove the pain of complicated grief, but it may make it more bearable and help people find new hope and meaning in their lives.

While the adoption of the term 'Persistent Complex Bereavement Disorder' in DSM-5 is an improvement on the terms 'Complicated Grief' and 'Prolonged Grief Disorder', if only because there are several forms of complicated grief that were not included in Prigerson's researches and there is more to PCBD than prolonged grief, it is disappointing to find the condition confined to a research category. Sufferers can, however, be diagnosed under the less rigorous category of an Adjustment Disorder and other cases may belong more appropriately as Separation Anxiety

Disorders. Either way DSM-5 has established the complications of bereavement as an important area of clinical relevance and research study. What it has not done is to recognise that bereavement is only one of the causes of grief and that by limiting PCBD to bereavement by death it is implying that death is the only cause of disorders of grieving.

Notes

1 American Psychiatric Association (APA). *Diagnostic and Statistical Manual of Mental Disorders* (4th ed.). Author, Washington, DC, 1994.
2 American Psychiatric Association (APA). *Diagnostic and Statistical Manual of Mental Disorders* (5th ed.). American Psychiatric Association, Washington, DC, 2013.

References

American Psychiatric Association (APA). *Diagnostic and Statistical Manual of Mental Disorders* (4th ed.). Author, Washington, DC, 1994.
Dyregrov, K. Do professionals disempower bereaved people? Grief and social intervention. *Bereavement Care* 24(1), 7–10, 2005.
Horowitz, M. Meditating on complicated grief disorder as a diagnosis. Symposium on complicated grief. *Omega* 52(1), 88, 2006.
Horowitz, M., Wilner, N. and Alvarez, W. Impact of event scale: A measure of subjective stress. *Psychosomatic Medicine* 41, 209–218, 1979.
Jacobs, S. *Pathologic Grief: Maladaptation to Loss.* American Psychiatric Association, Washington, DC and London, 1993.
Janoff-Bulman, R. *Shattered Assumptions: Towards a New Psychology of Trauma.* The Free Press, New York, 1992.
Kauffman, J. (ed.). *Loss of the Assumptive World: A Theory of Traumatic Loss.* Brunner-Routledge, New York and London, 2002.
Keltner, D. and Bonanno, G. A study of laughter and dissociation: distinct correlates of laughter and smiling after bereavement. *Journal of Personal and Social Psychology* 73(4), 687–702, 1997.
Kissane, D. and Bloch, S. *Family Focused Grief Therapy: A Model of Family-Centred Care during Palliative Care and Bereavement.* Open University Press, Buckingham, England, and Philadelphia, 2002.
Klass, D., Silverman, P.R. and Nickman, S. (eds.). *Continuing Bonds: New Understandings of Grief.* Taylor & Francis, Washington, DC and London, 1996.
Lindemann, E. The symptomatology and management of acute grief. *American Journal of Psychiatry* 101, 141–148, 1944.
Mawson, D., Marks, I.M., Ramm, L. and Stern, L.S. Guided mourning for morbid grief: a controlled study. *British Journal of Psychiatry* 138, 185–193, 1981.
Neimeyer, R. (ed.). *Meaning Reconstruction and the Experience of Loss.* American Psychological Association, Washington, DC, 2001.
Parkes, C.M. (guest ed.). Introduction and conclusions. Symposium on complicated grief. *Omega* 52(1), 1–112, 2006a.
Parkes, C.M. *Love and Loss: The Roots of Grief and Its Complications.* [Routledge], London and New York, 2006b.
Prigerson, H.G., Bierhals, A.J., Kasl, S.V., Reynolds, C.F., III, Shear, M.K., Newsom, J.T., et al. Complicated grief as a distinct disorder from bereavement-related depression and anxiety: a replication study. *American Journal of Psychiatry* 153, 84–86, 1996a.
Prigerson, H.G., Bierhals, A.J., Kasl, S.V., Reynolds, C.F., III, Shear, M.K., Day, N. et al. Traumatic grief as a risk factor for mental and physical morbidity. *American Journal of Psychiatry* 154, 617–623, 1997.
Prigerson, H.G., Frank, E., Kasl, S.V., Reynolds, C.F., III, Anderson, B., Zubenko, G.S., et al. Complicated grief and bereavement-related depression as distinct disorders: preliminary

evaluation in elderly bereaved spouses. *American Journal of Psychiatry*, 152(1), 22–30, 1995b.

Prigerson, H. G. and Maciejewski, P. K. A call for sound empirical testing and evaluation of criteria for complicated grief proposed for DSM-5. Symposium on complicated grief. *Omega* 52(1), 16, 2006.

Prigerson, H. G., Maciejewski, P. K., Newsom, J., Reynolds, C. F., III, Frank, E., Bierhals, E. J., et al. The Inventory of Complicated Grief: a scale to measure maladaptive symptoms of loss. *Psychiatry Research* 59, 65–79, 1995a.

Prigerson, H. G., Shear, M. K., Newsom, I., Frank, E., Reynolds, C. F., III, Houck, P. R. et al. Anxiety among widowed elders: is it distinct from depression and grief? *Anxiety* 2, 1–12, 1996b.

Prigerson, H. G. and Vanderwerker, L. C. Final remarks. Symposium on complicated grief. *Omega* 52(1), 92, 2006.

Ramsay, R. W. Bereavement: a behavioural treatment for pathological grief. In P. O. Sjoden, S. Bayes and W. S. Dorkens (eds.) *Trends in Behaviour Therapy* (pp. 217–248). Academic Press, New York, 1979.

Schut, H., de Keijser, J., van den Bout, J. and Stroebe, M. S. Cross-modality grief therapy: description and assessment of a new program. *Journal of Clinical Psychology* 52(3), 357–365, 1997b.

Schut, H. A. W., Stroebe, M., van den Bout, J. and de Keijser, J. Intervention for the bereaved: gender differences in the efficacy of two counseling programs. *British Journal of Clinical Psychology* 36, 63–72, 1997a.

Schut, H., Stroebe, M. S., van den Bout, J. and Terheggen, M. The efficacy of bereavement interventions: determining who benefits. In M. S. Stroebe, R. O. Hansson, W. Stroebe and H. Schut (eds.) *Handbook of Bereavement Research: Consequences, Coping and Care* (chapter 30, pp. 705–737). American Psychological Association, Washington, DC, 2001.

Shear, K., Frank, E., Houck, P. R. and Reynolds, C. F. Treatment of complicated grief: a randomized controlled trial. *Journal of the American Medical Association* 293(21), 2601–2607, 2005.

Sireling, L., Cohen, D. and Marks, I. Guided mourning for morbid grief: a controlled replication. *Behavior Therapy* 19, 121–132, 1988.

Stroebe, M. S. and Schut, H. The dual process model of coping with bereavement: rationale and description. *Death Studies* 23, 197–224, 1999.

Stroebe, W. and Schut, H. Risk factors in bereavement outcome: a methodological and empirical review. In M. S. Stroebe, R. O. Hansson, W. Stroebe and H. Schut (eds.) *Handbook of Bereavement Research: Consequences, Coping and Care* (pp. 349–371). American Psychological Association, Washington, DC, 2002.

Stroebe, M. and Schut, H. Complicated grief: a conceptual analysis of the field. Symposium on complicated grief. *Omega* 52(1), 53–70, 2006.

Vanderwerker, L. C., Jacobs, S. C., Parkes, C. M. and Prigerson, H. G. An exploration of associations between separation anxiety in childhood and complicated grief in later life. Journal of Nervous and Mental Disease 194(2), 121–123, 2006.

Wagner, B., Knaevelsrud, C. and Maercker, A. Internet-based treatment for complicated grief: concepts and case study. *Journal of Loss and Trauma* 10, 409–432, 2005.

Wagner, B., Knaevelsrud, C. and Maercker, A. Internet-based cognitive-behavioral therapy for complicated grief: a randomized controlled trial. *Death Studies* 30(5), 429–453, 2006.

World Health Organization. *International Classification of Diseases, 10th revision. (ICD-10)*. WHO, Geneva (ICD10CM categories give diagnostic criteria and codes), 2007.

CHAPTER 10

DANGEROUS WORDS

From *Bereavement Care* 26(2): 23–25, 2000.

As an editor of the journal Bereavement Care *from its inception in 1982 I have seen it grow from a small, in-house journal for Cruse Bereavement Care into a respected international journal with a worldwide readership many of whose papers are down-loaded from the Web. Despite this it has retained its objective to reach a wide range of professionals and volunteers who support bereaved people. Although all papers are peer-reviewed and of a high academic standard, the editors also expect them to be accessible and useful.*

I have chosen to include this short paper because it illustrates the educational func-tion of the journal as well as allowing me to ride a few of my own hobby horses.

> 'When I use a word,' said Humpty Dumpty . . . 'it means just what I choose it to mean, – neither more nor less . . . The question is, which is to be master – that's all'.
>
> —Lewis Carroll
> *Through the Looking Glass*, Chapter 6

Abstract

Some of the words and terms in common usage following bereavement are ambiguous or likely to be misunderstood. Words that need special caution include *grief, mourning, meaning-making, dependent, empathy* and various words used to describe the problems to which grief can give rise. The risk of misunderstanding is no reason to stop using these terms; problems can be avoided if we take care and clarify our usage when necessary.

Each one of us, when we use a word, knows just what we mean by it. Unfortu-nately, those who read it also think they know just what we mean by it. Often they are wrong.

In this paper I shall illustrate this point by reference to some words about bereavement that are commonly misinterpreted or misused. My intention is not to stop us from using these dangerous words, for most of them are very useful, but to attach some warning flags that will wave in our heads each time we meet or use the words in question, and warn us to watch out for misunderstandings.

Grief is the first word that comes to mind when we think of bereavement and it is probably the most useful. We all think we know what it means, yet there is very little agreement among experts regarding its definition. Some people use *grief* loosely to imply all of the distressing emotions that follow bereavement; sadness, anxiety, anger, guilt and much else. The problem with this is that it does not differentiate grief from the emotional reactions to other distressing events. Other people include the psychological processes through which people are supposed to pass over time, such as the so-called phases of grief. The problem here is the wide variety of opinions about these processes and the evidence that many do not follow a neat path through them.

Perhaps the most intuitive meaning, and the one that best distinguishes grief from other reactions, is also the simplest – grief is the intense and painful pining for and preoccupation with somebody or something, now lost, to whom or to which one was attached. It is distinguished from 'separation distress' by the intensity and duration that results from permanent loss.

Only if we can agree on the meaning of grief will our attempts to measure it by questionnaires and other means begin to make sense. At the present time we need to be particularly careful, when interpreting the results of such research, to examine just what is being included.

Grief is often used interchangeably with another dangerous word, *mourning*. This usage follows Freud's example in his famous paper, 'Mourning and Melancholia'. Freud's original paper ('Trauer und Melancholie' 1917) was written in German and translated by Joan Riviere. *Trauer* is ambiguous, used for both *grief* and its formal expression, thus *trauer tragen* means 'mourning dress'. On one hand, psychoanalysts have used the term *mourning* for 'the processes in which states of grief are eventually attenuated as the person recognises and adapts to loss' (Horowitz 1980). On the other hand, most social scientists reserve the term *mourning* for the public display of grief, which may have little to do with the underlying emotion (Gorer 1965; Rosenblatt, Walsh and Jackson 1976).

From time to time grief may take atypical forms that give rise to great suffering and disturbance of those functions that make life worth living. While these have all the characteristics of *mental disorder* there has been much resistance to applying this term to bereaved people. Because mental disorder is equated in the public mind with madness, or psychosis, and the consequent restriction of liberties and other negative attributions that accompany madness, it is assumed to stigmatise and disempower people. In fact most mental disorders are not psychoses and the appropriate use of psychiatric diagnosis can reassure people that they are not 'mad' and empower them to get the help they need (Dyregrov 2005).

There is little agreement regarding the words to be used for the disorders of grief. *Pathological grief, complicated grief, abnormal grief* and *morbid grief* have all been used to designate more or less the same thing. They all recognise the fact that grief sometimes takes forms that give rise to lasting distress and inability to function in the ways that make life worthwhile. It is the inconsistency and lack of agreement about just what is meant that has deterred the authors of the influential *Diagnostic Statistical Manual* (DSM) from recognising any of these terms (American Psychiatric Association 1994). As a result people suffering from these conditions have been deprived of the privileges of medical treatment and the compensation that they may deserve when others are responsible for their loss. Recent efforts to find consensus are currently close to fulfilment and it is hoped that the most frequent complication of grief, 'Prolonged Grief Disorder', closely defined so as to exclude those abnormal or atypical forms of grief that do not give rise to lasting suffering and impairment, will be included in the next edition of the DSM. *[As we saw in* Chapter 9, *this term was replaced in DSM-5 by yet another term,* Persisting Complex Bereavement Disorder.*]* The other terms should probably be dropped or retained only for forms of grief that do not meet accepted criteria. . . . The psychiatric problems of Major Depression, Anxiety Disorders, Post-Traumatic Stress Disorder and other psychiatric diagnoses that may be triggered by bereavement, should not be referred to as *Complicated Grief*.

A particular problem arises with the term *Abnormal Grief*. It is widely and incorrectly assumed that mental abnormalities are synonymous with mental illness but this is not the case. Indeed superior intelligence or other exceptional virtues are statistically abnormal but are not regarded as undesirable let alone pathological. Not only are many of the abnormal or atypical forms of grief compatible with a satisfactory and well-functioning life, but some of them may even benefit society. A mother may inhibit her own grief at the loss of her spouse in order to care for a newborn child. Her grief may then be abnormally delayed, but should not be regarded as pathological. Similarly, man-made deaths sometimes give rise to exceptionally intense but appropriate anger, which may itself lead to the righting of wrongs. Complaints against medical staff who cared for a dying person may be quite justified and should not be routinely dismissed as 'irrational'. Only if anger is unrestrained, inappropriate and likely to cause further injustice, suffering and/or cycles of violence can it be regarded as pathological.

Another word that is commonly used after bereavement is *trauma*. This term is often used loosely for any distressing event; some reserve it for situations of danger or threat to life, while others see it as any situation that challenges our ability to cope. Behind each of these viewpoints there is a theory trying to get out. Thus people who see trauma as caused by emotions will tend to use the first definition, those who explain it by stress theory the second and proponents of coping theory the third. Many of these types and theories of trauma can usefully be applied to bereavement but it is wisest not to take theory for granted, but to reserve the term *Traumatic Bereavement* for those bereavements that empirical studies have shown to be most likely to give rise to problems and the need for help, that is, unexpected *and* untimely losses, deaths by violence or mutilating illness, deaths by human agency, multiple deaths and disasters (Stroebe and Schut 2002).

It is not only words that confuse; non-verbal communication can also mislead us. Thus, we usually recognise emotions, and the assumptions that underlie them, by *empathy*. Carl Rogers (1961) identified empathy as one of the most important counselling skills, the means by which we get inside the heads of our clients and see the world from their points of view. This is, indeed, an important thing to do, but it carries with it the danger that we may then become blind to our clients' misperceptions of the world. Rogers was aware of that danger and warned against too close an identification with clients, but this advice is often forgotten. My recent studies show how frequently the problems that follow bereavement are rooted in misperceptions of ourselves and each other (Parkes 2006). For example, the widow who sees her late husband as the tower of strength who protected her from the dangers of the world may cause us, through empathy, to accept her view of herself as a helpless, childlike person who needs our protection from the world. From then on our empathy will be dangerous to the client and to ourselves, perpetuating the problem of dependency. For such a person it is not our empathic sympathy for their predicament that will help them, but our respect for their potential value and strength.

John Bowlby hated the word *dependent*, mainly because it is so often used in a pejorative sense. In a society in which 'love' is a virtue, 'dependency' is a vice

(1969). Yet both are aspects of attachment. 'You mustn't be dependent' we say, as if those who trust others more than they trust themselves had any option. Indeed by rejecting the clinger we make them more insecure and they then experience the need to cling all the harder. Alternative terms such as *reliance* are less likely to be seen as judgemental.

Many now see the main function of bereavement support as being to help people to find new meaning in their lives (Neimeyer 2001). Indeed there is something very appealing about the idea that, out of the ruins of bereavement, new meanings can emerge. The problem with *meaning-making* is that, like the word *stress*, it is so comprehensive a term that it can mean anything.

The brain is a machine for finding meaning. Each new 'sensation' arriving in the brain is matched with memories of previous sensations to enable us to identify and attach meaning to them, thus they become 'perceptions' and 'assumptions'. Throughout our lives we are adding to our library of memories, expanding our assumptive world and increasing our repertoire of solutions to problems. When, as after a bereavement, we are faced with a large gap between the world that we had taken for granted, our assumptive world, and the world that now is, we are forced to review and revise those assumptions, to undertake a psychosocial transition (Parkes 1993). In other words, we find new meanings in our lives. We will do this whether we get help or not, for humans are meaning-making animals.

Viewed in this way meaning-making cannot be an end in itself. Our problem as helpers is to ensure that the meanings that people now find are appropriate and rewarding to them and their families. On one hand rewarding meanings include paranoid ideas that others must be punished for their suffering; that a dead child is more important than those who survive; or that grief is a perpetual duty to the dead. On the other hand rewarding meanings include acceptance of death as a necessary aspect of life and recognition of and willingness to engage with the sufferings of others. These meanings transcend the littleness of 'I' and can be seen as spiritual meanings.

One type of meaning is found by *continuing bonds* to the dead. This may be constructive if it enables people to enjoy and make use of the memories of their times together, but it can also be problematic if, for instance, they see it as their sacred duty to grieve forever as a tribute to a dead partner or child.

We must beware of overemphasising meaning-making. It may well be true that some people have the capacity to achieve great things in the face of adversity, to discover meanings that enrich their lives and those of others. But we disappoint ourselves and undermine our clients if we expect too much of them. For many it is sufficient to survive and to be reasonably content with the restrictions of a world that is shrinking as their brains and bodies grow older. Likewise the terms *closure* and *resolution* are unhelpful if we expect the bereaved to forget the past and start again. 'The future is an illusion and the present too near at hand to be clearly understood, *only the past is real* and its reality increases as we and the world grow older' (Jackson 1948).

Words are the symbols we use to communicate meaning. They are useful only if the meaning they convey is shared between individuals. Much of the time minor differences, shades of meaning, are of little importance; indeed those who agonise about them are accused of pedantry. We even get away with incorrect usage, such as using the word *bereavement* to mean *grief*, when both parties understand what is intended. Problems only arise when sloppy or ambiguous language leads to misunderstandings or failure to communicate important issues. It is for this reason that we need to be on our guard.

References

American Psychiatric Association. *Diagnostic and Statistical Manual of Mental Disorders* (4th ed.). American Psychiatric Association, Washington, DC, 1994.

Bowlby, J. *Attachment and Loss. Volume 1, Attachment.* Hogarth, London; Basic Books, New York, 228–229, 1969.

Dyregrov, K. Do professionals disempower bereaved people? Grief and social intervention. *Bereavement Care* 24(1), 7–10, 2005.

Freud, S. Mourning and Melancholia, *The Standard Edition of the Complete Psychological Works of Sigmund Freud*, under the general editorship of James Strachey, in collaboration with Anna Freud, assisted by Alix Strachey and Alan Tyson. Hogarth Press, London, 1953– Volume 14, 239–258, 1917.

Gorer, G. *Death, Grief and Mourning in Contemporary Britain.* Cresset, London, 1965.

Horowitz, M. J. Pathological grief and the activation of latent self-images. *American Journal of Psychiatry* 137, 1157, 1980.

Jackson, H. *The Reading of Books.* Faber & Faber, 1948, p. 41.

Neimeyer. R. (ed.). *Meaning Reconstruction and the Experience of Loss.* American Psychological Association, Washington, DC, 2001.

Parkes, C. M. Bereavement as a psycho-social transition: processes of adaptation to change. In M. S. Stroebe, W. Stroebe and R. O. Hansson (eds.) *Handbook of Bereavement* (chapter 6). Cambridge University Press, Cambridge, New York and Victoria, Australia, 1993.

Parkes, C. M. (guest editor) Symposium on complicated grief. Introduction and conclusions. *Omega* 52(1), 1–112, 2006.

Rogers, C. R. *On Becoming a Person.* Houghton Mifflin, Boston, 1961.

Rosenblatt, P. C., Walsh, R. P. and Jackson, D. A. *Grief and Mourning in Cross-Cultural Perspective.* HRAF Press, Washington, DC, 1976.

Stroebe, W. and Schut, H. Risk factors in bereavement outcome: a methodological and empirical review. In M. S. Stroebe, R. O. Hansson, W. Stroebe and H. Schut (eds.) *Handbook of Bereavement Research: Consequences, Coping and Care* (chapter 16). American Psychological Association, Washington, DC, 2002.

CRISIS, TRAUMA AND TRANSITION

Since my childhood I have been fascinated by the task of finding out how things work. My toy cupboard was full of wind-up toys, model steam engines, broken clocks and other apparatus that had been 'tested to destruction'. In my primary school, aged nine, I learned the enthralling elements of anatomy. Sensing my interest my teacher encouraged me and I made regular visits to the local butcher who provided a bull's eye for dissection in the lesson on 'vision', a sheep's heart for the lesson on 'the heart and circulatory system' and a calf's kidney for the lesson on 'the uro-genital system'. Her tolerance was tested by 'the alimentary canal', a foul-smelling handful of chicken's guts wrapped up in newspaper. I shall always be grateful to this dear lady who opened my mind to the possibility of understanding how people work.

The human mind proved more difficult to understand if only because there was little that we could learn about what went on in it by dissecting soft, sloppy brains. To this day psychology is lagging behind other studies of the human mechanism as we are only now beginning to find ways of studying what goes on in the brain while we are thinking.

As we saw in Part 1, my early studies of bereavement were empirical, but theories were beginning to emerge and by the mid 1970s I was able to distinguish those aspects of the response to bereavement that were unique to loss of a loved person from the wider field of the losses and stresses that can be found in the range of traumatic events that do not involve attachment to a person. It was becoming increasingly clear that there was more to bereavement than grief and more causes of grief than those due to bereavement.

In this section we start by considering what is, probably, the most traumatic and horrific type of bereavement, bereavement by the murder of someone we love. We then turn our attention to systematic comparisons between responses to other types of traumatic loss. Do people grieve differently for the loss of a person, a limb or a home? By comparing reactions to one loss with another I began to uncover the regularities and differences that enabled me to dissect out the components of the human response to loss and change. Gradually my focus was to change from Attachment Theory, which explains much grief, to Transition (or Restoration) Theory that is concerned with changing what I term the *Assumptive World*. This last concept has wide relevance and proved most valuable in explaining the meanings which people find in life.

Part 2 ends with an account of an innovative family crisis intervention service that was set up in the East End of London in the hope of putting some of these principles into practice. But, although very popular with users and referrers, the service failed to attract the resources necessary to ensure its continuance.

CHAPTER 11

PSYCHIATRIC PROBLEMS FOLLOWING BEREAVEMENT BY MURDER OR MANSLAUGHTER

From *British Journal of Psychiatry* 162: 49–54, 1993.

Although it is more than twenty years since this paper was published, and many more since the first of these clients was referred to me for psychiatric help, I still recall many of them quite vividly and with pain. But my suffering is a small reflection of theirs. Hard though this was in the short run, these people proved rewarding to treat and I learned a great deal from them and gradually got used to overriding my own reluctance to get involved.

They taught me that, no matter how horrific the circumstances in which people have died, it is the life that they lived that matters most. By helping people to recognise that fact and by finding ways of helping them to live with their traumatic memories and imaginings they were gradually able to tolerate the shadow left by the death event.

Looking back I am grateful to these people for without that experience I might never have had the confidence and ability to face the mass deaths of disaster areas, particularly the mass murders of Rwanda.

Abstract

Bereavement by murder or manslaughter is often associated with a high incidence of factors which increase the risk of lasting psychological problems after bereavement. In this study it appears that self-perpetuating vicious circles often accounted for the persistence of symptoms, which fitted the diagnostic categories of post-traumatic stress disorders, anxiety states, panic syndromes, obsessive revenge-seeking and depression. Therapeutic approaches should be aimed at interrupting these vicious circles and fostering the work of grieving.

Situations of extreme stress provide the opportunity to study the onset and psychopathology of the psychiatric disorders to which they give rise. Bereavement following murder or manslaughter must surely be one of the most traumatic types of loss experienced. It has been the topic of several descriptive studies. These include Rynearson's (1984) study of people who attended a support group for those bereaved by murder, a similar study by Amick-McMullan and colleagues (1989), Burgess's (1975) account of six people seen by a nurse counsellor after a murder and several studies of children traumatised by a murder in the family (Black and Kaplan 1988; Pynoos and Eth 1984, 1985). There are also several reports of self-help groups for parents of murdered children (Klass 1988; Klass and Peach 1987; Redmond 1989). These studies describe a range of serious problems and support the view that the mental health of people bereaved by murder may well be at risk. Previous research indicates that any or all of the following factors (which are likely to be present after a murder) can increase the prevalence of psychosocial problems in the wake of bereavement:

(a)   sudden, unexpected deaths;
(b)   untimely deaths;
(c)   witnessing of horrific circumstances;
(d)   threat to the life of the survivor or other loss of personal security;
(e)   guilt at having survived;
(f)   intense anger or ambivalence; and
(g)   deaths by human agency, particularly when compensation is involved.

Parkes (1990) reviews the scientific literature in this field.

Method

It is with the aim of examining the interaction of these and other factors peculiar to bereavement by murder that a detailed study has been carried out of the case records of seventeen patients who were referred to the writer's psychiatric outpatient clinic at the Royal London Hospital for the assessment and for the treatment of psychiatric problems arising after a death which the family thought to be murder. Manslaughter has been included because in some cases this was the verdict of the court while many of the survivors continued to regard the offender as a murderer and to express deep resentment of what they saw as the derisory sentence imposed. If anything, the stress on the families of the victims seems to have been greater in these cases. Referrals to this clinic come from all parts of London, including several from a self-help organisation for parents of murdered children. Patients are always invited to bring a relative, and those who came were also interviewed.

Results

Only one of the seventeen patients referred was a man (he had lost his wife). Of the women, nine were mothers who had lost a child, two had lost a sister, two a friend, and one each a husband, mother and mother-in-law.

Six of the assailants had been a stranger to the patient (four of whom were never identified), six were relatives (three sons-in-law, two brothers-in-law and a son) and five were other acquaintances. The known assailants were all men.

The most common method of killing was stabbing (8); four victims were strangled, three shot, one beaten to death with an iron bar, and one burned to death with petrol. In two cases the body had been mutilated after death.

The apparent reason for the killing was unknown in four cases, attributed to psychosis in two (one depressive and one schizophrenic illness), marital jealousy in seven, psychopathology in one, a fight in a public house, a family quarrel and political vengeance.

Half of the patients were seen within a year of the death.

Reactions

Although the numbers are too small to justify statistical comparisons, this group of bereaved people had much in common with others who had suffered sudden, unexpected and untimely deaths such as those that result from road traffic accidents or disasters. Thus the immediate reaction was most often one of numbness, blunting or disbelief, and many had difficulty in expressing their grief. 'It didn't seem real,' 'I was knocked for six' and 'I couldn't believe it' were typical reactions. Episodes of intense distress were soon suppressed, and some used medication to reinforce their need to be in control: 'Melleril soon stopped me from crying.' Others found themselves unable to cry.

As with other sudden bereavements, the numbness did not prevent a high level of arousal. Restlessness and tension were pronounced, along with pressure of talk, bewilderment and incomprehension, which made it hard for people to find an effective outlet for their drive to action.

Strong feelings of rage against the perpetrator of the killing were common and one man, whose wife had been murdered, walked the streets with a loaded revolver in his pocket in an attempt to find the killer. (Fortunately the police got to him first.) Anger was also directed against the investigating officers who, at this stage, were often treating everyone with suspicion.

Communication of information at this early stage was often absent or chaotic, with conflicting messages being received about who had died and how. The police were sometimes suspicious of family members, reluctant to make allegations of murder and sensitive about the details of the crime. Distraught relatives who demanded information were met with silence, and some had been unable to discover what had happened until they read about it in a newspaper. News reporters were usually to hand, and while some had found them sympathetic and supportive, others had felt hounded and resented the intrusion. Despite these difficulties some families had been greatly helped by the sensitive understanding and support which they had received from individual policemen.

People who had witnessed the killing or discovered the body were preoccupied (or 'haunted') by the clear visual memory of the experience. Thus one woman whose daughter had died two and a half days after her former husband poured petrol over her and ignited it was haunted by the image of her daughter's burnt and swollen body, 'like a Michelin Man'.

Others had horrific images of what they imagined they would have seen. A fifty-year-old woman whose daughter had been hit over the head, raped and then strangled had a vivid image of the daughter's body lying on a slab. Vivid nightmares often had a 'haunting' quality, as in the woman whose landlady had been stabbed to death and mutilated by a psychotic man whose attention she had rejected. The patient had warned the victim of the risk she was taking and had been ignored. She had been so afraid of the man that she slept with a knife under her own pillow. After the murder the patient's main presenting symptom was a recurrent nightmare in which the murderer was pursuing her with a bloody knife and in which she ran screaming to the police, who refused to believe her.

Two young children, brought by the patient to attend an interview, who had witnessed the murder of a parent had apparently misunderstood the event and distorted their memory of it to fit their interpretation of what they had witnessed. Thus a four-year-old girl who had been told to 'go away' by the babysitter who had killed her mother with an axe subsequently said, 'Mummy cut herself shaving and was taken to hospital', and a girl of three whose mother had been stabbed to death by her jealous husband said, 'Daddy punched her' and later denied any recollection of the event.

Those who had not witnessed the killings were usually concerned to find out exactly what had happened; at the same time they were apprehensive and were easily dissuaded from visiting the mortuary or attending the inquest. Typically husbands persuaded their wives not to attend while attending themselves. Later they would be expected to give a detailed report of the medical evidence. This was usually regarded as helpful. Thus one woman was relieved to hear that her daughter had died from the first of five stab wounds in her back, and another was relieved to learn that there was no evidence that her daughter had been sexually assaulted before being strangled by the man who had lured her into his car on her way home from school. Feelings of guilt and self-reproach were commonly expressed, particularly when the killing had been carried out by a relative. In these cases there had usually been threats or intimations of danger, and surviving relatives blamed themselves for ignoring or underestimating these. One woman had been lured out of the house by an anonymous telephone call informing her that her husband was in hospital. After she left, her son-in-law (whose wife had left him to return to her mother on the previous day) broke into the house and killed his wife. The mother bitterly reproached herself for failing to protect her daughter.

An Asian woman had regularly left her school-aged daughter in the care of a brother-in-law who resided with them but whom she disliked. She had felt obliged to offer the hospitality of her home to this man who, subsequent to a quarrel in which her husband had threatened to evict him, had stabbed the daughter to death. The bereaved mother expressed intense reproach towards the killer, towards her husband for inviting him to stay, towards his family for not warning them of his previous delinquency and towards herself for leaving him in charge of her daughter. When members of her husband's family came to England, visited the killer in prison and gave evidence in his defence, she refused to have anything to do with them, and when the court committed him to a special hospital for psychiatric treatment she saw this as an outrageous failure to punish him for his crime.

An identical twin whose sister had been shot by her boyfriend felt that it should have been she who died.

Feelings of guilt could become an obsessional preoccupation, and sometimes led to self-punishment. One woman whose sister had been stabbed in the presence of the patient felt extremely guilty that she had run away when threatened by the assailant. Her sister's face had been spotted with blood and she later inflicted injuries to her own face in an attempt to punish herself for her cowardice. She also engaged in compulsive hand washing.

As long as the killer remained at large, the survivors were likely to be extremely anxious. The ten-year-old sister of the girl referred to earlier who was abducted on her way home from school was unable to sleep at night for fear of being murdered in her bed. She kept glancing over her shoulder for fear of being attacked from behind and, in succeeding weeks, this habit developed into a tic. Her mother aggravated the situation by becoming very anxious and overprotective; she too felt that she was waiting for the next attack.

People who have suffered major bereavements commonly lose the sense of invulnerability that enables most of us to move about the world without undue anxiety (see p. 160). It is hardly surprising that some of those bereaved by murder experienced chronic fear, shut themselves up at home, avoided people and places associated with the loss and were unable to go to work. The mother described previously was afraid to drive her car or to return to work; she became very tense and anxious and generally irritable.

As time passed most patients expected their symptoms to improve, but in fact feelings often seemed to remain unchanged or to get worse during the first year or so. Sometimes this occurred as the initial numbness and denial passed off, sometimes grief was 'kept alive' or renewed by the protracted legal procedures of the inquest, trial, appeal, compensation hearings and so forth, and at other times anniversaries or other events prevented patients from putting their grief aside.

The horrific circumstances of the death made it difficult for friends and relatives to know what to say and the social support systems on which many bereaved people can rely were often absent. Husbands and wives found it difficult to support each other. Typically the husband would feel a strong need to 'hold himself together', but could only succeed in doing this by distancing himself from his wife; as one put it, 'I can't stand her grief'. Those who were less upset than their wives were seen as uncaring, and those who were more upset as weak; either way, the husband and wife were unable to support each other at a time when both of them were in desperate need of help.

Other factors which undermined both partners were expression of irritability and the sheer duration of the distress. Partners who tolerated outbursts of rage and bitterness early in their bereavement found they lacked patience after some months, and there were many marital conflicts. Only one couple is known to have divorced, and this did not take place until several years after the bereavement. The truth often seemed to be that no matter how bad things had become at home, the prospect of a life apart was even more grim. Most couples seem to have stayed together in the hope of improvement.

The overall feeling was of sadness, bitterness and disillusionment, as if the powers that be had failed to provide the protection from danger which we all expect, and the very basis of a just society was in question. The legal processes resulting from the death were matters of great concern, but it was unusual for the sentence of the law to be regarded as appropriate to the magnitude of the crime.

Psychiatric diagnoses

Many of the symptoms reported by bereaved people in the wake of murder or manslaughter can be seen as those of a post-traumatic stress disorder (PTSD), as defined in DSM-III-R (American Psychiatric Association 1987). Thus, haunting memories, sometimes associated with nightmares of the murder and leading to fear and hyper-alertness, were common. Reminders of the murder (e.g. by the press) would evoke severe distress and often led to avoidant behaviour. Many of the bereaved patients could also have been diagnosed as suffering from anxiety states or panic disorders, with agitated depression as an additional alternative.

In view of the magnitude of the trauma inflicted on these bereaved families, it might be thought that prior vulnerability would have played little part in the causation of their psychiatric problems, but this was not the case. A systematic psychiatric history revealed that ten of the seventeen patients had evidence of previous insecurity. Most often this took the form of general shyness and lack of self-esteem which could be traced to problematic relationships with parents in childhood. These problems had continued in adult life, when insecure attachments had led either to intense, close and dependent relationships or to ambivalence and rejection. In a few cases these family problems had probably helped to set the scene in which the murder took place, for example by sowing the seeds of mental illness or relationship problems which ended in murder. Whether or not this was the case, such problems undoubtedly influenced the bereaved person's ability to cope with the bereavement and with the many difficulties which followed in its train. [*Presumably this was why they were referred to a psychiatrist*].

The most severely disturbed patient in this group was the elderly lady who had been lured out of the house by her daughter's husband. She had never been a secure person and suffered from diabetes, multiple sclerosis and osteoarthritis, which seriously limited her mobility and vision and threatened her life. Her retired husband was supportive, but she gave him a bad time. Members of his family had criticised her daughter in court, the charge of murder had been reduced to manslaughter and the assailant was already out of prison by the time the patient was referred to me. She would not allow her husband to contact his family or play the violin at home (because it made her cry); angry outbursts were frequent and, at times, had been violent. She was depressed, embittered and would probably have killed herself if she had had the means to do so.

Depression was a presenting symptom in most cases, with associated difficulty in sleeping, loss of appetite and weight and tearfulness in a minority. Two patients were abusing alcohol.

Course and treatment

Most of the patients were referred to psychiatric care within two years of bereavement and were seen by the writer for short-term psychotherapy. Only five of the seventeen had more than six interviews. An antidepressant drug (Mianserin) was prescribed in one case (the elderly lady described earlier) but without much benefit.

In four cases the patient's spouse was included in the therapy, and in two cases children were seen in family interviews while also receiving individual therapy from a child therapist.

In the psychotherapy sessions, patients were encouraged to review the events leading up to and following the death and to express any feelings that emerged. Most were asked to bring photographs of the deceased and any other artefacts, forms of funeral service and so forth which would help to 'bring the dead person into the room'. The therapist adopted a friendly but matter-of-fact manner without in any way belittling the powerful feelings involved.

Most patients were clearly improved by the time therapy ended, and none was worse. Anger and self-reproach remained, but they came to be expressed in creative rather than destructive ways. One man whose irritability had threatened his marriage after the death of a relative in a pub fight took part in a campaign which succeeded in bringing about changes in legislation on the carrying of offensive weapons. The man who had walked the streets with a loaded revolver in his pocket realised: 'If I had succeeded in finding my wife's murderer and killing him I would have been doing to this man's daughter what he had done to mine.' He subsequently spoke out in public against the reintroduction of capital punishment. Other survivors remained strongly in favour of capital punishment and critical of a legal system which they saw as sympathetic towards the culprit. Even so, the amount of unrestrained anger which they expressed at home diminished.

Post-traumatic symptoms seemed to respond to reassurance, although it is hard to know how many of them would have subsided spontaneously. Important factors seemed to be the recovery of a sense of control over one's life. Taking a history helped the bereaved to put things in perspective. Thus one woman who had herself been arrested on suspicion after two friends had been found stabbed was released when further investigations cleared her name and the assailant was sent for trial. Hounded by the press and distanced by the victims' families, she shut herself up at home in a state of continued anxiety and fear with typical symptoms of PTSD. She was much helped by the opportunity to talk through the events in detail and to attend the preliminary law hearing. After only four interviews she was free of symptoms.

The elderly lady referred to previously remained depressed but allowed her husband to start playing the violin again, and was much helped by attending a 'marathon' weekend-long group therapy session with a distinguished American psychiatrist *[Elizabeth Kubler-Ross]* at which her husband moved the entire group to tears with his playing.

People who had initially avoided too close a confrontation with places and people associated with the loss often seemed to benefit from deliberately finding out what happened. A woman whose son had been robbed and murdered while abroad visited the scene of the crime and talked to the investigating officers. This seemed both to reflect and to enhance her sense of control over the painful memories and imaginings which plagued her.

Given a little support from outside the family, relatives became more supportive. A patient who was seen only once subsequently wrote to say that when her family learned that she had been to scc a psychiatrist, they became so understanding that she did not need to return. The ten-year-old girl who had developed a tic improved rapidly and was soon sleeping through the night. In this case it is hard to know how much the improvement resulted from regular therapy from a child therapist and how much from the change in behaviour of her parents who, once they began to feel more secure, adopted more supportive and less coercive attitudes (e.g. by sitting with her when she went to bed and permitting her to sleep with the light on).

For a few people, the creation of fitting memorials to the dead was an important way of negating the loss. Thus the parents of the young man who had been robbed and murdered funded a project at his school to commemorate his name and purchased the villa in Spain where he had enjoyed his last holiday.

Discussion

It is hard to know how typical the bereaved people seen in this psychiatric clinic are of all those bereaved by murder. The fact that they had sought help from a psychiatrist suggests that their problems may have been worse than those of families who did not seek this help. Yet their symptoms did not differ markedly from those Rynearson described in his study of fifteen attendees at a support group who had not been referred for psychiatric treatment. The main difference between his sample and mine was that whereas Rynearson describes a marked improvement in most symptoms within six to eighteen months of the bereavement, the opposite was reported by my patients, most of whose symptoms had worsened in the course of the first year. This initial worsening of symptoms may well reflect a gradual reduction in the avoidance which is often pronounced in cases of PTSD, and it was reassuring to witness eventual improvement.

We have no means of knowing how the symptoms of either of these samples compare with those of people who do not seek help from support groups or psychiatrists. Are they resilient people who get all the help they need from family and friends, or could it be that they are more disturbed than the rest and try to limit their distress by avoiding situations in which they will be expected to confront the painful reality of their loss?

None of the phenomena described here are unique to bereavement by murder but, taken together, they show clearly why this type of bereavement is particularly conducive to psychopathology. The combination of sudden, unexpected, horrific and untimely death, with all the rage and guilt which followed and, often, the overwhelming of the family as a support system to the bereaved, is bound to interfere with normal grieving.

It does this in several ways: (a) by inducing post-traumatic stress – a kind of emotional shock which generates anxiety, depressive avoidance and vivid mental imagery; (b) by evoking intense rage towards the offender and all associated with him at a time when there may be little opportunity to vent that rage effectively; (c) by undermining trust in others, including the family, the police, the legal system and God; (d) by evoking guilt at having survived and at failing to protect the deceased. These consequences easily set in train vicious circles. Avoidance of confrontation or reminders ensures that grief will be delayed (Amick-McMullen *et al.*, 1989), feelings of helplessness easily become transmuted into withdrawal and depression, lack of trust causes people to turn away from sources of help and become socially isolated and feelings of guilt may cause them to engage in self-punitive grieving. The bereaved people in this clinic saw themselves as in a rut from which they could not escape.

The fact that with short-term therapy most did improve should not blind us to the fact that nothing can undo the memories or fill the gap left in the family by a murder. Some may well have benefitted from longer-term therapy if it had been available, and it is not possible to know the extent to which psychological trauma of this kind extended to relatives who were not seen, particularly children whose problems may well have been disregarded by their parents on the principle of 'least said, soonest mended'. Research into children traumatised by murder (Black and Kaplan 1988) suggests that some will be at special risk and may even pass on their problems to future generations.

From the point of view of the therapist, families who have been traumatised by murder can be a daunting prospect. We easily feel overwhelmed by their grief and helpless in the face of their helplessness. The sheer enormity of the outrage that has been committed against them may be hard for us to bear, and it is tempting for us to distance ourselves from their suffering. For our own sake as well as the families', we need to have a frame of reference, a way of thinking about their plight, which may not yet justify the term *plan*, but which is sufficient to enable us to 'hang in' with the pain of their chaotic experience.

The minimum desiderata for such a frame of reference may be: (a) the knowledge that, however horrific the circumstances, most people do eventually come to terms with them (order will emerge from chaos); (b) that neither the therapist nor the relatives can be expected to think about or cope with more than one problem at a time; and (c) that it is worth a little time working out what is most salient or important to consider at any time, bearing in mind that the bereaved person's agenda should take priority over the therapist's.

As the family members begin to share their thoughts and feelings, patterns will begin to emerge. The aim of psychotherapy is to address each of these patterns of reaction in a way which will help the individual to break out of the vicious circles. Taking the history initiates a process of confrontation in an atmosphere of support and reduces avoidant behaviour. By consistent reassurance of worth and respect for the bereaved family, the therapist helps to restore its integrity as a mutual support system to its members, and by staying calm and committed (and not over-reacting to the horror of the situation) a model of control is presented which can then be used by the bereaved.

A perpetuating factor in the obsessional rumination and recurrent dreams which haunt families bereaved by murder is the belief that such thoughts cannot be prevented. When people go to bed dreading nightmares, their dread creates the nightmares. The patient described previously who was regularly pursued by a man with a knife in her dreams was told that because we create our own dreams, she could choose how the dream would end. Several 'happy endings' were discussed, and she admitted that it had never occurred to her that she might control her own dreams. When seen three weeks later she was sleeping normally and the nightmares had not recurred.

To control thoughts is not to avoid them. In essence we are inferring that nothing is unthinkable, nothing is too painful or distressing to be excluded from our consideration. Given this encouragement, *the extraordinary becomes ordinary,* and the sufferer begins to accept reality, however painful this may be. Redundant basic assumptions about the world are called into question and replaced with new and more appropriate assumptions, and a new image of the self and of others is achieved. These may be less optimistic than the ones that preceded them, but they are in keeping with a fact of life that mostly we prefer to forget, that with all our civilised pretensions, man is still dangerous to man.

[Since this paper was published several major developments have undoubtedly provided improved support for families bereaved by murder or manslaughter in the United Kingdom. A self-help group, Support after Murder and Manslaughter (SAMM), has been set up and I have had the privilege of attending several of its meetings. They are surprisingly cheerful occasions and, although tears are often shed the mutual understanding obtained is considerable and the group has contributed to improve the care given by the police and legal system. This includes the creation of Family Liaison Officers in the police force who receive special training in the support of families faced with major crimes of violence (see p. 160). Whenever convicted killers are willing to do so, families can now meet and engage with them in a secure environment if they wish. This can help to dispel haunting fears and fantasies. The voluntary organisation Victim Support now offers the help of trained counsellors. Together these approaches have helped to restore confidence in a society which, at the time when this study was carried out, was often seen as uncaring and sympathetic towards the killers.]

References

American Psychiatric Association. *Diagnostic and Statistical Manual of Mental Disorders* (3rd ed., revised) (DSM-III-R). American Psychiatric Association, Washington, DC, 1987.

Amick-McMullan, A., Kilpatrick, D., Veronen, L., *et al.* Family survivors of homicide victims: theoretical perspectives and an exploratory study. *Traumatic Stress* 2, 1, 1989.

Black, D. and Kaplan, T. Father murdered mother: issues and problems encountered by a child psychiatric team. *British Journal of Psychiatry* 153, 624–630, 1988.

Burgess, A. Family reactions to homicide. *American Journal of Orthopsychiatry* 45, 391–398, 1975.

Klass, D. *Parental Grief: Solace and Resolution.* Springer, New York, 1988.

Klass, R. and Peach, M. R. Special issues in the grief of parents of murdered children. *Death Studies* 11, 81–88, 1987.

Parkes, C. M. Risk factors in bereavement: implications for the prevention and treatment of pathological grief. *Psychiatric Annals* 20, 308–313, 1990.

Pynoos, R. S. and Eth, S. The child as witness to homicide. *Journal of Social Issues* 40, 87–108, 1984.

Pynoos, R. S. and Eth, S. Children traumatised by witnessing acts of personal violence: homicide, rape, or suicidal behaviour. In R. S. Pynoos and S. Eth (eds.) *Post Traumatic Stress Disorder in Children.* American Psychiatric Association, Washington, DC, 169–186, 1985.

Redmond, L. M. *Surviving: When Someone You Know Was Murdered.* Psychological Consultations and Educational Services Ltd., Clearwater, FL, 1989.

Rynearson, E. K. Bereavement after homicide: a descriptive study. *American Journal of Psychiatry* 141, 1452–1454, 1984.

CHAPTER 12

PSYCHOSOCIAL TRANSITIONS
A field for study

From *Social Science and Medicine*, 5: 101–115, 1971.

A state without the means of some change is without the means of its conservation.

Edmund Waller, *Reflections upon the Revolution in France*

During the 1960s I was exploring some of the wider implications of our theories of bereavement by studying other types of loss such as loss of a limb and, with Roy Fitzgerald, loss of sight. From the outset it was clear to me that, while attachment theory had much to contribute to our understanding of the loss of persons, people were not attached to their limbs and eyesight in the same way that they were to people, nor did they grieve in quite the same way when these faculties were lost. A different theoretical model would be needed to explain these and other non-human losses.

The starting point was to ask 'What is lost?' In the case of bereavement that was obvious; it is a person to whom we are attached and, as we have seen, the biological roots of attachment predispose us to cry and to search for them even when we know that the search is pointless. In other losses searching can be a similarly meaningful response to the loss of an object or possession but it makes less sense when evoked by loss of a limb, loss of vision, loss of a job and so forth.

The examination of these problems caused me to re-examine our internal worlds in the hope of explaining our reactions to these other losses. The term psychosocial transitions *did not catch on but my underlying idea of the Assumptive World did. It is a simple concept that has profound implications. Since this paper was published the ideas it embodies have given rise to several other significant publications, the most notable being Janoff-Bulman's book* Shattered Assumptions: Towards a New Psychology of Trauma[1] *and Kauffman's multi-contributor book* Loss of the Assumptive World: A Theory of Traumatic Loss.[2] *For a recent update see Darcy Harris's paper 'New Understandings of Death and Grief'.[3] In the end the wheel was to come full circle for the theory that explained the response to non-human losses turned out, in addition, to advance our understanding of losses of humans and the whole concept shed light on the difference between the real world and our assumptions about it.*

Abstract

In drawing together ideas from stress research, crisis studies and loss research a new and more satisfactory conceptual field has emerged – the field of Psychosocial Transitions.

Such situations are seen as turning points for better or worse psychosocial adjustment. They often constitute natural experiments of great theoretical and practical importance. Grief is seen as a process of 'realization' by means of which affectional bonds are severed and old models of the world and the self given up. It tends to be avoided and accounts for resistance to change and depressive reactions to change.

The research field considered here represents a departure from the traditional disease-oriented field of psychiatry. Attempts to discover the aetiology of established psychiatric syndromes have rarely succeeded in demonstrating a one-to-one relationship between a syndrome and any of the many factors which have been postulated to account for it. Most investigators have come to accept that particular diseases are the consequence of the complex interaction of many different factors and that generalizations about any one are not possible. Others, particularly psychoanalysts, have continued to make generalizations about the constellations of aetiological factors which they regard as important, but have been unable to develop scientific means of testing the truth of these generalizations.

Despite all disagreements there remain certain situations and events which most clinicians continue to look for and to regard as at least partial causes of the mental disorders which occasionally follow them; these include disasters, bereavements, childbirth, changes of occupation, retirement, migration, major physical illness and disablement. They have been variously designated as 'stresses' or 'crises', but these terms are not altogether satisfactory. In the first place, the terms have come to have so wide a meaning as to give no clear indication of their limits. In the second place, there is, in their use, implication of outcome because a stressor is defined in terms of its effects. It seems better not to prejudge the question of whether or not a particular event will prove 'stressful'.

In a statistical and predictive sense, an event X may be regarded as a possible or probable source of stress if the proportions of the population having the sequence XY (where Y = disequilibrium) are known. In a substantive, retrospective sense, it may have been demonstrated that X *was* the source of stress, but in neither case does the concept carry us beyond a description of an actual or potential occurrence.

The notion of crisis is bounded by similar difficulties, although its dramatic quality encourages analysis. Thus, for example, we have Erikson's distinction between 'developmental' and 'accidental' crises (Erikson 1959). But the problem remains that an event which may be a crisis for one person can be a moment of unperplexing opportunity for another. Furthermore, both terms have strongly negative connotations. This makes it difficult to consider a positive outcome to an apparently critical event. Crisis can lead to the stars as well as to the grave. If the term is confined to a situation of 'imbalance between the difficulty and the importance of the problem and the resources immediately available to deal with it', the question has to be asked, how do we know when there is imbalance? The answer lies in the quality of the outcome. Thus a crisis occurs when there is imbalance and there is imbalance when there is a crisis. In itself the concept tells us nothing more than that there has been an unfortunate congruence of forces. It is essentially descriptive, retrospective and negative. Independently of 'stress research' an increasing number of studies have been carried out in recent years into the effects of major losses in people's lives. Stemming from Freud's attempts to link 'mourning' and 'melancholia' these have led dynamically oriented psychiatrists to study the effects of separating children from their mothers and the effects of bereavement in adult life and have caused them to develop theories of 'object relations' which relate mental illness to the development of unsatisfactory modes of coping with losses throughout the course of the lifespan (Freud 1917).

Whilst 'stress research' has been developed as a field by experimental psychologists and physiologists 'loss research' has emerged from clinical psychoanalysis and been developed by social psychiatrists. Because most losses can be construed as stressful and many stresses can be construed as losses there must be a considerable overlap between these two fields and there is a need to try to link them together.

But what do we mean by a loss? Are there not many events which can be construed as both gains and losses ('You are not losing a daughter but gaining a son.')? Does the bride who is left at the church lose the husband whom she has never had? Writers on this subject seem wary of specifying just what they mean by a loss. Perhaps this stems from the difficulty which we have in defining the frame of reference.

As I see it losses and gains are two ways of classifying changes in state. In the former case the end state is assumed to be worse than the initial state whereas in the latter case the end state is assumed to be better. The designation of a change of state as a loss or a gain is, therefore, dependent on an evaluation of outcome and there will occasionally occur major changes in state where the pros and cons balance out so well that they cannot be seen as either a gain or a loss.

Whenever a major change in state takes place the need arises for the individual to restructure his ways of looking at the world and his plans for living in it. Whether we construe the change as a gain or a loss it is likely to require effort. Old patterns of thought and activity must be given up and fresh ones developed. It is not only losses which are commonly believed to carry a risk of maladjustment; gains too can be hazardous. Promotions, engagements, the birth of a child, even winning the football pools have been blamed for the failures in adjustment which occasionally follow them. Whether the situation is seen as gain or loss one is tempted to think that the crucial factor may be the way the individual copes with the process of change.[4]

But what is it that changes? In the first place, the change is likely to take place in that part of the world which impinges upon the self. This is what Kurt Lewin has called 'the Life Space' (Lewin 1935). The life space consists of those parts of the environment with which the self interacts and in relation to which behaviour is organized; other persons, material possessions, the familiar world of home and place of work and the individual's body and mind in so far as he can view these as separate from his self. It does not include those parts of the world, the body and the mind with which the self does not interact (and this, of course, is most of the world, much of the body and a large part of the mind).

Changes in the life space are important or unimportant depending on their influence on the assumptions which we make about the world. For instance, sudden loss of vision involves a change in the life space which is important or unimportant depending on whether the individual believes himself to have gone blind or to have voluntarily closed his eyes. Out of the 'total set of assumptions which we build up on the basis of past experience in carrying out our purposes' we create our own 'assumptive world'.[5] A particular constellation of sensations is perceived as 'a window' only because we have had meaningful experience with windows in the past; the constellation has become a part of our assumptive world, enabling us to 'recognize' windows when we see them and to make correct predictions about their characteristics and their utility.

The assumptive world is the only world we know and it includes everything we know or think we know. It includes our interpretation of the past and our expectations of the future, our plans and our prejudices. Any or all of these may need to change as a result of changes in the life space.

The life space is constantly changing, novel stimuli, fresh combinations of events, unique communications from others are received and assimilated. Some of these changes fulfill expectations and require little or no change in the assumptive world; others necessitate a major restructuring of that world, the abandonment of one set of assumptions and the development of a fresh set to enable the individual to cope with the new, altered life space. If the change takes place gradually and the individual has time to prepare, little by little, for the restructuring, the chances that this will follow a satisfactory course are greater than they would be if the change was sudden and unexpected. Thus the transitions of maturation – growing in size, changing in appearance, becoming gradually older and more frail – are barely recognized as changes at all whereas the unexpected loss of a job or a wife is more likely to be recognized as a major transition.

Let us look more closely at those major changes in life space which are *lasting in their effects,* which *take place over a relatively short period of time* and which *affect large areas of the assumptive world.* I shall call these 'Psycho-social Transitions'. An example will help to illustrate some aspects of this approach. Loss of a job deprives a man of a place of work, the company of workmates and a source of income. It therefore produces several changes in his life space. What corresponding changes can be expected in the assumptive world? Clearly assumptions about the way each day must be spent will change, assumptions about the sources of money and security will change and the individual's faith in his own capacity to work effectively and to earn are also likely to change. His view of the world as a safe, secure place will change, his expectations of his future and his family will change and he is likely to have to re-plan his mode of life, sell possessions and maybe even move to a place where his prospects are better. Thus his altered assumptive world will cause him to introduce further changes in his life space, to set up a cycle of internal and external changes aimed at improving the 'fit' between himself and his environment. In order properly to understand the effects of loss of a job it is necessary to identify those areas of the life space *and* the assumptive world which will or should change as a consequence of the initial change in the life space.

A man is tied to his assumptive world. By learning to recognize and act appropriately within his expectable environment a man makes his life space his own. Anything which I can call 'mine' – 'my' job, 'my' home town, 'my' left arm, 'my' wife – becomes, to some extent, part of myself. To all of these things we are tied by bonds which (with Harlow) I have termed *affectional bonds* (Harlow and Zimmerman 1958). It is the nature of an affectional bond that it resists severance and any change in life space is likely to require of us the severance of affectional bonds. Hence resistance to change is to be expected whenever the change requires us to give up a part of the life space to which we are accustomed.

The assumptive world not only contains a model of the world as it is (John Bowlby calls this 'The World Model'), it also contains models of the world as it might be (these models may represent probable situations, ideal situations or dreaded situations) (Bowlby 1969). *[In later papers (see pp. 116–118) I was to change my mind. Models of the world that* might *be are not assumptions about the way it is and are better seen as belonging outside the assumptive world. On the other hand confident assumptions about the future certainly belong in the assumptive world as in the example that follows.]* Models of the world as it might be are used as a rehearsal ground for actions appropriate to these worlds. The bride-to-be rehearses in her mind the world which she hopes to create; she furnishes her home and peoples it with children. It may be almost as hard for her to give up models such as these as it is to give up objects which actually exist. Hence the girl who has planned for a marriage loses something very important if she is jilted. The change which she has to cope with is a change in her own assumptive world.

The comparison which is made between ideal models of the world and models of the world as it is perceived to be often makes us aware of gaps in the latter. These gaps represent unfulfilled wishes. A change in the life space may have the effect of closing one of these gaps. If it does so it will be construed as a 'gain' and the fact that the individual has already rehearsed in his mind behaviour appropriate to the new, more ideal world may enable the transition to take place smoothly.

However it is often the case that the transition from a deficient world to one which is, in some respects, more 'ideal' involves us in changes which were not foreseen. Unexpected deficits in our ability to cope with the new world give rise to awareness of fresh gaps and the situation which we have struggled to reach is found to be full of pitfalls.[6]

Any major change in the life space is likely to reveal many such pitfalls and to present the individual with the need to give up certain assumptions which had become a part of his mode of coping with life. It is no surprise to find that immigrants to another land often have great difficulty in making a successful transition and are frequently disappointed in the size and number of discrepancies between their ideal model of the 'promised land' and the new world as it is experienced.

The ability to recognize familiar objects and to orientate oneself within an environment implies a degree of mastery of that environment regardless of the extent to which the situation is actively controlled or altered. There is an 'active' component in perception. A sensory impression of an object 'out there' is compared with previous impressions of similar objects 'in here' and predictions made about the behaviour and characteristics of the external object. Many motor acts (e.g. following a moving object with the eyes) are carried out to facilitate perception and others have, as their goal, the achievement of certain sensations which are intrinsically pleasant. In fact sensory and motor phenomena, feeling and acting are so intermingled that attempts to separate them do violence to the real situation. A person is not the passive recipient of sensations from his life space; he creates his assumptive world by reaching out to his environment and sampling it, he reacts to his life space by moving within it, to keep it the same or to change it.

The fact that it is necessary to act in order to stay in the same assumptive world means that any change in the ability to move or perceive the world is likely to cause major changes in the assumptive world. But the ability to preserve our assumptive world depends on more than the intactness of our physical apparatus. Knowledge and skills are needed and in the social world in which we all live it is also necessary to depend on the abilities of others. In order to control others we make use of negotiable possessions such as money which themselves depend on our ability to render service to others. Taken together these capacities and negotiable possessions can be regarded as our 'potentialities'.

Permission, and often obligation, to make use of potentialities is given by society by the conferring of status and role (see Parsons 1953 for a clear account of the relationship between power, status and authority). It follows that major changes in potentialities, negotiable possessions, roles or status can be expected to lead to the need for major revision of the assumptive world.

Although it is possible to share parts of the physical world each man's assumptive world is unique to himself and no outsider can be sure of its extent. The individual can delineate his own assumptive world, but even here there are areas which are relatively inaccessible to introspection. When the assumptive world is made the object of introspection it is treated, for a time, as a part of the life space. Thus I may speak of 'my future' and 'my past' as if these things actually exist. Alternatively some change in the life space may cause me to 'question an assumption'; to objectify the assumption and examine it much as one might question a witness in a court of law. Such examinations are painful because of the threat which they represent to the established assumptive world. Moreover there are many assumptions which are not 'open to question' and history is full of examples of the lengths to which people will go to avoid changing their assumptive worlds.

Whether or not a particular area of the assumptive world is open to introspection depends, to some extent, on the setting and purpose of the introspection. Hence the importance of *rapport* in psychotherapy where the aim is to minimize 'resistance' to the admission to consciousness of otherwise unconscious assumptions. Psychotherapy exists to facilitate change in the assumptive world and it makes use of the relationship between patient and therapist as a 'test bed' in which old assumptions can be questioned and new ones be rehearsed. Insight occurs when a person recognizes a discrepancy between his assumptive world and his life space.

Rochlin has pointed out the part which grief plays in psychotherapy (Rochlin 1965). This is most obvious, of course, at the ending of therapy when the patient comes to realize the incipient loss of his therapist but losses also occur whenever a particular aspect of the assumptive world is found to be discrepant and needs to be given up. It has been suggested that the work of therapy and 'grief work' are one and the same thing, the painful reviewing of redundant assumptions and restructuring of the assumptive world.

The assumptions which are revised in psychotherapy may affect any or most areas of the assumptive world according to the extent to which therapy is 'focal'. Other life situations will tend to require the restructuring of only a part of the assumptive world although, following a major change in life space, it is more usual for several parts to be affected. Examples of events producing lasting changes of catastrophic proportion include incarceration in a concentration camp and the development of a fatal illness. In such situations persons affected usually attempt to avoid recognition of the true situation. False hopes are built up and retained despite glaring evidence of their falsity. This is so often the rule that Rochlin (1965) has concluded that 'acceptance and submission are a defence mechanism'. However there is also evidence that institutions which respect patients' defences whilst at the same time providing them with the opportunity to work towards a more realistic acceptance of the situation can enable many to face the prospect of their own demise and, despite this, to die in contentment.

In the end it seems that it is the person with the greatest trust in life who is best able to face death. But Aldrich has described the dramatic improvement which sometimes takes place in people with long-standing neurotic symptoms when they discover that they are about to die and I have come across several examples of this (Aldrich 1963). For these people death may be seen as the end of a fruitless struggle to master a life space which is seen as too difficult or dangerous.

Most changes in life space tend to affect one area of the assumptive world to a greater extent than others. We shall consider in turn events producing change in personal relationships, familiar environment, possessions, physical and mental capacities, roles and status. It is not possible here to describe in detail the process of reaction to each of the possible changes in these areas but I shall try to indicate some of the links between each class of event.

Changes in personal relationships are, perhaps, the area of greatest interest. They change at each stage of the life cycle, on going to school, leaving school, marrying, having children, on the marriage of children and, in more than half of those who marry, on the loss by death, separation or divorce of the spouse.

Studies of the reaction to loss by death of a loved person have thrown considerable light on the nature of grief, the painful process of 'realization' which normally follows a major bereavement. The transition takes place from a phase of almost global denial or 'numbness' through a phase of bitter pining and frustrated searching for the lost person (often with a sense of personal mutilation). This is succeeded by depression and apathy when the bereaved person finally 'gives up' hope of recovering the lost person and a final phase of reorganization when new plans and assumptions about the world and the self are built up. This sequence is now well documented (Lindemann 1944; Marris 1958; Parkes 1969, 1970). *[See p. 74 paragraph 1 for recognition of the problem with the phases of grief.]*

In this context 'grief' is seen as a relatively complex process which may follow a 'healthy' course towards a new and satisfactory assumptive world or may become blocked or distorted in some way. Two frequent pathological forms of grief are chronic grief (when intense yearning and depressive withdrawal fail to resolve in the usual manner) and inhibited or delayed grief (when the expression of grief is partially avoided or the need to grieve denied). In either of these forms pathological forms of identification sometimes occur and the bereaved person develops symptoms resembling those responsible for the death.

Reference must be made at this point to the work of John Bowlby who has spelled out, in great detail, the way young children respond to the loss of a mother or mother substitute (Bowlby 1960, 1961a, 1961b). A great deal of work has now been done in this important field and few people now doubt the potential dangers involved in lasting loss of a mother and the other changes in the child's assumptive world that usually accompany this.

Like the bereaved adult the young child whose mother has gone takes time to realize the loss. In grief he passes through the same periods of crying and searching followed by depressive withdrawal which have been found in the adult and he attempts to mitigate the pain of grief in play and at other times by clinging to other persons or toys which become a substitute for the lost parent. Children often express bitter anger towards lost parents at this time and this may continue in the case of temporary separations after the mother's return. The grief of the separated child has been clearly and painfully illustrated in a succession of films by James and Joyce Robertson (1952, 1958, 1969). These were made during periods of care in hospitals and residential homes.

As is to be expected the degree of emotional upset is greatest when the change in the child's life space is greatest and the film of John, an eighteen-month-old boy who spent three weeks in a residential institution while his mother was having a baby, reveals, in a direct and poignant manner, the features described earlier.

Despite the resemblance to adult grief 'the mourning processes of childhood habitually take a course that in older children and adults is regarded as pathological . . . This does not mean that a crippling of personality is the inevitable result; but it does mean that, as in the case, say, of rheumatic fever, scar tissue is all too often formed which in later life leads to more or less severe dysfunction' (Bowlby 1961b)

According to Bowlby the bereaved child is particularly liable to defensive processes which interfere with and distort his relationships with others. He may cling excessively and ambivalently to others often provoking rejection by the sheer intensity of his demands or he may reject all close relationships and permit himself only the most superficial of ties. Only consistent and unconditional affection over a long period of time can reassure the bereaved child and restore his trust in people and the world.

Anger, as we have seen, is likely to be a prominent feature of the bereavement reactions of children. It is also particularly pronounced in adults when the loss of another is interpretable as being a rejection or abandonment. This is particularly likely following separation or divorce. Far from idealizing the lost partner, as is usually the case following widowhood, there is a tendency to denigrate the other and to blame him for the breakdown of the marriage. This is necessary to enable the divorcee to maintain his own sense of mastery of his assumptive world. If the fault lies elsewhere a less radical change is necessary.

Two things seem particularly likely to predispose to marital breakdown, one is a major discrepancy between the assumptive worlds of husband and wife, the other is a determined effort by one partner to persuade the other to change which is interpreted by the other as a threat to his or her identity. In such circumstances it is seen as less painful to abandon the marriage than for both partners to change their assumptive worlds in a way which permits them a tolerable relationship. Either way the transition involves giving up one set of assumptions about the world and establishing another; grief is the inevitable consequence.

After changes in personal relationships changes in loved possessions are perhaps the most obvious source of grief. By loved possessions I mean those which we value for their own sake rather than for their negotiable value. They are the tools with which we exercise our function in the world and the extensions of ourselves which, after our loved ones, we cherish most dearly. They may include home, garden, car, cat, favourite jewellery, collections of books or antiques or other objects of 'senti-mental' value. Insurance will not prevent the grief which we feel if these things are lost, stolen or destroyed.

A sense of personal mutilation was described to the writer by a psychiatrist the day after his house had been burgled. Not only had he lost valued possessions of which he was very fond but his sense of the security of those possessions which remained was shaken. In the same way bereaved people often report fear of further losses. Wolfenstein (1957), in describing the reactions of tornado victims, has emphasized the frequency with which unrealistic fears of the disaster recurring are found. This is associated with loss of confidence in the world as a secure, reliable place.

It is a characteristic of disasters which have led to the destruction of a home that the survivors tend to build a new home in the same manner and the same place as the home which was lost, regardless of opportunities which might exist to build better homes elsewhere. It seems that the amplitude of the change threatened by the disaster is so great that the survivor must endeavour to reconstruct his assumptive world exactly as it was before the disaster.

The same problems arise when we come to consider other changes in the famil-iar environment. Marc Fried (1962) in an article entitled 'Grieving for a Lost Home' has described the reaction of 789 Boston slum dwellers to rehousing. Inter-views were carried out before rehousing and again two years afterwards. '46 per cent gave evidence', says Fried, 'of fairly severe grief reactions or worse'. Intense pining for the lost home along with psychological, social and somatic distress and outbursts of anger were typical and there was a tendency to idealize the old envi-ronment and to denigrate the new. Those inhabitants who, at the first interview, showed the most extensive knowledge of the environment, that is, those who were familiar with the largest area of their physical life space, were the ones who were most grief-stricken after the relocation.

This applied particularly to older inhabitants who had been living in the area for many years. The effects of relocation on old people may be very serious. To a frail old man or woman his or her own home and the presence of a clutter of familiar possessions helps to preserve a sense of security and orientation in a world which moves too fast. Old people, as Cumming and Henry (1961) have shown, tend gradually to disengage themselves from people around them and the loss of friends and relatives may give rise to little distress. But they are disturbed by changes in their physical environment. A paper by Aldrich and Mendkoff (1963) indicates that this can even affect mortality rate. A Chicago home for incurables was closed for administrative reasons. Among 182 patients who were relocated in other homes thirty were dead within three months, a mortality rate five times greater than expectation. Mortality was highest among those patients whose grasp on reality was most tenuous, particularly among the thirty-eight whom Aldrich rated as psychotic before relocation; of these twenty-four died within a year.

Other changes in the familiar environment which give rise to major alteration of the assumptive world are emigration and imprisonment. Both of these events have been the subject of research by social scientists and there is no space here to review the literature concerning them. Before emigrating the traveller builds up a set of assumptions about the new conditions he expects to experience. The degree to which these assumptions coincide with subsequent reality will determine not only the amount of change which he must undergo, but also its quality and content. The moment of arrival in the new environment, when the emigrant becomes an immigrant, is a dramatic and critical time. First impressions are often lasting impressions influencing modes of adaptation disproportionately to their validity or social importance. This is the period when the assumptive world is most sensitive to change and when the migrant is faced with the issues of whether to retain as far as possible the components of his former life space, or whether to change them in the light of the differences he perceives consciously and acknowledges intuitively.

Changes in physical capacities and body image usually go together. Thus disease, ageing and accident tend to produce loss of body parts and impairment of function although in a particular case one may be more salient than the other. Thus loss of an arm is likely to be viewed quite differently by a woman and a man. The woman tends to be primarily concerned with the effect of the amputation on her appearance; the man is more concerned with the loss of physical function and working capacity. In selecting an artificial limb the woman will choose a 'cosmetic prosthesis' with a realistic-looking hand even though this may be of little use to her. The man, on the other hand, chooses a bifurcated hook which, though it looks nothing like a hand, is much more useful than the 'cosmetic prosthesis'.

Most of the physicians and psychiatrists who have written about the psychological reaction to loss of a limb maintain that 'grief' is to be expected. Thus Wittkower (1967) says, 'Mourning is the normal emotional reaction'; Kessler (1951), 'The emotion most persons feel when told that they must lose a limb has been well compared with the emotion of grief at the death of a loved one'; Dembo, Ladieu-Leviton and Wright (1952), 'A person may mourn his loss'; and Fisher (1960), 'The reaction to loss of a limb, and for that matter the loss of function of a vital part, is grief and depression'. In none of these studies, however, is it clearly indicated just what it is that the amputee is mourning for.

An amputee loses a part of his visible body as well as the functions which previously he could perform by means of the body part. In any particular situation one rather than the other is likely to be seen as the predominant loss and a cause for grief.

There are many points of similarity between loss of a limb and the loss of a spouse, although in some ways, the two situations are not comparable. Thus the immediate reaction to amputation is often a state of numbness in which physical and mental feeling is blunted; this is soon succeeded by a phase of distress in which episodes of severe anxiety occur with pining for the lost limb or for those functions which are thought to have been lost. The amputee is preoccupied with fears that he will be unable to work or to walk, but at the same time he tries to avoid reminders and prefers his friends not to mention his loss. Depression, restlessness, tension, difficulty in concentration, insomnia, loss of appetite and loss of weight are common symptoms and the amputee tends to be irritable and to go over the events leading up to the loss in an attempt to find someone or something whom he can blame.

The so-called phantom limb bears much resemblance to the 'phantom husband' most widows describe. In both cases the lost object is not actually seen but the individual has the feeling that it is still present. This sense of presence is associated with a clear visual memory of the object which may take a long time to fade and which can usually be re-evoked by an effort of will.

Whether or not the 'phantom limb' has a physiological basis derived from the fact that the nerve tracts which once led to the limb are still present; it also has a psychological significance which would lead us to expect such a phenomenon even if no nerve tracts were present. It comes as no surprise to the psychiatrist to learn that surgical procedures which interfere with the continuity of these tracts do not necessarily eliminate the phantom limb.

Chronic pain in the phantom limb, which sometimes follows amputation, may be caused by complications in the stump. All too often, however, no such physical cause is found and there is reason to suppose that psychological factors play a large part in establishing and/or perpetuating the pain. Older patients who have great difficulty in coping with amputation and amputees who have been traumatized by such surgery in the past are particularly likely to develop pains of this type. In addition Kolb (1952) claims that identification with other amputees often plays a part. Whether or not phantom pain has a similar origin to the identification symptoms of bereaved persons which closely resemble symptoms formerly suffered by the person who has died it does seem to represent one form of pathological reaction to amputation.

Other difficulties which commonly follow amputations can lead to failure of rehabilitation. Chronic depression may cause the patient to give up trying to use his artificial limb so that he sits at home in an unhappy state of withdrawal. Conversely one may find the person who denies that loss of a limb is any problem at all. He is the hero of the ward, undertaking tasks which even an intact person would think twice about. He reacts with great indignation when he meets with any limitation to his activity, be it a task which he is now physically incapable of doing or a person who refuses to ignore his disability.

Similar difficulties have been described following other types of physical disablement. A study carried out at the Tavistock Institute of Human Relations by Fitzgerald (1970) has revealed the frequency of adjustment problems among the newly blind and once again we find problems of denial and depression which have many parallels in reactions to other types of loss.

Changes in psychological function can have similar effects to changes in physical function and psychiatrists are well acquainted with the grief and depression which brain-damaged patients go through if they are not so extensively damaged that they are unable to recognize the nature of their disability. Patients with loss of memory will sometimes invent a past which enables them to avoid realization of the extent of their loss. It is almost as if, lacking an assumptive world, they have to create one.

Belonging conceptually in the same class is the situation which arises when circumstances make it obvious that a person lacks certain psychological attributes which he formerly thought he possessed. Failure at an examination which one had expected to pass, inability to perform adequately in a situation where proper performance is expected, any situation in which an individual is brought face to face with deficiencies in his psychological functioning of which he was not aware is a cause of grief. To make a satisfactory adjustment the individual must give up one view of himself and his assumptive world and acquire another, more realistic one. Refusal to accept limitations which are obvious to others is seen in boasters who are perpetually demanding approval for qualities which they do not possess. Conversely those who are found wanting in some respect may give up altogether and become helpless, depressed and defeated. Once again we see avoidance and depression as the two main alternatives to acceptance of reality.

Physical and mental capacities enable a man to exert effective control over his environment. But a man can also make use of the physical and mental capacities of others provided he has negotiable possessions (e.g. money) with which they can be bought. Financial losses, therefore, result in loss of control over that section of the assumptive world which would have been controlled by money. The widow who loses her life savings in a slump is losing a set of assumptions about her own future life and maybe that of her children. In this context it is important to remind ourselves of the provisional nature of expectations. We build a set of plans to enable us to cope with a future which may or may not transpire. We are concerned first with maintaining that which we possess and we therefore insure against disaster. Second, we are concerned to obtain those things which we lack.[7] Negotiable possessions constitute an assurance that our plans are realistic and an insurance against possible disaster. Without them, we feel and are in danger, and our plans will have to undergo modification. It is for our assumptions about our lost future that we grieve.

It is no good being physically and mentally capable if there are no jobs available, as many men found to their cost during the Depression. Unemployment is a form of crippling which can be expected to have the same psychological effect as other forms of loss and it may be that society should become as sensitive to the damage inflicted on others by psychological mutilation as it is of the effects of physical mutilation. The tendency to recoil with horror from physical violence is particularly apparent where the punishment of crime is concerned. Imprisonment or a large fine, which produce extensive damage to the assumptive worlds of a man and his family, may be much greater mutilations than clipping his ears or flogging him. There are, in my opinion, great dangers for our society in this tendency to deny the violence which we employ.

Not that one advocates the restoration of corporal punishment. All that is being suggested is that we should become more aware of the mutilation which we inflict in the name of justice so that we can weigh it with greater sensitivity against the possible benefit to society of its infliction.

Studies of the psychological effects of unemployment, imprisonment, demotion, retirement and the transition from school to work are needed to determine the extent to which these changes in life space resemble and differ from other types of change. Studies of retirement have already revealed the depression which commonly attends this event and the need for adequate preparation is undoubted. Hill (1969) has pointed to the irrelevance of current methods of schooling as a way of building an assumptive world which is in accord with the life space of the school-leaver. It is no wonder that school-leavers often feel that they have been 'sold a pup'. Difficulties in making the transition may cause them to turn away from the adult world as a source of role models, to become 'unattached youths'. Much as the widow says, 'I don't think of myself as a widow', the young adult attempts to deny the fact that he is an adult. The fact that his coevals are going through the same identity crisis may mean that they are equally at a loss and so one gets the formation of social groups who are united in a collusive endeavour to become nothing, to 'drop out' of society.

The youth who gives up on life and takes a purely negative view of society is necessarily in a state of disorganization with all the depression and bitterness which this involves. But 'giving up' is an important phase of grief; it may be necessary to give up trying to retain a childish view of the world as perpetually loving and giving before one can allow oneself to discover one's capacity to survive despite competition from fellows and aggression from enemies.

In this, as in so many cases, fear of possible failure in the new life can retard the process of relinquishing the old. The appalling magnitude of the change in life space which we recognize and the change in assumptive world which we anticipate causes us to draw back, to 'look back in anger' at the implacable process of change which threatens to overwhelm and destroy us.

One piece of behaviour which, for some time, the writer found puzzling is the frequency with which men and women who have lost a limb speak with pleasure of their contacts with people worse off than themselves. At first it seemed that this reflected the sadistic counterpart of the envy which amputees often feel for those who are intact. But on enquiry it is found to be quite a different phenomenon. As a general rule the person who has recently lost a limb is preoccupied with the problem of his own future adjustment. Lacking any sound basis for prediction his thoughts range over a variety of possible models in which he often sees himself as perpetually crippled and helpless. It is only when he meets someone more seriously mutilated than himself who appears to be coping well and cheerfully with his disability that it becomes possible for him to look to the future in an optimistic and realistic manner.

It is for this reason that people who have successfully come through major transitions in their lives are often best able to help other individuals who are still caught up in the process of realization. In this paper it has been necessary to focus attention on the process of change which takes place within the individual in response to major changes in his life space. It is also possible, though outside the competence of the present writer, to extend the field to include the perspective of the larger units which go to make up society. Major transitions can affect all members of the family in which they take place, they necessitate the restructuring of the family unit and their effects may even spread to the work group and to the wider social setting. In the course of transition people are often brought into contact with others in a similar situation; hospitals can be viewed as communities whose purpose it is to facilitate the process of psychosocial transition – as can prisons, training establishments and certain types of emergency accommodation. The concept of the Hospital for the Chronic Sick as a transitional community has been well studied by Miller and Gwynne (1969). In a similar context, Menzies (1960) has described how a social system can develop within a hospital which protects nursing staff members from the anxiety of their patients.

Other studies have been concerned with the effects of major change within a large organization. The activities of the Tavistock team following the tip disaster in Aberfan are an example of this, but more frequently occurring, if less dramatic, than the Aberfan disaster are the major changes which occur within industrial organizations as a consequence of technological change. These have been the subject of several studies by staff members of the Tavistock Institute of Human Relations (Jacques, Rice and Hill 1951; Sofer 1955; Trist 1968; Trist, Higgin, Murray and Pollock 1962).

Finally there is the field of national and international relations. Major social changes and threats of major change are two of the most important factors by which governments are governed. Whether it is concerned to bring about change or to preserve the status quo (and issues such as birth control can be viewed from either perspective), a government needs to be aware of the effects of the psychosocial processes of transition and the means available to influence them. Just as intra-familial conflict commonly arises from the reluctance of family members to accept necessary changes in their life space so some international conflicts arise from the reluctance of nations to accept the need for change, be it change in territory or changes in other parts of their national life space. It may be that research in the field of psychosocial transitions will eventually have a contribution to make to the understanding of problems such as these.

To be a suitable area for research a topic should be of theoretical or practical importance, amenable to study and conceptually discrete. I have said enough in the foregoing pages to indicate the importance of this field from both theoretical and practical viewpoints. A word more is necessary, however, in defence of the methodological advantages and conceptual discreteness of the field.

Psychosocial transitions because, by definition, they affect large areas of the assumptive world and take place over a short period of time, are likely to be readily identifiable. They are often the subject of official statistics (birth, death and marriage registrations etc.) and are therefore amenable to epidemiological study. Because they comprise the transition from one relatively steady state to another they are often open to study before, during and after the transition thereby providing the investigator with a natural experiment comparable in scientific rigour to that of the laboratory experiment but without the ethical and theoretical drawbacks of the latter. Furthermore they often enable us to dispense with that bugbear of social science research, the control group, because a person who can be studied before and after change can be used as his own control.

Contrary to popular belief individuals who are undergoing psychosocial transitions are usually aware of their need for help and glad to collaborate in any research which provides them with an opportunity to discuss the problems which preoccupy them. They are also willing, and often able, to help others in similar predicaments and this has emerged as an important factor motivating collaboration with any research which is recognizably oriented to give help.

At the same time it must be recognized that those who are undergoing a major transition are peculiarly vulnerable to exploitation and easily hurt by insensitive research workers. It is, therefore, especially important that those who undertake this type of work should be more than ordinarily tactful and capable of using the scientific tools of research in a humane way. Because they are aware of the vulnerability of the person in transition others who are concerned for his welfare tend to adopt a protective attitude and it will be necessary first to convince them of the benign intentions of the researcher and of his ability to help rather than to harm the subject of his research.

'Stress Research' has been criticized for the imprecision of its meaning and the variety of concepts which it embraces. Clearly there is a danger that Transition

Studies, because of the variety of situations which can be conceived of as 'transitions', may be similarly criticized. But this very fact may greatly add to the importance of the field if it can, in fact, be shown that there are significant conceptual links between phenomena which, on the face of it, are widely diverse.

In order to point up the precision of the basic definition let us consider certain situations which are excluded from the field of study (though they may be eminently suitable for study under some other rubric). Maturation, because it is a gradual process of change, is not included, neither is aging, though a particular event which makes an individual suddenly aware of a change which may have taken some time to occur could be construed as a psychosocial transition. Frightening situations or transient illnesses which, though they may threaten life or cause extreme pain, give rise to no lasting effects on the assumptive world are not psychosocial transitions. Neither are lifelong states of deprivation, deformity or stigma (though they could, and have, been considered as stressful). Nevertheless the psychosocial transitions which occur in a family when a mentally defective child is born or when a daughter decides to marry a member of another race falls well within our frame of reference. Changes in work methods or the marketing of a new product are unlikely to represent psychosocial transitions as here defined unless they produce a major change in the life space of the population under study. Finally there is the possibility that adequate advance planning and preparatory training can transform what is potentially a major change in the assumptive world into quite a minor transition. This may complicate the field but it does not invalidate it any more than the discovery of a means of preventing rickets has invalidated the concept of rickets as a disease.

Only further research will tell us how powerful are the theories which will arise out of the further development of this field.

Acknowledgements

Thanks are due to Dr John Bowlby and Dr P.J.M. McEwan for constructive criticism of the drafts. This paper was completed in the course of research supported by the Department of Health and Social Security and the U.S. National Institute of Mental Health.

Notes

1   Janoff-Bulman, R. Shattered Assumptions: Towards a New Psychology of Trauma. The Free Press, New York, 1992.
2   Kauffman, G. Loss of the Assumptive World: A Theory of Traumatic Loss. Brunner-Routledge, New York and London, 2002.
3   Harris, D. Supporting clients through non-death loss and grief. *New Therapist* March/April, 14–19, 2014.
4   Tyhurst has used the term *transition state* in writing of the reaction to change but I prefer to regard transition as a process rather than a state and to reserve the term *state* for the relatively static situations which precede and follow the transition (Tyhurst 1957).
5   This contraction of Cantril's 'Assumptive Form World' is an attempt to broaden Cantril's concept to include conceptual as well as perceptual elements (Cantril 1950).
6   'Change is not made without inconvenience, even from worse to better', writes Johnson in the preface to his *English Dictionary*.
7   Deprivation is a relative thing but, on the whole, once essential needs are met, it is our view of others in the society in which we live which determines whether or not we feel deprived. I have no means of knowing what is mine by right but I know quite well that if Mr Jones has a Bentley then I should have one too. In acquiring a Bentley I am closing

a gap in my assumptive world rather than effecting a change. From the psychological point of view it might be more of a change to give up the idea of acquiring a Bentley than it would be to acquire one. One of the aims of advertising is to build assumptive worlds for people to live in.

References

Aldrich, C. K. The dying patient's grief. *Journal of the American Medical Association* 184, 329, 1963.

Aldrich, C. K. and Mendkoff, E. Relocation of the aged and disabled: a mortality study. *Journal of the American Geriatric Society* 11, 185, 1963.

Bowlby, J. Grief & mourning in infancy & early childhood. *Psychoanalytic Study of the Child* 15, 9, 1960.

Bowlby, J. Processes of mourning. *International Journal of Psychoanalysis* 42, 317, 1961a.

Bowlby, J. Pathological mourning and childhood mourning. *Journal of the American Psychoanalytic Society* 11, 500, 1961b.

Bowlby, J. *Attachment and Loss.* Volume. 1: *Attachment.* Hogarth, London, 1969.

Cantril, H. *The 'Why' of Man's Experience.* Macmillan, New York, 1950.

Cumming, E. and Henry, W. E. *Growing Old.* Basic Books, New York, 1961.

Dembo, T., Ladieu-Leviton, G. and Wright, B. A. Acceptance of loss – amputation. In J. F. Garret (ed.) *Psychological Aspects of Physical Disabilities.* U.S. Govt. Printing Office, Washington, DC, 1952.

Erikson, E. Identity and the life cycle. Selected papers. *Psychological Issues* 1, 116, 1959.

Fisher, S. H. Psychiatric considerations of hand disability. *Archives of Physical Medicine and Rehabilitation* 41, 62, 1960.

Fitzgerald, R. G. Reactions to blindness: An exploratory study of adults with recent loss of sight. *Archives of General Psychiatry* 22, 370–379, 1970.

Freud, S. Mourning and melancholia. *Collected Papers* 4, 152. Hogarth, London, 1917.

Fried, M. Grieving for a lost home. In L. J. Dahl (ed.) *The Environment of the Metropolis* (pp. 359–379). Basic Books, New York, 1962.

Harlow, H. F. and Zimmerman, R. R. The development of affectional responses in infant monkeys. *Proceedings of the American Philosophical Society* 102, 501, 1958.

Hill, J.M.M. *The Transition from School to Work.* A study of the child's changing perception of work from the age of seven. Centre for Applied Social Research, Tavistock Institute of Human Relations, London, 1969.

Jacques, E., Rice, A. K. and Hill, J.M.M. The social and psychological impact of a change in method of wage payment (The Glacier Project-V) *Human Relations* 4, 315, 1951.

Janoff-Bulman, R. *Shattered Assumptions: Towards a New Psychology of Trauma.* The Free Press, New York, 1992.

Kauffman, G. *Loss of the Assumptive World: A Theory of Traumatic Loss.* Brunner-Routledge, New York and London, 2002.

Kessler, H. H. Psychological preparation of an amputee. *Industrial Medicine and Surgery* 20, 107, 1951.

Kolb, L. C. Psychology of amputee. *Collected Papers from the Mayo Clinic* 44, 586, 1952.

Lewin, K. *A Dynamic Theory of Personality.* McGraw, New York, 1935.

Lindemann, E. Symptomatology and management of acute grief. *American Journal of Psychiatry* 101, 141, 1944.

Marris, P. *Widows and Their Families.* Routledge and Kegan Paul, London, 1958.

Menzies, I.E.P. A case study in the functioning of social systems as a defence against anxiety: a report on a study of the nursing service of a general hospital. *Human Relations* 13, 95, 1960.

Miller, E. J. and Gwynne, G. V. *A Life Apart.* Draft. Centre for Applied Social Research, Tavistock Institute of Human Relations, Doc., London, 1969.

Parkes, C. M. Separation anxiety: an aspect of the search for a lost object. In M. H. Lader (ed.) *Studies of Anxiety* (pp. 87–92). Headley, London, 1969.

Parkes, C. M. The first year of bereavement. *Psychiatry* 33, 442–467, 1970.

Parsons, T. A revised analytical approach to the theory of social stratification. In Bendix and Lipset (eds.) *Class, Status and Power* (pp. 99–128). Free Press, Glencoe, Illinois, 1953.

Robertson, J. Film: *A Two-Year-Old Goes to Hospital.* Concord Films, Nacton, Ipswich, 1952.

Robertson, J. Film: *Going to Hospital with Mother.* Concord Films, Nacton, Ipswich, 1958.

Robertson, J. and Robertson, J. Film: *JOHN, 17 months. Nine Days in a Residential Nursery.* Concord Films, Nacton, Ipswich, 1969.

Rochlin, G. *Griefs and Discontents: The Forces of Change.* Little, Brown, Boston, 1965.

Sofer, C. Reactions to administrative change. A study of staff relations in three British hospitals. *Human Relations* 8, 291, 1955.

Trist, E. L. *The Professional Facilitation of Planned Change in Organization.* Tavistock Institute of Human Relations, Doc., HRC 79, 1968.

Trist, E. L., Higgin, G. W., Murray, H. and Pollock, A. B. *Organizational Choice: Capabilities of Groups at the Coal Face under Changing Technologies.* Tavistock, London, 1962.

Tyhurst, J. S. The role of transition states – including disasters – in mental illness. *Symposium on Preventive and Social Psychiatry.* Walter Reed Army Institute of Research, Washington, DC, 1957.

Wittkower, E. Rehabilitation of the limbless: joint sociological and psychological study. *Occupational Medicine* 3, 20, 1967.

Wolfenstein, M. *Disaster: A Psychological Essay.* Routledge and Kegan Paul, London, 1957.

CHAPTER 13

WHAT BECOMES OF REDUNDANT WORLD MODELS?

A contribution to the study of adaptation to change

From *British Journal of Medical Psychology* 48(2): 131–137, 1975.

As we saw in Chapter 12, the assumptive world is a model of the world that we assume to be true. Major changes may invalidate these assumptions and face us with the problem of revising models that are now obsolete. This is easier said than done for our assumptive world is essential to our survival and all we have to go on.

In this paper I was able to draw on a wide range of clinical experience to analyse the various ways people attempt to solve this difficult task. This threw light on a new set of problems, many of which are common in clinical practice and have previously been seen as defensive 'denial' of reality. Rather than seeing these problems as symptoms of psychiatric illness I was coming to see them as reflections of a lifelong struggle to make sense of a complex and often unpredictable world.

Summary

When a life change has been expected, wished for or planned for and when it does not require too great an alteration to our assumptions about the world (world models) the necessary modification of these assumptions will usually proceed smoothly and realistically. When, however, circumstances are not ideal the old models of the world may undergo changes which give rise to further problems. Examples are cited of situations of change in which (a) the former models of the world are abandoned regardless of the continued relevance of some aspects of them; (b) models are modified in a partial and inappropriate manner, redundant parts being retained; and (c) models are encapsulated; they remain intact as alternative systems of thought or belief to which the individual can return if the alternative model proves unsatisfactory.

Among the various categories of events which are often classed as 'stressful' are those major changes in the life space which give rise to the need for a person to give up one set of assumptions about the world and to develop fresh ones. Events of this type have been designated as 'psychosocial transitions' and the reactions to which various transitions give rise bear sufficient resemblance to each other to justify us in studying them within a single frame of reference (Tyhurst 1957). Relocation of urban slum dwellers, amputation of a limb and bereavement by death are examples of psychosocial transitions which have been systematically compared (Parkes 1972a) but many other life changes could equally well be included: emigration, retirement, birth of a deformed or defective child or even unexpected promotion at work or receipt of a financial windfall. This does not mean that these events are always or necessarily deleterious in their effects and it is often the case that the completion of a successful psychosocial transition leaves the individual stronger, more mature and better equipped to cope with future transitions should they arise. But because psychosocial transitions are often turning points in life and adjustment and because a minority of those who undergo them develop physical or psychological symptoms or bring about social disorganization and suffering in the lives of others (Caudill 1958) they constitute an important field of study for social scientists. The characteristics of this field have been outlined elsewhere (Parkes 1971) and will not be reported here. This paper focuses instead upon one aspect of the reaction to psychosocial transitions, the changes which take place in the old assumptive world after an event which makes a large part of this internal model of the world obsolete.

The data upon which these generalizations are based derive from five main sources: studies by the writer of reactions to bereavement, amputation of a limb and terminal cancer, clinical psychiatric practice and the published studies of other workers.

World models and change

The nature of the world models has been well described by Bowlby (1969) who writes:

> The achievement of any set-goal requires that an animal is equipped so that it is able to perceive certain special parts of the environment and to use that knowledge to build up a map of the environment that, whether it be primitive or sophisticated, can predict events relevant to any of its set-goals with a reasonable degree of reliability . . . To call our knowledge of the environment a map is, however inadequate, because the word conjures up merely a static representation of topography. What an animal requires is something more like a working model of its environment . . .
>
> If an individual is to draw up a plan to achieve a set-goal not only must he have some sort of working model of his environment, but he must also have some working knowledge of his own behavioural skills and potentialities. Someone crippled or blind must make plans different from those made by the fit or the sighted . . . To be useful . . . working models must be kept up-to-date. As a rule this requires only a continuous feeding in of small modifications, usually a process so gradual that it is hardly noticeable. Occasionally, however, some major change in environment or organism occurs: we get married, have a baby, or receive promotion at work; or, less happily, someone close to us departs or dies, a limb is lost, or sight fails. At those times radical changes of a model are called for. Clinical evidence suggests that the necessary revisions of model are not always easy to achieve. Usually they are completed but only slowly, often they are done imperfectly, and sometimes not done at all. (p. 49)

It will be the purpose of this paper to look more closely at the ways models are revised.

Although some models of the world can be regarded as provisional and represent wished-for, dreaded or other possible situations, the models which I have subsumed under the term *The Assumptive World* comprise the individual's view of reality as he believes it to be, that is, a strongly held set of assumptions about the world and the self which is confidently maintained and used as a means of recognizing, planning and acting. It includes, for instance, the assumption that when I sit on something that looks like a chair I shall not fall on the floor, that when I go home at night my wife will be there to greet me and that when I get out of bed in the morning I can stand and walk about.

Assumptions such as these are learned and confirmed by the experience of many years. They enable me to make correct predictions about the world and to order my own behaviour accordingly. But sometimes the model proves wrong, my chair collapses, my wife is out or my foot slips on the mat and I fall over. These accidents may produce a transient feeling of frustration or anger but it soon becomes apparent that they are the exceptions that prove the rule; the chair can be repaired, my wife will return, the mat can be fixed to the floor. In all of these cases it remains possible to retain my former assumptive world unchanged.

Psychosocial transitions

Just occasionally, however, a life event can bring about a major change which, within a short space of time, renders obsolete a large part of my assumptive world; my wife is absent because she has died, I fall over when I get out of bed because my leg has been amputated (many amputees describe this experience) or I am unable to find a chair because my eyesight has failed – in such circumstances my established set of assumptions must be changed if I am to maintain a satisfactory level of functioning.

But although the event which produced the need to change may have occurred in a relatively short space of time the establishment of a fresh set of assumptions takes time and energy and it is likely to be a painful business. In the meanwhile my ability to function effectively is likely to be much reduced and those around me must make allowances for my incompetence. When, finally, I 'recover' from my period of mourning or rehabilitation (both terms carry similar implications), it is assumed that I shall have abandoned all those expectations and behaviour patterns which were only appropriate to my former life and that I will now have learned those new expectations and behaviour patterns which are appropriate to my current world.

Types of change in world models

Three possible types of change can occur in a world model: (1) it may be abandoned and cease almost completely to influence behaviour; (2) it may be modified or abandoned incompletely so that it continues to influence behaviour in major or minor ways for long or short periods of time; (3) it may be retained in encapsulated form independently of the new model and as an alternative determinant of behaviour.

Type 1 change

The first type of change, *abandonment of the former view of the world*, is sometimes seen as the ideal. The widow attempts to forget the past and start afresh; the cripple tries to put out of his mind the athletic prowess which he once achieved and focus attention upon the future which remains to him.

Insofar as these attempts result from realistic appraisals of the new situation and involve a change which it is within the individual's capacity to master they may lead to a satisfactory outcome.

Circumstances which favour such a successful transition are:

(a) *Minor losses* which do not require the revision of a major part of the assumptive world.

(b) *Changes for which the person is fully prepared* so that he has a relatively realistic model of the new world available into which he can move without hesitation. The surgical patient who has been given the opportunity to discuss in detail the purpose and effects of his operation before it takes place and has been instructed what to do if he should experience pain or other probable effects will tend to have a smoother postoperative course than one who is relatively unprepared. Thus Egbert, Battit, Welch and Marshall (1964) reported lower incidence of pain, halved consumption of pain-relieving drugs and early discharge from hospital in 'prepared' patients; and Lazarus and Hagens (1968) found less than half the incidence of postoperative psychoses among 'open heart' patients who had been prepared in this way.

(c) *Wished-for changes* which enable the old world to be given up without regret. Fried's study of the reaction to relocation of a slum population showed clearly that those who were most dissatisfied with the old area, or who disliked their neighbours, were less disturbed by the experience of relocation than others who had a strong positive attachment to the place and the people (Fried 1962).

(d) *An attitude to the world which enables it to be regarded as provisional.* People who adopt this attitude expect little from life and regard all commitments as temporary. The attitude is encouraged by certain religious and philosophical systems which emphasize the evanescent and unimportant nature of personal survival and foster the adoption of a state of emotional detachment from all changes of personal fortune. A Roman Catholic woman of fifty-five lost her sister from cancer and then developed an identical cancer herself. Treated by radiation she developed a venous thrombosis which necessitated the amputation of her left leg. Subsequently the wound broke down and she had another operation to shorten the stump. A humble, selfless woman, she admitted she never felt the need to cry about her own misfortunes but was concerned about the misfortunes of other people. When her leg got bad she faced up to the fact that she might lose it and in the end it was she who suggested amputation to the surgeon. She was properly instructed about the operation so that when she woke up to find that she still had a pain in her foot she was 'quite happy'. A year later she was 'living from day to day', crawling up and down stairs because her artificial limb was uncomfortable, but she was in good spirits, unworried and quite unself-conscious. She prayed regularly and said she was not afraid to die although she hoped that she would not for the sake of the family. She was fully occupied in housekeeping, cooking, making beds in a kneeling position and caring for her crippled mother, her husband and two unmarried sons.

But the consequences of abandoning old models of the world are not always beneficial to the person in transition or to others who may be affected by his behaviour. It is not uncommon, for instance, for a leg amputee, during the early weeks after the loss of his limb, to assume that he will never walk again. He may so far act on this assumption that he makes no attempt to use his prosthesis, to get a job or to resume any of the active pursuits which may still be well within his grasp. This global abandonment of the past is somehow easier to carry out than is the slow and painful process of finding out, little by little, which aspects of the old world model can be retained and which must be given up.

Type 2 change

We come now to the second type of change which can occur in the obsolete world model, *its modification or partial retention*. Even when a person makes a determined effort to turn his back on the past, to sell his former wife's possessions or to escape from reminders of what has been by selling up or emigrating, old assumptions continue to be made, expectations arise and habits of thought and action reassert themselves.

A widow who attempted to escape by going to live with her sister three months after the death of her husband could not get rid of the thought that he was sick at home waiting for her to return. A spinster of thirty-eight 'didn't give her another thought' after her sister died of cancer, but two months later broke down in a state of acute mania in which she carried on conversations with her sister. A man of thirty-six who put on a bold face after losing his leg from arterial disease and tried to avoid thinking about it alarmed his wife twelve months later when he climbed onto the roof of a house in the belief that he could return to his former occupation of roof tiler. Thus it seems that efforts to forget the past and to dismiss the old assumptive world from one's mind are likely to fail. It would indeed be sad if nothing which we have learned from one sphere of life proved to be useful in another and there are many aspects of one assumptive world which can continue into the next. The death of a husband does not mean that all the thoughts and behaviour patterns which were developed in interaction with him cease to be useful and most widows continue to use the memory of their husbands, their values, opinions, tastes and judgements, as a yardstick by which to measure their own behaviour and the behaviour of others. 'What would my husband have done?' becomes a guide for conduct and 'He would or wouldn't have liked this' a source of values. Insofar as these memories broaden her repertoire of solutions to problems they may be of value but there is also a danger that the blind adherence to outdated systems of thought may limit her freedom of action and autonomous development. This is the main problem which arises when old models are incorporated into new – we tend to build in aspects which are no longer valuable alongside other aspects which are of positive value. A young nineteen-year-old girl (Miss A.) who had lost her leg in a car accident impressed everyone by her determination to go to dances and date boys as she had before her accident, but her friends were embarrassed when she insisted on wearing a mini-skirt which revealed the mechanism of her artificial limb. Her refusal to compromise could then be seen as an unrealistic denial of the need to change her assumptions about herself. Fortunately she was subsequently able to realize that she was now more attractive in trousers or long dresses than in mini-skirts. Thirteen months after amputation she was 'going steady' with a boy who was unconcerned about her disability and treated her 'like anyone else'.

To be successfully modified the accuracy and usefulness of the world model must be subjected to repeated reality testing. In the example just given it was the recognition of embarrassment in her friends which caused Miss A. to question the assumption that she was still attractive in a mini-skirt. Similarly it is the painful realization that her husband is not coming down to breakfast which causes many a newly bereaved widow to stop laying the table for two; but she may forget this fact several times before she stops acting on the model that assumes that he is coming.

On the other hand, a model which is not challenged by reality will tend to persist. This is particularly likely if a person avoids situations which would force him to test reality; for example, the widow who leaves home so that she will not be reminded of her husband's absence will tend to go on picturing him at home and maintaining relatively intact the assumptive world which is associated with him. Other aspects of the world model are immune to reality testing because they exist at a conceptual but not a perceptual level. Thus, whereas the tendency to mistake others for a loved person who has died (which is common during the early post-bereavement period), is soon invalidated by closer scrutiny of the misidentified person, the 'feeling' that a dead husband is somewhere near at hand is not amenable to such examination and tends to persist. Likewise an amputee only has to look down to see that his foot is missing but this does not prevent him from feeling *as if* he still had the limb; and it may well be that this 'phantom limb', which is present in virtually 100 per cent of amputees during the first few weeks after amputation and only disappears slowly thereafter, is further strengthened by the presence of pathways within the nervous system which were formerly directly linked to the limb. The modification of the obsolete world model to fit the new was clearly illustrated by one amputee whose phantom limb had begun to 'shrink'. He now felt that he had a little foot halfway up his calf. When, however, he put on his artificial limb the phantom foot immediately 'zipped down' to coincide with his artificial foot.

One interesting way of modifying a model is by identification. A widow may no longer be able to interact with her husband but it may be possible or even necessary for her to take over certain roles which were formerly carried out by him. In so doing she may find that she is capable of performing these roles effectively because she remembers him performing the same roles and that she experiences a comforting sense of union with him or closeness to him. One widow spent a great deal of time decorating her house after her husband's death. This role, which had previously been performed by him, gave her much pleasure. She also learned to drive a car so that the vehicle which he had enjoyed driving could now be enjoyed by her. Unfortunately these roles, which were obviously potentially valuable achievements, were so overvalued that she got into financial difficulties and reality testing, in the form of her lawyer, led to a strict injunction that she cut down on her driving and decorating.

Type 3 change

The third type of change which may occur in the obsolete world model is *encapsulation*. Here the old model is retained unchanged alongside the new and the individual oscillates between them. A woman whose son was reported killed in action in Belgium reacted very severely but managed to mitigate her grief by clinging to the hope that the report was in error and that she would one day find him again. After the war she persuaded her husband to take her to Belgium to visit her son's grave. Returning home she said, 'I knew I was leaving him behind forever'. The encapsulation of an assumptive world is nowhere more clearly seen than in the phenomenon which Geoffrey Gorer terms 'mummification' (1965). He writes: 'the type of mourner whom I wish to describe preserves the grief for the lost husband or wife by keeping the house and every object in it precisely as he or she had left it, as though it was a shrine which would at any moment be reanimated.' Gorer cites Queen Victoria as the prime example of this type of mourning. After Prince Albert's death she had all the rooms which he had occupied in Osborne House photographed so that they could be correctly positioned after dusting; she arranged for his clothes to be laid out each day and his shaving water to be brought.

It would seem that the object of this behaviour is not, as Gorer suggests, to preserve *grief* but to preserve the *assumptive world* which existed prior to the bereavement, alongside the new, unwanted and usually resented world which threatens to replace it.

These attempts to retain an assumptive world which is now redundant seldom reflect a cognitive denial that the real world has changed. The woman who rocks the cradle of her dead baby knows very well that he is dead but she continues to behave in some ways *as if* he were alive. By so doing she is able to retain in some part a familiar, rewarding world which is vastly preferable to the strange, unrewarding and potentially dangerous world which surrounds her.

Encapsulation is particularly likely to occur if the life change has been preceded by a long period of uncertainty so that a provisional model of *the world as it may be* is built up alongside the model of *the world as it is*. Psychosocial transitions of this type are commonly seen when a person develops a progressive illness, particularly one which is likely to prove fatal. As the evidence of physical deterioration becomes more and more obvious despite drastic surgical and medical treatment, the patient may 'come to terms with his illness' in the sense that he questions his doctors about the nature of his condition, and if they give him direct and honest answers, seems to take in and accept the fact that he is going to die. One way he can do this is to maintain his obsolete assumptive world almost intact as a virtual 'escape route' to be used if the anxiety created by attempts to live with the reality of approaching death becomes intolerable. Thus a middle-aged man whose death was imminent said that a doctor had told him that 'just occasionally' a person will recover from cancer for no reason which we can discover. While he was able, most of the time, to say that he knew he had not got long left to live and to plan his life accordingly, he also developed an elaborate theory that death is a psychological phenomenon and that if he tried hard enough to force the illness to get better he would succeed. This enabled him to talk about the days when he would go home from hospital and make vague plans for the future. Another cancer patient, a young man who had repeatedly asked, and been told, the true facts about his illness complained to a junior nursing assistant that nobody would tell him what was wrong with him. The writer subsequently talked to him on the topic for a long time, answering direct questions such as 'How will I die?' as well and honestly as his medical knowledge would allow, only to be surprised by the patient's parting comment as he was wheeled back to the ward, 'Well I take it there's no doubt I shall return to college next term'. The patient died, peacefully, three days later.

The fact that there are some people, such as this man, who are able to deal with unwanted assumptions about the world by excluding them from consciousness does not mean that all people have the same ability. It would, for instance, be cruel to force every cancer patient to face facts about his illness which he was not ready to face. But it is the experience of many doctors and nurses who care for the dying that the patient who asks direct questions about his illness can usually cope with direct answers, particularly if these are given to him in a manner which does not magnify his anxiety but tends to reassure him that it is 'all right' to be helpless and ill and even to die.

Implications of these observations for care-giving professions

Within our internal worlds 'people' are likely to be more important than 'things' and because man is a social animal who is often strongly attached to and interdependent upon others in his life space, it is the loss of these significant others which is the most frequent cause of major disruptions of the assumptive world. Things which are closely associated with a lost person, clothes, personal possessions, photographs and so forth, which remain behind after the person has gone, may serve as a means of 'keeping alive' his memory. These 'linking objects' have been studied by Volkan (1970, 1971) who makes use of them in psychotherapy with people who have developed pathological reactions to bereavement as a means of focussing attention on the world which has been lost and evoking appropriate grief. Similar use can be made of dreams which also tend to provide a vivid image of the lost person which can be discussed, to bring about 're-grief work'. Both the dreams and the 'linking objects' reflect the lost person but, more than this, they reflect the whole set of assumptions which are now invalidated by the loss of that person and which, because they are a part of the internal world, cannot readily be relinquished.

By looking boldly at what has been lost the demarcation between the world that is and the world that was becomes clearer. Fitzgerald (1970) makes the point that partial blindness is more of a disability than complete blindness because it encourages the blind person to continue to attempt to function as if he could see instead of learning the skills appropriate to blindness. By minimizing the severity or permanence of his visual defect the partially blind person often maintains the assumptions appropriate to a sighted world long after these assumptions are no longer tenable. Only if he can be brought to examine the extent of his incapacity and to grieve for the world which he must give up will he be prepared to learn the use of cane, Braille, typewriter, guide dog and so forth, which between them can help him to achieve reasonable self-reliance and to build a new and worthwhile assumptive world to live in.

This example illustrates very clearly a common problem of psychosocial transition, the tendency to maintain the status quo at all costs and to avoid learning the tasks appropriate to a new unwanted world. Those who are in a position to give support and guidance at such times must be prepared to assist the other person to examine his assumptions, to clarify the model of the world which pre-dated the transition and the situation which now obtains in order to discover which aspects of it must change and which aspects can be retained. Although this is a painful and time-consuming business and requires of the helper patience, tact and understanding, it is also extremely rewarding work leading, as it usually does, to very obvious improvement in the competence and morale of the person who is changing. The implications of this approach to the understanding and care of bereaved people have been spelled out in Parkes (1972b).

References

Bowlby, J. *Attachment and Loss. Volume 1: Attachment.* Hogarth Press, London, 49, 1969.
Caudill, W. *Effects of Social and Cultural Systems in Reactions to Stress.* Social Science Research Council, New York, 1958.
Egbert, L.D., Battit, G.E., Welch, C.E. and Marshall, K.B. Reduction of postoperative pain by encouragement and instruction of patients: a study of doctor-patient rapport. *New England Journal of Medicine* 270, 825–827, 1964.
Fitzgerald, R.G. Reactions to blindness: an exploratory study of adults with recent loss of sight. *Archives of General Psychiatry* 22, 370–379, 1970.
Fried, M. Grieving for a lost home. In L.J. Duhl (ed.) *The Environment of the Metropolis* (pp. 151–171). Basic Books, New York, 1962.
Gorer, G. *Death, Grief and Mourning in Contemporary Britain.* Cresset Press, London, 1965.
Lazarus, H.R. and Hagens, J.H. Prevention of psychosis following open-heart surgery. *American Journal of Psychiatry* 124, 1190–1195, 1968.

Parkes, C. M. Psychosocial transitions: a field for study. *Social Science and Medicine* 5, 101–115, 1971.

Parkes, C. M. Components of the reactions to loss of a limb, spouse or home. *Journal of Psychosomatic Research* 16, 343–349, 1972a.

Parkes, C. M. *Bereavement: Studies of Grief in Adult Life*. Tavistock Publications, London, 1972b.

Tyhurst, J. S. The role of transition states: including disasters in mental illness. *Symposium on Preventive and Social Psychiatry*. Walter Reed Army Institute of Research, Washington, DC, 1957.

Volkan, V. 'The linking objects' of pathological mourners. Paper read to the American Psychoanalytic Association, New York, 1970.

Volkan, V. A study of a patient's 're-grief work'. *Psychiatric Quarterly* 45, 255–273, 1971.

CHAPTER 14

BEREAVEMENT DISSECTED – A RE-EXAMINATION OF THE BASIC COMPONENTS INFLUENCING THE REACTION TO LOSS

From *Israeli Journal of Psychiatry* 38(3–4): 151–156, 2001.

The new millennium seemed a good time to take stock and I received several requests to summarise the history of bereavement research.[1] In this paper, however, I attempted to take a new look at the basic principles underlying our understanding and to see how they could produce a unified model that would include the main theories and practical developments that had come out of our research and clinical practice. It was not possible, in the space available, to give full justification for the result which now seems simplistic; even so, the results are not without interest and go some way towards the integration of our thinking about a variety of losses.

In reviewing the medical, social scientific, philosophical and historical literature on bereavement Shaver and Tancredy (2001) conclude, 'Despite such prolonged and intense scrutiny, bereavement has yet to inspire a single, widely accepted explanatory framework.'

One reason for this may well be that bereavement has many consequences and no one frame of reference is likely to explain more than part of a complex whole. There has been an unfortunate tendency among theorists to label all of these consequences as 'grief'. Hence the instruments which have been developed as measures of 'grief', such as the *Texas Inventory of Grief* (Faschingbauer, Zisook and Devaul 1987) and the *Grief Experience Inventory* (Sanders, Mauger and Strong 1991) include emotions (such as depression) and symptoms (such as insomnia) which occur after many different life events and circumstances and are not specific to bereavement.

In an attempt to bring clarity to the field, I have dissected out the main psychological processes which commonly occur following bereavement and here consider how each one of them contributes to the mixture of reactions which then arise. Because the field is large it is only possible here to give an outline of the evidence and to provide references to further reading; nor has it been possible to include every current point of view. This said, the following ideas are offered in the hope that they will provide a nub around which other explanatory models can be integrated. Much of the evidence for these views will be found in Parkes (1996) and Stroebe, Hansson, Stroebe and Schut (2001).

In searching for the roots of human psychology it is, in my view, wise to start by examining the genome, the innate predisposition which we share with other social animals.

In all social animals bereavement by death usually gives rise to:

Alarm – this occurs whenever we perceive threat to our lives or to the lives of those to whom we are attached. The bodily and emotional changes which accompany it are well known and pervasive; they increase our ability to fight or flee (Cannon 1929 and many other authors).

Separation Reaction – It is a definition of social animals that they are part of an interdependent network of attachments. Attachments include behaviours and feelings which maintain closeness (e.g. smiling, following, clinging) and others which arise when we become separated (e.g. crying and searching). This repertoire of attachment behaviours is innate in origin, but modified by learning from its inception. Its primary function is to maintain security and maximise chances of survival. Only in the event of permanent loss is that function frustrated (Bowlby, 1969, 1973, 1980).

Change to the Assumptive World – All individuals share certain assumptions about the world and their place in it. For instance, in all social animals, each social group has a hierarchy (peck order); this is determined partly by individual attainment (e.g. aggressive display/submission) and partly by attachments to others of higher or lower status. Once established these places are maintained because they become part of the assumptive world of the group; everyone assumes that such and such is boss/boss's partner/boss's child and so forth until proved otherwise. Any situation which invalidates such assumptions requires a new Assumptive World to be established, a Psycho-Social Transition (PST) results (Parkes 1971, 1995). Note that only the Separation Reaction is peculiar to bereavement. Alarm arises in many other situations of threat and PSTs follow a wide range of life change events.

Although these three components can be viewed as separate and involve different psychological processes, they influence each other. Thus, following a death, all three influence the perceived security of the group, at both the individual and shared levels, producing non-specific arousal, vigilance, anger, anxiety and other reactions according to the magnitude of the event and the way the situation is perceived. They also interact with both innate and learned predisposition of various kinds and are affected by the many secondary changes which follow.

In human beings, to a larger extent than in other species, four factors profoundly influence the reaction to bereavement.

1   The ability to *imagine and rehearse complex models* of the world.
2   The ability to *postpone or avoid disturbing thoughts*.
3   The ability to *communicate models of the world*.
4   The ability to *communicate social expectations* of behaviour, thoughts and feelings.

Each of these is a mixed blessing which, while improving our overall chances of survival, also creates special problems and, may even, in certain circumstances, impair our chances of survival.

1   *The ability to imagine and rehearse complex models of the world.* The internal world of the human being is much larger and more complex than that of other species. In addition to the Assumptive World it includes a variety of Provisional Worlds, including Dreaded Worlds and Hoped-for Worlds which enable us to try out, in imagination, various alternative scenarios to deal with possible events. It also enables us to prepare for losses to come by (1) rehearsing the changes in the Assumptive World which will arise, thus facilitating the

PST, (2) grieving, in anticipation, for those losses which are inevitable but also (3) recognising what will remain. This can increase our preparedness as well as our sense of security and control (Parkes 1993).

> **Problem** – But it also causes us to worry and agonise when events are beyond our control and we are unable to anticipate positive outcomes. It faces us with the existential realisation that we, and those we love, must all die. The anticipation of a loss evokes similar distress to that produced by the loss itself and some people become obsessively preoccupied with dread and waste their time trying to postpone the inevitable (Bartholomew and Horowitz 1991).

2   Because intense distress can impair thinking, we have developed ways to minimise this by *coping (defence) mechanisms such as postponement, denial and avoidance.* These enable us to cope with emergencies without becoming paralysed by fear and to carry out day-to-day activities without undue anxiety (Folkman 2001). After bereavement most people oscillate between approach and avoidance thereby allowing the urge to search for the lost person outside of oneself to be gradually extinguished (by non-reinforcement) and the PST to proceed without disorganising distress (Stroebe and Schut 2001). Some basic assumptions are *myths* which preserve equanimity by illusions of invulnerability, exclusive protection and personal worth.

> **Problem** – At times, avoidance of important issues can impair our ability to cope with reality and postpone PST; at other times traumatic life events can rudely shatter our basic assumptions leaving us overanxious and disorganised in our thinking (Janoff-Bulman 1992).

3   *The ability to communicate models of the world.* These enable us to educate and otherwise help each other to cope with the world we meet. As a result, a world has come into being which is largely man-made and, most of the time, under our joint control, but our interdependence is greater than ever before. In the more developed parts of the world this enables even the weak and ignorant to survive. For the fortunate members of that world, survival is taken for granted and a new set of goals can give richness and meaning to life. The communication of an accurate model of the world is a major function of parenting.

> **Problem** – The enormous increase in the amount and complexity of the information which we need in order to achieve our goals means that few, if any, individuals can now control more than a small part of the world they meet. We are all aware of our (relative) weakness and ignorance and rely on them up there to look after us. It is a paradox that, at a time when our chances of survival have never been better, we have less sense of control and empowerment than ever before, with resulting insecurity. Insecure parents commonly fail to teach their children appropriate trust in themselves and others (Ainsworth 1991). At times of major loss and change this trust is easily impaired (Parkes 1995).

4   *The ability to communicate social expectations.* These influence our behaviour, thoughts and, to an extent, feelings. Social assumptions minimise the risk of conflicts between individuals, provide social sanction and support when

needed, and help to educate us into the roles and obligations expected of us thereby increasing our security and integrating us within society (Rosenblatt, Walsh and Jackson 1976).

Problem – Social assumptions can conflict with our felt needs. At such times we may either be expected to express emotions that we do not feel or to hide those that we do. Thus the felt need to grieve is often in conflict with social pressures to inhibit or express grief (Walter 1999). There is no one mode of grieving that suits everybody and counsellors must be sensitive to that fact and respectful of people's individual needs.

Psychiatric problems following bereavement

The traditional psychiatric diagnostic framework is based on phenomenology (symptom clusters or syndromes rather than root causes). For this reason it has serious limitations. Each of the major syndromes commonly found after bereavement are comprehensible in terms of the explanatory frameworks outlined earlier.

Anxiety/Panic – Anxiety is a natural part of the Alarm Reaction and also arises for many of the reasons postulated previously. Fighting and fleeing are inappropriate reactions to bereavement in human beings and the bodily symptoms which accompany anxiety are often misinterpreted as evidence of sickness. Thus anxiety often provokes more anxiety leading to panic. It is the most common reason for people to seek psychiatric help after bereavement (Jacobs 1993; Prigerson, Shear and Newsom 1996).

Response – Explanation, reassurance and instruction in techniques leading to relaxation and control can be expected to mitigate these problems as can any intervention which reduces insecurity (*v.i.*).

Depression – is often caused by negative assumptions and feelings of helplessness and hopelessness particularly following irrevocable losses and in those whose early experiences left them with little trust in themselves or others (Beck *et al.* 1979; Seligman 1975).

Response – Relationships which foster self-respect *and* appropriate trust in others will reduce depression. Cognitive therapies counteract habitual negative assumptions about the world (Fleming and Robinson 2001). Antidepressants may facilitate this (Jacobs 1993).

Chronic Grief – Much evidence indicates that severe, unrelieved grief is best seen as a disorder of attachment associated with dependency which itself reflects basic assumptions of personal weakness and reliance on others (Jacobs 1999; Parkes 1995).

Response – Relationships which empower the client and respect their true value and potential help them to reach the point when they begin to do the same.

Delayed, Inhibited or Avoided Grief – This is commonly caused by parents who are intolerant of closeness and other attachment behaviour. The child soon learns to keep their distance and to inhibit expressions of attachment. This leads to distrust of closeness, distrust of others, compulsive self-reliance or pseudo-independence (Parkes 1995). Avoidance also arises following sudden, unexpected and traumatic types of bereavement (*v.i.*).

Response – Therapy which recognises the clients' need for and simultaneous fear of attachment, and provides them with opportunities to recognise and value their own feelings (both negative and positive), will enable them, perhaps for the first time, to enjoy attachments to others (Lindemann 1944; Mawson, Marks, Ramm and Stern 1981; Schut, Stroebe, van den Bout and de Keijser 1997).

Post-Traumatic Stress Disorder – Haunting memories/mental images of horrific events which evoke disorganising panic and defensive avoidance. These, in turn, interfere with the examination and revision of the assumptive world which is an essential part of PST.

Response – Therapy (e.g. Eye Movement Desensitisation, Shapiro 1989) which, by repetitive confrontation, reduces the pain of imagery and enables the sufferer to stop avoiding it. This then opens the door to PST.

Implications for bereavement services

These considerations have important implications for the prevention and treatment of problematic reactions to bereavement which have been confirmed by research. Many of the responses recommended here are well within the powers of a bereavement counsellor or non-psychiatric health care worker; others require more specialist treatment.

Because many of the problems reflect insecurity and our prime source of security is the attachments we make to our own family it is no surprise to find that one of the predictors of poor outcome after bereavement is the perception of one's family as unsupportive. Yet people who make this attribution are also the ones who benefit most from counselling (Raphael 1977). It follows that one of the most important contributions which a helper can make is to provide the non-judgemental psychological and emotional support which people should expect from their families. Bowlby (1988) referred to this as the 'secure base' within which it begins to be possible for clients to tackle the problems about which they feel very insecure. This consideration will influence not only our verbal and non-verbal communication with bereaved people but also our choice of venue, duration of meetings, dress and much else.

It also implies that we should always attempt to understand and, where possible, relate to the client's surviving *family* who may need help in their own right and may both help and hinder our attempts to help the client (Kissane and Bloch 2002).

Because their own attachment needs are easily impaired by bereavement, *children* may be particularly vulnerable and we should always assess and, where necessary, ensure that their needs are met (Black and Urbanowicz 1987). There is a great need to improve services to bereaved children.

Once a secure base has been established those who deal with threats by avoidance may begin to feel secure enough to approach and share thoughts and feelings. Attempts to force the pace will only increase anxiety and slow down the process but reassurance and recognition of progress will foster emotional expression which, in this group, is likely to be therapeutic. But we should not overvalue the importance of the expression of grief. It is only likely to benefit a minority of the people who seek help from psychiatric and bereavement services and may even aggravate the problems of those who tend towards obsessive preoccupation with grief (Bonanno 2001).

Much more important is to help people to engage with the problems of changing their assumptive world, of finding new meanings and identity. The only way to change our assumptive world is to examine, little by little, what we have lost and discover what remains. When we do this we regularly find that many of the assumptions which were associated with the past remain true despite the loss.

Thus by letting go of what cannot be we become aware of what can be. This is the true meaning of grief work and it has little to do with grief and much to do with change.

The aim of counselling is not to help the bereaved to forget the past but to discover what assumptions from the past can be remembered, treasured and made use of and which assumptions are now obsolete and misleading. Assumptions to be retained will include aspects of the lost person who, in that sense, lives on in our memory. Klass terms this a continuing bond (Klass, Silverman and Nickman 1996). Following other types of loss it includes the view of the world which preceded the loss. Thus blind people can continue to relate to the world because they retain a mental image of the world in their mind's eye even though they can no longer see it; similarly the amputee can make use of an artificial limb because he learned to walk with a real one and carries that body image within him.

The principal means by which we can facilitate this change is by providing people with the *time and the opportunity to talk.* When they are explaining themselves to us they are explaining themselves to themselves, taking stock and building a new assumptive world. By reviewing what they have lost they discover what they can set aside and what they can carry forward. *Those whose assumptive world has been shattered do not rebuild the old one;* they discover a new one which may be less safe and cosy than the world which preceded it, for their myth of invulnerability has gone for all time, but the new assumptions are more realistic *because* they recognise the impermanence and vulnerability of all life. Sufferers often emerge wiser and more mature than they were (Schaeffer and Moos 2001).

The shattering of basic assumptions can destroy our sense of purpose and meaning in life; by the same token the creation of a new assumptive world gives rise to new meanings which are often richer and more vivid because they have been born out of the pains of grief. In that sense the psychosocial transition is a *spiritual experience* which we, the counsellors and therapists, are privileged to share.

Note

1   For a recent update, see for instance: Parkes, C.M. Grief: lessons from the past and visions for the future (updated). Special Issue on Bereavement: Contemporary Scientific Perspectives for Researchers and Practitioners. E. Zech and M. Stroebe (eds.) *Psychologica Belgica* 50(1–2), 7–26, 2010.

References

Ainsworth, M.D.S. Attachments and other affectional bonds across the life cycle. In C.M. Parkes, J. Stevenson-Hinde and P. Marris (eds.) *Attachment across the Life Cycle* (chapter 3). Routledge, London and New York, 1991.

Bartholomew, K. and Horowitz, L.M. Attachment styles among young adults: A test of a four-category model. *Journal of Personality and Social Psychology* 61, 226–244, 1991.

Beck, A.T., Rush, A. J., Shaw, B. F. and Emery, G. *Cognitive Therapy of Depression.* Guilford Press, New York, 1979.

Black, D. and Urbanowicz, M.A. Family intervention with bereaved children. In J.E. Stevenson (ed.) *Recent Research in Developmental Psychology* (pp. 179–187). Pergammon, Oxford, 1987.

Bonanno, G.A. Grief and emotion: a social-functional perspective. In M.S. Stroebe, R.O. Hansson, W. Stroebe and H. Schut (eds.) *Handbook of Bereavement Research: Consequences, Coping and Care* (chapter 22, pp. 493–516). American Psychological Association, Washington, DC, 2001.

Bowlby, J. *Attachment and Loss. Vol. I, Attachment.* Hogarth, London, 1969.

Bowlby, J. *Attachment and Loss. Vol. II, Separation: Anxiety and Anger*. Hogarth, London, 1973.

Bowlby, J. *Attachment and Loss. Vol. III, Loss: Sadness and Depression*. Hogarth, London, 1980.

Bowlby, J. *A Secure Base: Clinical Applications of Attachment Theory*. Routledge, London and Basic Books, New York, 1988.

Cannon, W. B. *Bodily Changes in Pain, Hunger, Fear and Rage* (2nd ed.). Appleton, London and New York, 1929.

Faschingbauer, T. R., Zisook, S. and Devaul, R. D. The Texas revised inventory of grief. In S. Zisook (ed.) *Biopsychosocial Aspects of Bereavement* (pp. 111–125). American Psychiatric Association, Washington, DC, 1987.

Fleming, S. and Robinson, P. Grief and cognitive-behavioral therapy: the reconstruction of meaning. In M. S. Stroebe, R. O. Hansson, W. Stroebe and H. Schut (eds.) *Handbook of Bereavement Research: Consequences, Coping and Care* (chapter 29, pp. 671–704). American Psychological Association, Washington, DC, 2001.

Folkman, S. Revised coping theory and the process of bereavement. In M. S. Stroebe, R. O. Hansson, W. Stroebe and H. Schut (eds.) *Handbook of Bereavement Research: Consequences, Coping and Care* (chapter 25, pp. 563–584). American Psychological Association, Washington, DC, 2001.

Jacobs, S. C. *Pathologic Grief: Maladaptation to Loss*. American Psychiatric Association, Washington, DC and London, 1993.

Jacobs, S. *Traumatic Grief: Diagnosis, Treatment and Prevention*. Taylor & Francis, New York, 1999.

Janoff-Bulman, R. *Shattered Assumptions: Towards a New Psychology of Trauma*. The Free Press, New York, 1992.

Kissane, D. and Bloch, S. *Family-Focussed Grief Therapy: A Model of Family-Centered Care during Palliative Care and Bereavement*. Open University Press, Maidenhead, UK, 2002.

Klass, D., Silverman, P. R. and Nickman, S. (eds.) *Continuing Bonds: New Understandings of Grief*. Taylor & Francis, Washington DC and London, 1996.

Lindemann, E. The symptomatology and management of acute grief. *American Journal of Psychiatry* 101, 141, 1944.

Mawson, D., Marks, I. M., Ramm, L. and Stern, L. S. Guided mourning for morbid grief: A controlled study. *British Journal of Psychiatry* 138, 185–193, 1981.

Parkes, C. M. Psychosocial transitions: a field for study. *Social Science and Medicine* 5, 101–115, 1971.

Parkes, C. M. Bereavement as a psychosocial transition: processes of adaptation to change. In M. S. Stroebe, W. Stroebe and R. O. Hansson (eds.) *Handbook of Bereavement* (chapter 6). Cambridge University Press, Cambridge, New York and Victoria, Australia, 1993.

Parkes, C. M. Attachment and bereavement. Second John Bowlby Memorial Lecture. In *Grief and Bereavement: Proceedings from the Fourth International Conference on Grief and Bereavement in Contemporary Society, Stockholm, 1994*. Swedish National Association for Mental Health, Stockholm, 1995.

Parkes, C. M. *Bereavement: Studies of Grief in Adult Life* (3rd ed.). Taylor & Francis, London and New York and Pelican, Harmondsworth, 1996.

Prigerson, H. G., Shear, M. K., Newsom, I. *et al.* Anxiety among widowed elders: is it distinct from depression and grief? *Anxiety* 2, 1–12, 1996.

Raphael, B. Preventive intervention with the recently bereaved. *Archives of General Psychiatry* 34, 1450–1454, 1977.

Rosenblatt, P. C., Walsh, R. P. and Jackson, D. A. *Grief and Mourning in Cross-Cultural Perspective*. HRAF Press, Washington, DC, 1976.

Sanders, C. M., Mauger, P. A. and Strong, P. A. *A Manual for the Grief Experience Inventory*. Consulting Psychologists Press, Palo Alto, CA, 1991.

Schaeffer, J. A. and Moos, R. H. Bereavement experiences and personal growth. In M. S. Stroebe, R. O. Hansson, W. Stroebe and H. Schut (eds.) *Handbook of Bereavement Research: Consequences, Coping and Care* (chapter 7). American Psychological Association, Washington, DC, 2001.

Schut, H. A. W., Stroebe, M., van den Bout, J. and de Keijser, J. Intervention for the bereaved: gender differences in the efficacy of two counseling programs. *British Journal of Clinical Psychology* 36, 63–72, 1997.

Seligman, M.E.P. *Helplessness*. Freeman, San Francisco, CA, 1975.

Shapiro, F. Eye movement desensitization: a new treatment for post-traumatic stress disorder. *Journal of Behaviour Therapy and Experimental Psychiatry* 20, 211–217, 1989.

Shaver, P. R. and Tancredy, C. M. Emotion, attachment and bereavement: a conceptual commentary. In M. S. Stroebe, R. O. Hansson, W. Stroebe and H. Schut (eds.) *Handbook of Bereavement Research: Consequences, Coping and Care*. American Psychological Association, Washington, DC, 2001.

Stroebe, M. S., Hansson, R. O., Stroebe, W. and Schut, H. (eds.) *Handbook of Bereavement Research: Consequences, Coping and Care*. American Psychological Association, Washington, DC, 2001.

Stroebe, M. S. and Schut, H. Models of coping with bereavement: a review. In M. S. Stroebe, R. O. Hansson, W. Stroebe and H. Schut (eds.) *Handbook of Bereavement Research: Consequences, Coping and Care* (chapter 17, pp. 375–404). American Psychological Association, Washington, DC, 2001.

Walter, T. *On Bereavement: The Culture of Grief*. Open University Press, Buckingham, 1999.

CHAPTER 15

ASSUMPTIONS ABOUT LOSS AND PRINCIPLES OF CARE

From Parkes, C. M. and Markus, A. (eds.) *Coping with loss: helping patients and their families* (pp. 131–138). London: BMJ Books, 1998.

The International Work Group on Death, Dying and Bereavement is an interesting group of experts in the field of thanatology who come from many academic disciplines and countries and meet every eighteen months or so somewhere in the world. As the name implies they work in groups to share research and clinical knowledge and to develop this emerging field. Several of the work groups have chosen a particular area of inquiry and listed the assumptions which can be made on the basis of current knowledge and the principles of care that can be derived from those assumptions. The lists are not particularly interesting but the discussion of their use is.

In this paper I made use of the IWG's approach in order to elicit the assumptions made by contributors to a book for members of the health care professions aimed at exploring the psychological issues they face in patients and their families. The principles of care which followed from these assumptions summarise the main conclusions from that book as well as illustrating many of the implications of the foregoing chapters of this one.

In the book in which this paper first appeared, we examined the psychological consequences of the many losses that are encountered by members of the caring professions in the course of their work and considered the implications of these for the care of patients, their families and ourselves. The defining characteristic of a loss is the grief to which it gives rise and the defining characteristic of grief, without which it cannot truly be said to be present, is pining, the feeling of missing the lost person, thing, situation or other object to which one has been attached. This is evident in situations as varied as the amputee's yearning to run and jump . . ., the separated partner's pining for a former wife or child . . ., the blind person's need to continue to watch television in preference to listening to the radio . . . or the unemployed person's longing for a job, the workmates he or she has lost and the self-image that came with these lost objects [*page references to these and other examples are given in the full text and shown here by . . .*].

Given this common ground we shall recapitulate by attempting to draw out the assumptions that it is reasonable to make in our current state of knowledge about the losses met with in medical practice and deduce from these the principles of care that follow. This approach has been used by the members of the *International Work Group on Death, Dying and Bereavement* as a means of reviewing current knowledge of the field and making recommendations (Corr, Morgan and Wass 1993). It combines a clear statement of current assumptions in a refutable form with a linked statement of the principles that follow, also in a refutable form. Hence it should stimulate further research as well as provide guidelines for action.

Assumptions	Principles of care
• Major losses are important experiences that can contribute to causing physical and psychiatric illness	Members of the caring professions need to learn how to reduce the risk
• Losses that have been expected and prepared for are much less likely to give rise to later psychiatric and other problems than losses that are unexpected	By sensitively imparting information and support we can help people to prepare for the losses that are to come
• Many of the losses that are met within medicine affect the lives of members of the families of our patients	It is the family, which includes the patient, that should be the unit of care
• Grieving people tend to oscillate between avoiding and confronting grief, problems arise when either of these ways of coping predomiantes	Some people need permission and encouragement to grieve and reassurance of the normality of grieving

People may also need permission and reassurance that they do not have to grieve all of the time. They may need opportunities and encouragement to replan their lives in a way that values the past |
• Anger and shame can complicate the course of grief	We need to reserve judgment and show understanding
• The minority at special risk can be identified before or at the time of a loss. These include those with traumatic losses, personal vulnerability, and lack of social support	Members of the caring professions are well placed to assess risk, to give support, and to advise those who need additional help how to get it
• Losses can affect the carer as well as the cared for. Doctors are not immune to grief	We need to become aware of our own reactions to our patients and their illnesses and to acknowledge and seek to meet our own needs for support

Contribution to other illness

A basic assumption that emerged repeatedly in the course of the book is the recognition that *major losses are important experiences that can contribute to causing physical and psychiatric illness*. Evidence to support this view was given in several chapters and the assumption would seem to be uncontroversial. The principle that follows from it is that *members of the caring professions need to take steps to acquaint themselves with the losses that afflict their patients*. Sadly we often fail to do this, either because we do not take steps to find out how our patients and their families are affected by the life events that are impinging on them or because, knowing the facts of the loss, we fail to discuss them because we are reluctant to upset or be upset by the patient. Thus, as reported in the preceding chapters, neither women undergoing mastectomy . . ., mothers having a baby . . ., or people in residential care who had suffered a bereavement . . . were encouraged to talk about the experience or asked how it will affect their lives.

Of course there would be no point in discussing these issues unless there was something that we could do to reduce the harmful effects of psychological trauma. Fortunately there are good grounds to believe that appropriate intervention can often reduce that risk . . . It follows from this that members of the caring professions need to ensure that such help is given when it is needed. This makes it important for us to ensure that doctors are trained to assess risk and take appropriate action.

Be prepared

Research into risk factors justifies the assumption that *losses that have been anticipated and prepared for are much less likely to give rise to later psychiatric and other problems than losses that are unexpected.* This has been shown to be true in regard to bereavement . . ., operative surgery . . . and terminal care. . . . The principle that follows is that *by sensitively imparting information and support we can help people to prepare for the losses that are to come.* Members of the caring professions are often in a position to do this but may fail to do so. Thus children are seldom warned of the likely death of a seriously ill parent . . . and surgical patients may be inadequately prepared for the consequences of the surgery . . . When anticipatory guidance has been given, however, the results are usually good.

Many of the losses that are met with in medicine affect the lives of members of the families of our patients, and sometimes their losses are as great as or greater than those experienced by the patient. For instance, patients with Alzheimer's disease or other psychotic illnesses may be blissfully unaware that they are ill at all while their close relatives may be suffering severe grief. . . . *Whenever a loss extends to affect the family it is the family, which includes the patient, that should be the unit of care.* This conclusion may seem obvious but members of the medical profession are so used to treating the patient as the unit of care that we regularly neglect the family. Thus, one study showed that eleven out of twelve families of psychiatric patients who had committed suicide would have liked some contact with the psychiatrist who had cared for the person who died but only one psychiatrist had initiated any such contact (Brownstein 1992). Even the simple process of recording who is who in the family by drawing a genogram (family tree) in the case notes is seldom done. A genogram displayed on a flip chart during case conferences and other meetings at which family needs are being considered is an effective way of helping the team to focus on family problems. In general practice, where it is common for doctors to get to know entire families over many years, genograms have proved particularly helpful (see Markus, Parkes and Tomson, 1989, for a more detailed account of their use).

Pendulum of grief

While grieving people tend to oscillate between avoiding and confronting grief, problems arise when either of these ways of coping predominates. Sometimes a decision to cope in a particular way arises out of the special circumstances of the situation. Thus a woman may feel unable to express her grief at becoming pregnant because she thinks that others will disapprove or a man may pretend that he is not upset by a diagnosis of cancer because he does not wish to be seen as a 'wimp'. . . . Conversely a widow may feel she owes it to her dead husband to grieve for him forever. In other cases the tendency to avoid or express grief reflects a lasting personality trait as in the 'avoiders' and 'sensitisers' . . . After major losses either type may suffer pathological forms of grief or become depressed. *The danger of these types of problem can be minimised by appropriate action.* Thus some people need permission and encouragement to grieve and members of the caring professions may be the only people in a position to give these. Our professional and confidential relationship may cause people to confide in us information that is known to few if any others.

People may also need permission and encouragement to stop grieving and reassurance that nobody needs to grieve all of the time. Grief is not a duty to the dead or a sign of virtue. Obsessive grief can sometimes become an excuse to avoid the dangers of confronting a potentially hostile world. Thus, it is easy to see why some people who have suffered a psychotic illness will shut themselves up at home and resist attempts at rehabilitation. If we blame or browbeat them we shall only increase their feelings of insecurity and fear.

Those who overreact to loss will benefit from opportunities to re-examine their negative assumptions about themselves and their world, to review and re-plan their lives in ways that value and build on the past and to venture forth into a world that seems more dangerous than it really is. Nothing succeeds like success and quite small beginnings can lead to a restoration of confidence that eventually allows great progress to be achieved. There is much to be said for John Bowlby's claim that *'the most important thing that we have to offer frightened or grieving people is a "secure base"'* (Bowlby 1988), a relationship of respect that will last them through the bad times with a person who has the time, knowledge and willingness to remain involved.

Complicated grief

Feelings of *anger and shame can complicate the course of grief.* For example, mental illnesses or sexually transmitted diseases carry so severe a stigma that patients and relatives often fear that they will lose the support of friends and family if they acknowledge its existence let alone seek help or support for themselves. This adds to any stress that may have caused the illness. We need to reserve judgement and show understanding if we are to create the situation in which they can face up to what has happened and talk through its implications.

While most people come through the losses in their lives without the need for help from outside the family there is a minority who need such help. *The minority at special risk can be identified before or at the time of a loss.* This has been demonstrated in several studies . . . The recognition of these risk factors enables us to give extra help when it is most needed and to conserve our resources when it is not. It follows that members of the caring professions are well placed to assess risk, to give support and to advise those who need additional help how to get it.

Risk factors include traumatic losses, personal vulnerability and lack of social support. Traumatic losses . . . include disasters and other situations in which losses are sudden, unexpected, horrific or culpable. Ill health often adds to vulnerability and may itself bring people into our care. We need to cultivate sensitivity to the possible psychological influences of the physical illnesses that come our way.

Other causes of vulnerability are childhood and old age. Each carries with it particular hazards which need to be understood if we are to give appropriate help . . . The hazards of losses in childhood often result from misguided attempts to protect a child, as when a parent conceals important information from a child or fails to seek psychiatric help for a child with learning difficulties. In old age it is more often the false assumption that losses are inevitable and that there is nothing to be done that deters old people from seeking help and care givers from offering it. Clinical depression often remains untreated and loneliness is assumed to be inevitable. Thus situations that may have been caused by loss result in further losses.

Sometimes the expectation of a loss can bring about a loss. A woman who has had a bad experience of pregnancy may experience high levels of anxiety and a propensity to depression which may spoil her next pregnancy. Similarly . . . fear of further damage to the heart can impair the rehabilitation of heart surgical patients and . . . an overprotective spouse can impair the recovery of a blind person. In such circumstances medical and nursing professionals may need to give extra support and reassurance.

. . . *Losses which impair communication disable the care giver as well as the cared for.* This makes it hard for us to support them if they are grieving or afraid. Above all we should take care not to allow our own feelings of irritation with the situation to spoil our relationship with our patients. It is not their fault that their behaviour is difficult.

Don't forget the care givers

In this, as in other clinical situations, we need to be aware of how our work is affecting us. . . . Losses can affect the carer as well as the cared for and *doctors are not immune to grief.* The obstetrician who witnesses the death of a pregnant woman, the psychiatrist whose depressed patient commits suicide and the general practitioner who has to break the news that a person whose backache has been misdiagnosed has an inoperable cancer are bound to be distressed.

We need to become aware of our own reactions to our patients and their illnesses and to acknowledge and seek to meet our own needs for support. In fact losses of one sort or another are so common in the lives of most doctors that it is good practice to hold regular meetings with a trusted group of colleagues at which we can support each other. If we do this we will come through the process of grieving and be able to return to the fray with renewed confidence. The very process of sharing genuine feelings with colleagues can help the group to cohere and leave us feeling more rather than less secure. We are no longer alone.

It is both the privilege and the penalty of being a part of a health care team that we will meet people who are suffering in the face of loss. If we back off or fail to recognise their needs we may miss the opportunity to help them through a turning point in their lives. We may also miss the opportunity to learn from them that *losses are often integrating factors in family life and, in the end, a source of new meaning and maturity.*

References

Bowlby, J. *A Secure Base: Clinical Applications of Attachment Theory.* Routledge, London, 1988.

Brownstein, M. Contacting the family after a suicide. *Canadian Journal of Psychiatry* 37, 208–212, 1992.

Corr, C.A., Morgan, J.D. and Wass, H. *Statements on Death, Dying and Bereavement.* International Work Group on Death, Dying and Bereavement, King's College, London, 1993.

Markus, A.C., Parkes, C.M. and Tomson, P. *Psychological Problems in General Practice.* Oxford University Press, Oxford, 1989.

CHAPTER 16

AN EXPERIMENT THAT FAILED

Perceptions of a family-oriented crisis service
by referrers and clients

From Perceptions of a crisis service by referrers and clients. *Psychiatric Bulletin*
16(12): 748–750, 1992.

*A psychiatrist colleague once startled me by observing: 'You don't think of psychiatry
as treating mental illness but of solving psychological problems'. Up until that moment I
had not thought of my approach as unusual, indeed it seemed to me to be quite natural to spend time working with my patients to understand the roots of their problems.
I assumed that, once we both understood the problems, the solutions would likely
become clear. Diagnosis was only useful insofar as it opened the door to understanding and helping with the problems. But that was seldom the case; indeed, many of
the people who came to my clinic occupied a grey area in which drawing the line
between mental health and mental illness became an academic exercise of little value.*

*My studies of responses to the traumatic life events that commonly brought people
into psychiatric care had made me aware that many of these crises impacted not only
the 'patient' but also other members of the family. Indeed, as we saw in the last chapter
it is not only the patient who suffers when dangers to life arise. At such times the family
is the natural source of support but, by the same token, when support is most needed
the members may be least able to provide it.*

*In 1973 I took up an appointment as Senior Lecturer in Psychiatry at the Royal Lon-
don Hospital. This included an honorary post as consultant psychiatrist with responsibility for a district service in Bethnal Green in the East End of London. It presented me with
the opportunity to introduce a service for families in crisis regardless of whether or not
any individual in the family was mentally ill. I hoped to provide a setting in which therapists and families could work together. I also hoped to reduce some of the pressure on
psychiatric beds which had become a serious problem in this area of 'hard psychiatry'.
While some of my psychiatrist colleagues were sceptical I was well supported by the
Professor of Psychiatry Desmond Pond and by the members of the Social Services
who were well used to working with families and keen to help. We were fortunate
to obtain a grant to pay for an office in the community and to employ a mature Community Psychiatric Nurse (CPN) to take overall responsibility for the day-to-day running
of the service and we were able to draw on the help of trainees who joined a rota of
psychiatrists, social workers and CPNs.*

I wrote:

> *The Crisis Service was set up in response to dissatisfaction with the status quo.
> Run as a joint Health and Social Services enterprise, it differs from traditional psy-
> chiatric services in accepting referrals from a variety of professional caregivers; in
> accepting individuals or families who are facing an emotional crisis regardless of*

*whether or not they are mentally ill; and in sending a multi-disciplinary team (usu-
ally of two members) into the home to meet the family. The team does not necessarily include a psychiatrist although one is included if mental illness is suspected.
Other team members may be social workers, community psychiatric nurses or
occasionally psychologists.*

(Parkes 1992)

In keeping with our aim to prevent psychiatric disorders we did not make a psychiatric diagnosis a condition of admission to the service but used as our criterion a
'family crisis'. Even so the GPs and social workers who made most referrals faced us
with families in which one or more members had long-term psychiatric problems and
those that did not were likely to have similarly long-term family problems. Losses had
played a part in triggering many crises but it was unusual for them to constitute the only
or even the main problem.

Case notes were problem and family oriented. All cases were reviewed within the
following week by a senior psychiatrist and social worker and a plan for intervention
agreed which most often involved several further meetings with the family.

Although it was necessary, for statistical purposes, to name one individual as the
key contact it was not assumed that this person was 'the patient'. By maintaining a
'family' orientation we tried to avoid the creation of scapegoats and to recognise
that the family is the unit of care for its members. This gave our staff a very different
perspective on the problems that presented and counteracted the usual tendency to
treat psychiatric patients in isolation from their families and to foster the isolation and
dependence on the medical system that often complicates the lives of the long-term
mentally ill.

As we shall see, the CIS was popular with both referrers and clients and in due
course it was extended to cover the whole borough of Tower Hamlets.

Abstract

Information was obtained from the case notes of 118 clients referred to the Tower
Hamlets Crisis Intervention Service (CIS) for the first time during 1984–1985, from
interviews with twenty-nine GPs, thirty SWs and twenty-three other professionals
who had made referrals during this period and from interviews with 107 clients of
the service.

The CIS is a part of the wider range of psychiatric and social services in Tower
Hamlets. Run jointly by the District Health Authority and the Local Authority
it offers the help of a multidisciplinary team (which may or may not include a
psychiatrist) to assess and support families in crisis in the borough. Referrals are
accepted from GPs, SWs and other professional caregivers and the presence of psychiatric illness in the family is not a condition of acceptance (although the presence
of a family living in the borough is). The therapeutic approach is eclectic but with
a special interest in the enhancement of family support. Clients of the service tend
to be young and female.

Although few of the clients referred to the service were psychotic the serious
nature of the crises referred to the service was evident from both the opinion of
referrers and from the clients themselves. Seventy-nine percent of clients were thought
to have a diagnosable psychiatric condition.

Both clients and referrers provided evidence to support the view that the service
provided by the CIS is effective, efficient, appropriate, equitable, acceptable and,

to most, accessible. It was thought less acceptable to the substantial Bangladeshi population in Tower Hamlets.

Contrary to expectation clients whose families did not attend meetings with the team benefited as much as those whose families did.

The service was also valued as providing training opportunities for members of the caring professions.

This paper reports an evaluation of an innovative Crisis Intervention Service (CIS) in an inner city borough (Tower Hamlets).

A companion paper (Parkes 1992) reported the views of Social Workers (SWs) and General Practitioners (GPs) regarding twelve services available to families in crisis in this borough. These SWs and GPs commonly see people in crisis although few of them think that the training that they received 'usually' prepares them to cope adequately with these crises. They had found the Tower Hamlets CIS the most helpful service for people in crisis; it was also the most accessible and the feedback received from the service most prompt and satisfactory. An emergency clinic at a psychiatric hospital provided a more rapid response than the CIS (which is only available during the working day) but was seen as less helpful and the feedback was poor.

There are many kinds of crisis service (Cooper 2008). Most are only open to people who have been diagnosed as mentally ill. They facilitate rapid admission to short-stay in-patient services with the backup of multidisciplinary teams working in the community. Others attempt to keep patients out of hospital by providing support to patients and their families in the community. Several of these have demonstrated striking reductions in the rate and duration of hospital admissions without detriment to the subsequent health or social adjustment of the patient (Langsley, Machotka and Cowenhalf 1971; Ratna 1978; Reynolds, Jones and Barry 1990).

The Tower Hamlets CIS was set up as a joint health and social services project in 1976. It provides a multidisciplinary team who visit families in crisis in order to provide assessment of their needs and, when appropriate, short-term support in the community. It differs from most other crisis services in attempting to prevent as well as treat mental ill health. Thus it accepts referrals from a range of professional caregivers and is not limited to people with overt mental illness, defining a crisis as any situation which creates distress in a family. The family is seen as the unit of care. Although the team is free to make use of the full range of psychiatric and social work services, the preferred method of treatment is short-term family therapy aimed at reinforcing or restoring the family as a support system to its members. Most assessment and treatment is carried out in the home. Case notes are 'family' and 'problem' oriented.

This paper reports the results of an evaluation of the service as seen through the eyes of referrers and clients of the service.

Method

Information for this evaluation was obtained in three ways:

1   By systematic analysis of the case notes of 118 clients referred for the first time to the CIS (94 women and 24 men) between January 1984 and May 1985.
2   By interviews with twenty-nine GPs, thirty SWs and twenty-three other professionals (82 in all) who had made referrals to the service during that period.
3   By interviews in their homes with 107 clients of the service who had been referred for the first time to the service during the period of study.

Full details of the interview schedules and samples together with the detailed results of the study in the form of a report to the DHSS are available. This paper can do no more than summarise the major findings.

Results

Eighty percent of clients were women with 79% under age forty (mean age: women 32, men 33). A half had partners (40% married, 12% cohabiting) with 29% single, 15% separated or divorced and 4% widowed. Reasons for referral as given by the referrers included 'threatened separation of family member' 50%, 'suspected or actual psychosis' 39% (or child – 13%), 'threatened or attempted suicide' 28%; 87% gave 'depression or distress in the family' and 18% other reasons. In all three-quarters of clients were said to have been referred because of a risk of suicide, violence or psychosis.

Although a psychiatrist subsequently made a psychiatric diagnosis in 79% of clients, psychoses were only diagnosed in 13%. Other diagnoses, in order of frequency were: personality disorder (21.5%), neurotic depression (14%), anxiety state (9.7%), brief depressive reactions (8.4%), alcohol dependence or abuse (7.5%) and phobic state (7.4%). Other conditions occurred in less than 5% of cases.

More useful from the point of view of management was the analysis of problems. This was carried out using a systematic method of data recording. Suffice it to say that nearly two-thirds of those with partners had major problems in relating to those partners whereas 41% of those without partners had suffered the long-standing loss, and a quarter the recent loss, of an adult person to whom they were attached. A third complained of social isolation or alienation from their families and a similar proportion of alcohol-related problems.

Problems with children were commonly reported and there was a small group of six adolescents all of whom had problems in relating to their parents.

Management

All clients were visited in their homes by a team of professionals (usually two in number). In 60% a psychiatrist was a member of the team, 55% a community psychiatric nurse and 52% a social worker. In addition to the client other family members were present at two-thirds of the initial (assessment) meetings, (38% spouses, 33% children, 16% parents and 11% siblings).

On average families received 6.8 visits from the team over a period of around twelve weeks. In addition 10% received on average of four and a half individual psychotherapy sessions. Antidepressants were prescribed for 13% of clients, major tranquillisers for 6% and minor tranquillisers for 3.5%. Twenty-nine percent were referred on to other agencies including 7% who were admitted for in-patient psychiatric care for a mean of forty-four days each.

Evaluation

1   *Effectiveness*. Seventy-eight percent of *referrers* thought that crisis intervention had led to the action they had hoped for. Seventy-nine percent thought that distress in the family had reduced or ceased, nearly a half thought that the risk of further crises had been reduced and in a quarter the need for psychiatric admission had been reduced or eliminated.

Three-quarters of *clients* had found the service 'helpful or very helpful' and two-thirds, asked 'How have things been since the team stopped visiting?' answered 'better' or 'much better' (17% said 'worse'). Among forty clients who were asked 'What do you think would have happened if you had *not* been referred to the Crisis Service?' a quarter said that they might have committed suicide, a quarter that they would have become mentally ill and 10% that they would have left home.

Features most often thought to have contributed to the effectiveness of the teams were support to and increased understanding by the family and the opportunity to talk through problems.

2   *Efficiency.* The annual cost of the service at the mid-point of the evaluation (1984–1985) was £35,000 or c. £300 per family. This compared with the cost at that time of a hospital bed of c. £20,000 but we have no way of knowing how much time these people would have spent in hospital if the CIS had not been available and the unending pressure on in-patient services in this district meant that any bed that is freed up from one source is quickly filled from another.

Could similar results have been achieved by sending only one professional? The team argues that at least two professionals are needed to meet the needs of a family and to avoid undue medicalisation. By sending a 'family' (the CIS team) to meet the client's family they attempted to provide a system of care which both supports and educates the family. They hope, in this way, to reduce the likelihood that the family will find itself unable to cope with future crises. In general this expectation is born out by the results of the study, although half the families reported 'some' and 29% 'many' further problems most of which had been resolved without the need for further professional help. Only 21% had been re-referred to the CIS between discharge and follow-up fifteen months later; these had required an average of only two further interviews half of them by one member of the team.

Unlike the 'open doors' described by Cooper (1979) there has been no tendency for the CIS to 'silt-up' over the years with long-term mentally ill patients who are more appropriately helped by rehabilitation services.

3   *Appropriateness.* Ninety-three percent of GPs, 97% of SWs and 83% of other professionals asserted that the client's home is the most appropriate venue in which to assess crises in the family. Only three caregivers, two of them consultant psychiatrists, thought 'hospital' the most appropriate place.

Most GPs and SWs thought a psychiatrist the most appropriate person to help families in crisis yet 40% of the teams did not include a psychiatrist. Close study of the reports on forty-six clients whose team did *not* include a psychiatrist revealed no misdiagnoses or mistreatments. None of these clients subsequently required admission, day care or out patient care and none were referred to the emergency clinic. No clients or referrers criticised the service for *not* including a psychiatrist although there were a few criticisms that the team, by including a doctor, may sometimes be medicalising normal life crises.

The short-term therapy was approved by half the clients who thought the number of visits was 'about right', a third would have liked more and 13% fewer visits from the team. Ninety-one percent agreed with the decision to end therapy and were satisfied with the advice given at that time.

Among fourteen psychotic patients referred to the service six were subsequently admitted for in-patient psychiatric care, one was referred to day hospital care and two refused further visits and further action was not deemed appropriate. The remaining five accepted and seemed to benefit from the care of the CIS and none was worse on follow-up. It would seem from these figures and from the comments of referrers and team members that, while many psychoses require hospital care there are some who will benefit from the family support provided by the CIS team and the involvement of the team was usually valued even if it subsequently led to admission.

4   *Equitability.* The service was criticised on the grounds that it does not accept referral of clients who are children, elderly or already receiving psychiatric care (unless referred by their psychiatrist). Staff argue that satisfactory alternative services already exist for these excluded groups. They see the CIS as complementing, not competing with, other services.

It was also suggested that the service should be open to clients without a family in Tower Hamlets. This questioned the basic assumption of a family-oriented service and caused the researcher to look closely at the thirty-four clients whose families declined or were not available to meet with the team. They seem to have benefited from and valued the help of the service as much as those with co-operative families! It may be that those who lack family support are in just as much, if not greater need, of counselling than those with family support but it also seems likely that individual one-to-one counselling would have been a more cost-effective way of meeting their needs.

5   *Acceptability.* The CIS attempts to become acceptable to the local population by visiting the client's home, operating from a base in the community, encouraging non-psychiatric referrals and not including a psychiatrist in 40% of teams. Only one referrer thought that a client had been stigmatised as a consequence of referral and 55% thought that stigma had been reduced (perhaps because psychiatrists, when present, often reassure families that the client is *not* mentally ill). Even so a third of clients had been apprehensive about the first visit and 13% had found this 'difficult' (two-thirds, on the other hand, found it 'easy'). Clients from ethnic minority groups may find the service less acceptable than those from the parent population because of the cultural differences that exist between clients and CIS staff (and staff of most other services). One GP who works mainly with patients from Bangladesh had made no referrals to the service on the grounds that he did not think it suitable for his patients and the proportion of clients from Bangladesh referred to the CIS (3.1%) is substantially smaller than the proportion in the parent population (c. 9%).

6   *Accessibility.* Most referrers rated the CIS as 'easily accessible at all times'. This was most apparent to social workers and other non-doctors whose direct access to other psychiatric services is limited because most of these will only accept referral from a GP or other doctor.

The CIS is not currently able to provide twenty-four-hour cover and most referrers think that this is unsatisfactory. On the other hand only 5% of clients were dissatisfied with delays in setting up the initial visit.

One referrer and several clients suggested that the CIS should be open to self-referral. This would improve accessibility but staff feared that it would lead to overload and to inappropriate use of a service which prefers to back up the open doors provided by GPs, SWs and the existing emergency clinic.

If primary carers are to continue to control access to the service it is important for them to have a good knowledge of it. Forty-seven percent of referrers agreed that there was a lack of publicity and, of the seven GPs who had made no referrals to the service, five requested further information and only one said that he would 'probably not' make a referral in the future.

Discussion

The CIS serves a population who are, in general, younger and more likely to be female and have partners than most psychiatric in-patients and long-term mentally ill people. It focusses, therefore, on a group who rather than being severely mentally ill themselves may have special potential for the prevention of mental illness in future generations. On the other hand the service may not be reaching the older, unattached members of the community whose need for psychiatric help is greatest.

In the absence of a satisfactory control group any conclusions drawn regarding the efficacy of the service provided by the Tower Hamlets CIS must be cautious.

Overall comments by both clients and referrers tended to be very positive and to reflect a high degree of satisfaction with the service for the purpose for which it was set up, crisis intervention. The findings strongly suggest, though they cannot prove, that the service substantially reduces the risk of suicide, mental hospital admission and family break-up, while improving the family's ability to cope with future crises. Working with the service was also seen as a valuable training experience for members of the caring professions.

Criticisms of the service were few. They included a wish for more information to referrers and more clarity in the information that is given to them about the service; several clients would have liked the support from the service to have continued for longer than it did and several clients and referrers thought that the service should be made available to a wider range of clients and should be extended to other districts. Doubts were expressed concerning the ability of staff from the United Kingdom to understand and communicate with families from Bangladesh.

These findings have proved useful in persuading the DHS to continue funding for a consultant in community psychiatry in the borough. A new psychiatric service for patients from Bangladesh is being set up with Sylheti-speaking staff and it is hoped that this group will take part as team members within the CIS when appropriate.

In 1981 the Crisis Intervention Service won the Joint Care Award for the best joint health and social service in Britain. Even so, during the late 1980s and 1990s public awareness of the dangers of child abuse along with criticisms of social services for failing to recognise or prevent such abuse gave rise to a major change in the distribution of social services. In Tower Hamlets the social workers were unable to continue to play a central role in the CIS. The Local Health Authority took over responsibility for the service and the community office was relocated within hospital premises. CMP retired from his leadership role in 1997 but returned to visit the Crisis Service five years later. The staff were as keen as ever and were surprised to learn that their service now bore little resemblance to the original. Like most psychiatric crisis services it provided domiciliary assessment and treatment of psychiatric patients on a one-to-one basis but the preventive and family orientation had ceased.

Acknowledgements

This study was carried out with the help of a grant from the Research Department of the Department of Health. Thanks are due to Dr Gillian Waldron for carrying out the diagnostic assessments, to Diana Bredenkamp for sensitive interviewing, to Ann Tyrrell for typing numerous handwritten drafts and to the clients and referrers who were kind enough to answer our questions.

References

Cooper, J. E. *Crisis Admission Units and Emergency Psychiatric Services.* Basic Books, New York, 1979.

Cooper, M. *Essential Research Findings in Counselling and Psychotherapy: The Facts Are Friendly.* Sage, London, 2008.

Langsley, D. G., Machotka, P. S. and Cowenhalf, K. Avoiding mental hospital admission: a follow-up study. *American Journal of Psychiatry* 127, 127–130, 1971.

Parkes, C. M. (1992) Services for families in crisis in Tower Hamlets: evaluation by general practitioners and social workers. *Psychiatric Bulletin* 16(12) 748–750.

Ratna, L. *The Practice of Crisis Intervention.* League of Friends, Napsbury Hospital, St Albans, 1978.

Reynolds, I., Jones, J. E. and Barry, D. W. A crisis team for the mentally ill: the effect on patients, relations and admissions. *Medical Journal of Australia* 152(12), 646–652, 1990.

DEATH AND DYING

I visited my dear friend, Dame Cicely Saunders, former nurse, social worker and physician, six days before she died in the hospice (St Christopher's, Sydenham) that she had created as a 'test bed', a new model of care for people approaching the end of their lives. Now it was Cicely's turn to test the death bed and she would not have been human if she had not been afraid. She knew that it was a myth to believe that 'everyone dies happy in a hospice' and she made no pretence that she viewed her death with equanimity. I had no certainty to assuage her doubts but it seemed to help us both that she had shared them.

We held hands and reminisced about the early days of hospice when nothing was set in stone. Each of the assumptions that had determined how people were treated at the end of life needed to be questioned and either reinforced or set aside. Nothing was taken for granted. We had the freedom to do it our way but were all too aware of our own limitations. I had the privilege of chairing a weekly meeting of the staff in which we challenged, argued and experimented. For instance: should doctors wear white coats? At that time we had doctors and medical students visiting for one month; we dressed them in white coats for two weeks, they then took off their coats for the next two weeks. They were surprised to find that patients were much more at ease and confiding with them in normal dress. In this, as in much else, it was the patients' views that mattered to Cicely and it was she who had the final say.

At our last meeting she thanked me for making the hospice 'respectable' by giving my support at a time when the medical establishment was suspicious of this young religious enthusiast who knew little about research. I had never thought of myself as an establishment figure but what she meant was that she had needed my credibility as a practical researcher to convince the establishment (in the person of the Queen's physician, Sir Harold Himsworth, KCB, FRS) to take her seriously. Cicely was a clinician first and last, and when she lectured it was about her patients. When politicians and other VIPs visited the hospice it was the patients who persuaded them that what we were doing was worthwhile and, in the end, it was not I and the other early researchers (notably John Hinton and Robert Twycross) who 'sold hospice' but the patients. They had experienced enough of the old model of medical care to appreciate the new. 'I love this place', said one patient, '. . . it's like a resort!' 'Yes,' said another, '. . . a last resort'.

I was surprised that, at our meeting, Cicely did not mention God, who had been central to her life in the early days, but I suspect she didn't need to. We had both changed over the years. She to become more tolerant of doubt, and indeed to admit her own, and I to become less aggressively atheistic and to share with her my speculation that God could best be found in the recognition of meaning in life and, by implication, death. We both recognised that we had been privileged to become part of an historical process.

I returned to the hospice on the day after her death to meet with the staff and attend a short service in the chapel. Len Lunn, the hospice chaplain and Cicely's confidante, shared with us his opinion that this remarkable lady had died peacefully in a way that, at her hospice, was unremarkable.

St Christopher's was a small institution and most of my researches in the first few years were small sample studies carried out on a shoestring budget. Today they have all been replicated by bigger and better studies. Indeed as I look back I am astonished that we achieved so much with so little. All I can say is that, with all its faults, St Christopher's and its researchers were 'good enough' to get things moving. These were the seeds from which an oak tree was to grow. Gradually, over the years, Cicely's four-page leaflet on 'drugs commonly used at St Christopher's Hospice', which was our first handout to visiting doctors, evolved into the massive *Oxford Textbook of Palliative Care*. A new speciality had been born.

At St Christopher's my work as a liaison psychiatrist was complicated by the fact that, although many of their problems were complex, most of the patients whom I saw did not survive for more than a few weeks; consequently it was not I but the nurses who conducted any psychotherapy that was needed. My main function was to act as a consultant to the staff and to provide them with insights into the problems of the patients and their families. Apart from studies of bereaved family members, much of my research was to evaluate the various kinds of innovative service that was being pioneered.

In Part 3 I have included only two of the many articles that resulted. The first reveals the wide range of issues faced by patients near the end of their lives and the second, published in 1979, gives a glimpse of the way the hospice was organised and the service viewed by the families whom we met.

CHAPTER 17

ATTACHMENT AND AUTONOMY AT THE END OF LIFE

From R. Gosling (ed.) *Support, innovation and autonomy* (pp. 151–166). London: Tavistock, 1973.

This was the second paper about my researches at St Christopher's Hospice. The first had compared doctors' predictions of the likely length of survival of patients admitted to the hospice with the patients' actual length of survival (Parkes 1972).On the whole we expected our patients to live twice as long as they did, but even if we had halved our guesses they would have been extremely unreliable. When this study was repeated thirty-one years later the results of doctors' predictions were no better (Glare et al. 2003).

I have included this second paper because it gives us a glimpse of St Christopher's Hospice during the first five years of its existence and before it became famous. At that time we had no home care service and patients stayed an average of thirty-two days on the wards. This gave time for the staff to get to know them and their families well. The introduction of home care halved the length of stay on the wards within a year. Henceforth it was the home-care staff who were to give most support to the families.

In the 1970s, and still today, most of the literature on the dying assumes that fear of death is the main cause of stress in people with life-threatening illness. As we shall see, my study threw doubt on that supposition. Indeed I was gradually to realise that, when care is good, it is probably less stressful to be a patient than to be a close relative. The patient's troubles were soon over, those of the family might just be beginning. It became part of my role at the hospice to fly a flag for the families and to attempt to reframe the family (which includes the patient) as the unit of care. This said, my focus in this paper was on the patient's fears and possible ways to alleviate them. Only in the final section did I make a plea for a new kind of professional trained to recognise the potentially competing needs of patients, families and staff. This orientation was to emerge more clearly in the years to come.

In Bowlby's theory of attachment behaviour (Bowlby 1969) an important component is the notion that the biological function of the child's first tie to its mother is protection from danger. The growing child, as he begins to explore and examine unfamiliar aspects of the world around him, refers repeatedly to his mother or mother-substitute for confirmation that what he is doing is safe; and his mother remains watchful for signs of danger while encouraging him in those activities which she approves as secure. In this way, as time passes, he becomes increasingly autonomous until both mother and child are able to tolerate prolonged separation from each other without undue anxiety.

Bowlby distinguishes this autonomy from the 'detachment' which occurs when a child has been deserted or left for a long period in an unfamiliar and therefore

potentially dangerous environment. 'Detachment' is the end result of painful grieving whose intensity far exceeds the tolerance of the young child; its character is
revealed by the way it affects the child's relationships with others including his own
mother if she should return. John, the two-year-old boy filmed by the Robertsons,
pointedly avoided his mother after only nine days of separation from her (Robertson and Robertson 1969). Whereas the 'autonomous' relationship is characterized
by trust and attachment behaviour is capable of being instantly renewed after periods of separation or in situations of danger, excessive separation on the other hand
leaves the child distrustful of relationships and either compulsively independent
('detached') or excessively clinging.

The persistence of such patterns can be expected to affect the nature of all subsequent relationships, but more especially it can be expected to determine how the
individual copes with situations of danger throughout his life. Much research is
needed to confirm and develop in full the implications of this theory. [*This has now
been carried out.*]

One situation of unequivocal danger is the situation of the person who is in the
late stages of an illness which is normally fatal and is not amenable to curative
treatment.

The information and experience described here were obtained in two ways: in the
course of clinical work with sixty-six patients with cancer and a few with multiple
sclerosis at a small in-patient unit for terminal care, St Christopher's Hospital, Sydenham, where many, but not all, patients have incurable cancers . . . and in the course
of a study of cancer care in South London. The special characteristics of care at the
in-patient unit and the effect of this upon the patients and relatives . . . accepts the fact
that many patients will remain within the institution until they die and it attempts to
provide a setting in which the physical needs of the patient can be met while providing
him with a good chance of realizing whatever capacity he may have for achieving a
satisfactory end to his life. . . . The average length of stay of patients in this unit is only
thirty-eight days and a prognosis of six weeks or less is a condition for admission.

The focus of attention is upon the interaction between patients and staff,
patients and relatives and relatives and staff and we attempt, by working at these
interfaces, to reduce the anxiety which is so often found in the dying patient and all
who are associated with him. We hope, by doing this, to improve the quality of life
that remains and to help the whole family to undergo the major changes which are
being forced upon them by the sickness and death of one of its members.

The patients seen by the writer are a small proportion of the total patient
population – in the region of 13 per cent. They are referred for a wide variety of
reasons by the hospital staff at the time of a weekly ward consultation. In many
cases one or two interviews are all that is carried out; in about one-third, however,
regular weekly interviews over many weeks enable the writer to help the patient
and/or his relatives through the inevitable phases of physical deterioration and in
so doing to study how they cope psychologically with the situation.

The second source of data is a study of cancer care in the boroughs of Lewisham
and Bromley. Two hundred men and women under the age of sixty-five who had
lost a spouse from cancer were interviewed between nine and twelve months after
the event, and a retrospective account obtained of the happenings leading up to the
death along with details of the reactions of patient and spouse.

Both of these studies have provided us with information about the medical
attendants and the institutions in which they worked, as well as information about
the dying patient and his relatives. In this paper attention will be confined to the
terminal period of care, the period from the end of active or curative treatment to

the death of the patient. In the Lewisham survey only 3.5 per cent of patients had died whilst still under active treatment. It is, therefore, the rule for cancer patients, unlike patients suffering from most other diseases, to be looked after by people who are not expecting them to survive or doing anything to prolong their life.

The end of active treatment is normally determined by the doctors who then inform the close relatives. It is not usually communicated directly to the patient at all except in institutions, such as St Christopher's, where an attempt is made to help each patient to become aware of the true situation. We have no means of knowing for certain what proportion of cancer patients realize from the outset that the termination of radio-therapy or similar treatment indicates that the doctors have given up hope of cure. In the Lewisham study 21 per cent of patients were thought by their spouses to have had full insight into their prognosis; but Hinton (1963), who asked direct questions of 102 patients in a general hospital during the months preceding their deaths, claims that 49 per cent 'soon showed that they were neither ignorant nor evasive of the fact that their illness might be fatal'.

During the terminal period the patient is impelled by conflicting pressures to deny and to accept the true situation. These pressures arise both outside and inside himself. Outside himself are the relatives (and often the doctors and nurses as well) trying to reassure him that all is well but also showing a singular reluctance to talk about the future. In addition it is often possible for him to witness the deterioration and death of other patients who are being similarly reassured.

The patient is himself most anxious to believe that he is getting better and to accept the reassurance of others. But he is losing weight and becoming steadily weaker; the varying physical symptoms which he has are getting worse, not better. The widespread use of morphine and diamorphine for terminal cancer may contribute to loss of drive. As time passes his appetite for food and all the other pleasures of life declines, while the drugs necessary to control his symptoms increase (78 per cent of cancer patients admitted to the in-patient unit are given diamorphine at some time during their terminal illness) and his wish to survive is likely to grow less. Even in the absence of severe pain or other distressing symptoms (which are seldom unrelieved in good circumstances of care), the will to live tends to decline as the disease progresses until the time comes when the patient does not greatly care what happens to him – the ego has lost its dynamic, both pleasure and distress are past and the patient can remain relatively peaceful and untroubled until death completes the process of dissolution.

It will be obvious, from what has been said, that the dying patient is at the centre of a changing field of forces which tend to press him, as time goes by, towards rather than away from realizing the fact that he is dying. His reaction, therefore, constitutes a process rather than a state, and the pattern which it takes will be governed by a number of internal and external factors.

Rochlin (1967) claims that no man can fully accept the reality of his own death and that all apparent acceptance is a defence. This kind of statement is, of course, impossible to prove or disprove and reflects the particular theoretical viewpoint of its author who sees the fear of death as the primary fear which underlies a great deal of human behaviour. Experience with terminal patients, however, does not suggest that the fear of death is either as simple or as all-pervading as Rochlin would have it. True, fears of one sort or another are very common but they can usually be attributed to one of a limited number of sources.

Among sixty-one patients seen by the writer during the past year forty-seven (77 per cent) discussed fears. The figures given in this chapter, of course, only include those fears mentioned to the writer. No systematic attempt was made to ascertain whether each patient had or had not each of the fears listed, and none was made to find out how frequent such fears were among patients who were not singled out to be seen by the writer. These [fears] could be classified into one of the following categories:

(a) Fear of separation from loved people, homes or jobs (38 per cent or more), for example separation anxiety, homesickness and so forth.
(b) Fear of being unable to complete some unfinished task or responsibility (10 per cent) – 'There's so much left to be done.'
(c) Fear of the consequences of the patient's death for his dependants (20 per cent) – 'What will become of them?'
(d) Fear of becoming dependent on others, of losing control of physical faculties, of 'being a nuisance' (23 per cent).
(e) Fear of pain or mutilation (7 per cent).
(f) In addition there were nine patients (15 per cent) who were fearful but who never specified what it was they were afraid of. Several seemed anxious to be reassured of their own worth, and one might conclude that, as religious persons, they were afraid of the judgement of God. More often, however, they seemed afraid of other unknown things that they must face at the time of or after death and of their incapacity to cope with these. It is this last fear, fear of the unknown, which comes closest to what most people mean by the fear of death.

In attempting to help the dying patient it is necessary to bear in mind each of these possible fears, even when they are not directly expressed. It is not always possible to deal effectively with all of these fears, but there are no cases for whom nothing can be done . . . [We can now consider] some of the ways effective help can be given.

In brief, *fears of separation and loss of loved persons and possessions* are a realistic and proper cause of anticipatory grief. With permission and encouragement from those around, the patient will often express appropriate sorrow and then go on to enjoy the life that remains to him.

Fear of failure to complete life tasks may lead the patient to carry out what Butler (1963) terms 'the life review'. This consists of a revision of significant problems in the patient's life in order, effectively, to deal with those that are soluble and to acknowledge and accept those that are insoluble. A psychotherapist who helps him to do this may be surprised at the speed at which chronic psycho-dynamic problems are 'worked through' as if the anticipation of dying has released the patient from the repetition compulsion. My own observations support Aldrich's (1963) contention that patients with lifelong neurotic symptoms may lose them at the time of a terminal illness.

Fears of ill that may befall one's dependants are sometimes realistic and practical arrangements may have to be made. Often, however, these fears hide a wish to retain caregiving roles for as long as possible. The dying wife and mother needs to be reassured that she is still needed by her family. As the illness progresses, however, she will find it increasingly difficult to meet these needs and in later stages the 'disengagement' which has been reported as characteristic of ageing (Cumming and Henry 1961) may take place. One mother who had previously tried to retain control of her newly married daughter later confessed to me that she preferred her daughter to keep her troubles to herself as she needed to remain 'peaceful'.

Fears of losing control of physical functions seem to derive mainly from fantasies of the effects of this loss of control on those around. Incontinence is seen as disgraceful, confusion as stupid and the expression of emotions as 'letting the side down'. Dying is itself sometimes seen as a disgrace. Patients who have been in pain are often more afraid of disgracing themselves by crying aloud than they are of the pain itself. One is reminded of the frightened parachutists described by Basowitz, Karchin, Persky and Grinker (1954) who were more afraid of disgracing themselves by not jumping than they were of killing themselves by jumping. Reassurance here comes from a realization that in this particular environment behaviour which would be disapproved of elsewhere is both expected and taken for granted. Even death itself is treated in a matter-of-fact way and permitted to take place in an open ward rather than being hushed up like a guilty secret.

Fear of physical pain or mutilation is often unrealistic, but when it is not, it may still be accepted if treated without alarm. If we react with disgust, horror or even pity to a patient he will soon come to see himself as disgusting, horrible or pitiful. If, on the other hand, we are not over-concerned by the appearance or malfunctioning of our patients' bodies they will learn to ignore them too. Ideally the patient needs to relinquish his attachment to his body as an attachment object. It helps if he can be reassured that the important part of himself remains.

Fear of the unknown or unfamiliar is a primary emotion. We see it in animals and young children and it is one of the factors Bowlby (1969) lists as a cause of attachment behaviour. For the cancer patient many things are likely to be unfamiliar and potentially dangerous or painful. If conditions of care are good, pain will rarely be allowed to become severe, and most of the distressing symptoms caused by cancer can be prevented or relieved. Many of the cancer patient's fears and fantasies are, therefore, likely to be unjustified, and the peace of a terminal ward will often convince him of this.

But however much he is reassured about the illness itself, the patient cannot know what will become of him after death and this remains a source of anxiety. Religious dogmas provide some vague notions but very little precise information about the life hereafter. Nevertheless it is probably no coincidence that the four best-known institutions for terminal care in London are all run by religious foundations.

The important reassurance which religious faith seems to give is a blanket assurance that life and death are meaningful – are part of a scheme of things which is benevolent towards mankind in general and towards the dying patient in particular. The Christian nurse or nun may not know exactly what happens after death but she does know that whatever it is will be 'all right'.

In an important sense the dying patient is in a similar situation to the young child when faced with a new, unfamiliar and therefore potentially dangerous situation. If he lacks strong convictions of his own regarding the situation he will turn to those whom he respects, doctors, nurses or close relatives, to see whether they are at ease or frightened. He is highly sensitive to the clues which they emit and easily frightened by their fears. On the other hand he can usually be reassured by them if they recognize his need for support. In practice it seems that the support which he needs most is the same support that a frightened child needs from his mother – bodily contact. The nurse or doctor in a terminal care ward frequently finds himself holding the hand or putting an arm round the shoulders of an anxious patient. Such behaviour is often more reassuring than any amount of reasoned discussion.

Bowlby (1969) lists the conditions which elicit attachment in the child: (a) conditions of the child: fatigue, hunger, ill health, pain or cold; (b) whereabouts or behaviour of the mother or mother-substitute, particularly if she is absent for any length of time, departing or discouraging of proximity; and (c) other environmental conditions or particularly alarming events or rebuffs from others.

Many of these conditions are likely to affect the terminal patient. Fatigue, ill health and pain, separation from loved family and friends and alarming and unfamiliar situations are the rule; and so it is not surprising to find a tendency to cling to those persons who are in the position of mother-substitutes, be they close relatives or medical attendants.

The terminal patient is not, of course, a frightened child and these remarks can only be applied in a general sense. In fact, there is great variation in the amount and type of support which each individual patient requires. However I can cite one example in which an infantile behaviour pattern became very obvious as death approached. This was related to me by a Scandinavian colleague who works in a cancer hospital. The patient was a young man of nineteen with leukaemia who had been born in Poland and been brought by his parents to live in Norway at the age of three. During his early childhood he spoke Polish, but after coming to Norway he was brought up as Norwegian and by the time he reached his teens he appeared to have forgotten how to speak Polish. His family members were extremely surprised when, in the last two weeks of his life, when he was very weak and exhausted by his illness, he chose to speak nothing but Polish so that a Polish nurse had to be found to help look after him.

As the child grows older he normally becomes able to tolerate increasing degrees of separation from his mother and to tackle the everyday problems and dangers of life without constant feedback of reassurance from a mother figure. But healthy development also requires that when problems and dangers exceed everyday levels of complexity the individual can make use of other members of society, usually those to whom he remains most closely attached, in order to find new methods of mastery. It is a sign of healthy autonomy that a person can ask for help when it is needed and can put himself in the hands of others when sickness makes him physically helpless.

The autonomous person trusts himself and trusts others. He shows what Ainsworth (1967) calls 'secure attachment' and Erikson (1963) calls 'basic trust'. He can even accept defeat and failure without losing faith in the ultimate goodness of things. 'After all,' one hears people say, 'it's not as if the world had come to an end'. And yet, for the dying patient, it seems that the world is coming to an end. The ability to face one's own demise seems to be the acid test of autonomy. And it is not only a test of the autonomy of the patient, it is a test of the institution in which he dies. To be truly effective an institution, be it a home or a hospital, needs to be [as one patient put it] 'a safe place to die in'. A place in which death is not seen as a great predator that is waiting to eat us all up but as a necessary and fitting end to the accomplishment of living.

Why do so many people fail to achieve a calm acceptance of their own coming death? At St Christopher's Hospice, where staff are much more 'open' with the patient than in most settings and a larger proportion of patients do achieve full insight, the commonest reason for failure seems to be lack of time. Whether he has been nursed at home or in a surgical or radio-therapy ward of a hospital, the patient and those around him are likely to have maintained an expectation of recovery until his illness has reached the point when he is so sick that he no longer cares what happens. This is not a bad way to die, but it does leave the surviving relatives with a feeling of strain and estrangement from the patient resulting from the enforced secrecy. 'We never had a secret between us before and I wasted a whole year by not telling him,' said one widow. Her husband discovered the truth shortly before his death thanks to a chance remark made by his daughter. He was very angry with his wife for not telling him herself and died a bitter and disgruntled man. His wife never had time to repair the rift.

Clearly it takes time for patient and family to work through the numerous problems attending a coming bereavement. Even when a patient becomes aware of the true situation in plenty of time he may not achieve the calm acceptance that I have described. Like the child in an alarming situation he may cling excessively or he may attempt a compulsive independence which makes his physical helplessness particularly pitiful. Both of these methods of coping may prevent the patient from receiving appropriate care. For instance, the patient who clings to his wife may refuse to enter hospital for fear of separation from her even though he knows that she is incapable of ministering to his needs. A sixty-one-year-old house painter had a haemoptysis in 1966 and was found to have a carcinoma of the bronchus for which he was treated by irradiation. He improved for a while but in the summer of 1968 he developed pains in his chest and again began to feel ill. Although he had not been told his diagnosis he became frightened and demanding, clinging to his wife and refusing to re-enter hospital for treatment.

Subsequently his condition deteriorated, the pain became severe and he developed persistent vomiting and diarrhoea. He would not allow his wife out of the house even to go shopping and insisted on being got out of bed and walked around the room at night with her support. He refused to allow a nurse to call and remained in a state of restless anxiety being nursed by his wife until his death on the night before Christmas. By this time she was praying for death to release him from his misery. Fortunately this kind of story is not common and the majority of cancer patients who choose to die at home accept the support of the general practitioner and district nursing services. The burden on the spouse, though great, seems to give her an opportunity to make restitution for any previous deficiency which may have existed in the marital relationship.

Compulsive independence is particularly problematic when the patient is forced by his illness to accept the help of others. AJ suffered from a condition which produced a gradually progressive paralysis of all his voluntary muscles so that he became unable to move at all and able to talk only in a whisper. Married, with two children, he had always been a strict, authoritarian Welshman with extremely high standards for himself and others. Obsessionally clean, he had difficulty in making close relationships and placed high value on self-reliance and self-discipline.

His father had died from the same disease and was said to have reacted to it by becoming aggressive and bitter towards AJ and his siblings. His wife asserted that he had never recovered from this and had become a person with little trust in the strength of others and a great need to control everything himself.

He reacted to his illness by becoming increasingly irritable and aggressive towards his wife and children. He was intolerant of his own helplessness, hated being helped and resented the people who helped him. As his ability to move diminished he attempted to exert an ever-more-rigid control over his family. At first his wife was very sympathetic and understanding, but she found herself having to protect the children from him and gradually became angry and resentful. One of his sons became withdrawn and lost all affection for him, the other continued to worry about him and suffered in consequence.

This was the situation at the time of his admission to hospital and it continued to spoil his weekends at home until his wife sought help from the ward staff. On the ward Mr J was cooperative and quiet. The nurses regarded him as a 'good patient' because he made few demands upon them and made every effort to help himself. He did not talk about his domestic difficulties and although he often seemed morose, particularly after his weekends at home, he was not unduly aggressive towards the nurses. I found him an intelligent man who was well aware of the nature of his condition and its inevitable outcome. He was annoyed when he heard that his wife had discussed his difficulties with me and remained stubbornly self-reliant, refusing to discuss his relationship problems. It was clear that he did not intend to trust anybody and he denied having any needs of his own. The only way I could get him to talk about himself was by asking for his help in studying the care of patients with his type of disease. Approached in this way he talked volubly and at length about the feelings of frustration engendered by the illness. 'You have to accept,' he said, 'but you must never give in. The physical has to be accepted but the psychological must not on any account be accepted.' By thus splitting mind and body he partially succeeded in retaining his independence.

I won't say that we solved Mr J's problem. He remained alienated from his family, but established very good relationships with the ward staff, who were prepared to respect the limits of his capacity for empathy. He was happiest when, along with two other patients who were in a similar condition, he went for an invalid holiday on the coast. There he found that he could still 'compete' with others who were 'in the same boat' and therefore 'understood'.

The self-defeating quality of this compulsively self-reliant reaction can be illustrated by a small, everyday event which must have been repeated, with variations, on numerous occasions. I was sitting talking to Mr J and I noticed that his hair had fallen forward and was getting into his eyes and causing him to blink. Because I knew of his resentment of dependency I hesitated to offer to comb it back, but when, after a few minutes, I did offer he replied, 'I wondered when you were going to do that.' I said, 'It must be difficult to ask people to do a thing like that,' and when he agreed I pointed out that it had also been hard for me to offer my help to so independent a person. He said that such situations make him feel angry, but because he cannot shout any more it is difficult to show people how he feels.

Both the clinging and the compulsively independent reaction to illness are readily understandable in terms of attachment theory and it is reasonable to postulate that both of them may result from the incomplete establishment of autonomy with attachment in childhood. But just as these attitudes in a patient may pose a problem to the institution, so the same attitudes in the institution may pose a problem to the patient. A patient whose relatives and nurses are over-solicitous may rightly get the impression that it is they who are clinging to him and not he to them. PM Turquet, in discussing [a draft of] this paper, has suggested that it is part of the patient's role to reassure relatives and staff that there is no need for anxiety.

This type of heroic stance may be sustained to the end and produces a reaction of gratitude and admiration in others. Mothering or maternal caretaking behaviour may be appropriate in its place, but the nurse who deals with her own inadequacies by infantilizing her patients and ignoring their needs for autonomy will fool nobody. Likewise the patient whose relatives and medical attendants insist that he is much more independent than he really is and who is constantly being adjured not to 'give up' and to 'fight on' must inevitably feel unsupported and a disappointment to all. Often, it seems, we attempt to cope with our own feelings of helplessness by clinging excessively or by remaining compulsively independent of our patients. Examples of the effects of this could be given, but the individuals in question would be too readily identifiable.

I now have some evidence from discussion with staff members that this kind of problem is particularly likely to arise when the member herself suffered deprivation experiences in childhood. Yet these very experiences may motivate some to take up this kind of work and a person who has successfully mastered the effects of childhood separation may be particularly well qualified to help others through a similar experience.

I do not think there are easy answers to the problems of staff selection and training but I agree with Miller and Gwynne that it is necessary for institutions to provide for both attachment and autonomy and for each to arise out of the patients' real needs rather than those of the staff – a thorny problem, but no more insoluble in the hospital than it is in the nursery. A home can be an overprotective warehouse or a liberal greenhouse. Some families are characterized by their tendency to cling and infantilize their members, others by leaving each other alone to cope with life in the interests of individual freedom and autonomy.

It seems to me that there is a need . . . in settings such as this for a new kind of professional – someone who is not identified as psychotherapist, psychiatrist or social worker in the accepted sense but whose role it is to work with and through members of staff to improve and support the fit between the institution and the patient. A hospital exists to meet the needs of its patients, but it will soon cease to exist if it does not also meet the needs of its staff. At present it often seems that the staff have to choose between sacrificing the patient and sacrificing themselves. Traditionally the psychiatrist and psychotherapist are called in to help the patient whom staff members find distressing or disruptive. He needs special sanction if he is to break away from this role and to help staff members and patients' families. Aspects of this role could certainly be performed by properly trained nurses, clergy and social workers. But the medical hierarchy has become so securely established in our minds that many people are unwilling to talk to anyone but a doctor about matters of life and death. Yet for these people he may be able to fulfil several important functions: he may support and reassure them in their handling of the situation; he may make suggestions and help them to solve problems; he may share feelings of grief or regret at failure and in so doing make them more tolerable and less the object of defensive behaviour; he may also help to improve the level of their performance by approving successful actions and by helping to establish an appropriate value system. Last and least he may need to take over the handling of the situation from them if it is clear that they are unable to manage.

References

Ainsworth, M.D.S. *Infancy in Uganda: Infant Care and the Growth of Attachment.* The Johns Hopkins Press, Baltimore, MD, 1967.

Aldrich, C.K. The dying patient's grief. *Journal of the American Medical Association.* 184, 329, 1963.

Basowitz, H., Karchin, H.J., Persky, H. and Grinker, R.R. *Anxiety and Stress.* McGraw Hill, New York, 1954.

Bowlby, J. *Attachment and Loss. Volume I: Attachment.* Hogarth Press, London, 1969. Penguin Books, Harmondsworth, 1971.

Butler, R.N. The life review: an interpretation of reminiscence in the aged. *Psychiatry* 26, 65, 1963.

Cumming, E. and Henry, W.E. *Growing Old.* Basic Books, New York, 1961.

Erikson, E.E. *Childhood and Society.* W.W. Morton, New York, 1963.

Glare, P., Virik, K. et al. A systematic review of physicians' survival predictions in terminally ill cancer patients. *British Medical Journal* 327, 1–6, 26 July 2003.

Hinton, J.M. The physical and mental distress of the dying. *Quarterly Journal of Medicine* 32, 1963.

Parkes, C.M. Accuracy of predictions of survival in later states of cancer. *British Medical Journal* 2, 29–31, 1972.

Robertson, J. and Robertson, J. *John: Seventeen Months: For Nine Days in a Residential Nursery.* Film with booklet. Tavistock Institute of Human Relations, London, 1969.

Rochlin, G. *Griefs and Discontents: The Forces of Change.* Little Brown, New York, 1967.

CHAPTER 18

TERMINAL CARE: EVALUATION OF IN-PATIENT SERVICE AT ST CHRISTOPHER'S HOSPICE

Part I. Views of surviving spouse on effects of service on the patient

From *Postgraduate Medical Journal* 55: 517–522, 1979.

This is another example of a small-scale study that had a large impact. In the late 1960s few people had heard of St Christopher's Hospice and many of those who had were suspicious. I recall one doctor who, not knowing of my involvement, told me authoritatively that most of our patients were '. . . knocked out by large doses of diamorphine (heroin)'. The fear of drug addiction made many doctors hesitant to use opiates and, when they did, it was after cancer pains had become so severe that large doses were necessary to relieve them. At St Christopher's research had shown that regular doses to prevent pain from building up enabled us to keep the dosage low most of the time. If the need did increase with the progression of the disease, this was usually without serious side effects and, given the poor prognosis, addiction was not a problem.

This paper, which focussed on the dying patient, along with the companion paper, Part II (not included here), which examined the influence of the hospice care on the principal family members, helped to answer these criticisms and to give a realistic picture of the likely consequences of our in-patient care.

Summary

The surviving spouses of thirty-four patients who died of cancer at St Christopher's Hospice have been interviewed about thirteen months after the patients' deaths. The information given [about the patients] is compared with that obtained from thirty-four spouses of patients dying from cancer in other hospitals and matched with the St Christopher's group.

Patients at St Christopher's were less often thought to have suffered severe pain and other distress than at other hospitals, but pain relief was not bought at the cost of drug-induced confusion and patients at St Christopher's remained more mobile than did patients at other hospitals.

Hospice patients were more aware of chapel services and prayers than at other hospitals. None was said to have been upset by these and most were glad of them.

Despite the frequency of deaths in the Hospice, patients at St Christopher's were no more likely to be thought to have been 'upset' by such events than patients elsewhere or to have found their interactions with other patients anything but helpful.

Introduction

The term *hospice*, originally designating a house of hospitality for pilgrims, has acquired a fresh meaning since the inception in 1967 of St Christopher's Hospice in Sydenham under its medical director, Dr Cicely Saunders. Essential components, in her view, are small autonomous units (maximum 50–70 beds) having a high nurse:patient ratio; a mixture of patients including some long-stay and some brief admissions for pain control as well as patients admitted for terminal care; a home-care programme serving patients at home; spiritual support for staff and patients but avoiding dogmatism and rigid answers; a tradition of flexibility and open communication between staff and staff, staff and patients and staff and families; minute attention to the relief of pain and other symptoms; full use of volunteers from the local community; willingness to teach and conduct research when and where possible; and support for the family before and, where necessary, after the patient's death. *[Most patients received, and still receive, all care without payment and the small minority of 'private patients' were treated in the same wards and manner as the National Health Service patients.]*

This is a report of evaluations of the effects on patients of in-patient care only. These were made by surviving spouses of patients who died at St Christopher's Hospice during 1967–1971. They are compared with evaluations by spouses of a matched group of patients dying in other hospitals in the area. Effects of the in-patient service on the patients' spouses are reported in Part II . . . *[The Home Care Service was introduced during the course of this study and was evaluated in separate studies (Parkes 1980 and 1985).]*

Method

The families reported here are two subsamples of the 276 who were included in a survey of the patterns of terminal care in the South London boroughs of Lewisham and Bromley. They were located through the death registrations of patients under the age of sixty-five years who had died from cancer during the period of study. Surviving spouses were interviewed in their homes on average thirteen months after bereavement and systematic information obtained regarding the patients' terminal illness and the reactions of patients and spouses to each phase of care. Further details of the sample, interview methods, reliability testing and findings of that study are published elsewhere (Parkes 1978).

For the purposes of this study contact was attempted with the spouses of fifty-seven patients who had died at St Christopher's Hospice and to ask them to agree to a second interview. One could not be located and one other declined; fifty-five were re-interviewed. It was then attempted to match each of the re-interviewed St Christopher's patients with a patient who had died in another hospital. Matching criteria were age, sex, socio-economic status, duration of terminal period and severity of pain before the terminal period (for the purposes of this study the terminal period was the period from the end of active treatment to death). Second interviews with thirty-four matched pairs were eventually obtained.

Difficulty in matching resulted from the inclusion in the St Christopher's sample of a number of patients who had died within a few hours or days of admission. Only a few patients who had had similar brief periods of terminal care in other hospitals could be found.

The second interviews were semi-structured. That is to say the interviewer obtained answers to specific questions covering each aspect of the care provided during the terminal period in hospital or hospice but also encouraged the respondents to talk freely about this period of their lives and recorded their comments verbatim.

Results

Demographic characteristics of the matched pairs are shown in Table 18.1 along with comparable figures for the total sample from which they are drawn. It will be seen that in both settings and both samples there is a preponderance of male patients of mean age fifty-five years and with a normal distribution across social class groupings. Matching for age, sex, social class, severity of pain before terminal period and mean duration of terminal period is quite good except for a rather larger proportion of patients said to have had severe pain before admission to St Christopher's. The matched groups resemble the full sample on most points, the main difference being the greater amount of pre-terminal pain said to have been suffered by 42% of the full sample of St Christopher's patients and 32% of the matched sample.

Further evidence of successful matching comes from analysis of the data from the first interview which refers to the period of care before the terminal illness. Among thirty-one different measures there were no significant differences between the matched groups.

The process of admission

Several questions concerned the process of admission and the view which the patient had of the hospital before admission. St Christopher's Hospice had not been open

Table 18.1 Characteristics of matched pairs and full sample of cancer patients dying in hospital or hospice

	Matched pairs		Full sample	
	St Christopher's	*Other hospital*	*St Christopher's*	*Other hospital*
n	34	34	55	100
Sex				
Female	35%	35%	40%	34%
Male	65%	65%	60%	66%
Mean age (years) (respondent)	54·9	55·4	49·9	55·0
Socio-economic status				
Group I	12%	9%	11%	13%
Group II	9%	21%	13%	18%
Group III	50%	44%	47%	49%
Group IV	21%	24%	20%	16%
Group V	9%	3%	7%	5%
Severe or very severe pain before terminal period	32%	21%	42%	28%

for very long in 1969–1970 and was not widely known in the neighbourhood, in fact only two respondents said that they had heard of it before the patient's referral. By contrast, twenty-seven (79%) of the respondents whose spouse had been admitted to another hospital had previous experience of the hospital which was usually the same general hospital in which the initial diagnostic admission had taken place.

In six cases spouses of patients who were subsequently admitted to St Christopher's Hospice paid an initial visit. They reported that they had seen all they wished to see and been satisfied with the answers to their questions. None of the twenty-six whose spouses were admitted to the hospice without prior knowledge of the place answered 'Yes' to the question, 'If you had (visited the hospice) would you have changed your mind about admission?'

Despite their ignorance of the hospice, only one patient was said to have been reluctant to be admitted. By comparison, eight who entered other hospitals were reluctant or very reluctant.

In only three cases (two St Christopher's and one other hospital) was there said to have been difficulty in finding a bed and the mean delay before admission was 3.6 days at St Christopher's and 2.7 days at other hospitals (four patients in each setting had waited for more than one week).

Ward unit

Three patients in each setting were cared for in single rooms. Of the remainder, those at St Christopher's were nursed in small partitioned units of four to six beds, whereas those in other hospitals were in larger units (most often these contained eleven to twenty beds but in twenty-four the patient had been nursed on a ward of more than twenty beds). *[At this time patients in most hospitals in the United Kingdom were still nursed in large 'Florence Nightingale' wards].*

Severe pain during the terminal period was said to have been suffered by 48% of patients at other hospitals, and in 36% this was mostly unrelieved. At St Christopher's Hospice, however, the proportion who were said to have suffered severe pain was 18% ($p < 0.05$) and in only 9% was this mostly unrelieved.

Reports of distress reflected those of pain but even when this was taken into account patients at St Christopher's were said to have suffered less distress than those at other hospitals. Thus, confining attention to twenty patients at St Christopher's and eleven at other hospitals who were said to have had little or no pain, three at St Christopher's (15%) and six at other hospitals (55%) had apparently suffered moderate to severe distress (Fisher's Test, $p < 0.05$).

Lest it be thought that increased relief of pain and distress at St Christopher's Hospice is bought by 'knocking out' the patient with large doses of narcotic or tranquillizing drugs, assessments of the overall level of consciousness and mobility in the two settings were also compared. These are shown in Table 18.2 from which it is clear that consciousness is no more likely to be impaired at St Christopher's Hospice than at other hospitals and that patients are rather more likely than at other hospitals to be out of bed throughout the major part of their period in hospital . . .

Religious aspects

St Christopher's Hospice is 'a religious and medical foundation' and it is appropriate to consider how the religious component was perceived by the patients and

Table 18.2 Reported pain, impairment of consciousness and mobility
in the patient

	St Christopher's	Other hospital	P
Pain rated as severe or very severe	18%	48%	< 0·05
Consciousness –			
Fully alert	33%	16%	
Some impairment	44%	61%	n.s.
Very confused or unconscious	23%	23%	
Mobility –			
Confined to bed	61%	87%	< 0·05
Not bed-bound	39%	13%	

their spouses. *[At this time prayers were said by nursing staff on the wards in the morning and evening and daily services held by the Church of England chaplain in the chapel for those who wished to attend. Visiting priests took a weekly Roman Catholic Mass and others from many denominations were encouraged to attend when needed.]*

There was no evidence that patients admitted to St Christopher's were selected or selected themselves for admission because of their faith. Thus only four were said by their spouse to have had a 'strong' faith in God compared with seven admitted to other hospitals (not significant) and only four were regular weekly church attendees compared with six at other hospitals (not significant).

It is unusual for a hospital to lack a hospital chapel but only seven respondents whose spouses had died at 'other hospitals' knew of the existence of such a chapel in their hospital and in no case had the patient attended a service in the chapel. By contrast, thirty-two of the thirty-four whose spouses had died at St Christopher's Hospice knew of the existence of a chapel (P< p < 0.001) and in nine cases (27%) the patient was known to have attended a service . . .

At St Christopher's Hospice twenty-one (62%) respondents were aware that ward prayers were said, thirteen said the patient was 'glad' or 'very glad', eight 'neutral' and none thought he had regretted or been upset by the saying of prayers . . . *[Although few patients were neither regular church attendees nor did they take part in the chapel services, the overall attitude of both patients and their families was neutral or positive about the religious slant. Even so the nursing staff eventually discontinued daily prayers.*

Given the number of deaths on the wards at St Christopher's it was important to assess the impact of these deaths on other patients here and at other hospitals where deaths were less frequent on the wards.]

The proportion of all patients admitted who stay until they die at St Christopher's Hospice (c. 92%) is very much greater than at most other hospitals and the median length of stay is only eleven days. Even so, only fifteen of the respondents (44%) were aware that a death had occurred on the ward during the patient's period in hospital and most were not, apparently, upset by this. Figures for other hospitals are remarkably similar, thus eleven respondents knew of a death on the ward but only two patients were said to have been 'very upset'.

Discussion

The evaluation of any system of health care is difficult and no method is ideal. In focussing on information obtained from the patients' spouses some sources of error have been reduced but not others. Doctors and nurses, because they are part of the system, are likely to be biased in its favour, and patients themselves, while they are at the mercy of the system, can hardly be expected to be able to make an objective evaluation. By obtaining the information from surviving spouses thirteen months after the patients' deaths it was hoped to eliminate some of this bias.

But it would be unrealistic to pretend that the husbands and wives of patients who have died in a particular hospital are completely unbiased in their attitude to that hospital. The fact that they are likely to have played a part in obtaining the admission in the first place plus their need to believe that everything possible was done to help their spouses may have distorted their judgements. Conversely the bitterness and resentment which is a common feature of grief may well have made some of them excessively critical.

It seems, then, that one must doubt the validity of the data, at least as it is expressed in absolute terms. Fortunately it is not with absolute levels that this study is mainly concerned but with a comparison of two systems of care in both of which it seems reasonable to assume that similar bias exists. It is a basic premise underlying the study that in the statistical analysis such biases will have cancelled each other out.

For this reason it was particularly important to ensure that the samples were well matched and some lengths were gone to to ensure that this was the case. The slight bias which crept in despite the attempts to match for 'pain before terminal admission' would tend to go against the hypothesis that patients at St Christopher's suffer less pain than patients elsewhere and need not, therefore, cause disquiet.

But the more rigorous the matching criteria the less likely it is that the matched subgroups are truly representative of the parent populations from which they are drawn. Table 18.1, however, indicates that the matched subsamples in this study were not much different from the full samples. The main discrepancies are found in the full sample of patients cared for at St Christopher's which differ from the matched subsample in containing more patients who had pain problems before admission and more who died within a few hours or days of admission. Despite this, the full sample was reported as having less pain in St Christopher's than the subsample. It seems likely, therefore, that the methods of pain relief in use at the hospice are likely to succeed even in patients who have had severe pain before admission and in those who are only in the hospice for a short time.

Critics of the provision of special in-patient units for the terminally ill point to three supposed disadvantages of such places: (1) The 'death-house' image. It is suggested that such places are likely to get a reputation as places where 'nobody gets out alive' and that this will deter people who need their services from accepting admission. (2) The 'depressing' environment. It is suggested that any ward which contains more than a few dying patients will become gloomy and that patients will communicate to each other feelings of depression and doom. (3) The 'upsetting' effect of deaths on the ward. It is suggested that patients in a unit with a high death rate are much more likely to become aware of the death of other patients than at other hospitals and that this will produce unnecessary fear and distress.

These are important criticisms which deserve to be taken seriously. The first cannot be answered from the present data because the author has no information from people who may have refused admission. The fact that some patients do improve sufficiently well to return home and that 'open days' at the hospice are held with the aim of reducing horrific fantasies may go some way to eliminate the danger. None of the relatives of patients in this study who knew nothing of the hospice before admission subsequently regretted having agreed to the patients' admission and the policy of encouraging patients and family members to visit the hospice in advance may have helped to reassure some of those who had doubts (but again, the author has no data concerning any who might have been 'put off' by such a visit).

As to the second point. The data reported here certainly dispel the notion that patients at St Christopher's suffer more distress than patients elsewhere or that interactions between patients are likely to be seen as unhelpful rather than helpful. Relatives too, as . . . shown in Part II, report feeling less worry and distress than at other hospitals so that the picture of the terminal unit as a 'slough of despond' certainly does not apply in this setting.

Despite the high death rate at St Christopher's Hospice more than 50% of the respondents seem to have been unaware of the death of another patient while their husbands and wives were in the ward. At first sight this seems remarkable until one recalls the small size of the ward units (4–6 beds) in which the patients at St Christopher's Hospice are nursed. Clearly, the chances of knowing what happens to the other patients is much greater in a ward of twenty to forty beds than it is when the only people you get to know well are your neighbours in a four-to-six-bed unit. It is not possible to know for sure how many patients succeeded in concealing from their spouses the fact that they were upset by the death of another patient but in view of the amount of contact which they had with other patients and their families it seems unlikely to have been a large proportion. Because the death of one or more other patients was known in fifteen cases at St Christopher's and eleven cases elsewhere why were patients not more often said to be 'upset' by this? A possible explanation was given by one widow who thought that her husband had been reassured by the occurrence of deaths on the ward . . . 'Because it all seemed so simple and caused no upset'.

The new approaches to the relief of chronic pain adopted by Dr Saunders have been described earlier but little systematic evidence for their effectiveness has previously been published. The assessments of pain the respondents made in this study are obviously subject to retrospective error but independent interviewers did, at least, agree quite well and there is no reason to believe that any bias which had crept in affected the assessments of pain at St Christopher's any more than those at other hospitals. There seems to be good reason to accept the overall assertion that patients under care at St Christopher's Hospice suffered less severe pain than patients at other hospitals and that this result was achieved without 'slugging' the patients with huge doses of drugs so that they were more likely to be rendered immobile or unconscious than patients elsewhere.

How much of the improvement in pain relief is attributable to drugs and how much to the relief of psychological distress is hard to say. Pain is a psycho-biological phenomenon and, whatever physical causes may be behind it, it is very likely to be aggravated by fear, tension and anxiety. Relieve the anxiety, and the pain improves, relieve the pain, and the patient grows less anxious. With so many interacting factors it is not possible to know how much weight to attach to any one of them.

Traditionally the church has had a recognized role in providing a context of meaning for death, a set of rituals which are assumed to provide support to the dying and the bereaved and a community of clergy and others who see it as their role to comfort them. In present Western society, however, it can no longer be taken for granted that beliefs, rituals or guidance from the 'religious' community will be offered or, if offered, will be acceptable.

The present data certainly confirm the small part played by religion in the 'other hospitals' to which patients were admitted. At St Christopher's Hospice most respondents were at least aware that chapel services and ward prayers took place and that most patients were visited by clergy. It was rare for them to have regarded any of these practices as harmful or intrusive and about 33% felt that they had been helpful or very helpful. Among those who took a positive view were several who had not previously expressed much interest in religion. This conforms to general experience at the hospice where the aim is not seen as a militant attempt to produce 'death-bed conversions' and where confirmations and baptisms are rare. Nevertheless most staff members have religious convictions of their own which they see as giving meaning to their work and as enabling them to become vehicles for the expression of God's love for the dying and the bereaved.

St Christopher's Hospice is often spoken of as a 'community', a network of concerned persons who, through personal interaction with each other and with the patients and family members who seek their help, support each other in facing the fears and griefs which often accompany death and bereavement. To evaluate this component of hospice care it is necessary to examine the way it was experienced by the husbands and wives of the patients . . .

This was reported in Part II in which it was shown that the spouses of St Christopher's patients differed significantly from spouses dying in other hospitals in spending more time with the patients, talking to more members of staff, other patients and visitors, reporting less anxiety and psychosomatic accompaniments of anxiety before the patients' deaths and being less worried about pain, others hurting or harming the patients or about revealing their own fears to the patients. In view of the fact that most people feel more secure at home than in a hospital it is interesting to note that, from a checklist, 78% of the spouses at St Christopher's agreed that 'the hospital is like a family' compared with only 11% in other hospitals (p < 0.001).

References

Parkes, C. M. Home or hospital? Terminal care as seen by surviving spouses. *Journal of the Royal College of General Practitioners* 28, 19, 1978.

Parkes, C. M. Terminal care: evaluation of in-patient care at St Christopher's Hospice. Part II. Self-assessments of effects of the service on surviving spouses. *Postgraduate Medical Journal* 55, 523–527, 1979.

Parkes, C. M. Terminal care: evaluation of an advisory domiciliary service at St Christopher's Hospice. *Postgraduate Medical Journal* 56; 685–689, 1980.

Parkes, C. M. Terminal care: home, hospital, or hospice? *The Lancet* 155, 19 January 1985.

PART 4

DISASTERS

Disasters are not to be recommended. They are cruel and horrible situations which do not happen so often that we grow accustomed to them nor are they so uniform that we can generalise with much confidence; every disaster, like every bereavement, is different.

My involvement with disasters started in 1966 in Aberfan, Glamorganshire, where, after a night of rain, with 'a roar like a jet plane', an avalanche of liquefied black coal waste buried the village school, careered through several houses and piled up against the railway bank. A hundred and sixteen children and twenty-eight adults died. The small Welsh village was inundated with newspaper and television reporters, soon to be followed by well-meaning crowds of sympathetic bystanders whose cars blocked the approach roads and hampered the rescue operations. Friends urged me to offer my help but I was reluctant to join the fray. I phoned the Director of Psychiatric Services who passed me on to the Community Physician, Dr Robin Williams. He invited me to meet with him to discuss how psychological support to the bereaved families could be organised.

Five days after the disaster struck I made my first visit to a small linear community, lying in a valley between steep hills and dominated by its sole source of income, the coal mine. Several great tips of waste hung over the village. One of them had left a silent black scar down the side of the mountain and a field of coal slurry at the foot. A few broken walls jutted out. Everyone I met, the GPs, clergy, police, administrators and bereaved people were numb. None of us knew what to do. By the time I was ready to drive home I too was numb.

Years later I took part in a role play exercise in which I played the part of a man returning from hospital where his child had died. 'How was it?' said the person playing my wife; those were the words my wife had used when I had returned from Aberfan. I couldn't speak; then the tears came.

I have dwelt on these details for they show how even professionals can be traumatised by disasters. But there is a positive side too, just as there is in all of our work. In the longer term there is something very uplifting about sharing in the struggles and eventual recovery of an entire community.

In 1966 we knew little about disasters and nothing about PTSD but the small team around Audrey Davey, the Welsh family caseworker whom I had recruited, achieved a great deal and was very well liked. At the time of the first anniversary a BBC television journalist (Fyffe Robinson) who visited the village to assess progress and found much to complain about said that 'Audrey Davey was the best thing that had happened to Aberfan'. This opinion was echoed by the chair of the medical committee who, when the first year was coming to an end conducted a straw poll of the bereaved miners who voted strongly for her appointment to be renewed for a second year. Recovery set in during the course of the second year. Derek Nuttall (see p. 173), another member of our team, was chosen to be the first chair of the community association that was able to overcome much of the paralysis of decision making that had bedevilled the first year. Five years later Aberfan acted as host to other communities in the mining valleys at a conference on community development in 'The Year of the Valleys' (Ballard and Jones 1975).

Aberfan (1966) was to be followed by the Axbridge air crash (1973), the fire at the Bradford Football Club (1985), the capsize of the ferry *Herald of Free Enterprize* (1987) and the terrorist bombing of Pan American Flight 103 over Lockerbie (1988); each taught us something different and helped to prepare me for the larger-scale disasters, the Rwandan genocide (1994), the Indian Ocean Tsunami (2004), 9/11 (2001), the London bombings (2005) and the tsunami in Japan (2011).

In this section I have focussed on care in the aftermath of disasters and the services needed to support survivors. But the disasters caused by terrorism were to raise a new set of problems that will be considered in Part 5.

Reference

Ballard, P. H. and Jones, E. (eds.). *The Valleys Call: A Self-Examination by People of the South Wales Valleys during the Year of the Valleys, 1974.* Ron Jones Publications, Ferndale, Rhondda, 1975.

CHAPTER 19

BEREAVEMENT FOLLOWING DISASTERS

From M.S. Stroebe, R.O. Hansson, H. Schut and W. Stroebe (eds.) *Handbook of bereavement research and practice: advances in theory and intervention* (pp. 463–484). Washington DC: American Psychological Association, 2008.

Although this is a recent paper I have placed it first in this section because it draws together many of the lessons that I have learned from working in disaster areas.

It provides a frame of reference that may make it easier for the reader to understand the complex situations which are discussed in the earlier papers.

The course of bereavement can be particularly problematic when a death is sudden, unexpected and untimely (Stroebe and Schut 2002). Deaths caused by a disaster inevitably fit these criteria. If multiple deaths are involved, bodies mutilated or unrecovered, children are among the fatalities, the survivors witnessed horrific events and/or blamed themselves or others, the process of bereavement becomes even more complex and difficult. Losses of property, homes and livelihood together with the social disorganisation and continuing dangers that often follow disasters add to the burden. It follows that psychological help from outside the family, often from outside the disaster-stricken community and sometimes from outside the country, will be needed and should be given priority by caring services, both professional and voluntary.

This paper draws on experience and published research to identify the principal variables that influence the reaction of people bereaved by disasters and to examine those interventions that can be expected, before, during and after a disaster, to reduce the risk of lasting problems in individuals, families, communities and nations. . . . The field of bereavement is not confined to any one discipline. Psychologists, sociologists, anthropologists, psychiatrists, counsellors and leaders of various religions have all made valuable contributions to our understanding of the many problems that beset bereaved people. The simplistic methods of 'bereavement counselling' of the early days are long gone. In their place we have more sophisticated and broad-spectrum approaches, which include the building of trust, assessment of psychological, social and spiritual needs and the provision of a range of services to meet those needs. These approaches have special value in response to the many problems of disasters.

My own experience of disasters grew out of my research into the psychological consequences of bereavement and out of my involvement with hospice bereavement services and with the national organisation Cruse Bereavement Care. Inevitably I shall be writing about that experience and about the British scene, but this does not mean that there are not other services in other countries that are worthy of emulation. Anyone who has worked in a disaster area will be aware of the stream of support, goodwill and commitment to which disasters give rise.

Rivalries diminish, prejudices are put aside and collaboration between individuals and organisations is often possible and can bring help to large numbers of traumatised and bereaved people.

In Britain, voluntary services for bereaved people are available, without charge, in most parts of the country. The largest and most comprehensive is Cruse Bereavement Care, but there are also many independent local bereavement services and most hospices have their own, although some make use of their local branch of Cruse. At the last count, Cruse had 5,400 volunteers, backed by 121 paid staff members, to support bereaved people across England, Wales and Northern Ireland *[By 2008 Cruse in Scotland was independent but remained closely allied.]* Cruse's Bereavement Volunteers (BVs), most of whom have themselves suffered losses, are carefully selected, trained and supervised in their work. Through its central and 240 local services Cruse responded to 177,452 enquiries during 2004/2005, corresponding to approximately one-third of registered deaths.

Bereavement services have developed separately from the field of traumatic stress. In recent years, however, the occurrence of disasters, such as airline crashes, in which many have died but few injured people or witnesses have survived, has focussed attention on bereavement and led to the inclusion of bereavement support workers in disaster teams. In Britain this has led to a close collaboration between Cruse Bereavement Care, the Red Cross and the police's new model *Family Assistance Teams* who provide front-line support in the face of major disasters. Staffed by Family Liaison Officers (FLOs) with special training in the support of families at times of crisis and disaster, these elite teams set a high standard of humane support while maintaining their roles in the detection and prosecution of major crimes. Because their involvement is limited to the duration of the emergency, collaboration with other organisations that are in a position to provide longer-term care is essential. In Britain, in 1966, at the time of the Aberfan disaster, Post-Traumatic Stress Disorder had not been identified, psychiatrists and volunteer counsellors were regarded with suspicion and services aimed at supporting disaster victims and bereaved families were virtually non-existent. By 2001, teams of FLOs and BVs were ready to be rapidly mobilised in response to 9/11, the Indian Ocean Tsunami and the London bombs of July 2005. Prejudice against psychiatric services continue but these alternatives have proved their worth and are now a regular part of the response to major incidents.

Although I have carried out little systematic research in this field I have been involved in the planning of responses, assessment of need and provision of help, after eleven disasters, over a period of forty years.

My experience ranges from small-scale disasters such as the consequences of a helicopter crash into an oil rig, which took twelve lives, to the Rwandan genocide, which took more than half a million. It includes local disasters such as the avalanche of coal slurry in Aberfan which killed 144 people (118 of them children), all from the same small village, to international disasters such as the bomb on Pan American Flight 103 which took 270 lives of people from twenty-one different countries. Over the course of my career major changes have taken place in the ways we view disasters, the resources available to deal with them and the interventions deemed appropriate.

Scale and spread

These variables of scale and spread influence the impact of the disaster and the services necessary to cope with it. Other factors which influence the response include the duration of the event, the type of damage and the culture and expectations of the affected population.

Differences of scale and spread are illustrated in Table 19.1. They have important implications for the organisation of a response (Parkes 1997). As a rough guide, a small-scale disaster is taken to mean fewer than 100 deaths and a large-scale disaster is taken to mean more than 1,000. Quite what the equivalent measures are for injuries and destruction of property has not been determined. Indeed some floods and other disasters cause extensive damage without any loss of life. Because these lie outside the remit of this volume they will not be considered here.

After small-scale local disasters the unit of care is the affected families but the community will also be affected. Psychosocial support can usually be managed by local services although it may be useful for them to seek out further expert advice and training. The disaster in the small town of Hungerford where, in 1987, a mentally disturbed gunman killed sixteen people and injured another fifteen before killing himself evoked offers of help from across the world. However, the local social services, with help from the local branch of Cruse Bereavement Care and other bodies, set up a 'Family Help Unit' to provide support and advice and to accompany bereaved people at the funerals and inquest. They were backed by a psychiatrist and had no need of more extensive help. The killer was a local man and the community as a whole suffered from becoming the centre of attention by the media and from the blaming and shame that followed.

In the wake of small-scale national disasters a local office in the disaster area and a telephone hotline is needed to provide information and short-term support as well as liaising with local services across the country. When, in 2002, a helicopter crashed into an oil installation in the North Sea, the twelve people who died were from several parts of the United Kingdom. They were all, however, employees of Shell Oil who rapidly mobilised its own occupational psychologist and psychiatrist to provide advice and support. I acted as consultant to that team. In such cases liaison with support services in other localities is needed and services are unlikely to become overloaded.

Liaison across national boundaries will be needed whenever an international disaster takes place even if small in scale. Consulates exist to assist and can be expected to respond appropriately. Leadership from the government in the country in which the disaster has taken place is the key to success but leaders too will be caught up in the psychological consequences of the disaster and may well lack the personal support that is offered to the bereaved families.

Table 19.1 Differences in scale and spread in recent disasters

Size of disaster	Local	National	International
Small	Hungerford Massacre	Shell Helicopter Crash	London Bombs 7/7/05
Medium	Aberfan	Capsize Zeebrugge Ferry	PA 103 Crash (Lockerbie)
Large	Bhopal	Genocide in Rwanda	9/11 (United States) and Tsunami (Indian Ocean)

In London, after the terrorist bombs on 7 July 2005, which killed fifty-six people in four locations, a helpline and Family Assistance Office was set up and staffed by FLOs from the Metropolitan Police, selected volunteers from Cruse Bereavement Care and the Red Cross. They were able to provide the range of expertise that bereaved families and survivors of the bombs needed. In the longer term they were able to refer those who needed it to appropriate specialist help.

Unlike those of small scale, medium-scale local disasters easily overwhelm local resources. In Aberfan the children who died were known to the local teachers, health care team and social workers, many of whom were themselves traumatised by the disaster. Lacking expertise in the field they were happy to accept the help of a small team of a family case worker, youth worker and unattached pastoral carer from outside the village who supplemented and themselves supported the existing psychiatric, psychological and social work teams. They, in turn, were supervised by a psychologist, a psychotherapist and a psychiatrist (CMP).

Medium-scale national disasters necessitate a national response although the spread of survivors across the nation may enable local services to meet most of their needs.

When, in 1987, the ferry boat *Herald of Free Enterprise* capsized outside Zeebrugge harbour, 193 people died, including passengers and crew, most of whom lived in the United Kingdom. Members of the crew and several passengers came from the port of Dover and it was here that a disaster office was set up with two support teams recruited from Cruse Bereavement Care and other organisations. One team, the 'Home Team', manned the office and provided support to the local people; the other team, the 'Away Team', travelled throughout Britain to meet with surviving family members, assess their need for support and to introduce them to local branches of Cruse and other sources of help.

Government involvement is crucial in medium-scale international disasters. When Pan-American Flight 103 was destroyed by a terrorist bomb, four days before Christmas 1988, over the village of Lockerbie in Scotland, there were no survivors from among the 259 passengers and sixteen crew. The dead came from twenty-one countries. Debris and bodies were scattered over a wide area and a large part of the fuselage crashed into Lockerbie destroying houses and killing eleven local residents. Psychological support in the locality was provided by local social services backed by Cruse. The largest number of dead came from the United States and the airline helped to set up mutual support groups in the United States, including a pressure group 'to discover the truth behind the bombing, seek justice for our loved ones, ensure the airline industry maintains and improves safety measures, educate the public about the incident and support one another'. Pan-American Airlines also set up a disaster team at Heathrow Airport to support its own air crews who were not only grieving for the loss of colleagues but were also threatened by the possibility of further bombs and the incipient financial collapse of the airline.

Large-scale disasters are seldom confined to one locality. An exception was the Union Carbide chemical plant in Bhopal, the capital city of Madhya Pradesh, where, in 1984, 3,800 people died and 2,800 were disabled by the escape of methyl isocyanate gas. The Indian government and Union Carbide organised medical care and an international appeal was set up to support the legal costs of the affected people, most of whom are poverty stricken, in a series of claims for compensation that have dragged on for more than thirty years. Little bereavement support seems to have been offered.

Large-scale national disasters are also likely to benefit from help from outside the affected nation. In Rwanda, the genocide of 1994, which killed more than half a million people, was the culmination of a series of massacres. Support services from abroad were only able to enter after the invading Rwandese Patriotic Front (RPF) troops succeeded in achieving control. The capital city, Kigali, was still under curfew and military control a year later, when a team from the United Nations Children's Fund (UNICEF) was able to set up a 'Trauma Recovery Program'. UNICEF opened a National Trauma Centre that, over the next five years, provided therapeutic services to 1,146 traumatised and bereaved survivors aged four to sixty-four. In addition, their trauma advisors trained 21,156 Rwandese teachers, caregivers, social workers, community and religious leaders and local associations from across the whole of Rwanda in bereavement and trauma support to children and adults. They eventually succeeded in supporting more than 200,000 multiply traumatised and bereaved children and their surviving families (Gupta 2000).

Large-scale international disasters inevitably require the organisation of support in all of the countries involved. The destruction of the World Trade Center in New York in the terrorist attacks of September 11, 2001 involved the loss of many people from outside as well as within the United States. To this day the number of dead is not known for sure and, at the time, a planned response was difficult. The initial Family Assistance Center soon had to be moved to larger premises. The British government acted on its own initiative to organise transport, accommodation and support for an estimated 300 British families who were invited to visit New York in search of missing persons. An account of the support given to these people by British police and bereavement volunteers will be given later in this paper. They liaised with the work of the Federal Emergency Management Agency (FEMA) whose 'Project Liberty' made use of more than 100 mental health care providers and numerous community agencies to provide free, anonymous, face-to-face counselling and public education services to more than a million New Yorkers (www.projectliberty.state.ny.us/).

The duration of a disaster can be a crucial factor in hampering support services. This is most obvious in war zones from which the Red Cross and other agencies may be excluded. On the other hand human beings can learn to cope with traumatic losses and the experience of recurrent typhoons, floods and high mortality from poverty and disease is associated with extraordinary resilience in many of the poorest parts of the world. Child bereavement advisor Dr Ann Dent and myself carried out an assessment visit to India in the wake of the Indian Ocean Tsunami of 26 December 2004. By early March 2005, three months after the disaster, the symptoms of PTSD and other stress disorders which had been prominent in the first few weeks had largely disappeared and the expectation of widespread traumatic disorder had not been fulfilled. (One Regional Health Advisor had predicted that 'almost all of the people affected by the Tsunami . . . will be suffering from some form of psycho-social trauma'). This does not mean that there were no problems, but the problems resulted from continuing displacement, unemployment, chronic grief and helplessness rather than from acute stress. Thus, we found evidence of sub-clinical or clinical depression, often associated with excessive alcohol consumption, in a substantial proportion of the fishermen who make up much of the affected population. *[This finding has since been confirmed by Tharyan 2005.[1]]*

Other cultural factors that may contribute to tolerance of trauma and loss are religious beliefs that emphasise the transience of life and the promise of rewards thereafter, along with social systems that minimise individualism and emphasise identification with the family or social group. Taken in conjunction with high birth and death rates among children, which are associated with less extreme reactions to the death of a child (Scheper-Hughes 1992), we may expect people in third world countries to be more tolerant of disaster than their Western counterparts.

But this should not lead us to assume that they are not in need of help. Cultural influences can increase as well as decrease vulnerability. For example, Yuksel and Olgun-Özpolot (2004) found remarkably high rates of persisting grief and PTSD in Turkey among parents of young men who had died or 'disappeared' in the conflict between Kurds and government troops, by comparison with parents whose children died from leukaemia. The attribution of martyrdom, by both sides of the conflict, seems to condemn these families to perpetual mourning. It would take us beyond the scope of this paper to consider a wider range of cultural variables. This important topic is covered in more detail by Parkes, Laungani and Young (1996).

The type of damage varies widely from one disaster to another. Perhaps the most important variable is the presumed cause of the disaster. Disasters that are attributed to human agency inevitably lead to much anger and recovery is complicated by the search for justice and/or revenge. In the immediate aftermath, outbreaks of ill-directed violence are not uncommon and may increase the risk of the initiation or perpetuation of a cycle of violence.

Most disasters give rise to a variety of traumata; these range from personal exposure to terrifying situations, witnessing horrific deaths, suffering physical injury, losing homes or property, losing one or more loved family members and experiencing communal chaos. This means that those who offer help need to be trained to understand and respond to this variety of needs.

Clinical and organisational implications

Given these great differences between disasters is it possible to prepare in advance for them and to mobilise appropriate resources when they occur? We can no longer assume that a course in 'stress management', 'post-traumatic stress disorder', 'anger management', 'critical incident stress debriefing', 'bereavement support' or 'community development' is sufficient on its own; all may be needed. This may sound like a tall order but, when we think about it, most of these skills should be part of the basic training of all caring professionals and bereavement volunteers.

Mental health care workers have an important contribution to make but their training tends to focus on the diagnosis and treatment of mental illness when it arises rather than its prevention. In disaster situations, as in all major life crises, opportunities exist for preventing illness before it becomes manifest and the services that have evolved in recent years to help people cope with bereavement and other trauma are preventive rather than psychiatric.

The focus on prevention has made us more aware of the social context in which mental ill health arises and this is of particular importance following disasters which, as we have seen, impact not only individuals and families, but communities and nations. International disasters, such as 9/11, cause armed conflict as well as mental illness and it is not unreasonable to hope that the right help given to afflicted communities may reduce the risk of both.

It follows that, in considering the clinical implications of traumatic bereavements at times of disaster, we need to look beyond the individual to include the family, the local community, the nation and the international scene.

Preparation for disasters

None of us knows when or where the next disaster will occur; all we can be sure of is that it will. For this reason, hospitals and emergency services all have their disaster plans, training programmes and disaster exercises. Yet only in recent years has proper attention been given to the need to take account of the threats to mental health and social stability that arise after disasters or to include within the disaster teams people trained in these fields.

The management of bereavement, trauma and stress should be part of the basic training of all members of the caring professions and all volunteers working with bereaved and/or traumatised people. Even in the absence of disasters these skills will be needed whenever we reach out to support people who have suffered traumatic losses. In addition, special training in disaster management should ensure that there are sufficient trained persons in each region to take a lead and provide the topping-up training that can enable a regular bereavement volunteer, social worker or counsellor to become part of a disaster team. This should include liaising with police, emergency and rescue services, training them in psychosocial skills and participating in joint exercises whenever possible. In Britain the police are now making use of psychologists and trainers from Cruse to train FLOs to support bereaved people and Cruse is using FLOs to help train their volunteers in crisis management. Special problems that arise in disaster areas need special attention. For a comprehensive source of information and links to major Web sites on disaster planning and management see: www.keele.ac.uk/depts/por/disaster.htm.

When we consider the response to disasters it is useful to break them down into four phases: impact, recoil, aftermath and long term. The term *impact* is here reserved for the period from the onset of the disaster to the arrival of the emergency services; *recoil* covers the period during which attempts at rescue take priority over everything else. This is followed by the *aftermath*, in which supportive services play a more active role, and *long-term care* during which disaster services are withdrawn. These phases are not clear-cut, particularly when the impact is spread out over a longer period.

Impact and recoil

The immediate response to disasters is one of confusion and chaos. All survivors become hyper-alert and, although high levels of fear are experienced, most show a capacity to remain calm enough to escape from immediate dangers and/or to assist in rescue operations. Panic is most likely to occur if people are trapped and can see no escape route; this can add to the danger and may cause more deaths. An 'illusion of centrality' may cause people on the periphery of the disaster to imagine that they are in the centre.

While dissociation (emotional numbing and the capacity to 'switch off' feelings) may enable some people to cope at times of emergency, it can also give rise to problems, as when people suffer episodes of amnesia or 'fugues' in which they are found wandering in a dazed state. Removal from the scene to a supportive environment may be sufficient to enable them to regain their bearings, but psychiatric help may also be needed.

The immediate response is the responsibility of the emergency services and attempts to save life and minimise further danger will take priority over most psychosocial needs. This said, there is much that can be achieved by providing background support and psychological first aid as well as using this time to assess future needs and adapt our disaster plan to this particular disaster.

Perhaps the greatest problem in this recoil phase is the chaos that is inevitable at this time and the feelings of helplessness that this evokes in would-be helpers, as well as in the victims of the disaster. I remember all too well my own feelings after my first visit to Aberfan. I found myself well able to cope while in the village but, while driving away after my first day, I had to stop the car three times in order to ventilate feelings of grief, anger and despair. I had little confidence in the value of my prior experience in this setting, little idea that my efforts would make any appreciable difference and insufficient confidence that I could control my own feelings. It was several months before I began to feel part of a team of dedicated individuals who could see that, for whatever reason, things were getting better.

Fortunately human beings evolved in a dangerous world and our sympathetic nervous system ensures that disasters generate the adrenalin, endorphins and other emergency responses that will get us through. We may be surprised at the enhanced alertness, energy and drive that we experience and we will find ourselves working long hours without flagging.

Even so, we need to guard against overload. When we become aware that we are over-stressed, for instance, if we begin to feel that we are drowning in the face of overwhelming demands, it helps to stop and wind down. I try to work out an order of priorities, deciding which tasks I must get on with now and which can be delayed, what things can be delegated and who I can draw in to help, how long I can carry on and when I must take a break.

This process of self-monitoring can be taught to colleagues and to traumatised clients who may feel even more overwhelmed than we do. They may try to snow us with information, bombarding us with one problem and not waiting for an answer before they start on the next. Again we need to 'flag them down', pointing out that neither they nor we can cope with more than one problem at a time and inviting them to consider which issue they need to deal with now. This helps them to focus and provides them with a model of action which they can continue to use.

Psychological first aid

The recoil phase is not a time to provide therapy; what people need, in the immediate wake of a disaster, is emotional support, information and instruction. By emotional support I mean the kind of reassurance that a mother can give to a frightened child; this has more to do with a touch of the hand and a smile than a facile assurance of security that may be no more than a pious hope. Information is needed to orient people and enable them to begin to adjust to the situation. Even if we are just as uncertain as they, it helps to share our uncertainty and to reassure them that nothing is being concealed. It is psychologically easier to deal with bad news than no news at all so we should rarely overprotect people by holding back information on the grounds that it may upset them. This said, it may be necessary to deliver bad news in 'bite-sized chunks' in order to give people time to digest and begin to process the implications of information that shatters their plans, hopes and assumptions about the world.

Information and instruction

Occasionally it may be necessary to give orders in order to take control of a situation. More often, however, it is wise to give information first so that people can understand why a particular instruction is being given. This is no time for democratic debate and we should recognise and fit into a military-style chain of command that can bring the situation under control as quickly as possible. The terrorist bombs of 9/11 were followed by a period of uncertainty. Despite a massive rescue operation it was a long time before it was known who had died. Urgent attempts to prevent further attacks led to the grounding of all passenger aircraft and the Foreign Office in Britain received numerous calls from families who were desperately seeking information about members who were missing in the United States. The Foreign Office responded by offering to pay the airfares and accommodation expenses of anyone who wanted to visit the States for four to five days in order to check out the situation. Most of the missing persons had worked or been visiting the Twin Towers. On 16 November I accompanied a team of FLOs to New York, on one of the first flights out of Heathrow, to prepare for the arrival next day of a team of experienced volunteers from Cruse Bereavement Care with their team leader, Dr Arthur O'Hara. We worked closely with these police officers and shared the Incident Room, which they set up. We all stayed at the same hotel as the families coming out under the Foreign Office scheme. To ensure effective liaison we formed units of one Cruse BV and two FLOs who met each incoming family at Kennedy Airport, escorted them to the hotel and provided the emotional support and information that they needed.

By the time the first families arrived, later on the first day, we had worked out where they might like to go and how to get there. We protected them from the intrusions of voracious press and television teams and accompanied them on visits to the site of the Twin Towers and to the Family Assistance Center that had been set up in Manhattan. Here they were able to search lists of names of patients in the New York hospitals, as well as to meet American and other families who were facing the same predicament. Most also visited the park in Union Square where candles had been lit, flowers displayed and notices put up. These notices varied from pleas for information about missing persons to expressions of sympathy, exhortations for world peace, demands for justice and nationalistic sentiments. By the time they returned to Britain these families had formed a relationship of trust with the support workers and this facilitated referral onwards to their local branches of Cruse Bereavement Care.

Both police and volunteers supported each other and were closely supervised and supported. The value of this became apparent in the second week when the capable and trusted head of the FLO team suffered a cardiac event and was flown back to Britain. Several FLOs subsequently expressed their appreciation of the support that they received from the BVs at that time. There can be no doubt that this was a very successful enterprise and much appreciated by the victims. Since then similar liaison has enabled us to support families returning to Britain from the Indian Ocean region following the tsunami of December 2004.

Aftermath

Once the rescue operations are at an end, the dead have been counted and the acute danger is over, psychosocial support services can play a more prominent role. By now we should have mobilised a disaster support team or teams depending on the scale and spread of the disaster. A chain of command should have been set up with members clearly apprised of their place and responsibilities within the team. An essential component is a centralised database on which is recorded relevant information about all victims and others affected by the disaster as well as the contact details and qualifications of all who have offered help. The team should operate from a disaster centre, which should also act as the information point, office and consultation centre for the affected population.

Bereavement support organisations have an important role to play at this stage and should be included in all disaster teams where deaths have occurred. But this does not mean that their volunteers and staff should confine themselves to problems of grief and mourning. Even outside disaster areas bereavement training and support should include the range of traumas and life changes that often follow traumatic losses. This makes well-trained bereavement support workers well suited to work in disaster areas. By the same token training in stress counselling in industrial or other settings needs to include the field of grief and bereavement.

Disasters usually attract numerous offers of help from volunteers, most of whom have little relevant experience or training. Some have their own religious or other agendas and there is a need for vetting to protect victims from unqualified intrusion from these people as well as from exploitation by irresponsible representatives of the news media. On the other hand both well-motivated, trained volunteers and responsible media have important roles to play and need to be welcomed and cherished.

Because it takes time to organise an appropriate response to disasters a mismatch often exists between the needs of traumatised persons and the resources available to meet these needs. Even when adequate resources are available it is important to introduce a form of psychological assessment or 'triage' to decide which individuals need priority attention. The 'illusion of centrality' often means that those most strident in their demands for help may not be the ones most in need. The 'risk factors' that enable us to identify individuals in need of psychological help following day-to-day bereavements are no different from the risk factors that predict psychiatric problems following disasters. They include the circumstances that make some bereavements more traumatic than others, the personal predispositions that make some individuals more vulnerable than others and the social circumstances that give support and meaning to the lives of some but not others (Stroebe and Schut 2002). Because bereavement workers are trained to identify these factors this makes them well qualified to carry out triage and focus resources where they are most needed.

All too often well-laid plans are delayed because of failure to provide the necessary resources. The 'Away Team' in Dover took nearly a year to visit and assess the needs of all the families at risk. Delays in funding, recruitment, training and deployment of staff reflect the real difficulties of creating, from scratch, a complex and expert team. Since that time (1987), public and government awareness of the need for psychosocial support after disasters has made it possible to act much more swiftly and effectively. The integration of psychiatric and psychological resources with trained BVs works very well and ensures that the majority of traumatised and bereaved people can receive the help that they need without recourse to expensive and scarce psychiatric services. But well-funded, centralised departments of psychological disaster management, such as the National Centre for Disaster Psychiatry at Uppsala University in Sweden, are needed to develop the organisational models and expertise that can prevent delays.

In the aftermath phase, psychologists and psychiatrists with experience in disaster areas are best employed in support of the front line of bereavement volunteers and counsellors and it is essential to organise one or more training days during which they can provide the 'topping up' training that is needed by less experienced colleagues.

Following an air crash in which more than 100 women had died, a training day had been organised by a local social service department who invited doctors, social workers and other professionals but failed to invite any volunteers or representatives of the local community. Subsequently the local people set up their own support networks and ignored those provided by the local authority.

Modern information systems are an important resource in disaster areas, even in parts of the world where few people own a computer. Mobile phones enable members of the disaster team to remain in touch with the office or incident room at all times and computers hold the database of victims and helpers as well as enabling team leaders to access and disseminate useful documents to the affected population.

Information and advice aimed at helping people bereaved by major disasters was placed on the Internet by the writer after the Indian Ocean tsunami and adapted for use after the London bombings of 7 July 2005. Cruse BVs working in the Family Assistance Centre printed it out and gave it to bereaved families. The feedback was very positive. The information covers commonly reported problems of trauma, grief, anger, guilt and life change. It is freely available on: www.cruse bereavementcare.org.uk.

The psychological interventions that are needed by bereaved people at this time are not intrinsically different from those required following other traumatic bereavements but the specialist therapists available in normal circumstances may well be in short supply following disasters, particularly in developing countries.

High levels of anxiety and fear are often aggravated by the physiological 'symptoms' to which they give rise (e.g. palpitations or breathlessness) and require traditional anxiety management programmes that are part of the stock in trade of volunteer bereavement services. Medical practitioners may need to provide authoritative reassurance that the 'symptoms' of anxiety are not an indication of illness. The diagnosis of PTSD is, or should be, included in the training of every bereavement worker, if only because it is eminently treatable. The 2005 report of the National Institute for Clinical Excellence (NICE) gives easily accessible guidance: www.nice.org.uk/pdf/word/CG026NICEguideline.doc. The NICE recommends that 'All health and social care workers should be aware of the psychological impact of traumatic incidents in their immediate post-incident care of survivors and offer practical, social and emotional support to those involved'. Routine screening should be carried out in all disaster areas using a suitable screening instrument such as that developed by Chou, Su, Ou-Yang and colleagues (2003).

Specialist psychological help should be considered whenever the symptoms are severe or disabling and persist for more than a month. (These criteria are among those necessary for the diagnosis of PTSD given in the American Psychiatric Association's *Diagnostic Statistical Manual*, DSM-IV, 1994.) Where available, techniques such as Trauma-focussed Cognitive Behaviour Therapies (CBT) and Eye Movement Desensitisation and Reprocessing (EMDR) will usually reduce haunting memories and fantasies to a tolerable level.

The horrific images that characterise PTSD are so painful and terrifying that sufferers will go to great lengths to avoid anything that reminds them of the loss. They also control their thoughts by keeping busy, distraction and rigorous self-control. Because thoughts of the lost person and the loss event can be counted on to trigger these images, people with PTSD find it difficult to talk about their loss or to grieve. This makes bereavement support difficult until the PTSD has been treated. At this point, however, the help of a BV who will 'hang-in' with the bereaved person as they begin, little by little, to rebuild their internal world can be invaluable.

PTSD in adults and children can also be treated by short-term 'Narrative Exposure Therapy' (Schauer, Neuner and Elbert 2004). As the name implies, this provides a structured method of life review to enable traumatised persons to regain purpose and direction in a life that has been ruptured by extreme traumatic stress. It is currently undergoing a randomised control study. Schauer's manual is accessible to the general public as well as to practitioners working in the fields of mental health, disaster, conflict resolution and human rights. Whether or not traumatised bereaved individuals have suffered from PTSD the risk of Complicated Grief (CG) is increased whenever a death is unexpected, untimely and shattering to a person's assumptive world (Parkes 2006a: 137–140). *[Since this was written Persistent Complex Bereavement Disorder has been identified, in DSM-5 (2013), as a category of response that is worthy of further research.]* Such deaths are the rule rather than the exception in disaster areas and they make the provision of bereavement support an essential component of disaster teams. The diagnosis and treatment of CG has been covered elsewhere in this volume (Chapter 9, pp. 63–70). Methods of treatment that can be accessed inexpensively by large numbers are of particular importance. It is, therefore, encouraging to report the promising results of an Internet-based treatment for CG (Wagner, Knaevelsrud and Maercker 2005). These researchers carried out a random-allocation study of the effectiveness of exposure to three modules; these included exposure to bereavement cues, cognitive reappraisal and integration and restoration. A large treatment effect was found.

Clinical Depression is another problem that is frequently encountered following disasters and other traumatic bereavements (Stroebe, Stroebe and Domittner 1988). It usually responds to Cognitive Behaviour Therapy (Sikkema, Hansen, Kochman, Tate and Defranciesco 2004) or to antidepressant medication (Pasternak *et al.* 1991; Reynolds *et al.* 1999; Zisook, Shuchter, Pedrelli, Sable and Deauciuc 2001).

Harris, Brown and Robinson (1999) have published well-conducted evaluations by random allocation of a form of 'befriending' that can be taught to volunteers. It has been tested on two samples of women, in one to prevent post-natal depression, and in the other to treat chronic depression. In both circumstances significantly lower levels of depression were found in the intervention groups and Harris suggests that 'befriending' may well have special value in the wake of bereavement, particularly when trained psychologists are in short supply, as they often are in third world disasters (Harris 2006).

Anger and aggression are natural reactions to man-made disasters. They seldom cause mental illness, but they may give rise to particular difficulties if the aggression is ill directed and they may even give rise to scapegoating, cycles of violence and armed conflicts. People will make allowances for bereaved people if their anger is sometimes disproportionate or ill-directed. But anger is not confined to the bereaved and community leaders easily get caught up in the wave of public rage that often follows man-made disasters. These problems have been spelled out in detail by members of the International Work Group on Death Dying and Bereavement (IWG) whose papers examine the consequences and implications of violent death (IWG 1997–1998) and the cycle of violence (IWG 2005).

Anger management is a skill that should be part of the training of all those in a position to provide support after traumatic loss, be it at individual, family, community, national or international levels. It should include understanding of the roots of aggression in both non-human and human animals (Lorenz's classic *On Aggression*, 1966, still has much to teach us), methods of conflict resolution and clear understanding of the circumstances under which necessary force should be used and the means by which its damaging effects can be minimised. Issues that increase the risk of further violence include misperceptions of the causes of violent acts, disproportionate immediate responses, the influence of legitimising authorities, destructive codes and polarising inflammatory strategies. Each can feed into a loop and increase the risk of a cycle of violence. By the same token interventions that correct the way violent behaviour is perceived, moderate the immediate response, support or counterbalance legitimising authorities, replace destructive with constructive codes, support mediation and moderate further violence (e.g. by removing weapons) can break the cycle at all levels (Parkes 2006b).

In Aberfan several public meetings broke up in fistfights during the early months after the disaster. It was a year before it became possible to deal more constructively with communal rage. As one woman said to me, after attending a group meeting focussed on anger management, 'This is the first time I was able to stand aside from my anger and see it as an inevitable consequence of the disaster, rather than being a part of me'. In that setting, attendance at the Board of Inquiry was seen as having therapeutic value. Although the Board attributed blame for the disaster on several named individuals, those who listened to the evidence did not see these people as enemies to be destroyed; rather it became evident to them that their guilt was a reflection of the human failings that we all possess.

Self-reproaches and guilt commonly co-exist with anger and aggression (Parkes 1998: 84). Some people seek to find someone else to blame for their own shortcomings while others blame themselves unreasonably for angry acts or for feeling angry. 'Survivor Guilt' is common and reflects the injustice of arbitrary deaths. Self-reproaches are more likely to become serious problems if warnings of disaster have been ignored or people have become aware of their culpability. A general practitioner told me that he had felt like a Roman Catholic confessor during the weeks that followed one man-made disaster. Such feelings may contribute to depression at the individual level and decline in morale at the group level. A community may come to see itself as 'rotten' or 'mad'.

It is a common experience that bereaved survivors of disaster are treated as heroes. If they express their guilt they are told that 'you should not feel like that', as if they could choose how they feel. These attempts at reassurance are not helpful. Two responses that do seem to help are showing non-judgemental understanding of the 'none of us is perfect' kind and encouraging the person to find a worthwhile way of making restitution, perhaps by bringing something good out of the disaster – 'If that's the way you feel what are you going to do about it?' In my experience, such expressions of confidence that something can be done have therapeutic value. Likewise, at a community level, action programmes may help to restore faith in a community. As one survivor put it, 'This disaster was caused by apathy and it is up to us to ensure that [this community] never becomes apathetic again'.

Communal rituals and memorials play an important part in all bereavement but take on added meaning when it is a community that is bereaved by disaster. They help to make real the fact of loss and to help people and communities to construct a new identity. As in bereavement counselling the aim is not to help people to forget the dead but to find a new place for them in the narrative of their lives and the life of their community. Community leaders play important roles by bringing home the seriousness of the situation and committing themselves to support the afflicted and involve themselves in the changes that must follow.

Ten days after 9/11 a service of prayer was held in St Thomas' Church, New York, to which the affected families were invited. The service was attended by Secretary General of the United Nations Kofi Annan, former United States president Bill Clinton and Prime Minister of the United Kingdom Tony Blair. A message of sympathy from Her Majesty the Queen was read out. The bereaved families were accompanied throughout the day by the disaster team. After the service they had an opportunity to meet the dignitaries and receive their sympathy. Although the occasion was an ordeal for several of the families it also brought home to all of us the historic significance of what had happened and a feeling of being more than the centre of attention – we felt loved and cared for.

Children in disaster areas are at particular risk, both as a result of the traumatic losses they have experienced and also as a result of the negative influence of disasters on their parents and peers. Pynoos and colleagues (1987), who studied the effects on children of sniper attacks on their schools, have shown that not only do children suffer post-traumatic symptoms in much the same way as adults, but the intensity and duration of these symptoms is much greater if the child was personally bereaved. It follows that support for parents and children should be a part of all disaster services and that disaster teams should include individuals who have been selected and trained to work with children. Although space does not permit a more adequate treatment of the special problems of children in disaster areas, the US National Institute of Mental Health provides useful guidance (2001).

Team support. All who choose to work in disaster areas need to be aware of the emotional cost of the work, to monitor themselves as described earlier and to provide and accept the mutual support that is needed at all times. 'Critical incident stress debriefing' was introduced to provide support to emergency services and later widened for use with victims of disasters (Mitchell 1983). More recently random-allocation studies have thrown doubt on the efficacy of brief, single-session interventions that focus on the traumatic incident (Van Emmerick *et al.* 2002; Wesseley and Deahl 2003). But this does not gainsay the need for regular meetings of staff at which the trust necessary to mutual support can develop, as well as the need for confidential one-to-one support. Although line managers have primary responsibility for supporting the team no one person can expect to be the sole supporter and team members should be able to choose the person in whom they wish to confide. Viewed in this way team support is a shared responsibility. Supervisors and support workers from outside the team both have useful roles to play, particularly when morale is at a low ebb or trust has been undermined.

Example: In one disaster area long-standing rivalry between the education department and the health department had caused the staff of each to operate independently of the other. It was necessary for the visiting psychiatrist to initiate joint meetings between the child psychologist and the family case worker before each realised that they were working with the same families! Prejudice soon dissolved once they began to share information and before long a good trusting relationship had developed.

It is also important to recognise that leaders also need support. This applies at all levels including politicians and military leaders who may find it difficult to acknowledge that they are not the supermen and superwomen that their juniors would like them to be. Faced with enormous responsibilities, and political pressures to take drastic action in the face of outrageous events, they need emotional support as well as reliable information and impartial advice. History suggests that they seldom get these.

Long term

As time passes the number of bereaved people who need continuing help can be expected to dwindle and it becomes possible to withdraw any support workers who have been introduced from outside the affected community. Although it may be administratively convenient to wind up the operation on a particular day, this should be resisted; needs do not change abruptly. Rather the team should be tapered off as soon as the need declines, the aim being to hand over to the indigenous support systems as soon as this is reasonable. It is not for the outsiders to colonise but to educate the local mental health and other professionals to take over.

It is unrealistic to expect that the members of the disaster team will simply return to the jobs they had before the disaster and carry on with their lives as if nothing had happened. It is not only the bereaved who are changed by disasters. It follows that winding up a disaster team should include recognition of the fact that many members will want to review the new directions that their lives are taking and to explore the opportunities that now exist for career and personal development. Some may want to train for a caring profession, others to take a break from caregiving.

And just as individuals are permanently changed by disasters so are communities and nations. Members of disaster teams may not see it as their role to engage with the political and administrative systems that supposedly control these changes but they often have insight into the psychology of the affected communities that these people lack. One sometimes gets the impression that, while psychologists and BVs are helping people to stand aside from their grief and make rational decisions, politicians and administrators are being blown hither and thither by the powerful emotions and pressures to which they are exposed.

Example: During the first year after the Aberfan disaster the discontent of the affected community was often expressed in attacks on 'them up there'. Administrators suffered so much abuse that a paralysis of decision-making took place and money that had been donated to the disaster fund went unspent. The end of the first year, however, marked a watershed. The need for individual support to bereaved individuals diminished to the point where it became possible to withdraw the disaster team one by one. At the same time it became evident that the community as a whole was recovering . . . This did not mean that there were not individuals who continued to suffer and a recent follow-up has highlighted the extent to which we failed to provide the sophisticated care that is possible today (Morgan, Scourfield, Williams, Jasper and Lewis 2003).

Following the first anniversary of the disaster two sociologists were invited to join with the local disaster team and community leaders to help develop a community development plan. After a successful public meeting, a community association was initiated and Derek Nuttall,[2] who had been the youth worker on the disaster team, was appointed as first secretary. Much else followed and Aberfan eventually became a forward-looking community. Five years later, it acted as host to the first of a series of conferences demonstrating the success of community development (Ballard and Jones 1975).

Conclusions

It would be a mistake to assume that satisfactory communal development is an inevitable outcome of disasters any more than we can expect all bereaved people to make a good recovery from traumatic losses. Kai Erikson analysed the consequences of the Buffalo Creek Disaster in which a flood inundated a chain of linear villages. In many respects, this medium-scale, local disaster resembled Aberfan. Erikson describes the 'loss of communality', which was still pervasive two and a half years later '. . . the people of the community no longer trust one another in the way they did before' (Erikson 1979).

There is no space here to analyse the reasons why this happened but the two examples, Aberfan and Buffalo Creek, do point up the possibility that things can go either way. Following disasters some individuals will grow in psychological, social and spiritual maturity while others will wither, so too will some communities and some nations. It is the task of all to foster creative responses to disaster and to minimise destructive responses. Bereavement research and interventions have gone some way to help individuals and families through these turning points in their lives. Is it too late to hope that the lessons learned can be successfully applied in the larger settings?

Notes

1   Tharyan, P. Traumatic bereavement and the Asian tsunami. *Bereavement Care* 24, (2), 23–26, 2005.
2   Nuttall remained in Aberfan for another two years, then left to become regional development officer and later director of Cruse Bereavement Care.

References

American Psychiatric Association. *Diagnostic and Statistical Manual of Mental Disorders* (4th ed.). American Psychiatric Association, Washington, DC, 1994.

Ballard, P.H. and Jones, E. (eds.) *The Year of the Valleys: A Self-Examination by People of the South Wales Valleys during the Year of the Valleys 1974.* Ron Jones, Ferndale, Rhondda, 1975.

Chou, F.H.C., Su, T.T.P., Ou-Yang, W.C., *et al.* Establishment of a disaster-related psychological screening test. *Australian and New Zealand Journal of Psychiatry* 37, 97–103, 2003.

Erikson, K.T. *In the Wake of the Flood.* Allen and Unwin, London, 1979.

Gupta, L. Bereavement recovery following the Rwandan genocide: a community-based intervention for child survivors. *Bereavement Care* 18, 40–42, 2000.

Harris, T. Volunteer befriending as an intervention for depression: implications for bereavement care? *Bereavement Care* 25, 27–30, 2006.

Harris, T., Brown, G.W. and Robinson, R. Befriending as an intervention for chronic depression among women in an inner city. 1. Randomised control trial. 2. Role of fresh-start experiences and baseline psycho-social factors in remission from depression. *British Journal of Psychiatry* 174, 219–224, 225–232, 1999.

International Work Group on Death, Dying and Bereavement (IWG). Document on Violence and Grief. Violence and Grief Work Group (R.G. Stevenson, chair). *Omega* 36(3), 259–272, 1997–1998.

International Work Group on Death, Dying and Bereavement (IWG). Breaking cycles of violence. *Death Studies* 29(7), 585–600, 2005.

Lorenz, K. *On Aggression.* Methuen, London, 1966.

Mitchell, J.T. When disaster strikes. The critical incident stress debriefing process. *Journal of Emergency Medical Services* 8, 36–39, 1983.

Morgan, L., Scourfield, J., Williams, D., Jasper, A. and Lewis, G. The Aberfan disaster: 33-year follow-up of survivors. *British Journal of Psychiatry* 182, 532–536, 2003.

National Institute of Mental Health. *Helping children and adolescents cope with violence and disasters: fact sheet.* NIMH, Washington, DC, 2001.

Parkes, C.M. A typology of disasters. In D. Black, M. Newman, J. Harris-Hendriks and G. Mezey (eds.) *Psychological Trauma: A Developmental Approach* (chapter 7). Gaskell, London, 1997.

Parkes, C.M. *Bereavement: Studies of Grief in Adult Life.* Routledge, London and Penguin Books, Harmondsworth, 1998.

Parkes, C.M. Breaking the cycle of violence. In Robert G. Stevenson and Gerry R. Cox (eds.) *Perspective on Violence* (pp. 223–238). Baywood, Amityville, NY, 2006a.

Parkes, C.M. *Love and Loss: The Roots of Grief and Its Complications.* Routledge, London, 2006b.

Parkes, C.M., Laungani, P. and Young, B. *Death and Bereavement across Cultures.* Routledge, London and New York, 1996.

Pasternak, R. E., Reynolds, C. F., Schlernizauer, M. *et al.* Nortriptyline therapy of bereavement-related depression in later life. *Journal of Clinical Psychiatry* 52, 307–310, 1991.

Pynoos, R. S., Frederick, C., Nader, K., Arroyo, W. *et al.* Life threat and post-traumatic reactions in school-age children. *Archives of General Psychiatry* 44, 1057–1063, 1987.

Reynolds, C. F., Miller, M. D., Pasternak, R. E. *et al.* Treatment of bereavement-related major depressive episodes in later life: a controlled study of acute and continuation treatment with Nortriptyline and interpersonal psychotherapy. *American Journal of Psychiatry* 156(2), 202–208, 1999.

Schauer, M., Neuner, F. and Elbert, T. *Narrative Exposure Therapy: A Short-Term Intervention for Traumatic Stress Disorders after War, Terrorism, or Torture.* Hogrefe & Huber, Cambridge, MA and Göttingen, Germany, 2004.

Scheper-Hughes, N. *Death without Weeping: The Violence of Everyday Life in Brazil.* University of California Press, Berkeley, CA, 1992.

Sikkema, K. J., Hansen, N. B., Kochman, A., Tate, D. C. and Defranciesco, W. Outcomes from a randomised controlled trial of a group intervention for HIV positive men and women coping with AIDS-related loss & bereavement. *Death Studies* 28(3), 187–210, 2004.

Stroebe, W., Stroebe, M. and Domittner, G. Individual and situational differences in recovery from bereavement: a risk group identified. *Journal of Social Issues* 44, 143–158, 1988.

Stroebe, W. and Schut, H. Risk factors in bereavement outcome: a methodological and empirical review. In M. S. Stroebe, R. O. Hansson, W. Stroebe and H. Schut (eds.) *Handbook of Bereavement Research: Consequences, Coping and Care* (chapter 16). American Psychological Association, Washington, DC, 2002.

Van Emmerick, A. A. P., Kamphuis, J. H., Hulsbosch, A. M. and Emmelkamp, P. M. G. Single session debriefing after psychological trauma. *Lancet* 360, 736–741, 2002.

Wagner, B., Knaevelsrud, C. and Maercker, A. Internet-based treatment for complicated grief: concepts & case study. *Journal of Loss & Trauma* 10 409–432, 2005.

Wesseley, S. and Deahl, M. Psychological debriefing is a waste of time. *British Journal of Psychiatry* 183, 12–21, 2003.

Yuksel, S. and Olgun-Özpolot, T. Psychological problems associated with traumatic loss in Turkey. *Bereavement Care* 23(1), 5–7, 2004.

Zisook, S., Shuchter, S. R., Pedrelli, P., Sable, J. and Deauciuc, S. C. Buproprion sustained release for bereavement: results of an open trial. *Journal of Clinical Psychiatry* 62(4), 227–230, 2001.

CHAPTER 20

PSYCHOSOCIAL EFFECTS OF DISASTER
Birth rate in Aberfan

R. M. Williams and C. M. Parkes

Reprinted from *British Medical Journal* 2: 303–304, 1975.

Aberfan had been an important lesson for me but I did not feel confident to write about it until other disasters had given me some standard of comparison. It did occur to me, however, that Dr Williams, as the community physician, was in a position to carry out a study of birth rates after bereavement using statistics similar to my earlier studies of death rates after bereavement (see Chapter 5). This revealed a sharp rise in the birth rate which, over the next five years, equalled the number of children killed in the disaster. When we published this paper it attracted attention in the press and gave rise to angry correspondence from readers who confirmed a point that we had made, that you cannot replace a dead child. Even so, it does appear that a process of restoration was taking place in the community as a whole.

Summary

An increased birth rate occurred in Aberfan during the five years after the disaster there in 1966. It was not confined to the bereaved parents.

Introduction

On 21 October 1966, in the Welsh mining village of Aberfan and its companion village Merthyr Vale, 116 children and twenty-eight adults were killed when an avalanche of coal slurry engulfed the village primary school and several houses. Some of the psychological damage produced was reported by Lacey (1972). Using statistics now available from the Registrar of Births and Deaths we have plotted changes in the birth rate during the five years before and after the disaster.

Method

Birth rate is measured as births per 1,000 population. Thus an increase may result from either a rise in the number of births or a fall in the population. The fall in the population of Aberfan due to the disaster would therefore be expected to be associated with a rise in the birth rate even if the number of births remained the same.

In attempting to find whether there was a rise in the birth rate attributable to increase in births among those of reproductive age it was necessary to exclude from consideration the children who died in the disaster. To do this, population estimates from 1967 onwards were increased by 116. On the other hand, the twenty-eight adults who died were included in the population estimates because many of them would have been of reproductive age. Between the 1961 and 1971 censuses the population of the Aberfan and Merthyr Vale ward fell from 5,459 to 4,642. This was accounted for by ex-migration because during the same period there was an excess of 219 births over deaths (discounting the 116 child deaths in the disaster). The total number of ex-migrations was therefore 920, or ninety-two a year. In calculating the yearly population we assumed that this rate of attrition was steady and subtracted from it the excess of births over deaths for each year.

We also calculated the number of children who would have been born in Aberfan and Merthyr Vale had the trend in the birth rate for the years 1962–1967 continued. During that period there was a mean decline of 3.6 births a year. The mean number of births a year over the five-year period was 80.6. Starting from the midpoint of the quinquennium, 1965, and assuming an expected 80.6 births during that year, we subtracted 3.6 births successively year by year.

For comparison we obtained birth rate figures for the other seven wards which, with Aberfan and Merthyr Vale, make up the County Borough of Merthyr Tydfil (population 54,530 in 1971).

Results

Figure 20.1 shows the changes in birth rate in Aberfan and Merthyr Vale corrected for population change due to the child deaths in 1966, as described earlier. During 1962–1967 the changes in birth rate mirrored those for the rest of the borough, which had a slightly higher overall rate. No effect of the disaster on birth rate would have become apparent until the second half of 1967, and, in fact, there was

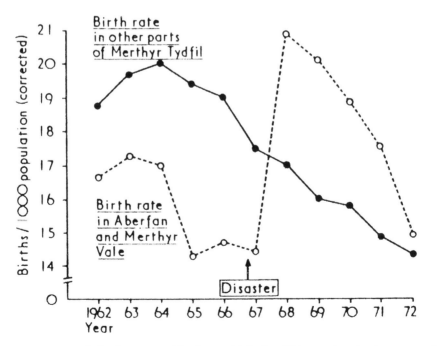

Figure 20.1 Yearly birth rates in Aberfan and Merthyr Vale ward and other parts of Merthyr Tydfil during 1962–1972

Table 20.1 Expected and actual births in Aberfan and Merthyr Value

Year	Expected No. (See Text)		Actual No.		No. to Bereaved Parents	
1965	80·6		74			
1966	77·0		75			
1967	73·4		72		3	
1968	69·8		103		6	
1969	66·2		98		4	
1970	62·6	}313·0	91	}445	3	}17
1971	59·0		83		1	
1972	55·4		70		3	

no significant change during that year. In 1968, however, the birth rate increased sharply from 14.38 per 1,000 to 20.80 per 1,000, and it remained above the rate for the rest of the borough until 1972, the last year for which figures are available.

Table 20.1 gives the number of births which took place each year in Aberfan and Merthyr Vale from 1968 to 1972 compared with the number expected when assuming a linear decline, as explained previously. Over the five-year period 445 children were born, 132 more than expected. To find whether this increase was confined to parents who had lost a child in the disaster we compared the birth registers with the death roll. Surprisingly, only fourteen pairs of bereaved parents had had one or more further children during 1968–1972. Between them, they had given birth to seventeen children (three other bereaved families had left the area and could not be traced).

As in the rest of the population, the number of births to bereaved parents reached a peak in 1968 and declined rapidly thereafter. Thus only a small proportion of the increased birth rate in Aberfan after the disaster was attributable to the bereaved parents.

Conclusions

By 1972 the number of children killed in the disaster had been replaced and the birth rate had fallen to near the pre-disaster level. It had not, however, fallen to the level which would have been reached had the decline indicated by pre-disaster figures continued. The increase in births was not confined to the bereaved parents but was spread over the whole population.

Clinical studies have indicated risks to children born to replace a dead child. Cain and Cain (1964) claimed that such children may be overprotected and expected to live up to the idealized memory of their dead sibling, and Paul and Grosser (1965) and Welldon (1971) reported that they may suffer lasting identity problems. These workers independently concluded that such misidentification may even cause schizophrenia in later life, which, if verified, carries important implications for preventive psychiatry. But these studies were based on a few cases referred for psychiatric help and give no indication how great the danger to health may be in the average child-bereaved family. Nor do they tell us anything about children born to parents who have not been bereaved (most in this study).

A common observation in disaster areas is that those who survive are strongly motivated not only to repair the damage but to bring something positive out of the ruins. As Barton put it, 'When conditions are favourable, the therapeutic community response sets in motion enough helping behaviour to reduce rapidly the deprivation of the victims of collective stress, thereby restoring the situation to its prior equilibrium. It is possible that the effects will even go beyond that to produce a net improvement, an "amplified rebound" from disaster' (Barton 1969).

In Aberfan and Merthyr Vale the disaster gave rise to a community development programme, which is now viewed as a model. Journalists and others who visit the area find a mature and responsible community, whose morale is probably higher than it has ever been (Nossiter 1973).

In the light of these changes it seems reasonable to conjecture that the increased birth rate in Aberfan and Merthyr Vale observed during the first five years after the disaster was mainly a consequence of a process of biosocial regeneration by couples who had not themselves lost a child. This process cannot bring back the children who died or remove all the scars of bereavement; there are, no doubt, some in the community who have suffered lasting damage. But it does provide grounds for recognizing that psychosocial transitions of this kind are not entirely destructive in their effects when viewed from the perspective of the community in which they occur.

References

Barton, A. H. *Communities in Disaster*. Doubleday, New York, 1969.

Cain, A. C. and Cain, B. S. On replacing a child. *Journal of the American Academy of Child Psychiatry* 3, 443, 1964.

Lacey, G. N. Observations on Aberfan. *Journal of Psychosomatic Research* 12, 25–67, 1972.

Nossiter, B. D. *The Washington Post*, May 27, 1973.

Paul, N. L. and Grosser, G. H. Operational mourning and its role in conjoint family therapy. *Community Mental Health Journal* 1, 339, 1965.

Welldon, R. M. C. The 'shadow of death' and its implication in four families, each with a hospitalized schizophrenic member. *Family Process* 10, 281, 1971.

CHAPTER 21

HELP THE HOSPICES TSUNAMI PROJECT

Consultant's report and recommendations

Consultants: Colin Murray Parkes and Ann Dent

Parkes, C.M. and Dent, A. Help the Hospices Tsunami Project: consultant's report and recommendations. Prepared for Help the Hospices, 2004.

Although this report received limited circulation within hospice circles in the aftermath of the Boxing Day 2004 tsunami in the Indian Ocean it was circulated more widely, along with other documents, after the similarly massive tsunami in eastern Japan in 2011 in which 15,883 people died, three nuclear reactors melted down and huge numbers were evacuated from their homes. It is included here along with extracts from the project notes to give readers a feel for consultant work in disaster areas. In this case the two consultants were given a brief to assess the needs and make recommendations for the use of a contribution to the needs of the affected population.

The Tsunami

On 26 December 2004, a magnitude 9.0 earthquake off the northern tip of Sumatra gave rise to a tsunami, which inundated the adjoining coast line up to 3,000 miles away. Aftershocks continued to occur in the region and another major earthquake (Richter 8.7) took place on 27 March in islands in the same region but did not give rise to another tsunami.

As of 4 March 2005, 283,100 people were killed, 14,100 were still listed as missing, and 1,126,900 lost their homes in ten countries in South Asia and East Africa. (USGS Earthquake Hazards Program). UNICEF estimates that children comprise more than one-third of total deaths (UNICEF 10.1.05) and subsequent reports indicate that in many areas more women than men died.

Dead, missing and displaced (USGS 4.3.05)

Indonesia 126,602 dead, 93,638 missing, 514,150 displaced (BAKORNAS 22.3.05)
Sri Lanka 31,229 dead, 4,100 missing, 500,000 displaced (OCHA 29.3.05)
India 10,749 dead, 5,640 missing, 112,558 displaced
Thailand 5,395 dead (including 1,953 foreigners, 1,925 Thai and 1,517 unidentified), 2,952 missing, N/K displaced, some 14 victims remain hospitalised for trauma, while another 9,174 are in need of counselling and a further 1,000 require prescriptions to overcome depression (OCHA 11.3.05).
Maldives 82 dead, 26 missing, 21,663 displaced
Malaysia 68 dead, 6 missing, 8,000 displaced

Somalia 150 dead, 5,000 displaced, 102,000 affected
Myanmar (Burma) 60–80 dead

Mental health

Several authoritative assessments have emphasised the danger to mental health likely to result from the tsunami, thus:

> Almost all of the people affected by the Tsunami . . . will be suffering from some form of psycho-social trauma.
>
> (WHO Regional Health Advisor, Indonesia)

> The most urgent intervention now is a psychosocial or mental health one. This is the most prevalent concern.
>
> (Dr Julia Suryantan, CWS Indonesia's Senior Program Officer for Health and Nutrition)

> 50% or more of those effected could suffer from clinically significant distress or psychopathology.
>
> (Stevens and Slone, US National Center for Post Traumatic Stress Disorder (PTSD))

> Considering that approximately 1 million people may . . . be affected by the disaster, we may expect 500,000 people will need psychosocial support, and up to 100,000 people will require skilled mental health intervention for trauma-related stress disorders.
>
> (WHO Recommendations for Mental Health in Aceh 27.1.05)

Aims of the project

To assess the needs of people bereaved by the tsunami.
To assess the extent to which these needs are being met by existing services.
To make recommendations for actions to alleviate further suffering of bereaved people.

Methods of assessment

- **Collection of information from published sources.** CMP spent several weeks trawling the Internet to obtain as much information as possible about existing services.
- **Personal inquiry from individuals working in the affected area.** A large number of e-mails were sent to officers of the various organisations engaged in providing support and most replied.
- **Visit to areas affected by the tsunami to meet those organising services and to visit the towns, villages and refugee camps.** AD and CMP spent a week in affected parts of Tamil Nadu [India] where we consulted with doctors, psychiatrists, psychologists, social workers, staff of non-governmental organizations (NGOs), community leaders and selected tsunami-bereaved people.

Limitations of the study

In view of the enormous scale of the disaster, the difficulty in obtaining access to accurate information, the continuing threat of further earthquakes and other dangers in the affected region and the relatively small resources available to us, we cannot pretend that we can give a comprehensive view of the situation or offer solutions to all of the numerous problems that continue to arise.

The area of greatest need is undoubtedly the northern tip of Sumatra, Indonesia, but this is also the area that has received the greatest support from other countries and one of our informants expressed the opinion the situation in Sumatra is 'quite chaotic and there are hundreds of NGOs [Non-Governmental Organisations] and orgs claiming to be "Trauma Experts" and no coordination or collaboration amongst them'. Our original intention was to go to Sumatra but we needed and failed to obtain the support of an approved organisation on the scene. This, in itself, is not surprising given that there are no palliative care or bereavement services in Sumatra and little awareness of any need for such. The Indonesian government is suspicious of foreign intervention and originally set a target of 26 March – three months after the tsunami – for the withdrawal of all foreign aid agencies not contributing to long-term reconstruction. This deadline was extended by a month but reduced the chance of effective intervention in that country.

In Sri Lanka the UK/Sri Lankan Project is already doing great work and we have the benefit of a close relationship with Professor Bill Yule who was on site during February. He has kindly provided CMP with a day-to-day diary of his activities, which is the next best thing to visiting the island ourselves. We decided that we can draw on his knowledge of that country in making our assessment.

This freed us up to visit India where hospice and other palliative care services are well developed and, in contrast to Indonesia, we were able to obtain the full collaboration and support of local professionals. As in Indonesia and Sri Lanka the highest death rates were among women and children of fishermen living in villages along the flat lands on the coast. Unlike Indonesia, this is an area relatively well provided with excellent medical services. It cannot, therefore, be taken as typical of the whole disaster area.

An important limitation of any study in which 'experts' from one culture are asked to assess the needs of people from another is the recognition that it is dangerous to assume that cultures are so uniform that lessons learned in one culture will necessarily apply in another. This does not mean that we have nothing to offer, but that we should collaborate actively with local people who can help us to decide what we have to offer and how relevant it is to their needs. This issue is considered in detail in CMP's edited book *Death and Bereavement across Cultures* and forms the basis of WHO's recommendation that existing resources should be adapted to ensure that they are 'culturally appropriate and relevant to local needs'. An important aim is to 'strengthen the capacity of community organisations and community leaders in the provision of psycho-social support' rather than to take over the care of the affected population (WHO Recommendations for Mental Health in Aceh). We accept this recommendation.

Findings of the study

Full details of our findings are available in our 'Project Notes' *[see Appendix]* and CMP's 'Assessment of Services'. Here, we shall give a concise summary of our major conclusions and the grounds on which they were reached.

1   **The initial prediction of widespread damage to mental health in the affected population has not been substantiated by subsequent observations.** Thus, Dr Prathap Tharayan, Professor of Psychiatry at the Christian Medical College (CMC), Vellore, writes:

> I myself had visited Nagapattinam [the area of India in which the greatest loss of life took place] 2 weeks after the tsunami struck and had spent a week there with a team of nurses and counsellors from CMC. At that time nearly everyone had symptoms of acute stress and many who had lost loved ones were in the acute stages of grief. Most survivors were apprehensive and hyper-vigilant and had recurrent images of the tsunami at night along with the sound the tsunami made (a high pitched noise like a speed boat) that prevented them from sleeping [similar reports have been published from many other parts of the tsunami-affected area]. Many of the rescue workers had flashbacks of dead bodies that they had helped recover and bury in mass graves. We provided psychological first aid as well as training for some local volunteers in bereavement counselling.
>
> About two weeks ago, another team from the department spent a fortnight in Sirgali Taluk and conducted more training workshops for local NGO counsellors. Their report was that the acute stress symptoms had settled down and though there were many grieving normally, the psychological consequences were less than at our first visit. Children were back at school and seemed to be overcoming their fear though they still drew pictures of the tsunami when asked to draw.
>
> (E-mail 7.3.05)

In Thailand, Thavich Jitprasarn, the director of the primary school in Baan Nam Khem – one of the villages worst hit by the tsunami – said his pupils were gradually beginning to feel better.

> Children move on very quickly, but many of them still don't really want to talk about what happened . . . The older children, especially, are finding it difficult to cope, the little ones don't understand everything fully.
>
> (BBC News 29.3.05)

Probable explanations are that predictions made from western cultures, where death is a rare event and trauma exceptional, are less dire in societies in which mortality rates remain high, fishing is still a high risk occupation and people have large families because they expect children to die. Two other factors are the social support that is still provided by extended family networks and the community at large (by contrast with the relative lack of such supports in the West) and the excellent medical and psychiatric services, which provided Trauma Counselling where needed.

Even so, psychiatric problems remain and, in Tamil Nadu [the coastal strip most affected by the tsunami], seem to be mainly attributable to loss of homes, loss of meaningful occupation and bereavement. These problems were most apparent in the displaced persons camps where men, whose self-esteem and purpose in life rely largely on their prowess as fishermen and wage earners, find themselves passive recipients of aid and unable to influence their own futures. There is evidence of sub-clinical depression and excessive alcohol consumption which, when combined with bereavement or other vulnerability, sometimes reaches clinical levels. This then has a secondary effect on wives, particularly those who are already suffering severe grief. As in the West women are more in touch with their feelings and more willing to ask for help. This gives the impression that they are more distressed than men and in greater need of psychological services. We suspect that it is in fact the men who are at greater risk.

Children, though resilient, are very sensitive to the problems of their parents, teachers and peers. We obtained an overall impression that, thanks to the fact that most children are now back at school with the same teachers and friends and supported in the community by caring adults, *the majority* are doing well. This said, children who have suffered traumatic losses do not always show their feelings and we received reports that in some places children's needs were being neglected. Several of our informants reported that adults in Tamil Nadu do not acknowledge their children's grief or know how to cope with its manifestations; boys (like all men) are encouraged to suppress their feelings, schoolteachers are given no guidance on how to help bereaved children and there are no other services for such children.

2   It is our impression that, in keeping with the recommendations of WHO and other authoritative bodies, the main focus of psychological care has been on providing trauma counselling and therapy.[1] This is well founded in research and quite rightly seen as the first priority in disaster areas. Less well recognised but also founded on good research is the need for special attention to be given to the needs of people who have suffered traumatic bereavements. Evidence to support this view is summarised by CMP in Appendix I, *Evidence-based Bereavement Support*. This shows that, although there is no reason to believe that all bereaved people need or will benefit from support from outside their own network of family and friends, people who are at special risk, including those who have suffered unexpected and untimely (i.e. 'traumatic') bereavements, do benefit from appropriate interventions. Scientific studies suggest that the most effective therapies embody a personal relationship with the client that is sensitive to emotional, cognitive and cultural issues.

To our knowledge, formal bereavement services do not exist in any of the areas affected by the tsunami and some of the professionals in India to whom we spoke questioned if they are needed in a society in which family and communal support for bereaved people is still good and there is widespread acceptance of the vicissitudes of life. Several Indian palliative care services, however, include bereavement care among the services they provide and the team based at the Christian Medical College in Vellore includes training for volunteers on 'bereavement counselling' among its activities in the tsunami-affected villages under its care. It seems that whatever model of care is provided it will need to be tailored to the culture and circumstances of the affected population.

Recommendations

Our remit is to make recommendations for the improvement of services to people bereaved by the tsunami. While this remains our primary objective we recognise that bereavement is only one of the several major losses and traumas by which people exposed to the tsunami have been afflicted. Services provided for people bereaved by death should not be separated from services provided for people suffering other types of loss and *vice versa*. We believe that an understanding of bereavement and its problems sheds light on many other life situations and traumata.

While, for some purposes, it is useful to have special organisations serving bereaved people only, for the psychiatrists, psychologists, social workers, counsellors and volunteers working in disaster areas, training is needed to enable them to help people suffering the effects of trauma, bereavement, major life change (Psycho-social Transition), depression and other problems. This should include training in the recognition of manifestations of grief and distress in bereaved children and provision of appropriate help. Training in bereavement support, therefore, should be part of, but not alternative to training in these other areas.

1   We recommend that funding be sought for one-week workshops on bereavement care to be given in the tsunami-affected area. Participants would be professionals with senior roles in the organisation and provision of services and training in psychosocial care. Requests for workshops should be made by the organisations responsible for providing services in the affected areas and at least 50% of the workshop leaders should come from those areas. Costs will vary but should include fees and expenses of organisers and speakers together with bursaries to cover travelling expenses and accommodation for any participants who are not able to cover these costs from alternative sources. These are to be piloted in Tamil Nadu, preferably at the Christian Medical College, whose staff have expressed an interest in applying and have offered their facilities and collaboration.

2   Because local professionals lack the funds to attend overseas conferences, we recommend that a limited number of bursaries be made available to senior professionals from the tsunami-affected area who are involved in the training and supervision of front-line workers to attend the Seventh International Conference on Grief and Bereavement in Contemporary Society, which will be held on 12–15 July 2005 at King's College, London, UK. This presents a unique opportunity to meet others from around the world and share experiences, knowledge and research results through a series of seminars and workshops. Several sessions will focus on the needs of tsunami survivors.

3   Regardless of whether or not recommendation 2 is approved, we would also recommend that Help the Hospices host a one-day workshop, during the Monday preceding the conference, for any professionals or volunteers who are working with people bereaved by the tsunami.

4   We understand that Help the Hospices is already funding the translation and dissemination of relevant literature for people working in Sri Lanka with tsunami victims. We applaud this use of funds and would be glad to help develop similar literature for use in other tsunami-affected countries.

5   Amanda Aitken, who regularly provides reviews of resources on the Internet for the journal *Bereavement Care*, has prepared a review of the resources on the World Wide Web available to people working with tsunami survivors. We recommend that she be reimbursed for the costs of this work. This will be used to enable her to upgrade her computer facilities.

6   CMP has prepared a short advice leaflet 'For People Affected by the Tsunami and Similar Traumatic Losses' which has been published in English on the Cruse Bereavement Care Web site for bereaved people returning to English-speaking countries from the tsunami area. Professionals in India are currently considering its suitability for use in the tsunami-affected parts of India. If a suitably modified document can be agreed some funds for translating it into native languages in the tsunami area and, possibly, publishing as a leaflet for circulation locally would be of value.

7   There is a need for systematic research to assess the continuing needs of the tsunami-affected populations, to guide service provision and to enable lessons to be learned from this disaster that will improve planning for future disasters. CMP has already been asked to advise on suitable methods of assessment and we recommend that funds be made available to support the costs of such work by responsible bodies.

Final considerations

The longer-term consequences of the tsunami are still not clear and we shall not lose interest in further developments once this initial project is concluded. The continuation of earthquake activity near the epicentre of the 26 December earthquake is cause for anxiety, not only because of further danger to the affected areas, but also because it keeps alive the fears of traumatised people and may contribute to the perpetuation of PTSD and other problems. CMP has recently been approached by Dr Estefanus, a consultant physician from Anugerah Hospice in Java, Indonesia, who has himself visited Aceh and is willing to assist in any attempt to carry out a similar assessment in that region. We shall continue to monitor developments and may seek funds for further action.

The proposals listed here will contribute to improve the quality of the care provided to people bereaved by the tsunami. It may also lead to the development of bereavement services in the affected countries and we have already contributed to encourage the development in Vellore of a bereavement service linked with the developing palliative care unit. Through its link with the well-regarded Christian Medical College in Vellore, this bereavement service could become a model for the development of similar services elsewhere in India. Professor Tharyan and his staff are already well versed in bereavement work and will provide a useful resource for the further development of this work. We hope to provide continued support and AD, who is a Trustee of *Weston Hospice Care*, at Weston Super-Mare, UK, has proposed a twinning arrangement between the two hospices.

We wish to express our thanks to the donor who has made this work possible, to the many professionals and bereaved people who have helped us and to those who provide continuing help to the people whose suffering we have witnessed.

APPENDIX – EXTRACTS FROM PROJECT NOTES

[Before meeting those directly affected by the tsunami it was important to find out all we could about cultural issues and the services already responding to the disaster in Tamil Nadu.]

18.3.05

Having travelled to *[Chennai, capital of Tamil Nadu,]* India we went to . . . Loyola College to meet Dr Udaya Mahadevan, Head of Social Work, . . . and several colleagues who have been providing support to tsunami victims as part of the response of the government of Tamil Nadu.

[They informed us that] on the whole the Tamils are a peaceful group and the tensions of the past have quite gone away. They tend to believe in astrology and the situation has been made much worse by one famous astrologer who predicted that this would be a bad year for men and committed suicide after the tsunami because he could not bear facing the worse disasters that are to come.

In the past the sea was their friend, a goddess, 'Karam Hama'(trs. Sea Mother), who provided them with their livelihood. Now they have been betrayed by their god. The fact that 80% of Tamil fishermen are Christian does not prevent this superstition. Their Christianity is a thin veneer covering older beliefs.

The family and community support systems are not what they used to be, with many young people leaving their homes and neighbourhoods to follow educational and occupational activities elsewhere. This said there is communal support for grieving in the form of the Opeara – a tradition in which people hug and support bereaved people and share their grief. Suicide among young people has been on the increase for several years and is attributed to examination pressures.

. . . In Chennai there were 100 identified dead and 100 still missing. Relatives of missing persons are unable to claim death benefits because of the stringent criteria that have been set up to prevent false claims. The physical damage is enormous with homeless now in temporary accommodation. Allocation of this has taken account of the importance of maintaining community links. Fifty-six percent of the exposed population are disturbed. Most of their department's 100 child development centres have been destroyed and several of the teachers killed.

They explained that there are no bereavement services *per se* in Tamil Nadu but they run training programmes in trauma counselling and psychosocial counselling. Moneys have been provided for building temporary homes and to replace some of the fishing boats that have been lost, but the distribution of funds is uneven.

A major political crisis has arisen because developers, who are thought to be in collusion with the government, want to take this opportunity to turn the fishermen off the coast in favour of tourism. The fishermen are ambivalent about going back to sea but have no alternatives and there is no proposal to retrain them. Some of the displaced persons' accommodation is twelve kilometres inland, making it more difficult for fishermen to return to work, even if they still have boats.

Cases of PTSD are being identified and treated with good results. Anger is not yet a problem but survival guilt is expressed by children and adults. Many children have refused to return to school, although this is getting better. Many fishermen are too afraid to return to the sea. Counsellors are trying to reassure them but are not being believed. There has been a sharp rise in problems of drugs and alcohol in both men and women. (In Tamil Nadu the wives of fishermen often drink alcohol.)

Schoolteachers are being trained in trauma support and numerous volunteer counsellors have already been trained. . . . CMP asked if they thought there might be some value in some workshops to train people to develop bereavement support services. They showed great interest and seemed fascinated to learn about the variety of such services in the United Kingdom.

We then moved on to visit the headquarters of Action Aid in Tamil Nadu, which was situated in a low-cost building in central Chennai. We were welcomed by some enthusiastic and impressive young Indian women who were proud of what they have achieved. They have trained more than 100 volunteer counsellors to provide one-to-one support (focussed on empowerment) and have developed a variety of community support programmes. Despite this they recognise that the help is still patchy . . .

After leaving them we visited the sea front at Chennai where we found many people staring out to sea. Washed up on the shore were numerous garlands which had been thrown into the sea as a tribute to its power. This is a common tradition and has nothing to do with the tsunami except to confirm the importance of the sea on the lives of these people. When the bodies of Hindus have been cremated their ashes are thrown into the sea, not the Ganges.

19.3.05

Mr Santhosh Clement came to our hotel and will accompany us during our trip south. He is a young experienced Indian psychologist who, before the tsunami, was working with AIDS sufferers and has been helping to set up a palliative care unit at the Christian Medical Care (CMC) Hospital in Vellore.

[He informed us that] . . . following the tsunami a variety of NGOs descended on the area to provide support of varying quality. Some areas were inundated with too much help, others got nothing at all; it was chaos. Now the NGOs have mostly gone home and the government of Tamil Nadu has instigated a proper plan for the long-term care of those who need help. All charities are asked to register (as we have done on behalf of Help the Hospices) and to work together. CMC, Action Aid and others have each been allocated specific villages for which they are now responsible. Santhosh is in charge of the training and support of psychosocial care in four large villages. He knows the area well, speaks good Tamil and has spent time providing one-to-one care; consequently he is the ideal guide for us and we have spent a great deal of time talking about the situation today.

We drove from Chennai to Pondicherry and spent the rest of the afternoon talking, arranging visits and planning the next three days. Santhosh confirms our impression that palliative care services in this country do little to support bereaved people. He also confirmed that traditional family support systems are breaking down, particularly in the cities and towns. On the other hand he has been impressed by the effectiveness of both the community supports and the coping strategies of the rural fisher folk who are most affected by the tsunami. They are totally dependent on the sea but also used to its dangers. Fishing from small boats, men can be lost at any time and often are. Their families live with that danger and their communities regularly provide support to those who are bereaved. Thus, the tsunami is just another example of the outrages of nature that they have come to expect. Women grieve in a natural way and most of them seem to cope well.

Men, on the other hand, do not expect to lose wives and children. When faced with bereavement they are not allowed to cry; they adopt a macho attitude, keep a stiff upper lip and drink too much. Alcoholism is now a serious problem. They also suffer from high blood pressure and sexual problems, notably loss of libido. He confirms CMP's impression that Indians tend to somatize their problems. Santhosh thinks men are now more in need of counselling than women.

20.3.05

Drove, with Santhosh, to visit the four villages in Nagapattinam supported by CMC. This was our first direct contact with the affected population and it proved to be deeply moving and made us apprehensive for the future. The first village we visited, Tirumavaisal, is largely ruined. It consisted of single-storey, cement-walled bungalows thatched with reeds. Many of the roofs are gone and the walls smashed to the ground by the weight of water. Broken palm trees litter the ground and open spaces are denuded of foliage. Some trees have survived and their vivid green contrasts with the grey and white skeletons of homes and habitat.

In the houses that remain people sit and children play much as ever, but broken boats are everywhere visible on the foreshore and even those that seem, at first glance to be intact, are found, on closer inspection, to have great gashes in their hulls. As a backdrop, a lovely sandy beach with distant waves. In this area five fishermen go out in each boat, with nets, to catch the prawns and fish that come close to the land. Larger boats are used for deeper fishing but these were not seen.

The local head man told us how the first wave alerted people to the danger without doing much damage and some people escaped by running to higher ground or clinging to trees. It was the second wave that did the most damage being more powerful. Most of the houses were immersed and 180 people drowned. By the third wave the survivors had climbed onto the roofs of those houses that were still intact and no more were lost. Today, nearly three months on, none of the fishermen have returned to the sea although all say that they will do so when the proper compensation has been paid.

In the course of the day it became clear to us that in recent weeks most of the many NGOs who came in the aftermath of the tsunami have left. Much of the money which was handed out in well-meant but irregular and unpredictable fashion to poor people who have always lived from hand to mouth has stopped and the population is now subsisting on government aid. Some fishermen have received payments and others none; some have received new boats from NGOs but have sold these because they have already been promised new boats by the government and will lose them. Having nothing to do, they drink away their aid money and become increasingly dissatisfied.

The situation resembles that which commonly causes compensation neuroses and chronic unemployment in other settings – people are afraid that if they return to work they will lose out and are gradually being sucked into a state of passive dependency. This is likely to get worse unless an equitable agreement can be reached between the government representatives and those of the fishermen. But much of the anger is irrational and may be a reflection of unresolved grief.

We visited the home of a woman in her forties who had lost one of her twin sons. She looked anxious and insecure, is suffering long-standing anxiety, which predates the tsunami, but is now much worse. Her husband is an alcoholic and stood sheepishly by as we talked with his wife. She cannot sleep and fears the return of the water.

A younger sister was asked to talk to us and appeared very nervous. CMP tried to put her at her ease by admiring her dress but she then took fright and walked out of the room. It appears that CMP had broken a taboo that men should not comment on such things. As we left she was waiting outside and gave him a reassuring smile as if to say, 'I understand and am not offended'.

More tragic was the case of a middle-aged woman who lost her daughter and granddaughter. When we arrived her mother was lying on the floor of her small, dark, house in an attitude of despair. She left as we entered and was replaced by her daughter who crouched in the corner and cried throughout our meeting. Her doctor has prescribed an antidepressant but she will not take the tablets as she does not believe that they will help her. She describes her despair as continuous and unrelieved, a clear indication of clinical depression. Her extended family is very solicitous but unable to get through to her. CMP tried to persuade her to take the tablets as they will assuredly help her, but she was too depressed to respond. Her family and friends may persuade her. Her husband is an alcoholic and stood sheepishly by as we talked with his wife. Santhosh says that he no longer cares for his wife.

A twenty-two-year-old girl with a baby now aged four months had lost her husband. She seemed cheerful but would not talk about the tsunami. A bright girl who will do well.

We drove on to a refugee camp, a grim line of corrugated iron shacks, where large numbers of men sit around doing nothing while the women look after the many kids and do the household chores. Again, most men are fishermen although some are migrant labourers who normally work in Singapore and have returned to be with their families and to claim benefits. This serves the village of Kodalayar where many lost their homes, but the head man was away so we did not stay for long and moved on to a third village, Kottamedu, where there had been little structural damage and no loss of life but all the homes were flooded, possessions were lost, boats destroyed and the land salinated so that nothing will now grow there. People gathered round to tell us of their plight and morale is low.

Finally we visited a large refugee camp. Hepatitis has broken out and CMP examined one of the first cases and confirmed the diagnosis. CMC has provided lavatories but these are not being cleaned and smell badly; these people normally excrete in the woods and by-ways and such refinements are unfamiliar to them. They refuse to clean the lavatories (which is the job of people of the lowest caste).

We met Matthew, a tall social worker who is initiating mutual support groups. No special services are provided for bereaved people but there had been a special meeting of them this day. We were about to leave when 'Dr John' arrived. He is concerned about a man who has taken to the bottle using the compensation money, which he received for the death of his wife and two children. He says he is denigrated by others who are jealous of his 'wealth'. Seen with Dr John, he said that he wants more money so that he can get a wife. She will stop him drinking and he will then be able to return to his work as a labourer. CMP expressed sympathy for his loss and gently suggested that he is more likely to be able to attract another wife if he stops drinking. He admitted that he misses his wife and children terribly and feels socially isolated in this camp. He drinks to escape. Having talked this all through he appeared much less belligerent and we parted the best of friends.

21.3.05

Nagapattinum is the largest town in India to be badly affected by the tsunami. Built on the waterfront it was badly hit by the second wave; many houses were destroyed. We drove to the hospital for an appointment with Dr Venkatachalam, Director of Health Services for the large district . . . He explained that, in this area, the main source of income is fishing and most men are part of the fleet of large boats that go out for three days at a stretch with crews of up to twenty men. Almost all the boats have been lost and it will take between six months and two years to replace them.

Many men have lost their homes and are living in the large refugee camp near the foreshore. Although his department has managed to provide a high standard of health care the fishermen are unable to return to work, the aid from abroad is now drying up fast and people are losing faith in the government's ability to support them. Bereaved people are having a particularly hard time and there has been one suicide of a widower among the families of 5,000 who died.

The director assigned two staff to accompany us to the refugee camp, which houses 2,000 people in shacks with corrugated iron walls and roofs. It is situated quite near the sea and vulnerable to any future tsunami. This fact did not seem to be a major source of anxiety to the refugees, who seem to have accepted the reassurance that they have received.

We talked at length with a group of refugees. They told us that the houses are much too hot, there are no fans and they are uninhabitable after the sun has come up. The men all want to return to work and say that they are not afraid of the sea, but there are no boats for them. They sit around all day; when the sun goes down some play volleyball but most do nothing. There is an outbreak of chicken pox affecting all age groups. They hate waiting like this and fear that, now that most of the aid workers have gone, they will be neglected. Conditions in the camp are poor with one dilapidated shack in use as a medical post and a tiny hut as a temple. There is one large television set for the 2,000 people in the only large meeting hall. The best thing is the school, which is situated in the camp and run by the same teachers whom the children all know.

Walking around it was clear that the children are indeed quite happy while the adults appear depressed and hopeless. They take little interest in sports or other activities and greeted CMP's questions about the volleyball team as trivial.

We visited the ruined area of the town where most of the sites of houses have been cleared but the large, wrecked fishing boats fill the landscape, like beached whales. Some of them have been swept by the tsunami into the housing areas and are now wedged between ruined buildings. Some enterprising survivors have transformed a couple of wrecked boats into homes with newly improvised thatched roofs. Houses here were bungalows built of bricks with rush-thatched roofs. Many of the brick walls are down, but where the walls were not destroyed the thatch has now been replaced and life goes on. A new bridge is being built, a new school is completed and people are hard at work building new houses on the sites left bare by the tsunami. Nobody seems to fear another tsunami. A specimen house has been built within the refugee camp as a symbol of hope.

We talked to a man who had lost his wife and mother. His house is still habitable but his two children are in the refugee camp with their friends. He visits them there every day and cooks their food. Asked how high the wave came he said it was higher than his bungalow. He looked sad but not overwhelmed and clearly has a plan of life worked out. While we were talking two friends came to join in and we realised that he is certainly not alone.

On the foreshore a number of canoes made out of thick, curved, timbers of a light wood have been repaired and some of the men use them to catch fish for their families, but not enough to sell.

A local man told us he had lost his two daughters and wife, but now felt he had recovered and wanted to get back to fishing. He showed us where a mass grave had been dug on the shore where both identified and unidentified bodies had been buried.

Returning to the hospital we met the senior hospital administrator who told us proudly of the rescue operation which took place after the first wave hit the ground floor of the hospital. The second wave arrived ten minutes later by which time every patient had been removed to higher ground and not a single life was lost. Most of the hospital is in ground floor blocks that were flooded to a depth of three or four feet. The building was already old and he showed us the plans of the brand new hospital that will be built from charitable donations.

22.3.05

Drove to the Christian Medical College (CMC), Vellore the campus of which is beautifully situated in open woodland. We were welcomed by Dr Prathap Tharyan, Professor of Psychiatry, who had helped to arrange our trip.

We lectured on the subject of traumatic bereavement to an audience of about thirty medical students and staff of the hospital . . . After the lectures we dined with the faculty members including the staff of the palliative care unit. This has been providing home care for two years and has eleven staff members. We met their medical director, Dr Reena George, also their chief nurse, chaplain, junior doctor, social worker and administrator and were most impressed. They reacted very positively to Ann's offer to arrange a link with a hospice in Bristol of which she is a trustee.

23.3.05

CMC Hospital is a large and prestigious hospital and medical school two kilometres from the college. Ann was asked to talk to a group of around thirty paediatric nurses on the issues surrounding child death. In India children are not told of their impending death, families do all the caring and nurses have few opportunities to be alone with children. She was introduced to the head of Child Health, who was keen to support further training. Doctors and nurses desperately need more books and leaflets. She was shown round the paediatric intensive care unit (11 beds) and the other paediatric wards which were all very busy and spotlessly clean.

Ann then joined CMP in the offices of the palliative care team. Palliative medicine is still developing in India and faces many problems. It can be difficult to achieve good symptom control when drugs, beds and community nurses are scarce. The palliative care service in Vellore is set within a busy oncology department and cares for patients and their families within a twenty-mile radius.

. . . We visited the site of the future in-patient palliative care unit. This is in the grounds of a large and beautiful Catholic meditation centre; a peaceful place where we walked in silence through a courtyard filled with the sound of caged birds. That centre is providing the land and premises and its nuns will act as nurses in the unit. It is some miles from the busy hospital in quiet pleasant surroundings. It is hoped that the hospice building will be completed by the end of 2005. In collaboration with the palliative care unit, an order of Roman Catholic nuns will run the hospice, and carry out nursing duties . . .

Most of our recommendations were implemented and we had the pleasure of meeting again with Santhosh Clement, Reena George and others who were supporting victims of the tsunami at a post-tsunami workshop on bereavement needs in emergency situations and in the course of the Seventh International Conference on Grief and Bereavement in Contemporary Society that took place in London from 12–16 July 2005, seven months after the tsunami.

Note

1   Trauma counselling and therapy is aimed primarily at anxiety management, prevention of PTSD and treatment of anxiety/panic disorders and PTSD. These conditions commonly occur in disaster areas and respond well to these interventions.

PART 5

WAR AND TERRORISM: BREAKING THE CYCLE OF VIOLENCE

In October 1993 I retired from my post as senior lecturer and honorary consultant psychiatrist at the Royal London Hospital. Friends sent me retirement cards with pictures of old men fishing and I thought that might be interesting. But not interesting enough.

In the same month I had been invited to celebrate the tenth anniversary of Cruse in Northern Ireland. Peace talks had broken down and the Irish were experiencing the worst death toll since the early 1970s with twenty-three civilians killed, nine in the IRA Shankill bomb and eight in a Loyalist shooting on Halloween night (after calling 'trick or treat') at a Greysteel's pub in County Derry. These events had stirred my sympathy for the affected Irish but it was the hideous genocide that took place in Rwanda in early 1994 that changed the direction of my researches.

I visited the capital city, Kigali, to help set up a trauma recovery programme at a time of chaos, when law and order had broken down, the invading army was still on full alert and maintaining a nightly curfew and revenge killings were commonplace. The atmosphere brought back teenage memories of Britain in 1940 and shattered any illusion I might have had that the world is a safe place. It left me with an angry need to understand how an entire nation could become drawn into such murderous violence.

This feeling was reinforced by visiting New York in 2001 in the wake of the 9/11 terrorist attacks. I was a member of a team of Cruse volunteers who worked closely with family liaison officers from the Metropolitan Police to meet and support the relatives of British people lost in the collapse of the Twin Towers. With them, I met Kofi Annan, director general of the United Nations, and told him of the work in Rwanda. Subsequently I wrote to him on behalf of Doctors for Human Rights urging him to set up a United Nations Genocide Prevention Focal Point. 'This would act as a watchdog, alerting you and the member nations of the build up of tensions likely to lead to future genocidal conditions and drawing on the experience of genocide scholars, lawyers, politicians and others to reduce that risk . . .' On 7 April 2004, the tenth anniversary of the start of the genocide in Rwanda, he announced the creation of the post of special advisor on the prevention of genocide, 'to ensure that the Security Council is informed fully and in a timely manner about situations of threats of genocide which also represent threats to international peace and security'.

These experiences convinced me that the growing body of knowledge of the psychosocial consequences of trauma, death and bereavement has important implications for our understanding of the responses to terrorism, genocidal killings and other armed conflicts. The publications included in this section will give the reader a feel for work in conflict areas and some idea of the way our thinking is developing. But we still have far to go if the trajectory of these lessons is to be maintained.

CHAPTER 22

GRIEF AND RECONCILIATION

Extracts from an address to celebrate the tenth anniversary of the foundation of Cruse Bereavement Care in Northern Ireland

In September 1993 a car bomb exploded outside the Cruse shop in Belfast. The windows were shattered but the shop stayed open. On 3 October 1993, as president of Cruse, I gave an address at the special service held in St. Anne's Cathedral, Belfast, to celebrate the tenth anniversary of Cruse Bereavement Care in Northern Ireland. In addition to Cruse counsellors and supporters, the lord lieutenant along with senior clergy of each main religion attended the occasion. The lesson was taken from the first book of Kings, chapter 17 v. 10–16 in which the prophet Elijah visits the village of Zarapheth during a time of famine and asks a starving widow and her son for hospitality.

> *And she said, 'As the Lord God liveth, I have not a cake but an handful of meal in a barrel and a little oil in a cruse; and behold, I am gathering two sticks, that I may go in and dress it for me that we may eat it and die'. And Elijah said unto her, 'Fear not, go and do as thou hast said; but make me there of a little cake first, and bring it unto me, and after make for thee and for thy son. For thus saith the Lord God of Israel. The barrel of meal shall not waste nor shall the cruse of oil fail until the day that the Lord sendeth rain upon the earth'. And she went and did according to the saying of Elijah: and she, and he, and her house did eat many days. And the barrel of meal wasted not, neither did the cruse of oil fail . . .*

In the tale of the widow's cruse, there are two caregivers; there is the prophet Elijah, who cares for the widow and her son, and there is the widow who cares for the prophet. We are here today to celebrate ten years of the work of Cruse Bereavement Care in Northern Ireland, ten years in which the many volunteers who give their time to Cruse have cared for hundreds of widows, widowers, children and others bereaved by death. Those of you who know about bereavement will not be surprised to hear that many of those who offer themselves so wholeheartedly as counsellors to the bereaved have themselves been bereaved. They have learned from their own experience how much the bereaved need support through the long valley of grief and, in due time, they have become guides to others. Like the widow of Zarapheth, they are motivated to reach out to others in misfortune.

We are never more in need of our friends than we are after a bereavement, yet this is also a time when many of those we thought of as friends will disappoint us. They don't mean to. Perhaps they avoid us because they are afraid of upsetting us, of making things worse – 'What can you say?' They know they can't give us the one thing we most want, the dead person back again. They feel helpless and useless, so they back off. In consequence bereaved people often feel that they are being treated like lepers, as if bereavement were infectious. They now understand the meaning of the phrase 'Laugh and the world laughs with you, weep and you weep alone'.

Belfast has had more than its fair share of traumatic bereavements and Cruse has been in the forefront of support to victims of bombings and other man-made violence. The anger which follows such events is very understandable and can become a power for good or bad according to the way it is expressed.

In the course of my work as a psychiatrist in London, I was consulted by a man whose wife had been murdered by the babysitter's boyfriend whom she had interrupted while he was robbing her jewellery box. During the next few days her husband, in his rage, was roaming the streets of London with a loaded revolver in his pocket, searching for the killer. If he had found him he would probably have killed the man. Fortunately the police got to the murderer before he did. Six months later this man appeared on television speaking out against capital punishment for murder. He said that it had suddenly occurred to him that, if he had found and killed the murderer, he would have been doing to this man's child exactly what the man had done to his own four-year-old daughter.

In Ireland we have seen, only too often, the dreadful consequences of the vicious circle of violence which can arise when violence begets vengeance. But we also know of some notable bereaved people whose anger, far from leading them to seek vengeance, has drawn them into the peace movement. This is creative grieving. It's no good saying to a bereaved person 'You mustn't be angry.' Anger is a normal human emotion which needs to be expressed. But there are creative as well as destructive ways of expressing grief.

When people are bereaved they often lose faith; they may rail against God. C. S. Lewis, the Christian theologian, in the diary which he kept after his wife died and subsequently published as *A Grief Observed*, says 'Don't speak to me of the consolations of religion . . . go to Him when your need is desperate . . . and what do you find? A door slammed in your face, and a sound of bolting and double-bolting on the inside. After that, silence.' That was his experience and I am not suggesting that it is everybody's experience. But we have to accept people the way they are. It is no good arguing with the desolation that is grief. All we can do is to hang in there with the bereaved, to allow the waves of grief to break over us and to hope that, little by little, as the grief subsides, they will find new meanings in life and in God.

And by and large they do. One of the exciting things about bereavement counselling is to see people emerging from grief. Grief is not like the measles; you don't recover from it and go back to being the person you were before you suffered the bereavement. We are all permanently changed by grief. But the changes which take place need not be changes for the worse. Out of the fire of grief can come wisdom.

Never again will bereaved people be able to pretend that all is well with the world. Never again will they be able to ignore the griefs of others or deny the reality of death. They have learned the harsh facts of death the hard way. But in doing so they may become more sensitive and more compassionate to the griefs of others, and develop a deeper understanding of the meanings of life and death.

Society has an unfortunate tendency to pity the bereaved, to belittle them and to see them as broken reeds who have nothing to contribute. But I believe that those who have come through the pains of grief and have found new directions in their lives are often more valuable to society *because* of their experience.

Reference

Lewis, C. S. *A Grief Observed*. Faber (first published by N. W. Clerk), London, 1961.

CHAPTER 23

GENOCIDE IN RWANDA

From *Bereavement Care* 14(3): 34, 1995.

In 1995, in the wake of the conflicts in Serbia, Croatia and Bosnia/Herzegovina (B/H), I was invited by the distinguished psychologist Atle Dyregrov to attend a conference on traumatic bereavement in Norway. I gave a lecture on 'Working with Victims of Traumatic Bereavement' and we then divided into groups in order to help with some of the problems brought by the participants. Among the members of my workshop were ten people, one of whom was a young Muslim social worker from Bosnia/ Herzegovina. She asked our group how she should help a small community in which she, as well as most of the other women, had been raped, and most of the men had been murdered by Serbian troops. We were all horrified by her story and I suggested that we try to get our heads round the problem by each taking the role of one key member of that community and then talking together from that person's point of view. In the course of the next two hours the social worker briefed us and we became wives, children, teachers, an imam, a journalist and, in my case, a community elder whose life had been spared because he was too old to fight.

As we talked, the community gradually ceased to be an object of pity and became instead familiar, like an extended family. We were, in a sense, making the extraordinary, ordinary. I was already an 'elder' and it was all too easy to see, in my mind's eye, a gang of Nazi thugs, the bogeymen of my childhood, raping and murdering my friends and family. Although the experience was hard for all of us, I shall never forget the strange sense of solidarity, indeed gratitude, as if this young woman had invited us into her home during a time of great suffering. The feeling was mutual and by some mysterious process our willingness to share made the social worker feel understood and accepted. Rape is a very alienating experience and it takes courage to talk about it. Our willingness to accept her and her damaged community, to welcome them to our world, healed something, and, as she put it, gave her the courage to return. We had no simple answers to her predicament but the very act of sharing the horrors had made them seem manageable.

At the final plenary session a Jewish psychologist, who had himself lost most of his family in the Holocaust, expressed his appreciation of the workshop and said that, if only something similar had been provided immediately after World War II, much of the lasting suffering among Jewish survivors might have been alleviated.

The conference ended with a barbecue party by the waters of the fjord. As the sun went down and the wine took effect, we danced and sang together to the music of many nations. I think that this may have been the time when I became an internationalist, proud to be a part of the community of the world despite its horrors.

Atle was pleased with the evaluations of our work and it was not long before I heard from him again. 'Colin, I want you to go to Rwanda. UNICEF has set up a trauma recovery programme there; they need your help.' What could I say?

During the first week of April 1995 I visited Rwanda as the guest of the United Nations Children's Fund (UNICEF). My brief was to speak at a conference and to meet some of the people who are providing counselling and support to the huge numbers of people who were bereaved and otherwise traumatised in the genocide which took place during April and May 1994.

Rwanda is only slightly larger than Wales. It has a population density not much different from England but without the industrial base to support it. A hilly country with a wonderful climate which allows two harvests a year, it should be an Eden but for the terrible heritage of violence that has been eating at its heart for thirty-five years.

I spent the first two days talking to aid workers, several of whom were Rwandans who had lost members of their families. These included a schoolteacher, who had been attending a conference in Nairobi when the massacres broke out and returned to find that her husband, parents and five children had all been killed, and a young psychologist who had recently moved with most of his family to Belgium. He had left his son [and mother] in Rwanda to complete his schooling. The boy was lost, along with many of his classmates [and his grandmother].

Their stories are typical of a country in which up to a million [recent estimates are 800,000] men, women and children have been slaughtered in a systematic attempt at genocide which appears to have been organised by a corrupt government in an attempt to destroy its political opponents and remain in power.

Readers will be familiar with the story. In the context of an uneasy truce in the civil war, which has been going on in Rwanda since 1990, the United Nations along with all of the countries surrounding Rwanda finally persuaded the president of Rwanda to agree to hold democratic elections the outcome of which would have led to the downfall of the government in power. Three days later, the plane in which the president was travelling, along with the president of neighbouring Burundi, was shot down by missiles whose origin has never been established. The ruling family, who were Hutus, blamed members of the Tutsi tribe and within twenty-four hours had initiated the systematic killing of their Hutu political opponents as well as of all men, women and children who were thought to be Tutsis. Within the next fourteen days the killing spread throughout Rwanda and massacres took place in most towns and villages. . . . [Many] people are said to have been slaughtered by means of fragmentation grenades which were thrown into the churches, schools and other places where the terrified victims had taken refuge. The doors were then thrown open and anyone left alive finished off with clubs and machetes.

There then followed a mopping-up operation in which local militia regularly searched the homes, work places and hospitals to find and kill any of the 'cockroaches' who had survived the massacres. Parents hid their children in holes in the ground or left them unaccompanied in the bush (for a child accompanied by a Tutsi parent would be killed). As a consequence there were, when I visited, still 40,000 children in Rwanda and 45,000 in surrounding countries who had literally 'lost' their parents. Most of them had witnessed horrific events.

During the first month the rate of killing exceeded that achieved by Hitler in his gas chambers, but this genocide was not carried out by professional guards but by local militia and neighbours of the Tutsi minority. The arrival of a victorious Tutsi army brought an end to the genocide but triggered a mass exodus of two million people who are now living in refugee camps in the surrounding countries. Some took refuge in a 'safe zone' set up by the French and subsequently handed over to the current government. The army's attempts to force the refugees to return to their home villages triggered another massacre.

I visited Rwanda on the eve of the first anniversary of the genocide. Five thousand bodies which had been dug up from mass graves were to be reburied in a cemetery overlooking the capital city of Kigali. Dignitaries from Africa and other countries were in attendance and the world press were present in large numbers. The Hotel Mille Collines was a crowded fortress with guards in every corridor but the streets were sparsely populated and the shops closed because of the national holiday. Only a few street children and amputees begged for money or tried to sell cigarettes. A curfew came into force at 5 p.m. but this did not deter anyone with a vehicle bearing the UN emblem from driving and I was able to spend evenings with hospitable members of UNICEF staff.

Our conference took place on the day preceding the burial service and enabled us to draw attention to the need for counselling and support of the numerous people who had been psychologically traumatised by the war and the massacres. Leila Gupta, who is in charge of UNICEF's trauma recovery programme, is setting up a network of people across Rwanda who will have been trained in bereavement and trauma counselling. She has a mammoth task and the financial resources of UNICEF are already overstretched, but if youth and enthusiasm count for anything then this team deserves to succeed.

The burial ceremony was extraordinary. A small group of us from UNICEF, along with other officials, drove in our UN vehicle onto the pitch of a football stadium in which the seats were occupied with huge coffins each of which contained twenty or so bodies. In this strange setting it was as if the dead had come back to watch the petty antics of the living. We milled about and talked in hushed tones while gangs of sweating men loaded the coffins onto giant trucks for the two-hour drive to the burial ground. The procession drove slowly through the streets which were lined with all the population of Kigali, past the ruined churches and the shell-torn signs of war, through the hovels of the shanty towns and through the fields of cassava and coffee bushes which line the thousand hills of this fertile and overpopulated land.

Nobody who visits Rwanda can fail to be captivated by it. This made it all the harder to witness the blank expressions on the faces of the tens of thousands who lined the streets to watch the procession. Nobody cried or smiled or waved. Even small children stood in silent family groups along with their older brothers and sisters, their thoughts locked up within their heads.

Arriving at the lovely hillside burial site we were ushered to seats beneath a covered canopy which was sprayed with scented water to offset the acrid aroma of the dead *[I still cannot bear the smell of rose water]*. Ten thousand others stood or sat in the bright sunshine, silent onlookers who shed no tears and talked quietly among themselves. An endless line of trucks unloaded their grisly contents onto baulks of timber which had been placed in readiness across long trenches. A small choir sang cheerful songs about Jesus and the bright sunshine seemed indecently obtrusive. The archbishop spoke briefly as the body of the late president together with the coffin of an unknown victim of the genocide were lowered side by side into the ground. There followed a long succession of speeches in various tongues. We did not stay until the end; one of our party was feeling sick and the rest of us were glad of the excuse to slip away.

I lingered on in Kigali for three more days, typing reports, broadcasting on the radio (probably my most important contribution) and swimming in the hotel pool along with press men, aid workers and the UN human rights officers (who have the impossible task of monitoring abuses which, if reported to the authorities, often lead to more abuses of human rights, for the system of law and order has broken down).

On the journey home my plane broke down in Nairobi which gave me the opportunity to fulfil a life's ambition to visit a game park. The park was all it should have been and I pretended to be a tourist, but my heart was not in it.

These experiences made a deep impression and changed the direction of my studies in the years to come. I remained in touch with Leila and her colleagues. We met again at several international conferences and I joined Doctors for Human Rights and took part in international work groups on 'Traumatic Bereavement', 'Cycles of Violence' and 'Armed Conflict'. I returned to Rwanda in 2012 to interview survivors and study the peace process for the book 'Responses to Terrorism: Can psychosocial interventions break the cycle?' (see Chapter 22).

CHAPTER 24

REFLECTIONS ON CRUSE'S RESPONSE TO 9/11

Extracts from the diary of Colin Murray Parkes

From *South West Herts Bereavement Network Newsletter,* 2002.

11.9.01

. . . the news pictures from New York came through of the hijacked airliners, filled with fuel, crashing into the World Trade Center and the Pentagon. For the rest of the day there was continuous news coverage of the aftermath but it took a long time for its implications to sink in. The whole thing was beautifully filmed, giving the impression that it was a disaster movie; only when I caught sight of the look of abject fear on the face of one of the people fleeing from the collapse of one of the towers did it strike home. I cried.

15.9.01

The Annual Conference of Cruse Bereavement Care . . . was held at the Institute of Education in London. Virginia Bottomley MP was giving an excellent paper during the morning when a call came through from the Foreign Office requesting us to mobilise a team of volunteer counsellors to go to New York to support the 200+ British citizens who had lost people in the disaster. They would be flown out there at government expense. I explained the situation to the meeting and, within an hour, we had forty names of volunteers willing to go, out of a meeting of 163 people.

16.9.01 Sunday

Up at 6 a.m. to catch a flight from Gatwick to New York to prepare the ground for the Cruse counsellors who will fly out tomorrow. At the airport I met up with twenty-one police officers from the Family Liaison Unit; they are employed to collect evidence and give emotional support to families following murders and other serious crime. We got to know each other in the airport and on the plane and I got on reasonably well with their leader, Detective Chief Superintendent John Godsave. He is every inch a policeman – stocky, direct, curt and accustomed to being obeyed. His two deputies, David and Duncan, are more human and will be more closely involved with the day-to-day running of the team of which we are a part.

Arriving in New York we were bussed to a plush hotel, the Millennium UN Plaza, in midtown Manhattan. We were welcomed and briefed by Tom Harris, the British consul. Much of the southern end of Manhattan has been cordoned off as a crime scene which, we are told, will make it impossible for visiting families to get near the wreckage of the World Trade Center.

By now few people have much doubt that the missing persons are dead but the rescue operation is continuing. One of my tasks is to find a suitable place where the families can lay flowers.

17.9.01

During the morning we were taken in two minibuses to Union Square where flowers and candles have been placed along with pathetic pictures of missing people and requests for information. There are impassioned pleas for peace alongside declarations of support for America. The pleas for peace predominate.

We were accompanied by Mae Ling Harris, the consul's wife. A lovely lady in all senses. I sat next to her and she chatted about diplomatic life in New York where Mayor Giuliani has brought crime under control and made the city much safer than it was last time I visited.

On to the Family Center at Pier 94 where families of the missing persons are going. The Center is a huge place, like an aircraft hanger, and is staffed by eager volunteers who kept stopping me and asking if they could help. People coming to the centre are bringing toothbrushes and other household articles belonging to the missing persons for DNA testing. They can consult the computerised missing persons register and ensure that their relative is on the list. There are dangers of duplication because each country has its own list and nobody knows for sure how many people are indeed missing . . .

I visited the British Consulate to explain our role to the staff, then back to the hotel for a formal welcome from the British ambassador and his wife.

Went to Newark Airport to meet and welcome the Cruse counsellors in the evening. Their plane was delayed and we were all very tired by the time we got to bed. I woke up at 2 a.m. (7 a.m. British time) to phone Patricia.

18.9.01

Jet lagged on waking but soon revived and much relieved that the BCs are here. Patrick Shannon, the acting Chief Executive of Cruse, had sent a briefing note with the BCs appointing Artie O'Hara as our Team Leader. He is a fellow psychiatrist who has been responding to terrorist attacks in Northern Ireland and serves with me on the Council of Cruse. I was apprehensive that this might lead to conflict between us but he is as keen as I am to be of help and we get on well. I shall continue as consultant to the team.

At the morning briefing in the Incident Room at the hotel, John, 'the Guv', gave a clipped welcome to the new troops who were startled and amused by his orders for the day. He told them, clearly and precisely, what roles he and his fellow seniors were to play and left them in no doubt that he expected instant obedience to his commands. After only ten minutes he handed over command to David, his team leader, and left to attend to other business . . . *[Unfamiliar as we were to this authoritative style I can see his point. Disaster areas are no place for democratic decision-making.]*

Families are beginning to arrive and have, so far, been welcomed by the FLOs, leaving the BCs free to be briefed by me. During the afternoon they were taken on a tour of the town, leaving me free to organise rooms, phones and so forth . . .

Most of the planning of the team is done in the Incident Room, a large L-shaped room one half of which can be used for briefings, writing reports and so forth while the other houses the duplicator, shredder, two laptops, printer and so forth. We all carry mobile phones which enable us to keep in touch at all times.

The BCs are shaping up well. Lynn Franchino has been appointed to run the supervision and the team has been meeting to discuss its roles without me being needed. Each BC is linked with two FLOs and have begun to accompany them on some of their visits to the airports to greet families. David confided that several of the police are prejudiced against counsellors but I hope that this distrust will dissipate when we get to know each other.

19.9.01

. . . During the afternoon an influx of families who have arrived in time for the service of prayer tomorrow necessitated calling a group of the counsellors back from their exploration of the town. They had been trying to discover a suitable view point from which families can see the ruins of the towers. Lynn Franchino, with two FLOs and a bereaved family, reported that the FLOs had talked an American policeman into letting them into Ground Zero, the vicinity of the ruins. The smell is appalling and nearly made her vomit but the bereaved family, who wanted very much to get closer, were not, apparently, distressed. The FLOs went closer than the family and saw human body parts.

Reviewing this in our group we agreed that, even if this is permitted it would rarely be appropriate to expose a family to these sights and smells. We have, however, established that by travelling by the subway to Fulton Street Station and walking south down Broadway families can get a reasonable view of the wreckage without being exposed to anything more horrible than the press.

When the Guv found out that his officers had disobeyed his order to keep out of Ground Zero he was furious and cancelled the evening briefing.

20.9.01

Last night's infringement of Ground Zero nearly blew up into a diplomatic incident and the two officers involved will face disciplinary proceedings when they return to the United Kingdom. The other officers seem unfazed by this and one gets the impression that events of this kind are taken in their stride. One whom I spoke to thought that the officers concerned deserved to be disciplined.

This morning two large motor coaches carried us with nine or so families and the staff of the consulate to the consul's beautiful residence overlooking Central Park. Here we were given soft drinks and nibbles and had a chance to chat to each other. One bereaved lady said she was 'dying for a drink' so I burgled the consul's drink table and poured a stiff gin into her orange juice!

There was a steady downpour of rain as we got back into the coaches to be transported to St Thomas', a cathedral-sized church in the Gothic style with a fine stone altar screen. The press was there in force but we were admitted through a side entrance and sat, with the families, in the front of the nave. I was in the fifth row. While we waited the organist played a concert of lugubrious modern music which did little to raise our spirits. After twenty minutes a procession of dignitaries arrived to sit in the front row. They included Bill Clinton with Kofi Annan, the Secretary-General of the United Nations. Tony Blair was caught in the traffic and we had to wait another twenty minutes before he appeared with his wife Cherie and the service could start.

This was a beautiful event. Largely thanks to the singing of a large choir who performed several modern works. . . . Tony Blair gave a moving reading and an equally moving message from Her Majesty the Queen was read out. She quoted, without attribution, Colin Parkes' dictum 'grief is the price we pay for love'.

After the service we were ushered into a back room, with the families, to meet the dignitaries. I felt greatly honoured to meet Kofi Annan, who wore a serious face as he met each of us. He has a soft handshake and did not let go as he asked me about our work. I told him of my contribution in Rwanda and he looked surprised and said, 'Oh, you were there too were you?', then moved on with a perplexed expression on his face. I think he is not proud of his contribution to that enormity.

Tony Blair gave me a brief handshake and said 'Thank you'. He looked haggard, anxious and in a hurry. He was obviously behind schedule and soon left us to go on to Washington, DC to meet George Bush. [*With hindsight it is not hard to imagine the weight of responsibility that he bore at that time. His role was to assure President Bush of the sympathy and support for the United States of the British nation. Was he aware of the danger that he would be sucked into a cycle of violence?*] . . . Bill Clinton was doing a great job answering a bereaved relative who had the temerity to ask him what he would do if he were still the president. His reply lasted twenty minutes.

Returning to our hotel we continued our deliberations with the families over tea. Despite the length of the earlier formalities all opted to come and, by the end of the day, I had met most of the bereaved relatives and established friendly relations. It was very evident that their grief is oscillating. At times they look very sad, and some cry, at other times they cheered up and overall, in the course of the day, the mood lightened. I found myself pointing out that today's ceremonies meant that the world was grieving with them and several families seemed to find comfort in this idea. Personally I often had a feeling of depersonalisation as if we were all drifting on a tide of grief. I talked with one family whose son had been killed in one of the hijacked aircraft. They needed to know that he had been killed instantly and would not have suffered.

21.9.01

Went with two BCs, Pam Snowden and Shirley Hill, to visit the scene of the disaster. We emerged from the Fulton Street subway station to the din of road drills and lorry engines. Police are everywhere and marshalling the crowds to keep moving down the one side of Broadway that is open to the public. Television cameras are in evidence and ready to swoop on anyone who looks distressed. A constant stream of lorries is carrying rubble away from Ground Zero where a mound of rubble can be seen.

Some people were crying and Pam was the first of us to give way soon to be followed by me. The smell is not as bad as I had feared and the smoke, which was very evident two days ago, now seems to have diminished. Even so the sight is of a vision of hell.

We walked south down Broadway and the rescue operation could be easily seen along Fulton Street and Maiden Lane. On our left many of the shops were closed and everything on the right (west) side of the road is closed and coated with grey dust. Along the streets leading to the disaster area are parked emergency vehicles of all kinds. Many of the surrounding buildings have been reduced to tangled wreckage and others have been burned out. Further out from Ground Zero many of the skyscrapers have lost some or all of their windows. The empty frames stare out like puncture wounds. Along Maiden Lane a twisted mass of girders rears into the sky like the ribs of a giant skeleton. Cranes are at work scooping out the rubble and an endless stream of workers in hard hats and face masks comes and goes. Groups of them can be seen leaving the work face to stand around at a distance, where it is safe to remove their face masks and shout above the din to each other.

Fortunately the prevailing wind is from the east and the only smell was of dust but the atmosphere was oppressive and it was with a sense of relief that we escaped from the disaster area to relax and recover our composure on the Staten Island Ferry. While we sat and talked together the Statue of Liberty slipped slowly by and Shirley revealed that she has secondary cancer and has postponed her third course of radiotherapy to come here. Now it was her turn to cry, but she was not alone. I shall not forget the face of this gentle lady, in her late fifties and evidently underweight, talking softly about her need to connect with the griefs of others in the time that remains to her. While I sat with my arm round her I had the strangest feeling that she represented all of the griefs that we have witnessed and shared.

At the evening briefing we were addressed by Dr R. Shepherd, the Forensic Pathologist from St George's Hospital who has been sent over by the Foreign Office to liaise with the Americans. He gave us what information he could about the casualties. It will be for us to decide how and what to pass on to the families. It is now clear that few more intact bodies will be recovered from the wreckage, that the identification of those that remain by DNA and other means may take up to a year *[This information proved pessimistic, the identifications were soon completed]* and that, due to the corruption of the bodies, it may not be possible to extract useful tissues after the first few weeks.

. . . It is strange how each of us perceives the situation differently. The pathologist sees it as an exercise in identifying bodies, the police see it as a crime scene and I see it as the last resting place of thousands of people whose bodies might best be left undisturbed. Meanwhile huge numbers of people are digging frenetically in the vain hope of rescuing more people. All of this only prolongs the agony of the bereaved who want to know if they can now start grieving. I have spoken to adults of all ages; they know the score and want to be told what to do. A few are enraged and hitting out wildly. They upset the authorities who are trying to regain control of an uncontrollable situation.

The United Nations is united, almost for the first time. President Bush has set in motion the process of polarisation which is typical of the run-up to war with his 'all who are not with us are against us' speech. This is just the kind of divisive rhetoric which brought about the genocide in Rwanda *[This paragraph was omitted from my report to the SW Herts Bereavement Network, but it proved all too prescient]*.

I am tired and I want to go home. My work here is done and we can reduce the number of BCs here next week. Half the team is willing to stay and there will be no need to train a new batch. So I have booked a flight home tomorrow night.

[In retrospect, I left because I had no wish to tread on Artie's toes. Although support for families subsequently went smoothly and was much appreciated, John Godsave, 'the Guv', developed cardiac symptoms during the second week and was flown home. Morale in the police unit is said to have dropped sharply, but they were well supported by their Cruse partners and this incident seems to have consolidated mutual trust which was to continue in the years to come and led to a closer relationship between Cruse and the police service.

During the following month (October) I suffered a recurrence of asthma and a blood test showed me to have an indolent form of Chronic Lymphatic Leukaemia (CLL). The asthma soon improved, the CLL caused no symptoms and my lymphocyte count also improved gradually over the next decade. Were these illnesses precipitated by the stress of 9/11?]

11.9.02 [One year later]

Met up with several of the Cruse team from New York before the service of remembrance in St Paul's Cathedral. Princes William and Harry came, the young men looking very correct while their sun-tanned father was peering round at the congregation. During two minutes silence for the dead 3,000 white rose petals snowed down from the whispering gallery. Very effective and followed immediately by a beautiful Nunc Dimitis set by Geoffrey Burgon in 1941.

Had no opportunity to meet the bereaved families again but chatted to several members of the Police's Family Liaison team after the service, including their former Chief Superintendent John Godsave. He has recovered from his heart attack and was looking very well [*but has been*] retired from the police force.

While I was waiting to be interviewed briefly by the BBC, an onlooker suddenly shouted 'Babylon the Great is fallen' at the top of his voice before being swiftly removed by the police. The cathedral remained standing.

CHAPTER 25

MAKING AND BREAKING CYCLES OF VIOLENCE (ABRIDGED)

From R. G. Stevenson and G. Cox (eds.) *Perspectives on violence and violent death* (pp. 223–238). Amityville, NY: Baywood Publishing, 2007.

This paper was my first attempt to cross the boundary between clinical studies of the persisting violence that can follow violent deaths and the cycles of violence that can give rise to terrorism and war. In undertaking so ambitious a task I was helped by colleagues from the IWG who brainstormed together to create a useful model.

Some of the most harmful consequences of violence arise when a cycle of violence becomes established. In order to break cycles of violence we need to analyse the causes of such cycles. Yet violence evokes such strong emotions that it clouds our thinking and inhibits analytic thought. Indeed there is something 'calculating' about the very exercise in which we are engaged in this chapter. Like the anatomists who first dissected the human body, we need to find a way to touch the untouchable, to think clearly about the unthinkable, to inhibit our own revulsion from so dangerous a task.

Everyone has their own 'solution' to the problem of violence, which usually consists of identifying an enemy and defeating it. Another is the idea that the best way to break cycles of violence is to forbid violence, yet how can we enforce that prohibition if we are not willing to use violence itself? Police forces may need to use violence to apprehend a serial killer and 'peacekeeping' forces may need to use violence to protect themselves and to bring peace. Each discipline tends to develop its own model. Soldiers seek military solutions, clergy seek religious solutions, politicians seek political solutions and economists seek economic solutions. Some of these solutions sometimes work, but none of them provides a comprehensive or integrated view; all are, to some extent, simplistic, they attempt a simple solution to complex problems. And, as we shall see, some simplistic models do more harm than good.

In this paper a model will be described which explains many, but not all, of the cycles of violence and illustrates how they can and have been broken. The examples are either derived from actual cases or from systematic research. They show that, although the causes may be complex, they are often comprehensible and, although solutions may not be easy, they are often possible . . .

[Individual acts of violence rarely give rise to cycles of violence. It takes more than one person to perpetuate violence.]

Family and interpersonal level. Two or more individuals perpetuate or repeat acts of violence or abuse. These often involve circular 'traps' in which short-term relief from rising tension leads to perpetuation of conflict, for example marital tensions leading to alcohol abuse leading to repeated violence or sadomasochistic sexual relationships. Although, at the outset, such cycles usually involve two individuals, others are soon drawn in to take sides.

Small group/community level. In many species cyclical changes in hormone levels trigger aggression against co specifics at certain times each year; these lead to combats which come to an end as soon as one of the combatants submits or runs away, they seldom end fatally, for example rutting of stags in the spring. In humans, it is reasonable to assume that similar hormonal changes predispose young people, particularly males, to engage in aggressive, challenging behaviour. Young females may encourage conflict by favouring winners.

A large difference between humans and other species is, of course, the opportunity to achieve status by other means than combat. Psychological battles . . . take the place of physical conflict, and the takeovers, feuds and 'broken hearts' that result are seldom fatal.

Although few societies in which a small scale of 'clan' or 'tribal' organisation is established still exist, they were, over the long period of human evolution, the main unit of social organisation. Most societies lived in peace much of the time but sooner or later conflicts over territory, food or available mates would arise. Repeated battles against neighbouring tribes met the purpose of extending or maintaining territory; they also widened the gene pool by enabling the victors to claim mates from another tribe. Young males, who did most of the fighting, were also rewarded with 'warrior' status. This enabled some tribes to survive while less martial tribes perished. Thus, in evolutionary terms, the cost to the community of the death of some warriors was balanced by the survival of the clan/tribe.

Large-scale societies attempt to forbid or limit internecine feuds at the small group level with varying success. Within many societies subcultures see themselves as outside the law, 'outlaws' or gangs which resemble the clan or tribe. They are particularly likely to arise when central government breaks down and/or the rewards of obedience to higher authority: wealth, jobs, security, and so forth are denied, for example in the poor areas of major cities with high levels of unemployment and little hope for the future. Gangs often use drugs and/or alcohol to reduce fear or increase excitement; this in turn reduces inhibitions against violence, which is usually directed against other gangs or supposed enemies who may then become victims.

National level. Coups and revolutions occur when a powerful group within a large-scale society attempts to wrest power from the leaders. If the conflict is not soon resolved cycles of violence may become established and we have a civil war. Even when the conflict is resolved the seeds of future violence may have been sown. Because the emergent power is likely to enact severe penalties against future revolt the defeated parties may become 'outlaws' as described earlier. For a revolution to become a civil war two things are needed: 1) a balance of power between the contending parties such that neither can win a decisive victory, and 2) the contending parties need to be unwilling or unable to find a way to share power.

International level. When a powerful large-scale society attacks a weak or small-scale society the conflict is soon over although, as seen previously, the seeds of future conflict may have been sown and acts of resistance or 'terrorism' may continue. Wars arise when two or more powerful countries use violence against each other and, as in civil wars, the contenders cannot reach agreement to share power.

Although, at first glance, the differences between wars and smaller scales of conflict seem great, they become less so when we consider the important roles leaders and young males play. At all levels of analysis, except the individual, it is a small number of leaders who have the power to stop the conflict or to allow it to continue. Likewise, at all levels of analysis, it is young males who do most of the fighting.

A model of the cycle which crosses levels of social unit

With this in mind members of the International Work Group on Death, Dying and Bereavement (IWG) have developed a common model of cycles of violence capable of throwing light on the cycle at all levels above the individual. The model also suggests points at which intervention may break the cycle.

The IWG is a group of clinicians, researchers and educators, from many countries, who develop research and practice dealing with death, dying and bereavement. Our work brings us face to face with the consequences of cycles of violence (see Figure 25.1). It is this involvement that motivates the IWG to find ways to understand and find solutions to the problem. A more detailed account of the model described here has been published in *Death Studies* (International Work Group on Death, Dying and Bereavement 2005) . . .

Although the circumstances listed in the cycle tend to occur in sequence, each influences all the others.

Violent behaviour seldom occurs out of the blue. It is usually preceded by a period of rising tension during which preventive intervention is possible.

Examples:

- Mothers who serially abuse their children are often themselves under stress. Only when she 'gets to the end of her tether' does a mother, who may genuinely love her child, suddenly find herself losing her temper and hitting the child against a wall. Social workers may be able to form a

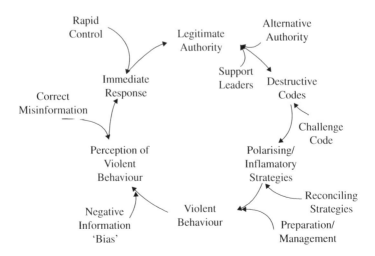

Figure 25.1 Cycle of violence

relationship of trust such that, whenever the mother becomes aware that her level of tension is rising, she will contact the social worker for immediate support and guidance.

- At an international level the United Nations has appointed a Special Adviser on the Prevention of Genocide whose role is to ensure that the Security Council is informed fully about threats of genocide, which also represent threats to international peace and security.

Violence is most likely to lead to retaliation and the initiation of a cycle if it is excessive, disproportionate, cruel or inhumane. When violence is threatened it may be possible to persuade or train those who are to carry it out to keep it to a minimum consistent with their aims. This is particularly the case when the violence is planned in advance. Rules of punishment and rules of engagement may authorise violence, but they also constitute opportunities for minimising it.

Examples:

- The abolition of corporal punishment in schools.
- Use of non-lethal methods of crowd-control (such as 'foam baton rounds' in place of conventional ammunition).

Those who carry out acts of violence need to monitor the consequences of their acts if they are to keep their violence to a minimum. This is easier in face-to-face combat than in conflicts that, with modern weapons, can be carried out without ever seeing the 'enemy'. In these circumstances the temptation to 'over kill' in order to be sure of success regularly leads to death and injuries to non-combatants. Agreements can forbid or limit the use of weapons likely to give rise to excessive consequences.

Examples:

- Legislation against the right of ordinary citizens to own or carry lethal weapons.
- International agreements against development, ownership and use of weapons of mass destruction.

Perception of violent behaviour

It is the perception of an act that determines the response. Following acts of violence the magnitude of the impact and interpretation of the event is influenced by witnesses and how information is communicated to others. Thus, child abuse is often perpetuated because the abused child is afraid to reveal the abuse or because it is disbelieved. On the other hand some children exaggerate or imagine abuse that has not happened (False Memory Syndrome). This can lead to 'witch hunts' that drag on and lead to more injustice. Clearly accurate and impartial reporting and open-minded listening are essential if communication is to succeed and an appropriate response to be made. In psychiatric circles this is referred to as 'reality testing' and involves very much more than the communication of factual information.

Similar failure of communication can take place at other levels, as when newspaper reporters play down or, conversely, exaggerate the magnitude of an event and the dangers associated with it or when prejudice clouds our interpretation of the information we receive.

But accurate reporting does not necessarily solve the problem. While modern weaponry may make it hard for combatants to witness the consequences of their actions, modern media of communication have the opposite effect. On September 11, 2001 hijacked airliners crashed into every home in the world in possession of a television set. Although the total number of deaths was about 100th of the number who died in the genocide in Rwanda, and no greater than the number who die on the roads every week in the United States, the perception of the outrage was much greater after 9/11 and its impact and consequences quite disproportionate. We cannot blame the mass media for showing these pictures but a great deal more could have been done to put them in perspective. In a few months the acts of a handful of religious extremists started a succession of wars, which are still not over.

Judges, whose experience of the adversarial system trains them to see both sides of every case, statisticians who are trained to weigh up the significance of large numbers, historians, who are trained to see events in their historical context and psychotherapists, who are trained to take a family history and to hear what is not being said as well as what is, may be better placed than others to get such things in proportion. Journalists have so much influence that a high standard of training and performance should be required and monitored outside of political and other partisan influence. Schools should teach children how to read, understand and evaluate news.

Example:

[An account is given of the murder case described on p. 198.]

. . . In 1966 an avalanche, caused by the collapse of a spoil heap from the local coal mine in the village of Aberfan, resulted in the death of 116 children. In the weeks that followed, anger was spilling in all directions and three public meetings broke up in fistfights. Reporters from the *Merthyr Gazette* worked closely with the Disaster Response Team to scotch rumours and to provide distressed people with accurate information and opportunities to express their feelings in ways that would not add to their problems (e.g. in a poetry column). Subsequently the newspaper received a well-earned award for the quality of its support to the community. Many villagers attended the Board of Inquiry and found that the impartial examining of witnesses changed their perception of what had happened. Even when blame was attributed they could now acknowledge that those responsible were fallible human beings, not outright monsters.

(Parkes 1976)

Immediate responses to violence

Fear and rage are natural responses to threat along with a tendency to seek out others in mutual defence. In the environment of evolution, such behaviour often enabled people to survive and even today this is sometimes the case. Unfortunately, misperception of the situation, pressure to take immediate action for fear of worse to come and the escalation of fear which may infect crowds or other groups of people may lead to intemperate responses that aggravate the situation and lead to a cycle of violence. Vilification and immediate retaliatory acts against a supposed enemy, triumphalist behaviour by victors and attributions of martyrdom to victims may all contribute to escalate the violence.

It is of crucial importance that those responsible for keeping the peace take immediate action to advertise their presence and to take control of the situation, prevent further violence and give emotional support to those affected. This may include neighbours and others not directly under threat.

Example:

Murders are often carried out by family members. This sometimes makes investigating police officers suspicious and uncommunicative in their handling of bereaved families and aggravates bitterness and anger. In the United Kingdom special training is now provided to Police Family Liaison teams who are expected to provide emotional support at the same time as carrying out their investigative roles. One such team [as described on p. 160] worked closely with bereavement volunteers from Cruse Bereavement Care to provide 'psychological first aid' to traumatised families from the United Kingdom who were flown to New York in the wake of 9/11.

Legitimising authorities

Cycles of violence seldom persist without the support of an authority or authorities who legitimise further violence. These may include parents, political leaders, religious leaders, military authorities, cult leaders, insurgent leaders and gang leaders. They may perpetuate the violence by direct command of military or other force, by exaggerating the danger in order to obtain popular support for retaliation, by reminding people of past wrongs and humiliations and by 'monsterising' the 'enemy'. These acts may be necessary responses to real dangers but they may also be unnecessary or disproportionate response to minimal dangers.

Unnecessary or disproportionate responses are likely to occur if the leader seeks to buttress an insecure power by uniting others behind him/her and against a common enemy. It then becomes unpatriotic to oppose the leader.

At times of violence parents and other leaders are often themselves traumatised and their ability to make wise decisions impaired. Some are more vulnerable than others; they may have personal problems, have suffered trauma in the past or lack emotional support. Only too often, those at the top of the tree are supposed to support people below them and to have no need for support for themselves. Having, in a crisis, adopted a particular stance it may then be difficult and/or politically disastrous for them to change their minds. It follows that every effort should be made to give psychological support to leaders following violent events and to dissuade them from drastic actions that may exacerbate the problems they face.

To varying degrees all leaders are subject to pressures and influence from power groups and from others. At times of violence such pressures are often in the direction of retaliation and leaders who temporise are seen as weak. Opposition groups may vie with the leader for public support for aggressive action, each group adopting more extreme positions. Military leaders and political leaders who find their main support from the military are particularly likely to seek military solutions to their problems.

Other groups are likely to oppose violence and to offer alternatives to retaliation. Indeed some constitute *alternative authorities* with the role of limiting the power of the parents or other leaders. These include legislative authorities such as social workers, religious leaders, judges, peacekeeping forces, arbitrators (who are authorised to make decisions about disputed issues) and mediators (who facilitate negotiation in the hope that contenders will reach agreement). All of these bodies can, at times, break cycles of violence.

Examples:

- After the death of his wife, a caring but insecure father found it hard to cope with a nine-year-old son whose grief was reflected in rebellious behaviour. He exerted his authority by the only means he knew, beating the boy. His son responded by becoming increasingly bitter and by bullying other children. When a schoolteacher informed the social services the son was placed on the 'at risk' register and the father was induced, by the threat of judicial action, to accept the guidance of a social worker. He subsequently learned to obtain his son's cooperation by rewarding good behaviour in preference to coercion. The cycle of violence was broken, the relationship between son and father improved and the child's bullying ceased.
- In Britain the monarch, unlike her ministers, is relatively free of pressure from the electorate and often acts as a close advisor to her Prime Minister. In December 1861, at the height of the American Civil War, Britain's aged, gout-crippled Prime Minister, Lord Palmerston, learned that a British ship, the *Trent*, had been intercepted by an American Union warship and two Confederate envoys, Mason and Slidell, taken into custody. Reaction, in the press, to this insult to the British flag was strong and, under pressure from his Foreign Secretary (John Russell), Palmerston showed the Queen a draft of a belligerent letter to the American Secretary of State. This would probably have led to extension of the war, with Britain taking the side of the Confederates and France drawn in to support the Union. Queen Victoria and Prince Albert, who was already suffering from the typhoid fever that would kill him two weeks later, persuaded Palmerston to accept a redraft of the letter; this provided the Americans with an opportunity to deny hostile intent and avoid an escalation of the war.

(Weintraub 1996)

- Although the United Nations was criticised for its failure to prevent the genocide in Rwanda, the presence of small numbers of UN peacekeeping officers *(see p. 202)*, who moved rapidly to trouble spots in the wake of the genocide, probably helped to break the cycle of violence which had [recurred] over twenty-five years.

Acts of legitimising authorities, which may increase the risk of cycles of violence, include concealment of relevant information or plans, misrepresentation of dangers and adoption of double standards. Leaders who act covertly often encourage others to do the same, trust is undermined and all sides tend to expect the worst. Conversely, open awareness reduces suspicion and the paranoid assumptions that encourage further violence.

Examples:

- After their daughter died George and Mary each responded in their own ways, Mary by crying and seeking attention, and George by refusing to speak about his daughter, going to the pub and getting drunk. Mary accused George of not caring and George, who felt helpless and threatened by his wife's clinging, continued to distance himself from her. The affection that they had previously felt for each other seemed to dissolve. As time went by the tension between them increased and they took out their bitterness by abusing each other verbally and, at times, physically. Eventually Mary sought the help of a psychiatrist and her husband agreed to attend with her. The psychiatrist reminded them that anger is a natural reaction to bereavement and invited each of them to reveal how they felt about their daughter's death. Once George realised that he was not under attack or being blamed for his daughter's death he 'confessed' that he felt a failure as both husband and parent. He had backed away from his wife because he did not know how to help her. His frankness had an immediate effect on his wife who realised that, in his own way, her husband cared just as much as she.

- Documents about the Cuban Missile Crisis (Chang and Kornbluh 1999) show how the danger of a nuclear war was greatly increased by the fact that both sides kept their intentions secret and deliberately set out to mislead the other. This led to each side assuming the worst and making plans for pre-emptive strikes against each other. Only when Kennedy and Khrushchev spoke directly and corrected these misperceptions of each other's intentions could trust be established and a basis for agreement reached. Even then both sides continued to conceal their negotiations from their followers in order to take credit for the outcome.

Destructive codes

[In subsequent research I have recognised that, although destructive codes undoubtedly contribute to cycles of violence, they are best considered as part of the context in which acts of violence take place and they then affect all of the choice points on the IWG's cycle.]

Our brain is an organ one of whose main functions is to take in huge amounts of information and simplify it to the point where we can comprehend the world around us and cope with it successfully. One way of doing that is to adopt shorthand 'codes' to represent complex aspects of reality. Most of them we take for granted; they become axioms that form the basis of our assumptive world, the world that we assume to exist. Among these codes are assumptions about 'friends' and 'enemies', 'good' and 'bad' and 'right' and 'wrong'. 'Friends' we can trust, we can count on their loyalty at times of trouble; they will help to defend us from our enemies. On the whole we assume that friends are good and right. When they are not we forgive them their failings; we tend to idealise them. 'Enemies', on the other hand, are not to be trusted; they will harm our allies and us, they are bad and in the wrong. When they are not we ignore the discrepancy; we tend to monsterise them.

Although these codes are always simplifications of reality there is nothing wrong with having them, indeed we could not survive without them. Even so it is important to recognize that they can never be anything more than approximations to reality, the best we can manage. And there are times when they become destructive and contribute to cycles of violence. Cycles of violence are likely to persist if maintained by the belief that my side is 'right', just and good, while the enemy is wrong, unjust and bad. Strangers and foreigners are often assumed to be dangerous and easily come to be seen as enemies. When we treat them as enemies it is not surprising if they do the same to us, thereby confirming and perpetuating the belief system (Hence the saw, 'give a dog a bad name and it will bite you').

Codes of justice range from concepts of 'fairness' in personal relationships to more general belief in a rule of law based on human rights and assumed to be maintained by the ruling power. Codes of morality distinguish good from bad. Codes of honour guide assessment of worth and esteem. Codes of propriety define what is proper, decent and correct. These codes, though all concerned with value, may conflict or compete with each other. Thus, the code of honour among young men may value bravery and pride above moral codes of gentleness and humanity. Indeed there are times when ruthlessness and cruelty to an enemy is seen as right by one side and monstrous by the other. At a family level codes which perpetuate cycles of violence include family myths such as 'spare the rod and spoil the child' and 'children are wicked by nature and the sin must be beaten out of them for the sake of their immortal souls'.

Cycles of violence are most likely to persist if buttressed by strongly held, inflexible belief in codes that permit or encourage violence. Destructive codes include:

Codes, such as 'an eye for an eye', which encourage retaliation;
Codes which are exclusive, the only true faith and denigrate other faiths;
Codes which foster a belief in the superiority of a person or group that makes them entitled to special privileges;
Codes which permit, reward or encourage cruelty, killing, suicide or martyrdom.

It follows that anything that persuades people to question, abandon or modify destructive codes will reduce the chances of violence becoming cyclical. Tolerance of people different from oneself may not come easily, but can be taught, so can respect for the positive codes of others, establishment of new codes that foster humility and tolerance while discouraging extremism and violence. This is easier said than done for it is our codes that give us our identity. Question them and you devalue us. Even so some remarkable successes can be cited.

Examples:

- Mahatma Ghandi developed his code of non-violence in South Africa. He wrote in his autobiography: 'It is necessary to revive the eternal law of answering anger by love and of violence by non-violence; "Hate the sin and not the sinner" is a precept which, though easy enough to understand, is rarely practised, and that is why the poison of hatred spreads in the world . . . It is quite proper to resist and attack a system, but to resist and attack its author is tantamount to resisting and attacking oneself . . . It is the acid test of non-violence that, in a non-violent conflict, there is no rancour left behind, and in the end the enemies are converted into friends. That was my experience in South Africa, with General Smuts. He started with being my bitterest opponent and critic. Today he is my warmest friend' (Prabhu and Rao 1945). The application of Ghandi's policy of passive resistance to British domination of India became a non-destructive code that succeeded in producing major social change in India and eventual independence. There was very little violence on either side and the change has left a legacy of mutual respect between the two nations.
- The Roman emperor Constantine, in 313 CE, pronounced the 'Edict of Milan' declaring that 'complete toleration' should be given by the state to anyone who had 'given up his mind to the Christians' or any other cult. This brought an end to a long cycle of persecution of Christians (Johnson 1976).

When codes are written down, or 'codified', they become more rigid, reduce ambiguity and simplify decision-making. Most religions codify both moral codes and codes of propriety. Believers then have a simple guide to what is right. Unfortunately different religions adopt different codes and even within the major religions there is considerable variation from fundamentalists to liberals in the flexibility with which the codes are applied. Codes of justice and human rights are codified as laws and these are usually assumed to apply to leaders as well as followers. This said, leaders often have the power to change laws. Cycles of violence may be created or broken by changing the law.

Examples:

- Marriage guidance counsellors often make use of a 'contract' which both sides can agree to and which, if kept, will reduce the chance of further conflict.
- Most civilized countries now acknowledge such human rights as the right of people accused of an offence to hear the evidence against them and to be entitled to legal defence in a court of law. Even so, following 9/11, the British government introduced legislation allowing the indefinite detention, without such trial, of foreign nationals who are thought to support 'terrorism'. Although this attempt to deprive foreigners of their human rights was intended to break the cycle of terrorist violence, it may have had the opposite effect. By undermining Britain's ethical position it supported the destructive code of some Moslems that Britain is a corrupt country ruled by Satan. The British legislation has recently been successfully challenged in the European Court of Human Rights.

Polarising, inflammatory strategies

All of the foregoing factors influence the formation of strategies which sometimes inflame the situation and establish or perpetuate a cycle of violence. Perpetuation is particularly likely if the strategies result from an assumption that there is *no alternative to a violent response*. This is likely to be associated with scapegoating, that is focussing on a *single assumed cause* (e.g. Arabs, Jews, religious extremists) who can be defined as monsters or 'enemies' and defeated.

A cycle of violence is most likely to be established if either the balance of power is such that neither side can be defeated or, having demonstrated their superior power by threatening or defeating the enemy, the powerful then

- attempt to humiliate, punish or take revenge, or
- fail to deal with underlying causes of the conflict (e.g. injustice, poverty or exploitation).

By depriving the weaker side of any chance of an acceptable existence hatred is generated, destructive codes established and the probability of future violence increased. Conversely, anything that allows all parties to live an acceptable existence, respects their world view and attempts to put right the underlying causes of conflict will reduce the chance of further conflict.

Examples:

- The film *One Flew over the Cuckoo's Nest* demonstrated how the abuse of power by the staff of a mental hospital could lead to resentment and eventual retaliation by the patients in their care. Although fictional, the film explains why the removal of physical methods of restraint, the unlocking of doors and the creation of 'therapeutic communities' in such institutions during the 1950s and 1960s, contrary to the expectations of older staff (who were locked into a destructive code), led to a reduction in violence and improvement in symptoms and relationships between staff and patients (Jones 1982).

- After World War I the humiliation of Germany sowed the seeds of bitterness and, in the end, led to World War II. Two years after the end of World War II, on 5 June 1947, Secretary of State George C. Marshall spoke at Harvard University:

  I need not tell you gentlemen that the world situation is very serious. . . . the United States should do whatever it is able to do to assist in the return of normal economic health in the world, without which there can be no political stability and no assured peace. Our policy is directed, not against any country or doctrine, but against hunger, poverty, desperation, and chaos. Its purpose should be the revival of working economy in the world so as to permit the emergence of political and social conditions in which free institutions can exist (Marshall Plan Speech 1947).

  The Marshall Plan provided Germany with opportunities of economic recovery and broke the cycle of violence.

When violence starts it usually involves only a small number of people. They may be extremists or people who misperceive a situation as exceedingly dangerous. For the reasons given here, violence evokes violent responses and before long others are likely to be drawn in to take sides. This polarisation is usually a gradual process but it may be accelerated by the magnitude of the perceived threat and by group or individual pressures. Leaders who insist that 'all who are not for us are against us' are attempting to force people out of the middle ground. Consequently those who advocate peaceful alternatives may be framed as less committed to the group's welfare, as appeasers, disloyal, naïve or cowards. Such behaviours increase polarisation and may foster cycles of violence. On the other hand those who resist such pressures or oppose extremism may help to break a cycle of violence. If polarisation is the centrifugal force driving people towards the poles, then centrism is the centripetal force that pulls them together. Those who insist on maintaining a middle ground can encourage centrism.

Examples:

- In the case of George and Mary cited earlier, their surviving children sided with Mary and George felt increasingly isolated and bitter as a result. He had now lost not only his daughter but his entire family. Their psychiatrist, on the other hand, refused to take sides or to judge either party. By holding to the middle ground he implied that it was possible for George and Mary to do the same. Instead of justifying their positions by attacking each other, they each tried to understand the other's point of view. Once the door to honest communication was open each parent realised the extent to which their grief had driven them to defend themselves and set up a cycle of distrust. They came to understand that they were needed by and had something to give to the other.
- In May 1986 Nelson Mandela, who had been in prison for twenty-three years, received a visit from a group of Commonwealth leaders. His

account of this meeting illustrates that it is possible for a leader, who had been seen as an extremist, to demonstrate a moderate or centrist position without betraying his cause:

> I told them . . . that I was firmly committed to a non-racial society. I told them I believed in the Freedom Charter, that the Charter embodied principles of democracy and human rights, and that it was not a blue-print for socialism. I spoke of my concern that the white minority should feel a sense of security in any new South Africa. I told them I thought that many of our problems were a result of lack of communication between the government and the ANC [African National Congress], and that some of these could be resolved through actual talks. They questioned me extensively on the issue of violence, and while I was not yet willing to renounce violence, I affirmed in the strongest possible terms that violence could never be the ultimate solution to the situation in South Africa.
>
> (Mandela 1994: 629–630)

The meeting marked a turning point in the negotiations that were to lead to the abandonment of *apartheid* in South Africa and to Mandela's emergence as the first black South African president and the first man to govern a democratic, multi-racial South African society.

Conclusions

Some have claimed that it is the 'animal' nature of man that explains both the occurrence of violence and its perpetuation. Yet, as we have seen, aggression between non-human animals of the same species is rarely fatal. Furthermore all social animals share with human beings the tendency to make attachments to parents, children and, in most cases, peers. This inhibits aggression and facilitates social intercourse. Hence it can be argued that it is our 'animal' capacity for love that provides us with a natural tendency to abhor violence. Viewed in this way cycles of violence are an aberration. They are certainly not inevitable and should be preventable. Mankind is not doomed by his animal nature; we may treat strangers with suspicion but they need not remain strangers for long, indeed, as Ghandi maintained, it is natural to turn strangers, and even enemies, to friends.

Over the years we have developed systems of justice and social organisation that have reduced violence at family and community levels in many parts of the world. Where this is not the case this often reflects social injustice and 'structural violence' that leave the disempowered no perceived alternatives to violence. The wholehearted adoption of international law and justice, the universal establishment of codes of human rights and the fostering of 'internationalism' as an alternative to 'nationalism' would all tend to break the cycles of violence that destroy the peace of the world.

Scientific and technical developments have resulted in most of us living in a world that is largely man-made. Thanks to these developments we are now, in theory, capable of eliminating poverty and creating a society in which human rights can be guaranteed . . .

Given the global danger of cycles of violence in an age when weapons of mass destruction are available, it is surprising that similar attention has not been paid to the study and legislation that are necessary if we are to eliminate these cycles. Part of the difficulty may lie in the fact that no one scientific discipline covers the field. The model developed here integrates knowledge from several different disciplines.

This is a field in which psychologists, sociologists, political scientists, historians, economists, journalists, theologians, ethicists, military scholars and many others need to learn to work together. If they will take the trouble to reach out beyond the limits of their own restricted vision they may discover that cycles of violence are neither inevitable nor irreversible.

References

Chang, L. and Kornbluh, P. (eds.) (1999) *The Cuban Missile Crisis*. National Security Archive, Washington University. Retrieved from www2.gwu.edu/~nsarchiv/nsa/cuba_mis_cri/, (Accessed 20 June 2014).

International Work Group on Death, Dying and Bereavement (IWG). Breaking cycles of violence. *Death Studies* 29(7), 585–600, 2005.

Johnson, P. *A History of Christianity*. Penguin Books, Harmondsworth, p. 67, 1976.

Jones, M. *The Process of Change*. Routledge & Kegan Paul, London, 1982.

Mandela, N. *Long Walk to Freedom: The Autobiography of Nelson Mandela*. Abacus, London, 1994.

Marshall Plan Speech. Office of the Historian, US Government. Retrieved from https://history.state.gov/departmenthistory/short-history/truman, 2014.

Parkes, C. M. Preface and Postscript to *In the Wake of the Flood* by Kai T. Erikson. Allen & Unwin, London, Boston and Sydney, 1976.

Prabhu, R. K. and Rao, U. R. *The Mind of Mahatma Ghandi*. Mudranalaya, Ahemadabad, 1945. Retrieved from www.mkgandhi.org/momgandhi/main.htm, 2014.

Weintraub, S. *Victoria*. John Murray, London, pp. 294–295, 1996.

CHAPTER 26

CAN THE CYCLE OF TERRORISM BE BROKEN?

From Synthesis and conclusions. In C.M. Parkes (ed.) *Response to terrorism: can psychosocial approaches break the cycle of violence?* (pp. 230–235). London and New York: Routledge, 2014.

You never change things by fighting the existing reality. To change something, build a new model that makes the existing model obsolete.

—Richard Buckminster Fuller

In 2006 I attended a meeting on 'Terrorism and Human Rights' organised by the Clemens Nathan Research Centre (CNRC) at which Lord Guthrie, former Chief of Defence Staff, had given a revealing and very interesting paper (CNRC 2007). Present at the meeting was a former psychiatrist colleague, Hugh Freeman, an editor of the British Journal of Psychiatry *whom I had met from time to time over the years. He recruited me to join an academic study group focussing on the causes and responses to terrorism. This gave me the opportunity to continue the work initiated in the IWG, reported here in the last chapter, and, in due course, we put together the outline of the multi-contributor book from which this chapter is taken. Sadly Hugh died shortly after the outline had been accepted for publication by Routledge and I was left with responsibility for editing the book and contributing several chapters. These included three about Rwanda co-authored by Peter Hall, chair of Doctors for Human Rights. I have chosen the following as it sums up the major conclusions arising out of our work.*

The reader will by now be aware that the contributors to this volume each bring their own frame of reference to the task we face and my role as editor is not to force them all into the same bed. Indeed any attempt to do that would soon bring home the impossibility of one person speaking for us all at this point in our discourse.

Anthony Glees reminded me that

the purpose of this study was to take two public policy issues, terrorism, and counter-terrorism, and see how a group of experts, predominantly drawn from psychiatry and psychology, would approach them in a critical format and advance novel but hard-nosed solutions. As such, the book is a contribution to public policy, and to its being debated, rather than to the further study of psychiatry, or thanatology. This book is about experts reaching out, moving beyond their comfort zone and arguing normatively, not just positively, about a major issue of our time.

(Personal communication 2013)

He is right, but we need to be careful what we mean by 'counter-terrorism'. Most of our contributors have seen our responses to terrorism as extending beyond the obvious steps to obstruct and eliminate terrorists, important though that may be, to examining the roots of terrorism and of the 'natural' responses in the hope of finding more radical solutions to the problems to which they give rise.

With these words in mind I shall test the tolerance of both my fellow contributors and my readers by taking advantage of this opportunity to summarise what I see as some of the lessons I have learned and highlighting some of the challenges that remain.

It seems to me that much of it comes down to security. Our attachments to all that we love, our families, our Gods, our homes and homelands, all function to keep us and our genes safe in the world and as such they are our most precious possessions, our most priceless treasures. So are those attachments of the attackers and their supporters. Both terrorist attacks and the insecurity which causes them upset the balance between our security and that of the people whom the terrorists hope to, and may indeed, represent.

It is natural and indeed quite proper for the attacked to defend themselves, and in some circumstances it would be suicidal not to. That's what 'security forces' are for. They have to find the right balance between meeting violence with the violence necessary to maintain our security without shattering the security of peaceful others and that can only be achieved by understanding and respecting *their* sources of security. It is sad that the term *security staff* has come to mean officials with guns who protect our gates, rather than friendly people who make us feel welcome and, like good parents, combine the roles of protector, supporter and informant.

Relevant to the response to terrorism is the model of the police's Family Liaison Officers (FLOs) who, in Britain, have now replaced the macho detectives who investigated violent crimes and controlled disaster situations. They recognise that it is quite possible to combine the roles of investigating officer and family supporter to people in crisis. They enter homes and meet families who are facing great trauma and loss with empathy and kindness even when they expect their overtures to be rejected. This does not mean that they deny the need to take control, like good parents, when it is important to set limits; and that sometimes means meeting violence with firmness and strength.

In this book we have seen how, faced by the loss of those they love and trust, human animals are programmed by evolution to experience powerful impulses to actions which may themselves increase the danger. But these impulses can also save us and without them none of us would be alive today.

There is a measure of truth in the saying that love is blind and it is no surprise to find that we, like the terrorists, overvalue the people, communities and Gods to whom we are attached. Myths of the superiority, wisdom and strength of our own family and tribe are inevitable and we enjoy the pride, the enhanced self-esteem and sense of security that comes from such relationships. Sadly these myths are also likely to be associated with negative myths about outsiders, their inferiority, impurity and enmity. These enable us to exploit and even kill them without undue self-reproach. It seems that love cannot make the world go round but it can make it grow pear-shaped.

We saw how Catholics and Protestants in Northern Ireland and Hutu and Tutsi youngsters in Rwanda joined with others in riots with enthusiasm and some of those who subsequently joined the terrorist sides took pleasure in hunting and killing their supposed enemies. We also saw how each side tends to overestimate its own strength, courage and resources while underestimating the strength, courage and resources of its opponents.

We have seen how important it is to distinguish a deadly event from our perception of the event and from the way we respond to it. What actually happens in a terrorist attack and what we see happening are two different things – the news has usually been chosen by informants (notably the media) and what we make of it is determined by our choice of informant, by the emotions evoked and by the sum total of memories and assumptions out of which we recognise and make sense of our world. The chances of distortion are great and we all experience something different. Yet we must act together if we are to respond.

Between the moment of perception and the moment of response there comes a pause. Our brains are alerted, we are never more 'switched on'. During that pause we digest the information we receive, followers look to leaders and leaders to followers, and out of that interaction comes a group reaction which may be quite different to the reaction of any one of us alone. We find ourselves drawn towards others who share our myths and united against the supposed attackers and their supporters. Polarisation often escalates the conflict and leads to retaliation and another turn of the wheel of deadly violence, but awareness of that danger can change our responses.

Group interaction can also lead to de-escalation. We do not have to be pawns in the hands of our emotions and the cycle of violence is not inevitable. Our studies have shown how children can be helped to stand aside from the traps in which they are entangled and to resist the magnet of violence. Is it possible that adult education can meet the same challenge? We saw how, in both Rwanda and Northern Ireland, substantial numbers of people have become disillusioned with the use of deadly violence and have accepted leaders who offer alternative ways to find security and, with it, peace. Are there ways to speed up disillusionment with violent solutions?

All change is painful, even change for the better, and changing patterns of attachment are the most painful of all. We have seen that such change is a process of grieving akin to the grief we experience whenever we lose something or someone we love. In both Northern Ireland and Rwanda the peace process has been slow because it takes time, patience and group process to change the attachment patterns and the obsolete assumptions on which we have learned to depend.

In Rwanda new leaders achieved power by force of arms and social change was enforced by law. Many of those who were held responsible for abuses of genocide and other crimes by their neighbours were punished but the punishment was not excessive and retribution is now virtually at an end. Security was largely brought about by non-coercive means, many of the new leaders are women, few are warriors, and security is enhanced by education, by community involvement and by economic support and advice from other countries. Little by little new myths have taken the place of the old destructive ones. Now support from outside is dwindling and the Rwandese are becoming autonomous. Even so, although twenty years have passed, the cycle of deadly violence continues to rage in nearby countries and in Rwanda fear of a return to the old patterns of attachment is undermining the trust that would make possible a true democracy.

In Northern Ireland it was leaders in Great Britain and the Irish Republic who met and worked together in the European Union and started to understand each other that eventually extended to the warring parties. Moderates initiated the process but not until extremist leaders, in Sinn Fein/IRA in particular, took significant initiatives to end the war did substantial de-escalation take place. They met with neutral commissioners and led the way, persuading their followers to decommission their weapons and their minds. The long-standing attachment to these leaders enabled new myths to grow out of the old. The Omagh bomb proved the acid test of community commitment to the new assumptive world and left the remaining terrorists isolated and discredited. Here too economic security and the support of allies trusted by both sides, notably the United States, helped to foster the security that is the *sine qua non* of the psychosocial transition to new patterns of attachment.

These issues were well summarised on 13 September 2012 when one of our contributors, Lord Alderdice, addressed the General Assembly of the UN in a debate on 'Strengthening the Role of Mediation in the Peaceful Settlement of Disputes, Conflict, Prevention and Resolution'.

He said:

> . . . powerful feelings affect the way that we think. Even when it is to our disadvantage we cannot just dismiss our feelings. Powerful emotions actually affect not just what we think but the way that we think; they disturb our capacity for rationality and acting in our own best self-interest. This is true also of groups, communities and whole nations of people . . .
>
> In every part of the world where I have studied the outbreak of terrorism and profound violence, I have found at least one group of people who feel that their culture, their values and their people have been treated unfairly and profoundly disrespected. When they have been unable to right what they perceive to be this terrible wrong, they have turned to violence, not out of rational self-interest, for their people rarely benefit from the violence; they usually suffer terribly.
>
> This is one of the mistakes that people from stable societies often make in addressing violence in other places. They try to interpret the events using a rational actor model, when what they are observing are 'devoted actors' motivated not by social and economic drivers but by 'sacred values' – by which I do not mean religious values but values that transcend economic benefit – the value of the life of my child is a sacred value. I cannot trade that without losing part of my very humanity . . .
>
> Forgiveness, like trust and reconciliation, is not a prerequisite for starting the process of addressing such conflicts, but is a result of a successful process of doing so. However, while trust tends to grow out of the experience of working together in a human relationship with the other side, forgiveness is much less common, much more difficult and very painful.
>
> The key element in building trust, achieving agreement, ending violence, and eventually contributing to reconciliation is the construction of a process through which by direct engagement with each other, the two or more, sides begin to see 'the Others' as human beings who have their positive as well as negative elements. If you treat others as less human than you and your people they will feel able to treat you and your people as less than human too.
>
> These then are some of the key issues in mediation work with groups in violent conflict: The power of the past – with repetitions and reactions to hurts, over centuries not just years. The impact of the emotions – I react not out of rational self-interest but emotionally, and often to my cost. The toxic effects of injustice and humiliation – resulting in devoted actors, who, if they find no other way may react with self-destructive violence in what they perceive to be a higher cause. If you humiliate me, I will remember it forever and find it hard ever to forgive. The need to construct a robust process through which I begin

> to relate directly to 'the other side' as human beings with good in them as well
> as bad, and recognizing the faults on my own side in the past and the present.
>
> (Alderdice 2012)

The recognition that social scientists can throw new light on old problems does not mean that we have all the answers. Psychology and psychiatry have lagged behind other sciences but that does not mean that our contribution is valueless. Much of our theorising has been speculative and it will require more research and interaction between the various schools of psychology, sociology and psychiatry before we can truly call our work in this field 'hard-nosed'.

In the Introduction to this volume I asked if palliative care, the body of knowledge that has revolutionised the care of patients and families faced by deadly illness, has something to teach people in communities faced by deadly terrorism. In both situations people face threats to their survival and the loss of others. A recent IWG workshop concluded that in both situations people need (1) to obtain reliable information, (2) to face the painful reality of death, (3) to find a safe place, (4) to make secure relationships, (5) to relinquish long-standing assumptions about the world (decommission mindsets), (6) to grieve, commemorate and value the lasting bonds that remain to those people and other objects of attachment that are now lost, (7) to apologise and make restitution for any failures, (8) to forgive or accept the failures of others, (9) to let go of what they cannot have on the way to accepting and enjoying what they can have (reconciliation), and (10) to prepare for future threats, losses and change (IWG 2011). In palliative care it is the support with all of these problems that can often bring relief of distress, calm reflection, peace of mind, security in the face of death and maturity in its aftermath. Could similar kinds of support be developed for people faced with deadly terrorism?

Given that resistance to changing mindsets results from fear, the first step may be finding ways to support the front line of responders. Brian Rowan acknowledges the dangerous and stressful time in his life as a journalist reporting the Troubles when

> . . . the BBC offered me some counselling, and I can remember feeling insulted, thinking that this offer in some way suggested weakness on my part. Many years later, I realise that the penny was beginning to drop in terms of what was being asked of those involved in the reporting of our conflict/war.
>
> (Rowan 2014, p. 163)

For journalists' sake and for ours, they may be wise to think again.

Of course, psychiatrists and psychologists are also caught up in their own assumptive worlds, blinkered by the limitations of the human brain. We have our own attachments and agendas; others may be right not to trust us. One object of this volume is to put our cards on the table. To let others judge and share in the insights and assumptions that we make, to disagree, to take what is useful and junk the rest. We are all in this together.

Lord Alderdice has acknowledged the very different roles required of the politician and the psychotherapist. And yet he remains a good example of a psychiatrist who has, patiently and unobtrusively, made use of his skills in both fields to play a significant part in a peace process. Professor Gersons and Mirjam Nijdam have shown that psychologists can support politicians and help to minimise the psychological impact of threats that could easily impair their judgement and decision-making at a time when these skills are most needed.

In the past fifty years hospices and other palliative care services have sprung up all over the world. Is it possible that, fifty years from now, leaders, communicators and communities faced with life-threatening violence will obtain similar support, not from psychiatrists or specialists in palliative care, but from a new kind of psychological, social and spiritual care that is now, as Albert Najambe would put it, 'pushing out'?

References

Alderdice, J. Speech to the General Assembly of the United Nation Organisation. Retrieved from www.yumpu.com/en/document/view/11399117/speech-to-the-united-nations-general-assembly-13-the-lord-alderdice. 27 May 2014.

Alderdice, J. Strengthening the role of mediation in the peaceful settlement of disputes, conflict, prevention and resolution, 2012.

Clemens Nathan Research Centre (CNRC). *Foreign Policy & Human Rights.* CN Research Publications Martinus Nijhoff, Leiden, the Netherlands, 2007.

International Work Group on Death, Dying and Bereavement (IWG). Can individuals who are specialists in death, dying, and bereavement contribute to the prevention and/or mitigation of armed conflicts and cycles of violence? *Death Studies* 35(5), 455–466, 2011.

Rowan, B. Responses to terrorism: The role of the media. In C. M. Parkes (ed.) *Responses to Terrorism: Can Psychosocial Approaches Break the Cycle of Violence?* (pp. 151–163). London and New York, Routledge, 2014.

FINAL CONCLUSIONS –
LOVE IS THE KEY

With the warm breath of my mentors, John Bowlby, Margaret Torrie, Cicely Saunders, Mary Ainsworth and her namesake, Patricia Ainsworth (now Parkes), urging me on, I find myself in the last chapter. What lessons have we learned? What doors opened?

The information explosion that has resulted from the discovery of the Internet opens the door to the dissemination of knowledge across the world. It is tempting to see that accumulation as a progressive process that will inevitably lead to a happier world, but this may be naïve. For most people the sheer quantity of information is indigestible; much of it is unreliable and even more irrelevant to our particular needs. We all live at the periphery, vainly trying to piece together a meaningful narrative for our own lives and that of our nearest and dearest, but dimly aware that there are massive changes looming over which we have little or no control.

Even the scientists, who keep their heads by demanding high standards of evidence for their beliefs, are bemused by the sheer number of peer-reviewed journals and articles therein that make it difficult to develop grand theories that take all of the relevant evidence into account. Even within the narrow focus of bereavement research there is little or no consensus among the 'experts' because, faced with a mass of evidence, we tend to focus our attention on the data that confirms our preconceptions, to remain locked into the paradigms, the habits of thought, of our own assumptive worlds.

Re-reading the papers recorded here I am aware of a feeling of urgency that has pushed me to move too fast in the eager search for answers. There are times when I would have been wise to go more slowly, to await larger samples and better methodologies. But my work has made me all too aware of the brevity of life and I have been impatient to complete my own with some kind of closure, yet I suspect that that is impossible. All I can hope for is to draw attention to some ideas that others can use in the endless quest to make sense of seemingly senseless suffering. Suffering that, one way or another, is tangled up with love. Apparently *'Le cœur a ses raisons, que la raison ne connaît point'* (Pascal 1671). 'The heart hath its reasons that the reason knows not.' But what if Pascal was wrong? Perhaps reason can be used to know the heart. Attachments have a logic of their own and we all need to understand the logic of the emotions which so often conflict with the reason by which we try to live. Rather than being the context of suffering, love can become the key to our understanding it better and helping those afflicted by it.

It has been a privilege to witness and play a part in the inception of attachment theory and to dispel some of the confused thinking to which attachments give rise. Grief may be a high price to pay for love, particularly when the idealisation of the loved person, god, nation or other entity is disappointed or destroyed. But it is a necessary part of our psychological heritage and, like the pains of childbirth, a price worth paying.

My initial hope, that studying one major stress, bereavement, and its consequences would enable us to understand the roots of mental illness, has not yet been achieved, though I still hope that it will be. Hopefully you and I now understand the roots of one mental illness, Persistent Complex Bereavement Disorder (PCBD), as the *DSM-V* reluctantly calls it. By assigning it to a special category 'for further research' and refusing it a code number the authors have excluded sufferers from the privileges of medical diagnosis. I suspect that the reason for this hesitation is a dawning awareness that once they accept that bereavement by death can be a cause of PCBD there can be no logical reason not to accept that other major losses can cause the condition. Like the revolution in medical care that took place when the discovery of bacteria overturned the humeral system, this opens the door to a system of psychiatric diagnosis based on psychological causes rather than emotions. It also brings closer the day when recognition of the fact that we are all vulnerable to grief and its consequences will undermine the stigma that results from attributions of mental illness. Love and loss, it seems, have many and varied casualties.

We saw, in Part 2, how the study of bereavement has been extended to shed light on a wide range of loss events, in Part 3 the care of the dying, and in Part 4 disasters. Studies of responses to amputation and other non-death losses helped us to recognise the dual process, the two overlapping psychological processes reflected, on the one hand, in the painful search for the lost person or object, and on the other, with the complicated revision of the assumptive world that is necessary whenever major changes take place in our lives and it is necessary to discover new meanings. At such times the right help can reduce the risk of paranoid or excessively defensive attitudes while fostering the increase in emotional strength and maturity that is often an impressive outcome of major losses. The concept of the 'assumptive world' has wide relevance extending into philosophy, sociology, theology and other disciplines.

Although evaluations of support for unselected bereaved people by poorly selected and untrained volunteers have proved disappointing, much can be achieved by proper selection and training and there is evidence that specific training for specific problems can reduce suffering. We saw in Chapter 17 how the inception of a professional service for families in crisis that minimised the risk of medicalising normal life crises was a popular step that deserves further study, as does my dream, in Chapter 26, of a similar service for journalists, politicians and military leaders faced with disasters or terrorist attacks; and I still hope that, with the right training, advisors and members of the caring professions can develop the necessary skills. A forthcoming multi-contributor *Handbook of Loss, Change and Transition*, to be edited by CMP, Darcy Harris and Jeffrey Kaufman, is already in train and aims to do just that.

Readers may find Part 5, in which we take a hard look at cycles of deadly violence and the extreme forms of attachment that feed them, too speculative to be regarded as science. Yet the arguments are compelling and it is included here in the hope that it will encourage others to 'take the ball and run with it'. It has been a privilege to work with researchers and clinicians from many related fields to cross the boundaries between academic disciplines and to apply the psychosocial understanding that has arisen from studies of loss and change to the problems of disaster and armed conflict.

Love and loss, it seems, can contribute to some of the darkest, saddest and most painful aspects of life. Indeed, the cost of commitment can be very high. Any simplistic and sentimental ideas we may have had that love solves all problems must be set aside. And yet our commitment to care, which is another aspect of love, may also hold the key to solving those problems and to discovering that the price of love can be a price worth paying.

Reference

Pascal, B. (1671). *Les Pensées*. Section IV On the Means of the Belief (277).

INDEX

Aberfan 165–6, 173–4, 176–9

adolescents 58; crises 132

Ainsworth, Mary 21, 57

alcohol *see* drugs

amnesia 165; *see also* fugues

amputation 79, 90, 98–9, 106–11, 120, 230; and phantom limb 99; *see also* hallucinations, hypnagogic

anger 8, 74; in children 97; creative 86, 198; destructive 198; and disasters 164, 190, 198, 213; disproportionate 75, 190, 213; after murder 214; normal 198, 216; pathological 75; peace motive for 198; rage 83; rejection and 97; and restlessness 10; transcendence 4; and violence 198; *see also* bereavement problems, anger; violence, cycles of; PCBD; PST

anger management 164, 166, 216–17; on line 169

anxiety: autonomic symptoms of 27, 118, 169; after bereavement 15, 24, 84, 118 (incidence 25; symptoms 27, 29, 118); after disasters 186; disorganised thinking 117; 'escape route' 112; and felt security 57, 116, 127; in helpers 38, 101; helping 119, 127, 140; after other losses 99; management of 169; panic 118; *see also* attachment(s), anxious ambivalent; avoidance; fear(s); generalised anxiety disorder; palliative care; post-traumatic stress

anxiety states (disorders) *see* generalised anxiety disorder

aggression *see* anger

armed conflict 195–228; in Bosnia/Herzegovina 199; in communities 210–11; in Northern Ireland 195, 197–8; in Rwanda 195, 199–202; in New York (9/11) 195, 203–8; *see also* grief; murder/manslaughter; traumatic bereavement; violence, cycles of

assumptions: basic 57–8, 61; continuing bonds 120; dangerous 58; in depression 118; destructive/constructive codes 216–18; early childhood 58; group 116; helpless/hopeless 118; holding on to 8; about loss 123–7; perception 93; in polarisation 218; of potential value 94; of psychiatrists 226; questioning 95, 137; and real world 90; redundant (obsolete) 89, 113; shattered 61, 90, 95, 117, 120, 170; social 113 (conflicting 118); unconscious 95; *see also* assumptions, changing; assumptive world(s); codes; linking objects; myths; re-grief work

assumptions, changing 61, 70, 92–6, 95, 112–13, 116–20, 129; decommissioning mindsets 224; in disaster areas 170; dual process 230; letting go i; in life cycle 96; maturity 120; in Northern Ireland 224–5; in palliative care 224; preparing for 109; in PGD 170; in psychological first aid 166; in psychotherapy 95; in PTSD 119, 170; in reality testing/realization 91, 110–13; recognising potential value 94; resistance to 93–5, 116; in social animals 116; at St Christopher's Hospice 137; turning points 91; types of 108–12; wished for 109; *see also* amputation; blindness; PST; stress; trauma

assumptive world(s) 79, 90, 123–8; and affectional bonds 93; attachments and 58; and the brain 76; control of 94; definition 92–3; encapsulation 112; 'fit' 93; habits of thought 94; and life space 92; making sense of 224; parental influences on 57; preserving 94; and psychiatric problems 57; recognising discrepancies in 95; of scientists 229; and secure base 61; and status 94; *see also* bereavement, losses (non-death); PGD; world models

attachment(s) 1, 7, 16, 45, 50–61, 229;
  adult 61, 85; and autonomy 140;
  behaviour 17, 18, 21, 53, 116; biological
  roots 90, 139; to body 143; changing
  224; to clients 63; and culture 48–9;
  at end of life 139; gender and 58; to
  God(s) 223; to home 79, 109, 223; to
  leaders 225; to a limb 79, 90; love 53;
  and monotropy 49; networks 106; in old
  age 59; to places 109; and psychiatric
  disorder 55, 60–1, 66; science of 56;
  security and 21, 57, 59, 119, 144; sexual
  59; in social animals 20, 220; and social
  support 59; and status 116; survival
  value 21; of terrorists 223; to therapists
  61, 225; and violence 230; to vision 90;
  see also amputation; attachment(s) and
  bereavement; attachment(s), disorders of;
  attachment(s), patterns of; nurturance
attachment(s) and bereavement 61, 66
attachment(s), disorders of 55, 60–1, 66,
  75–6, 118; *see also* separation anxiety
  disorder
attachment(s), patterns of, 53–4, 57–8,
  75–6; anxious ambivalent 58–60;
  avoidant 58–9, 118; clinging 146,
  dependent 48, 76; disorganised 58; *see
  also* avoidance; strange situations
autonomy 139–40; *see also* compulsive
  independence
avoidance: alternating with approach
  (oscillation) 117; to minimise fear/
  anxiety 117; of grief 21, 118–19; by
  postponement 117; of reality 100; of
  reminders 88; response 118–19; of
  traumatic memories (after murder/
  manslaughter 87–8; in PCBD; in PGD
  66; in PTSD 66); *see also* denial

bereavement: in childhood 119, 184; coping
  with 117; definition 20, 74–5; experts
  229; and grief 20, 115; and mourning
  74; preparation for 125, 145; recovery
  from 198; by suicide 125; and trauma 75;
  see also bereavement losses (non-death);
  disasters; grief; loss(es); mortality after;
  research after; PST; stress; suicide, risks
  of; traumatic bereavement/loss
bereavement, helping 25, 75; communicating
  120, 125; facilitating grief 119; family
  119, 125; meaning making 75, 198; *see
  also* bereavement services
bereavement problems: anger 8, 14, 82, 97,
  126, 198, 216; conflicts 18; and shame
  126; stigma 198
bereavement, responses to 115–122; closure
  229; early 9–18; influence of parenting
  on 51–72; loss of mother 96, situational
  20; *see also* complicated grief; depression;

drugs; generalised anxiety disorder;
  genocide; grief; murder/manslaughter;
  PCBD; PGD; PTSD
bereavement risk assessment 24–7, 68
bereavement services: for children 119;
  counsellors/volunteers 24–7, 119, 184, 230
  (cost effectiveness of 29–30; evidence for
  184); for families 230; in hospice/palliative
  care 22–30, 149; in India 187; psychiatric
  168; at St Christopher's Hospice 22–30;
  see also Cruse Bereavement Care;
  disaster(s); bereavement, helping; group
  support; medication
bitterness *see* anger
blindness 99–100, 107, 113, 120, 123, 127
blunting of feelings *see* numbness
Bowlby, John x, 21, 229; attachment
  behaviour 8, 139, 143; attachment theory
  1, 53; dependency 75–6, goal-corrected
  behaviour 17, 107; monotropy 53;
  mother, loss of 96, 116; phases of grief
  7–8, 96; secure base 119, 126; world
  model 97, 107
breaking bad news 166
broken heart *see* mortality

caretaking *see* nurturance
changing assumptions *see* PST
child 1, 143; abuse of 136, 211–13, 215,
  217, 219; and (non-human) animals
  11, 220; bereaved 28, 58, 83, 88,
  96–7, 119, 125; carers 61; cultural
  differences (in mortality 48, 53; after
  disasters 184, 191; in parenting 48, 59);
  development 56, 139–40; education of
  224; ethics of researching 43–4; PCBD
  in 68; and genocide 200–1; security
  56, 59; separation from parents 57, 60,
  96; stress response to 59; therapy 87;
  vulnerability 127; *see also* adolescents;
  attachments; family; complicated grief,
  roots of; grief, basic components, roots
  of; separation anxiety disorder; strange
  situations
child, loss of 58, 76; continuing bonds 76;
  in disasters 156–62, 163–72, 176–84,
  191, 200–1; by murder 81; psychiatric
  disorders 65; sacred values 76, 82, 225;
  and therapists 146; *see also* PGD
chronic grief *see* PGD
CNRC (Clemens Nathan Research Centre)
  222
codes 216–17; constructive 216–18;
  destructive 216–18; of justice/law 217;
  morality 217; of propriety 217; *see also*
  human rights
cognitive: and emotive help 23, 69, 184;
  and love 51; problem-focussed therapy
  96 (and gender 69; for PCBD)

cognitive behaviour therapies: for complicated grief 170; for depression 118, 170; for PTSD 169, 170

communication 73–8, 76, 116; and child abuse; across cultures 46, 49–50, 135; defects 127; in dysfunctional families 69; influence of media 212–13; and interdependence 117; after murder 83, 214; non-verbal 75; *see also* mediation

community 5; association 158; clergy 154–5; family crisis services 125, 129–31, 160–1; of prognosis 141; psychiatric nursing 132; structural violence 220; therapeutic 155; transitional 101; volunteers 149; *see also* disaster(s), community responses; Tower Hamlets Crisis Intervention Service

complicated grief (CG) 60, 63–71, 126–7; in childhood 96; chronic 96, 118; delayed 96, 118; in DSM-5 63–71; inhibited 96, 118; index of (ICG), intervention 173; morbid 74; pathological 74; roots of 51–62; treatment of 69; unresolved 190; *see also* PCBD; PGD

compulsive independence 118, 145; in caregivers 146; in childhood 140; *see also* avoidance

continuing bond(s) 18, 21, 76, 120; *see also* attachment(s)

coping 16, 91–2, 94, 117, 145–6; cultural influences on 189; theory 75; veterans 101; *see also* avoidance; cognitive therapies; compulsive independence

crisis *see* trauma

critical incident stress debriefing 172

Cruse Bereavement Care 5, 160; after disasters 160–2, 165, 167, 169, 195, 203–8; in Northern Ireland 197–8; Web site 169, 185

crying 7–8; cultural influences on 46; after disasters 206; excessive 25; inhibition of 21, 143; after losses 12, 20, 116; seeking attention 215; survival value 7; tranquillizers 83; *see also* attachment(s)

culture, influence on: extremism 225; response to bereavement 20–2, 45–50, 117–18; response to disasters 160–1, 182

cultures: Apache 21, 46–7; Bosnia 199; Buddhist 48–9; Caribbean 47; Dayak (Borneo) 48; Egypt 21; Hindu 46; Ifaluk 21; Judaism 46, 199; Maori 46; Muslim 49, 199; Navajo 21, 46; Netherlands 48; Northern Ireland 194, 197–8, 204, 223–4; Samoa 48; Shinto 49; Tahiti 21; *see also* Rwanda

death/dying: community 5; facing 5; at home 145, pain 145 *see also* life threatening illness, palliative care

defence, psychological 16; acceptance 95, 141; group 213; in psychotherapy 95; *see also* avoidance, coping; denial; grief work; myths; reminiscence; worry work

denial 8, 14, 112; of blindness 99; coping 16; of disability 110; disbelief 14; disregard 14; function of 117; 'mummification' 111; *see also* avoidance; numbness

dependent 75–6, 118; fear of becoming 142; *see also* compulsive independence

depression: and alcohol problems 163; after amputations 98–9; after bereavement 28, 64, 81, 86, 88 (cultural influences on 47; gender influences on 28); after disasters 171, 183, 185, 190; distinction from grief 66, 115; after illness/disability 99; after loss of roles 100–1; measures of 27; in old age 127; personality 127; suicide, risk of 132; *see also* assumptions; bereavement, responses to; disasters; hopelessness; MDD; trauma, responses to

disaster(s) 157–93; accidents 82–3; bereavement after 159–75; duration 163; human agency 164; psychological insurance 100; international 164; self-monitoring 165; tsunamis 180–93; types of (scale and spread) 160–3; *see also* 9/11; Aberfan; armed conflicts; homes, loss of; trauma; traumatic losses

disaster(s), community responses 173; anger 170–3, 213; birth rate 176–9; chaotic 182, 188; communality, loss of 173–4; community development 158, 173, 179; consultant roles 180–93; cultural influences 163–4, 182–3, 187; disorganisation 158; goodwill 159; Inquiry, Board of 213; memorials 171; paralysis of 173; regeneration 179; rituals 171; shame 171; sociologists role 173; *see also* Aberfan; tsunamis

disaster(s), mental health after 91, 164–5, 181, 183, 190; in children 172, 183

disaster(s), management of 157; anniversaries 208; bereavement volunteers 167, 188; emergency services 165; family assistance teams (police) 160, 167, 214, 223; disaster response teams 217; family centre 204; incident room 204; leadership 166, 171–2, 203–4; media 167, 213; mutual support groups 190; non-governmental organisations (NGOs) 188; preparation for 164–5; psychological first aid 165–6; relocation 183; staff support 167; team support 172–4; supervision 205; training for 165, 185; viewing the site 205; VIPs 205–6; *see also* anger management; bereavement services; critical incident stress debriefing; disaster(s), community responses; trauma services

disaster(s), psychological responses: aftermath 158, 167–72; anger 97, 171, 207, 213; of children 178, 178, 184; delayed 157; depression 191; fears 97, 191, 213; gender issues 183–4; guilt 171; of helpers 165–6, 172; heroism 171; hope 207; impact 159, 165, 203; of leaders 173; long term 172–3; recoil 166; resistance to change 97; *see also* grief

disbelief/disregard *see* denial

dissociation 165

DSM (Diagnostic Statistical Manual of Mental Disorders) 63–71 *see also* MDD; PCBD; PGD; PTSD

dreams 4; after bereavement 12–13, 88–9; recurrent 88–9; use in therapy 113

drugs (including alcohol and tobacco): abuse 6; and armed conflict 210; after bereavement 28; after disasters 188; *see also* medication

dual process model 69, 230; orientation (loss and restoration) 69; oscillation 69; use in therapy 69–70

empathy 75, 223

ethics 27, 38; of research into bereavement 38–44

evaluation 40, 44; of bereavement services 23–30, 38–44, 230; of crisis intervention service 129–35; of palliative (hospice) services 42, 148–56; of therapies 69

evolution, genetic: of attachments 7, 20–1; of emergency responses 166, 213, 223; environment of 47, 52; of grief 21; of sympathetic nervous system 166

evolution, social 6, 210; of palliative care/ medicine 138; of warriors 210

family 129; cultural influences 49, 56, 183–4, 187, 189; (extended 56, 59; vigil 52;) myths 214, 223; police attitude to 83; in PSTs 101–3, 140; shared grief 88; socio-economic influence 47; genograms (family trees) 125; unit of palliative care 125, 130–1, 139, 149

family after bereavement: after murder 214; risk assessment 25–30, 126–7; role change 142; after suicide 125; *see also* bereavement services

family after disasters 161–2, 199; case worker 162, 172; family assistance centre 161, 167, 169, 195, 203; family problems 84, 86, 127, 132, 145, 184; conflicts 102, 145, 170, 209; violence 220;

family services, 86–8, 126, 184; counselling 119; family liaison teams/ officers (FLOs) 20, 38, 160, 167, 195, 203, 223; general practice 125; mediation 219; psychiatric, 139; therapy 131, 213; *see also* FFGT; palliative care; Project Liberty; Tower Hamlets Crisis Intervention Service

family support or lack of: to bereaved 25–8, 65, 119, 126, 164; after disasters 159; to dying 56

fear(s) 213–14; and alcohol 210; and anger 4; of bereaved 97; after disasters 97, 165, 169, 186, 203; of dying 6, 21, 84–5; expressed by dying patients 139–45, of failure 101; of further losses 99, 127; judgement of God 142; management 165–6, 226; panic 165; and pain 154; paralysed by 117; of separation 142; *see also* anxiety; anxiety, management of; PTSD; separation anxiety disorder

FFGT (family-focussed grief therapy) 68, 119

forgiveness 225

Freud, Sigmund 7; 'mourning' 16

fugues 13, 165; *see also* dissociation

gender: aggression and 210–11; attachment patterns and 58; help seeking 58, 135; sex hormones 210; and mortality 31–7; and personality 58; responses to interventions after bereavement 29, 48; symptoms after bereavement 42; *see also* grief, gender influence of

generalised anxiety disorder (anxiety states) after losses 64, 75, 81, 85, 118

genocide *see* armed conflict 48

GEI (grief experience inventory) 115

grief: in adolescence 215; anticipatory 51–2, 142; broken heart 31–7; care- giver's 61, 127, 165–6; in childhood 184; closure 76; continuing bonds 21–2, 75; coping 198; definition 2, 74, 115, 123; after disasters 163, 167–70, 183; as duty to the dead 75, 126; evolution of 21; function of 16; gender influence of 46–7, 58; 'healthy' 96; and maturing 198; measurement of 52, 65–6, 74, 115; medicalisation of 65; and mourning 74; after murder/manslaughter 83–5; the price of love 1, 3, 47, 206, 229–30; sensi- tizers 126; social influences on 118; stop- ping 126; triggers of 5; turning points 5; universality of 20–2, 46; *see also* assump- tive world(s); attachment(s); avoidance; bereavement; grief, features of; grief and mental illness; grief work; mourning; separation anxiety (distress) grief, basic components of 9–19, 115–22; consequence of attachment 1, 61, 96, 234 (crying 8, 12, 206; pining 2, 74; protesting 8); roots of 5–62; *see also* searching

grief, features of: acceptance of 3, 5; anger 7–8, 75, 126, 153, 198, 207; avoidance of 3, 5, 21, 88, 118, 126; cultural influences on 43–50, 164; delayed 67; depersonalisation 206; inhibited 66; letting go 101, 120; and meaning 4, 198; mitigation of 53, 59; mummification 111–12; obsessive 45–6, 126; oscillation 125, 206; pain of 4, 120; phases of 7, 74, 96; realization 91, 96; and reconciliation 197–8; repression of 5, 46–7; sharing 187, 207; *see also* avoidance; defence, psychological; searching

grief and mental illness 21; abnormal 65; in DSM 63–4, 75; interventions 64; prevention to 68; therapy 5, 41, 68, 95, 113, 116–18; vulnerability 84, 230; *see also* complicated grief; Index of Complicated Grief; PCBD; PGD; psychotherapy

grief, psychophysiology of 18; fMRI scan studies 18

grief work 16, 21, 95, 120; *see also* re-grief work

group: depression 171; hierarchies 116; pressure 162, 214, 219; process 224; irrational 225; myths 217; response to perceived attack 213, 224; security 116

group support 24, 57; in disasters 162; 'marathon' therapy 87, after murder/ manslaughter 81, 87; mutual (self help) 81, 89, 123, 162, 190; for peace 224; social 101, 163; at work 101, 127; workshops 199; *see also* anger management; family; IWG

hallucinations, hypnagogic 15 *see also* illusion(s)

Harvard Bereavement Study 27

home, separation or loss of 27; homesickness 142; *see also* strange situations

hope 4–5, 16, 70, 109; false 95, 166; giving up 141; of survival 57–8, 111; forlorn 207; *see also* breaking bad news; spiritualism

hoped-for worlds 116

hopelessness: after bereavement 118; and depression 118; after disasters 191; and poverty 210

hospice *see* palliative care

human rights 217

hyperactivity *see* restlessness

identification 4, 14, 111; identity problems 178; symptoms 66; *see also* empathy; amputation, and phantom limb

illusion(s): Buddhist view of the world as 48–9; of centrality 168; of invulnerability 117; of lost person 11; of safety/security 195; *see also* hallucinations; myths

Index of Complicated Grief (ICG) 65, 69–70, 120

insecure attachment *see* attachment, security and

internal models of the world *see* world model(s)

IWG (International Work Group on Death, Dying and Bereavement) 123, 170, 209, 211, 222, 226

Laboratory of Community Psychiatry 25

Lewis, C. S. 17–18, 198

life space *see* assumptive world(s)

life threatening illness: acceptance of 141; awareness of 144; coping with 145; fears of patients with 139–45, non-verbal communication 143; religious faith 143; *see also* palliative care

linking objects 113

loneliness 59, 127; *see also* dependent; support, social

loss(es) 79; clear visual memories of object 10–11, 13, 15, 83, 99; and gains 92; of meaning 67–8; responses 92; sense of presence 15, 99; *see also* amputation; assumptive world(s); bereavement; blindness; disaster(s)

love 229; animal capacity for 220, attachment or 48, 53; beauty of 54; blind 223; commitment 52; compassion 5; and death 51; detachment from 48–9; functions of 223; global 45; of God(s) 223; and grief 1, 20, 51–62, 64, 224; and health 52–3; idealisation 229; key 229; logic 51; meaning of 4–5; measurement of 52; object 3, 53; parental 59; patterns of 53; places 137, 223; possessions 97; price of 206, 229–30; qualities of 53; risks of 53, 117, 223, 230; romantic 53; rules of 52; and security 52, 70, 171; and suffering 229; symphony 61; theory of x; ties of 17, 52; transference 61; transience 51; a 'virtue' 75; *see also* attachment(s); monotropy

Maori bereavement 4–5, 46

martyrdom 164, 213, 217

MDD (major depressive disorder) 75; and alcohol problems 163, 170; antidepressants 118, 170; 'befriending' 170; after disasters 190; guilt 171;

mitigation 118; in old age 127; role of volunteers 170; *see also* cognitive behaviour therapies

meaning-making 4–6, 49, 62, 70, 76, 198, 228, 230; and attachments 57; and continuing bonds 76; maturity 127; and spirituality 120, 138, 143, 154–5; in therapy 70; *see also* loss(es), of meaning

medication: for life threatening illness 108, 141, 154, 192; for traumatic bereavement 86; post-operative 109; for psycho-social transitions 108; *see also* drugs; opiates; tranquillizers

mediation 215, 225

memorials 15, 87; after disasters 171, 226

memories of lost person/object 15, 110; and the brain 76; in children 83; clear visual memories 10–11, 13, 83 (correlates of 10; after murder 81; perceptual set 11); happy 4, 65; idealised 178; intrusive (haunting) 4–5, 83, 85, 195; preoccupation with 6; reminiscence 16; treasuring 70, 120; *see also* amputation, and phantom limbs; avoidance; linking objects; PTSD; sense of presence

monotropy 53

mortality after bereavement 31–7; rates, influence on response to losses 45, 52–3, 183; in old age 98; *see also* gender

mourning 16, 74, 111; ambiguity of 74; customs 47; 'guided' 69; for martyrs 164; and melancholia 91–2; *see also* grief

murder/manslaughter: responses to 81–9; influence on mental health 81–3, 85–6; psychological reactions to 83; psychotherapy and outcomes 86–7; risk factors 82; social/marital relations 84–5; *see also* family services, family liaison teams/officers (FLOs); Rwanda; SAMM

myths 4, 120, 137; basic assumptions 117; family 217; perpetuating cycles of violence 217; positive and negative 223–4; revising 224–5

Narrative Exposure Therapy 169–70

nostalgia 15

numbness 14, 83; after amputation 99; and arousal 83; after bereavement 14; *see also* PCBD

nurturance 53, 58–9, 61; *see also* attachment(s)

object relations theory 91–2

opiates 148; *see* also drugs; medication

palliative care 56, 70, 136–56; bereavement care in 160; evaluation of 148–56; facing death 226–7 (individual and community 226); family services 23–4; at home 25,

145, 147, 149, 192; in India 182–4, 192–3; myths of 137; social club 25; *see also* bereavement services; death/dying; life threatening illness; St Christopher's Hospice

palliative medicine *see* palliative care

panic disorder *see* generalised anxiety disorder

PCBD (persistent complex bereavement disorder) 230 *see also* PGD

peace 4, after 9/11 204; international 167, 195, 212; in Northern Ireland 195, 198, 224; in Rwanda 224; and transcendence 4; *see also* violence, breaking the cycle

peaceful death 49, 112, 141–3

peacekeeper(s) 209, 214; arbitration 214–15; Marshal Plan 219; mediation 225–6; psycho-social 226; UN 202, 215

PGD (prolonged grief disorder) 18, 69–70, 74–5, 170, 230; an adjustment disorder 70; persistent complex bereavement 63–4; disorder treatment of 69–70; *see also* complicated grief

play: in poetry 4; music 86–7, 205; myth 4; role play 157

perceptions 94; *see also* assumptions

polarisation 170, 218–19, 224; in run up to war 207; *see also* violence, cycles of

post-traumatic stress 88, 90; anger 88; and mental health 85–6; Victim Support 89; *see also* PTSD

Prigerson, Holly 64–70, 118

Project Liberty 163

PST (psychosocial transitions) 90–114; anger 101; attachments changing 225; definition 92–3, 102–3, 106–8; facilitating 113; implications 102–3; in institutions 101; meaning-making 76; outcome 107; preparation for 103; resistance to 6, 91, 93–4, 97, 101–2, 106–13; shattered assumptions 90; as a spiritual experience 120; transference 61; turning points 91, 107; *see also* assumptive world(s); disasters

psychiatric disorder: after loss xii, after threat of loss xii, and cycles of violence xii *see also* MDD; PCBD; PGD; PTSD; separation anxiety disorder

psychotherapy 95; after loss/crisis 23, 47, 95, 130–2, 171; in armed conflict 213, 226; changing assumptions 95, 118–19; 'complicated grief treatment' (Shear) 69–70; cultural ruts 50; after disasters 162, 169, 184; emotion focussed (affective) 48, 69; after murders 81, 86–9; in palliative care 138, 142; to patients (counter-transference) 61; *see also* cognitive behaviour therapies; evaluation; FFGT; linking objects;

mourning, 'guided'; Narrative Exposure Therapy; psychiatric disorder
PTSD (post-traumatic stress disorder) 63–4, 81; after disasters 163; symptoms 64, 119; after traumatic bereavements 81

rage *see* anger
reality testing: after losses 14, 67, 111; in childhood 13; codes (approximations) 216, 222; in the dying 112, 141, 226; in therapy 89, 111, 212; *see also* avoidance; denial; disasters, resistance to change; PST
re-grief work 113
religion(s) 46, 49, 198; beliefs 163; Buddhist 48–9; Christian 109; clergy 209, 214; 'consolations' of 198; extremists 168, 213, 218; fear of judgement 142; Hindu 46; Islam 49, 199; Judaism 46, 199; moral codes 218; Shinto 49; tolerance 49, 197; view of death 109, 143; Western 49–50; *see also* cultures; spirituality; St Christopher's Hospice
reminiscence 16, 67
research 229; into attachment 53, 56, into bereavement 54–5, 59, 90–3, 102, 119 (ethics of 38–44, 52; methods 8, 43–4, 52; training interviewers 40–1); in disaster areas 170, 184; family crisis intervention 130–5; into other loss and change 102–3, 115, 124–5; into a palliative care service 138–55; into responses to terrorism 222–7; *see also* CNRC; IWG
restlessness 9–10, 13; after amputations 99; after bereavement 15, 18, 83
Rwanda 161–3, 195, 199–202, 222–4; inhibition of grief 46, 50; peace process 224 Trauma Recovery Programme 163

St Christopher's Hospice 139, 149; evaluation of family care 155; evaluation of patient care 148–56; pain relief 151–4; spiritual care 151–2, 154–5; *see also* palliative care; bereavement service
SAMM (Support after Murder and Manslaughter) 89
scapegoating 218
searching 7–19, 90, 116–17, 163, 230; components of 8–13; extinction by non-reinforcement 117; and finding 15, 18; for meaning 62; in prolonged grief disorder 18; psychophysiology of 18; in social animals 7, 18, 20
secure base 59, 61, 119, 126–7, 156
security (safety) 57, 223; after bereavement 21, 48, 116–19; coercion 224; and

control/empowerment 117; in counselling 226; economic 225; in family 119; forces 223; of government 210; in groups 224; international 211–12, 220; of leaders 214–15; in life threatening illness 59, 70, 226; after murder/manslaughter 82–9; in old age 98; sources of 56, 59; staff 223; in therapy 166; *see also* attachment(s), security and; PST (psychosocial transitions); secure base
Security Council 195, 212
seeking *see* searching
separation anxiety (distress): fear 142; in grief 74, 116, 123
separation anxiety disorder 60, 70; diagnostic criteria 60; *see also* complicated grief
separation behaviour 7; in social animals 116
separation from attached persons: in immigrants 59; in life-threatening illness 59; separation and divorce 96–7
separation from parents: in adolescents 58; in adults 57–8; in childhood 57, 59, 67 (influence in adult life 57–8; on health 52–3, 57); in infants 7, 20, 59, 140; in social animals 7, 20, 52; *see also* attachment disorders
shame 126
shattered assumptions *see* assumptions, shattered
social support *see* support, social
social work(-ers) in bereavement services 24–5, 215; in child abuse 211; in crisis intervention 129–36; in disaster services 162–3, 165, 185, 187, 190; in palliative care 192; in war zone 199
spiritualism 11–12, 15
spirituality 103; devoted actors 225; sacred values 225; *see also* transcendence
status 94, 116, 210; with avoidant attachments 58; gender and 58; socio-economic 47, 149–50; of warriors 210
stigma 65, 74, 126, 134, 230
strange situations 57–8, Strange Situation Test 57
stress 91–2; *see also* loss(es)
supervision: of bereavement research interviewers 41, 44; of bereavement volunteers 160; of disaster teams 162, 167, 172, 185, 205
support, social: cultural influences on 183; effect on loneliness/grief 59, 126; group 24, 57; after murder/manslaughter 85; in old age 59
suicide: ideas or threats of 12; risks of (after bereavement 25, 68; with PGD 65)
survival prediction of 139
survival guilt 88

terrorism *see* armed conflict
Texas Inventory of Grief 115
threats of loss: and cycles of violence xii; and psychiatric disorder xii
tolerance 217–18
Tower Hamlets Crisis Intervention Service 129–36; acceptability 134; accessibility 134; appropriateness 133–4; criticisms 135; effectiveness 132–3; efficiency 133; equitability 134; threatened or attempted suicide 132
tranquillizers 151; *see also* drugs; medication
transcendence 4, 62, 76, 'sacred' values 225
transition(s) *see* psycho-social transitions
trauma 79–136; acculturation 47–8; basic assumptions 57; helping 86–8; preparation for 124; *see also* amputation; armed conflict; disasters; loss(es); post-traumatic stress; traumatic bereavement; traumatised persons; traumatology
trauma services: anger management 170; critical incident stress debriefing 164, 172; Cruse Bereavement Care 160, 162, 198; family crisis services 125, 160–1; Internet based 185; NICE recommendations 169; role play 199; police family liaison officers 160, 223; psychological 169; Red Cross 163; trauma counselling 173, 184; UNICEF 163, 195, 200–1; *see also* Tower Hamlets Crisis Intervention Service
trauma, responses to 96, 169; anger/rage 83; bewilderment 83; cultural influences 163; depression 185; haunting memories 4, 4–5, 83, 85, 195; hyperactivity 83; numbness 83; rumination 88; helping 125; *see also* dreams
traumatic bereavement/loss 57, 90, 126–7; in childhood 81, 88, 172, 184; helping 88–9, 118–20, 126; *see also* armed conflict; disasters; family liaison officers; grief, avoided; murder/manslaughter

traumatised persons: helpers 88, 162; parents 59; *see also* amputation; traumatic bereavement/loss
traumatology 56
triage 168; *see also* bereavement risk assessment

Victim Support 89
violence: apartheid 220; in families 209–11; international; myths, positive and negative 223; in nations 209, simplistic 'solutions' 209, 218; in small groups 210
violence, breaking the cycle 222–27; attachment security 223; crisis intervention 212; depolarisation 224; forgiveness 226; human rights 220, 222; impartial support 219; insight (disillusionment) 224; Marshall plan 219; mediation 215, 225; multidisciplinary response 220–1; negotiation 220; peace processes 226; reconciliation 225–6; restitution 226; rules of engagement 212; social justice 220
violence, cycles of 209–21; IWG model 211–20 (violent event 211–13; perception of event 212–13; immediate response 213–14; legitimising authorities 214–16; destructive codes; polarisation 216–19; retaliation 211–2)
violence, reactions to: group responses 213, 224; hunting 224; martyrdom 164, 213; misperceptions 213, 224; over-reaction 213; in social animals 210, 220

war *see* armed conflict
widows and widowers *see* grief, gender influence of
world model(s) 93–4, 108, 116–17; dreaded 93, 116–17; hoped for 116–17; ideal 93, probable 93; provisional 116; redundant 106–14; wished for 94; *see also* assumptive world(s); PST
worry work 16

26505059R10140

Printed in Great Britain
by Amazon